MULTIPLE CASE STUDY ANALYSIS

Multiple Case Study Analysis

ROBERT E. STAKE

THE GUILFORD PRESS
New York   London

© 2006 The Guilford Press
A Division of Guilford Publications, Inc.
72 Spring Street, New York, NY 10012
www.guilford.com

Printed in the United States of America

This book is printed on acid-free paper.

Last digit is print number: 9   8   7   6   5   4   3   2   1

Library of Congress Cataloging-in-Publication Data

Stake, Robert E.
    Multiple case study analysis / Robert E. Stake.
        p. cm.
    Includes bibliographical references and index.
    ISBN 1-59385-248-7 (pbk.)—ISBN 1-59385-249-5 (cloth)
    1. Education—Research—Methodology. 2. Education—Europe,
Eastern—Cross-cultural studies. 3. Case method. I. Title.
    LB1028.S733 2006
    370.'7'2—dc22
                                                2005017005

Preface

The Design of Multicase Projects

Whether leaning toward standardization or diversity, almost every educational or social service program will be far from uniform across its different situations. To understand complex programs, it is often useful to look carefully at persons and operations at several locations. The multicase project is a research design for closely examining several cases linked together. It is also a design for studying an issue or phenomenon at sites that have no programmatic link. This book is an introduction to the study of multiple cases within a single research project.

In an overview of multicase research based on broad experience, Robert Herriott and William Firestone (1983) concluded that the method was applicable to policy study and social science generalization as well as to description of complex programs. They acknowledged, however, that searching for better policy is somewhat in conflict with searching for understanding of what happens within a collection of individual cases. In this book, I identify choice points for making a study more productive of generalizations or more descriptive of current operations. And, more often than not, I support the view that program administration, public support, and legislative policy making can be more insightful when based on case-specific understanding of local functions (Parlett & Hamilton, 1976).

MULTICASE METHODS

The multicase study is a special effort to examine something having lots of cases, parts, or members. We study those parts, perhaps its students, its committees, its projects, or manifestations in diverse settings. (The definition of a "case" is discussed in greater detail in Chapter 1.) One small collection of people, activities, policies, strengths, problems, or relationships is studied in detail. Each case to be studied has its own problems and relationships. The cases have their stories to tell, and some of them are included in the multicase report, but the official interest is in the collection of these cases or in the phenomenon exhibited in those cases. We seek to understand better how this whole (in this book, I am going to call the whole—the entity having cases or examples—a "quintain") operates in different situations. The unique life of the case is interesting for what it can reveal about the quintain. The quintain can be an organization, and we study its different parts. The quintain can be a campaign, and we study its instances. The quintain is something that we want to understand more thoroughly, and we choose to study it through its cases, by means of a multicase study.

To carry out the study of the quintain, we need to organize separately our data gathering and reporting of the individual cases. These case studies will have one or a few research questions (issues) in common and will have others particular to each. The issues are important problems about which people disagree—complicated problems within complex situations. Our readers need to be given the opportunity to know how the study of issues that cut across cases contributes to understanding the quintain.

Deciding on issues for the quintain and the cases helps us define data sources and data-gathering activities. We are likely to make observations, to conduct interviews, to get observations of things we cannot see ourselves, and to review documents. Examining these data, we will often revise our issues. New issues emerge. Case study work is often said to be "progressively focused"; that is, the organizing concepts may change a little or a lot as the study moves along.

Usually it will be important to seek out and present multiple perspectives on activities and issues, discovering and portraying the different views. Seldom will it be necessary to resolve contradictory testimony or competing values. Even contradictions may help us understand the quintain.

To understand the quintain better, we try to observe each case in its ordinary activities and places. We try to minimize intrusion, often avoiding the special tests and assessments that are characteristic of survey and laboratory study. We recognize that case study is often subjective. We rely heavily on our previous experience and our sense of the worth of things. We try to let our readers know something of the personal experience of gathering the data. And we use techniques to minimize the misperception and the invalidity of our assertions.

We seek an accurate understanding of the quintain, although this understanding is necessarily incomplete. Sometimes we generalize across the cases. Some comparison across cases is inevitable. We and our readers generalize about the quintain at the outset of the study, and modify the generalizations somewhat as a result of acquaintance with the cases. Sometimes the cases are selected for us; sometimes we choose them. When we choose, it is often better to pick the cases that most enhance our understanding than to pick the most typical cases. In fact, highly atypical cases can sometimes give the best insights into the quintain.

We use ordinary language and narratives to describe the quintain. We seek to portray its cases comprehensively, using ample but nontechnical description and narrative. Each case report may read something like a story. Our observations cannot help being interpretive, and our descriptive sections are laced with and followed by interpretation. We offer readers the opportunity to generate their own interpretations of the quintain, but we offer ours too.

STEP BY STEP

In this book, the primary illustrations for research on multiple cases will be the country cases of the Step by Step case study project. Step by Step is an early childhood education program that has operated since 1994 under the auspices of the Open Society Institute, founded by philanthropist George Soros. Step by Step began as a 2-year project in 15 countries in Central and Eastern Europe, but has since expanded to an ongoing effort in about 30 countries; the majority of these are still in the former Soviet bloc, but a few countries in other areas (e.g., Haiti) are also now included. The Step by Step program is described more fully in Chapter 5 with the help of Sarah Klaus, the executive director of the Step by Step Program, and Cassie Landers. I offer my sketch of it in Figure P.1.

Many education and other social service programs operate in different places and under different conditions. Step by Step teacher training occurs in Mongolia, Estonia, Bosnia and Herzegovina, and the vast triangle of countries in between. Although the Step by Step programs in indi-

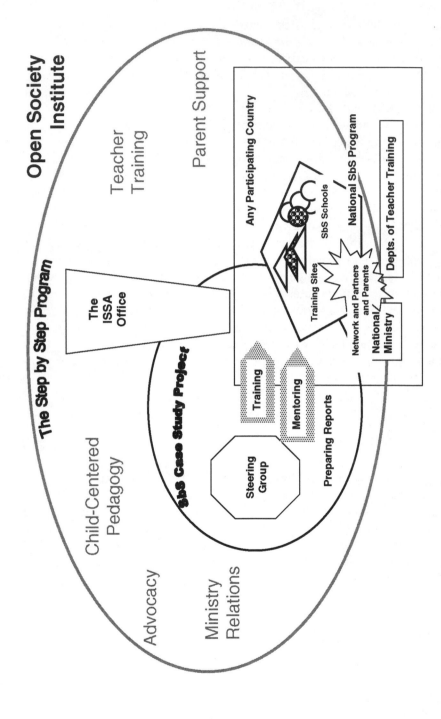

FIGURE P.1. The Step by Step (abbreviated SbS) program and its case study project.

vidual countries all emphasize child-centered teaching, the Step by Step personnel in Mongolia work with "yurt schools" that move with the herds, and the personnel in Slovakia have worked to reduce the school segregation of Roma children. (The Roma are more widely, although pejoratively, known in English-speaking countries as "Gypsies"; they are a long-oppressed ethnic minority in Europe.) To understand the multinational, highly diverse Step by Step program, therefore, one needs to know the communities, the customs, and the differentiated pull of the economy at each place. To provide a better understanding of the program's experiences was the task for its multicase study.

In the Step by Step multicase project, the country cases were linked by common sponsorship, purposes, and program standards. But the teachers, the parents, the local authorities, and the countries' ministries of education, though similar in some ways, were dissimilar in ways that differentially shaped the adaptation of the methodology to the national curriculum, the involvement of parents and the community, and the program's sustainability. To administer, to participate in, or to appreciate the program, one needs to know its grand sweep and the complexity of its experience in a number of cases (Crabtree & Miller, 1999). Professional skill depends on recognizing and accommodating individual differences, whether the cases are children or countries.

Three of the Step by Step case studies are included in this book in their entirety (see Chapters 6–8); the different formats of these reports as prepared by the respective research teams have been retained. I was particularly impressed with the extent to which these studies captured the diverse experiences of teachers and schools following Step by Step principles. But I chose them also because I was the research mentor for all three. Each had a very different story to tell. Each fit differently but nicely into the innovations and principles of the Step by Step program.

STUDYING PHENOMENA

The Step by Step case study project is a good example of multicase research on a diversified program, but it is not a very good example of researching a phenomenon. Studying phenomena can be similar to studying programs. Many phenomena take on different lives or forms, depending on the particular hosts or local conditions: sibling rivalry, treatment of children with autism, responses to new drugs, and international terrorism, to name a few. It is important to examine the common characteristics of these phenomena, but it is also important to examine situational uniqueness, especially complexity and interaction with back-ground conditions (Geertz, 1973; Simons, 1980). As policy making is extended to cross-continental phenomena, such as teacher training in the European Union or home nursing care across the United States, the importance of unusual customs and habitats makes knowledge of individ-ual cases a necessity for the public, the authorities, and the professions (Creswell, 1998).

Sibling rivalry seems a simple enough concept, but is it different when one of the children in a family is adopted? Is it the same when the siblings are greatly different in musical talent in a family recognized for artistic performance? Is it manifested differently when one brother is the governor and another is the president? One can find quantitative vari-ables, such as stress within the family, paternalism, or amount of peer sup-port, to help explain the behavior in general, but one needs to work with both the general and the particular. One fails to understand the phenom-enon unless the explanation holds up in most individual situations. Examining situational complexity is a vital part of social science re-search.

This book describes the design of multicase projects. It does not repeat the design of single-case studies as described in Eckstein (1975), Merriam (1998), Stake (1995), and Yin (1994); it builds on them. As I see it, the ideas of multicase methods will not make sense unless single-case study makes sense, both conceptually and experientially. This book relies heavily on the instruction and illustrations to be found in the liter-ature. The situation here is one of working with a set or collection of case studies so that they effectively illuminate a common program or phenom-enon.

I started writing this book in December 2004 and finished it in April 2005. As the end neared, Rita Davis improved both the logic and typography. Reacting to my prospectus and drafts were Marya Burke, Brinda Jegatheesan, Saville Kushner, Barbara Metcalf, and George Stanhope. Many others made the thinking and the publication possible, especially Jack Easley, Gordon Hoke, C. Deborah Laughton, Linda Lee, and Luisa Rosu. Finally, I would like to express my gratitude and appreciation for the students with whom I have worked throughout my career. I dedicate this book to all of my students, listed below:

1958–1963: Iris Abel Clement Adelman Jack Anthony Laura Armstrong David Balk S. A. Balu Mildred Bartos Harrell Bassham James Beaird Roberta Beaird Jaswant Bedi Lanny Beyer John Bianchini Glenn Boerrigter Marie Bombardier Linda Bond Alan Booth Norman Bowman Vilma Bravo Lynette Breining Marianne Brennan Sue Brigden Rus Brown Jo Buck Mary Anne Bunda Shirley Burnham Evelyn Caha

James Callan Harry Canon Amy Carter Janice Chang Shu-wan Chiu Marta Civil
Joann Cohn Trey Coleman Jim Condell Rebecca Conrad Jim Craigmile Larry Cross
Mats Danell Jo Day Fred deWit Glen Dey Geoff Driver Hubert Dyasi Jack Edling
Paul Elliot Ivan Ellingham Joe Ellis Terry Elofson George Fernandez Joe Fisher Walt Foley
Steven Foster Kerry Freedman Jo Friedman Robert Frogge Oren Glick Jerry Gage
Rita Gentry Art Gilbert Radnar Gilberts Cristina Gillanders Susan Giurleo Gene Glass
Corrine Glesne Pearl Goldenstein Bill Goodrich Marcus Green Arden Grotelueschen
Janice Hand Alfred Hall Neil Hartman Tom Hoemke Robert Hopmann Marty Hotvedt
Ernie House Betsy Hutchins Hiroshi Ikeda Dee Irwin Elsa Iverson Ruth Jaenike
Stan Johnson Joyce Jones Nephat Kathuri Mary Kennedy Tom Kerins Cathy Kim
Rex Knowles Saville Kushner Gabriele Lakomski John Lawson Joe Liggit Henry Lippert
Suzanne Little Robert Littrell Duncan MacQuarrie James McCabe
Doug McKie Martin Maehr Marty Maehr Tom Maguire Mohamed Mahmoud
Gary Marco Tom McHale Bill Mehrens Monika Meinhold William Merz David Merrill
Ebert Miller Xiao Kang Mo Naftali Mollel Ragnhild Nitzler John Norton Linus Ogene
Ernest Olson Lorraine Pallecen Ioannis Paraskevopolis Jim Pearsol Bill Peterson
Dwain Peterson Jon Peterson George Pinckney Kijong Rhee Anne Sadayasu
Phyllis Safman Barbara Schneider David Schramm Tom Schwalbe Charles Secolsky
Yaron Siach-Bar Finbarr Sloane Doug Sjogren LuAnn Smith Nick Smith Philip Smith
Aminata Soumare Joe Steele Richard Stafford Orin Stratton Wallace Strong
Rich Sudweeks Sherry Sullivan Deborah Switzer Sauli Takala Lucille Tempero
Pat Templin Paul Theobald Graham Thompson Harry Torrance Rosalie Torres
Deborah Trumbull Barbara Tymitz Diane Ursliner George Uhlig Ursula Walsh
Bill Watkins Larry Weber Bill Webster Nancy Wehrbein Eric Weir Don Weiss
Bill Zoellick **1964:** Ernest Anderson Janice Arms Clarence Ash Glenn Bedell Gary Beeb
Mary Louise Berndt Don Brown Ken Brynjolfsson Rodney Charron
Akiko Chiba Catherine Crocker David Cundiff Jessica Daniels Dewitt Davison
Don Draayer Orpha Duell Norman Ehresman Lila Eichelberger James Elliott
John Emswiler Paul Fardy Gerald Faust Ann Fox Gail Friedman Howard Garver
Joseph Gehrman Mary Ann Glasgo Verna Godman Dorothy Goebel Tom Goodale
Sharon Gotch Charles Gray Marcus Grice John Guthrie Margot Hall Don Harrington
Robert Harris Ruth Harris William Haskel Glenn Hayes Betty Henry Joe Hoffman
William Holloway Charles Hooper Larry Hovey Odette Howard Judith Jackson
Robert Kansky Holly Kapple Ann Kenward Girvin Kirk Sister Kliebhan Alfred Kolmos
Patricia Komiss Maureen Kortas Nuanpen Kosolsreth Hilda Llewellyn Howard Marston
Patricia Macnamara Raymond MacQueen Roger Marcum Sister Maureon Naomi Meara
Alice Mischke Karl King Moody Christy Murphy Sharon Myers Katherine Nicholas
Kukumi Pac Janet Palmer James Peace Thomas Powers John Pyper Hal Scholle
Philip Reidford Jean Renfro Fred Richardson Barbara Rosenquist Leon Rottman
Herschel Rowe David Ryckman Severino Santos Paul Scher Richard Schwartz
Faye Shaffer Jay Shores Donald Smitley Frederick Stewart Robert Stoneburner
Warren Suzuki James Talley Peter Taylor Lucille Tempero Henry Timko
Greg Trzebiatowski Glen Wiley Peter Zansitis Russell Zwoyer **1965:** Ronald Avery
Alan Balter Sheila Barker Norman Brust Theodore Beastall Gene Bell Wilma Boswell
Bob Broule Dennis Colbert Bryan Cooke John Cox Roscoe Daniell Mariann Donley
Paul Fardy Bill Fole Joyce Gore Charles Gray Harry Herder Lloyd Hicks Roger Hoffman
Paul Holland Robert Koonz Maureen Kortas Kenneth Kyle Walden Lewis

Rich Linnenburger Patricia McNamara Richard Malter Marilyn Melton Carl Midjaas Dorothy Popejoy James Prince Mildred Ransom Ataullah Rauf Barbara Rosenquist Carmelo Sapone Henry Scherich Donald Scherrer Lewis Selvidge Paul Sparks Gordon Stone Larry Stoneburner Michael Tremko Robert Wall John Wernegreen Ruth Whitmarsh Carolyn Yashko **1966:** John Ahlenius Henry Alexander Tom Anderson Louis Audi Aline Bateman Frank Bobbitt David Chasin Laura Coleman Joe Connelly Carole Crawford Catherine Crocker Linda Davis Steve Davis Tom Deem Anabeth Dollins J. H. Duthie Valerie Ann Farrell Mary Jean Feeney Richard Fleisher Louis Fornero Dominick Frigo Lee Gaines James Gallagher Vincent Gambino Donald Gill David Goddard Clarence Goldenstern Lawrence Grant Stewart Griffeth James Gryder Gordon Gundy Kathleen Gunning John Guthrie Darrell Helm Don Henkel Bruce Hertig Laurel Hertig Lowell Hillen Glen Hubele Richard Hult Patricia Jacobowski Martin Jason Alfred Lindsey George Madden Charles Mader Jack Marcussen Virginia McCormick Richard McCuo Tom McGreal Tom McNamara Fred Menz Marion Milbrandt Patricia Monoson John Muhm Victor Nafranowicz Paul Nelson Genevieve Painter Rudolph Pohl Evalyn Rapparlie Marianne Roderick Isaac Rogers Stan Rubin Stephen Rudin Karen Sauln Henry Slotnick Ralph Smith James Tawney Stephen Tilton Ron Tschudy William Ullery Gerald Unks Robert Wall Billy Wilbanks Kenneth Wyatt Victor Zavarella **1967:** John Adams Sandra Addy Nizar Al-Talib Francis Archambault Bob Aukerman Larry Bailey Emmet Beetner Thomas Bligh Allen Boehm Ed BonDurant Norman Bowers Thomas Breen James Brown Grace Burton Bill Buss Joyce Cantileno Ronald Carter Alan Caskey Joseph Cunningham Sharon Davis Michael Ellis Tom Goins Marc Gold Hermyne Green Keith Hanson Arthur Hasbargen Brad Hastings Carol Helwig Harold Holmes Karen Hoppens Charles Horn Charles Huth Jack Hutton Robert Irwin Eugene Johnson Charles Joley William Kachadorian Dan Kiley Thuridur Kristjansdottir Pash Ladd Joseph Laoye Kenneth Lawson James Leach Alfred Mannebach Glen Martin Glen Maw Mary McJunkin Richard Metzcus Donald Monroe Barry Moore David O'Bryant Stanley Patterson G. G. Petersen Thomas Pike Jacobo Pino Donald Piper Charlene Poch John Preston Eleonor Prueske Vicente Quiton Eldon Rebhorn Wallace Roby Stan Rubin Kathleen Runchey Bruce Rusk Herman Saettler Howard Schmidt Jerraald Shive Thomas Sinks Judith Slaughter Del Stauffer Joe Steele Roland Stoodley Richard Swanson Jon Tate Arthur Thompson Edwin Vernon Edward Vertuno Terry Weech Keith Weese John Wernegreen Jack Wiley Susan Wirth Floyd Wyrick Tom Yawkey Michael Zieky **1968:** John Adams Ed Anderson Sue Auger Terry Auger Wayne Becker Emmet Beetner Howard Bers Thomas Bligh Lloyd Brewer Mason Bunker Carol Burden Tasso Christie Alan Coller Tim Craig Sharon Davis Bernard Dodds Colin Dunkeld James Duthie Carl Edstrom Dan Feicht Bill Flottman Kurt Froelich Foster Fuller Arthur Gillis Dale Good Nancy Goodwin Dick Griffiths James Gulden Carol Helwig Lloyd Hicks Gary Hoeltke Hugh Inglis Gary James Larry Kennedy Odette King Leonard Kirk Dan Knifong Glen Kunzman Ira Langston Joseph Laoye Dorothy Lloyd Donald Lund Violet Malone James Marine William Marshall Duncan McQuarrie Walter Miller Sandor Molnar Barry Moore George Oetting Alphonso Palmiotto Sally Pancrazio Doug Patterson Margaret Pjojian John Preston Vicente Quiton Joe Rice Eui Do Rim Andrea Rothbart Mike Royer Pam Rubovits Stanley Rumbaugh Kathleen Runchey Donald Rutschmann Sandra Savignon Paula Schutt Peter Simmons Henry Slotnick Kathryn Smith Del Stauffer

Patricia Stoll Stephen Storch Gary Storm Carl Tausig Eugene Thomure Graeme Watts
Philip Wickersham Esther Williams Mary Yeh Raimonds Zuirbulis **1969:** John Alden
Ali Ammadi Tom Andre Julianne Anthony Gary Arsham Charles Atherton
Karop Bavougian Edward Bellamy Dick Bennett Anna Bezdek Alfred Blatter
Dorothea Blue Rebecca Bock Robert Borucki Don Bosshart Mack Bowen
Mary Anne Bunda Robert Clarke Howard Crombie Sylvia Crooks Gerald Curl
James DeYoung Carlene Doran Christopher Edginton John Fiore Dennie Franklin
Diane Frey Sheila Goldberg Matash Golshan Dale Good Dennis Gooler Richard Grubb
Jim Gulden Arlen Gullickson Thomas Higgins Doris Jefferies Stuart Jenkins
Carol Jugovich Ed Kelly David Kives John Kleberg Robert Knol William Kornegay
Reynold Krueger Raymond Kulhavy Glen Kunzman Joe Lamos Glenn Lose Dorothy Loyd
Bart Luedeke Allen Matsunaga Barry McGaw William Moss Joseph Pechinski
Adrian Peterson Dallas Preston Charles Render Dave Rockenbeck Todd Rogers
James Roland Margie Ross James Saunders Gale Schiamberg Lori Shepard
Terry Shepherd Martin Siegel Carl Slater Mary Lee Smith Nick Smith Paula Smith
Margaret Snowden Bernadine Stake Patricia Thomas Dick Thornes Adrienne Turbow
Janice Unruh Robert Waggener Art Walker Jeanne Walker Ona Weizmann
Tim Wentling Averill West Norman Wetzel Judi Whalley Conard White Amy Williams
Jirawat Wongswaddiwat Blaine Worthen Nitza Yarom Mary Yeh Cherry Yin
Raimonds Zuirbulis **1970:** John Adam Al Avner Don Bosshart John Brown
Marie Conlon Tom Curtis Alex Davidonis Marsha Dolven Louise Gentle
Nancy Goodwin Dennis Gooler Glen Hamilton Rose Hamman Lee Hertzman
Janet Hidde Ron Hildebrand Richard Hofstrand James Ingersoll Steven Karten Dan Kau
Cinda Kochen Shirley Koeller William Kornegay Etha Kristjansdottir James Kusick
Dave Martin Rosemary McConkey Curtis McKnight Duncan McQuarrie Jim Mitchack
Anna Moore Joan Moore John Murdock Carole Narigan Gerald Niewoehner Nick Pallizi
Carol Perez Taweewat Pitayanon Rick Powell Marion Sahni Nedra Sarnow
Hae Kyun Song Helen Spotts Fred Vallier Patricia Valoon Peter Valora Terry Wilmot
Chumporn Yongkittikul Mary York Alan Young Bob Young **1971:** Kenneth Brasel
Alicia Cieslar Terry Crooks David Davison Vincent DeLeers Mack Faite Craig Gjerde
Frank Green Everett Harris Carl Hay Pulsri Kanokvichitra Wayne Lockwood
Ruth Lungstrum George Malo Dave Myrow Wook Park Chieh-min Ping Nancy Pjojian
Larry Ruby Jerry Schoenike Heather Sharman George Shirk Marty Siegel Nick Smith
Richard Tate David Terry John Toney Robert Wolf Patricia Wood Chin Wen Yao
Makonnen Yimer **1972:** Edna Albert Barbara Barnes Marvin Barth Kathleen Brophy
David Bowling Ellen Bush Eleanor Daniel Douglas Dirks Gene Dolson Evelyn Domingo
Irene Dowdy Wayne Dvorak Paul Elliott Diane Essex Linda Girard Tom Grayson
Herman Green Holly Hollingsworth Marty Hotvedt Truman Jackson Daniel Kamanda
Stephen Kemmis Laura Klemt Marilyn Martin William Marzano Lynn Misselt
Ernie Olson Allen Ottens Lisa Parker Elaine Pavelka Orest Pyrch Teli Rajendra-Prasad
Eleftherios Rasis Flora Rodriguez Helen Rose Barbara Rosenshine Farideh Salili
Ali Shahabi Carolyn Shevokas Susan Vess Patrick Walsh Eric Weir Robert Wirsing
1973: Arthur Boynton Sanford Farkash Barbara Francis Fred Gbegbe Joseph Green
Donald Keefe George Lowrie Robert Means Ernie Olson Gillian Ortony
Floyd Pennington Mary Pollock Helen Rose Steve Rugg James Stamper Dennis Wiseman
1974: Stephen Alessi Rick Amado Bonnie Armbruster David Barr Barry Biddle
Linda Bock Jon Bowermaster John Carleton Darrel Caulley James Chan Kathy Dalgaard

Brian Dallman Warren Dastrup Judy Dawson Charles Evans Mary Jensen Sharon Johnson Toni Lissy Perry Main Lynn Misselt David Murphy Rose Owens Robert Rose Uzi Selzer Susy Soung Rich Sudweeks John Surber Neil Wilcof Bill Zoellick **1975:** Leslie Ansel Sylvia Atallah David Belsheim Jane Bertschi S. Boonruangrutana Ella Bowen Jonné Browne Fedeserio Camarao Paul Christenson Herschel Cline Barbara Core Dwight Davis Beth Dawson David Domino Ivan Ellingham Owen Gaede Leslie Gerstman Mike Greenwood Nick Hastings Susan Hutchison Colin Hook Mike Horwitz Eloise Jackson Roger Johnson Barry Jones Mary Ann Jones Barbara Kremer Sid Levy Jean Ann Linney Louise Meyer Holiday Milby Donald Moore Tony Moriarty Diane O'Rourke Joe O'Shea Linda Perkins Al Phelps Jim Pichert Wayne Predura John Robinson Amanollah Safavi Joan Sattler Pat Scheyer Dick Schreck Bob Schwartz Shelley Schwartz Ronaid Schworm Constance Shorter Louise Singleton Fred Slate Jeff Slinde Marcia Smith Suzanne Smither Iris Sutherland Marc Tabackman Marilyn Terrill Barbara Tymitz Charlotte Waters Rose White Mark Williams Tse Yung **1976:** Marli Andre Stephen Bell John Berryman Anthony Chan Charlotte Claar Judy Dawson Mercedes Graf Del Harnisch Warren Johnson Turee Olson Gail Parks Judy Riggs Hassan Marshad Fred Noyes Howard Rosen Chuck Secolsky Derek Taylor Tom Watkins Richard Zollinger **1977:** Marli Andre Bob Blomeyer Norman Bowman Darrell Caulley Judy Dawson Mel Hall Elaine Hwang Shirley Johnson Jennifer McCreadie Turee Olsen Oli Proppé Delores Schoen **1978:** William Ade Michael Agone George Arakapadavil Kathryn Au Elka Block Steve Bopp Joanne Broadbent Rob Brown Linda Carl Tony Chan Margaret Connolly George Davidson Hamideh Elmi-Gharavi Carmen Espino-Parij Patricia Gatto Rick Gammache Ron Hage Judy Harrison David Hedges Robbe Henderson Dennis Hengstler Elaine Harpine Tom Kerins Shirley Kessler Gary Laumann Jim Lichtenstein Lynne Lichtenstein Jennifer McCreadie Sue McKibbin Robert Mitrione Patricia Morris Tom Morris Sue Moulder Maria Murillo Bruce Olsen Ralph Reynolds Ina Robertson Gail Rooney Ivan Ruiz Tom Seals Joan Sextro Angela Taylor Graham Thompson Cindy Tyska Elizabeth Weiss **1979:** Chris Accornero George Arakapadavil David Balk Richard Birarda Bonnie Boyle Linda Brandau Judi Catlett Rebecca Dyasi Steve Everett Eskandar Fathi-Azar Bobbie Flexner Dick Franz Lynn Grady Gail Halliwell Jim Healy Sue Hill Kathy Johnson Bob Kenny Alice Ann Kingston Kyoko Miyazaki Connie Nast Jesús Negrete Daphne Persico Gene Peuse Oli Proppe Gail Rooney Debbie Rugg Rosemary Sutton Jeff Tank Cindy Tyska John Wakefield Basimalla Yesuratnam **1980:** Timir Adhikari Alice Arnold Betty Bahadori Jennifer Bahowick Subrahmanya Balu Deva Bhattacharyya Bob Blomeyer Annette Buckmaster Bill Bursuck Joshua Cleon Larry Colker Vicki Conrad Barbara Creamean William Ebomoyi Titus Eze Dennis Fisher French Fraker Kerry Freedman Jo Friedman Antonio Gonzalez Marjorie Inana Andra Johnson Lynn Juhl Vijaykumar Kapse Hrolfur Kjartansson Joan Knickerbocker S. Krishnamurthy Gabrielle Lakomski Anna Lichtenburg Astray-Jose Miras Marilyn Munski John Noonan Judy Osgood Jim Pearsol Keith Pharis Brandt Pryor G. N. N. Rao Naomi Richmond Irma Serres de Miras Carol Smith Margarito Soliz Al Spiegler M. Singh William Tirre Deborah Trumbull Laxmi Verma John Wakefield Alice Williams Sonia Williams **1981:** Christine Brieland Sandra Allarie Eileen Broderick Juan Callejas Jean Chen Avon Crismore Steve Dunbar Barbara Eibl Ivan Ellingham Anne Goudvis Sue Hill Neal Hocklander Joanne Huff Jacqueline Jones John Ketchen Akemi Kurachi

Sally Lowenstein Anna Magnusdottir Phillip Marks Sandra Mathison Paul Mayberry Jennifer McCreadie Alinde Moore Patricia Morris Mary Mulcahy Sylvia Munsen Marilyn Munski Rick Orr James Pearson Becky Pharis Hallie Preskill Oli Proppe Dan Robertson Elizabeth Rucinski Kathy Ryan James Shearl Vickie Sigman Kathleen Sullivan Deborah Trumbull Sonia Williams **1982:** Naser Al-mahmoud David Appenbrink Claire Blanchard Carmen Browne Eva Coffey Avon Crismore Dagny Fidler Beth Grane Robert Hale Janice Hand Gail Harrison Don Kachur Khalil Khalili Dave Larkin Helga Larusdottir Jane Maitland-Gholson Mary Manthei Noreen Michael Doug Musser Linus Ogene Mary Power Carol Rhea Maria Sepyrgioty Sauli Takala Rosalie Torres Denise Ward **1983:** Linda Benjamin Susan Brigden Connie Della-Piana Sam Fillipoff Elizabeth Goldsmith-Conley Lois Habteyes Golie Jansen Harry Liang Mitch Ludwinski Martha Markward Robin McTaggart Noreen Michael Tom Reischl Terry Rogers Sheena Selkirk Jonnie Shobaki Sheila Simard Penha Tres Barbara Waters Carolyn White **1984:** Cathy Desser Bob Francis Peg Hess Elsa Iverson Brandt Pryor Edwin Ramos Loretta Reinhart Penha Tres Carolyne White **1985:** Mike Bach Janet Brine James Callan Rey-Mei Chen Gary Coons Brenda Crimmins Carolyn Cuttill Brad Elzinger Dennis Fehr Jim Finn Paula Finn Cheiko Fons Lorne Gripp Dianne Guthrie Patte Howard John Hughley Golie Jansen Michael Jeffries Briane Kangas Mellen Kennedy Nancy Lauts Anita Law-Bergman Swati Lal Jupian Leung Steve Lichtenstein Neia Lively Robert Long Annabelle Munkittrick Peter Napper Marcia Rubin Linda Russell Kathy Ryan Peter Stainton Wendy Strachan Anne Sikwibele James Strauss Donna Walraven Kathy Westbrook Glenn Whittington Bob Winton **1986:** Benita Berros Emer Broadbent John Chenault Cynthia Cole Pat Decoteau Cindy Duffy Shirley Faughn Adrian Fisher Jim Frasier Alan Freeman Ramona Hao Cheryl Harper Ann Hulsizer Sasi Jungsatitkul Tom Kidd Anna Kindler Jerry Kuroghlian David Metzer Mark Moilanen Bill Parker Phil Scherviett Candy Shaeffer Penha Tres Bonnie Weller Janice Winek **1987:** Anita Booze Liora Bresler Candace Clark Francine Clark-Jones Jeffrey Ediger Warren Ellis Gale Fiehler Walter Foster Don Kiraly Linda Mabry Paul Nelson Bernice Magnus-Brown David Metzer Nancy Miller Arvin Moden Naftali Mollel Stella Oertel Eleanor Pobre Douglas Rokke Georgia Smyrmou Deborah Switzer Paul Theobald Elma Tuomisalo Corrine Walker Lihni Zhang **1988:** Linda Barratt Kelly Brennan Liora Bresler Anita Booze Carl Cooper Carol Crook Timothy Dowler Dawn Gerriets Cindy Herring Jane Hoegl Grant Holkestad Philip Holmes-Smith Jennifer Johnson Nephat Kathuri Lily Kaye Cora Kinoshita Richard Kramer Glenn Leskiw Mark MacDonald Aminata Maiga David Metzer Ziaokang Mo Paul Nelson Giordana Rabitti Alicia Rodrigues Jeanne Shaw Alan Thomalla Pat Tracy Deborah Victor **1989:** Jean Allen Ceola Baber Brenda Blanchfield Malinda Colgan RaVonda Dalton-Rann Celia Dickerson Loretta Dodgen Sandra Drury Warren Ellis David Feagins Bert Goldman Dot Harper Patricia Harris Marsha Heck Helen Hotz Dee Irwin Faye Jernigan Janice Jetton Beth Lawrence Jean Luce Linda Mabry Marcy Maury Carole Meshot David Millsaps Milton Morrison Rita O'Sullivan Anne Patterson Mary Penta Sandy Powers Giordana Rabitti Vivian Radonsky Kristin Rauch Sylvia Robinson Donna Simmons Claudette Smith Phil Smith Melba Spooner Paula Stanley Lorraine Stewart Marcia Tharp John Watson **1990:** Sondra Burman Mark Clayton Tom Grayson Jim Hall Geraldine Heath Deb Hlavna Bonnie Hudson Ken Jerich Margaret Levin Chien-Cheng Lu Sue McGinty

Tony McMann Frank O'Connor Charles Ramer Ki jong Rhee Cindi Rucinski
Craig Russon Justine Schoeplein Shin young Shin Kim Tong Richard Traver
1991: Valerie Chang Sara Davis Warrick Easdown Colleen Gilrane Elizabeth Hess
Chao-Sheng Hsu Ken Jerick Chien-Cheng Lu Mary Mathieu Masaki Moriyama
Suzanne Oliver Larisa Pandit Tom Rogers Merle Wallace Glyn Westcott
Deborah Winking **1992:** Cleo Arthur-Boswell Yvonne Austin Marilyn Benjamin
Warner Birts Ervin Bond Marilyn Booker David Boudreaux Charlotte Branson
Jenna Caldwell Deb Ceglowski Enid Collins Phyllis Cowens Linda Culberson
Gloria Davis Sara Davis Doris DuBois Marci Dodds David Espinoza Dale Fink
Carmilva Flores Joan Forte Barbara Forte Erin Fry Sue Glossop Mary Goosby
Rob Gorham Lyndia Gray Mary Ann Grice Karen Grover Lois Gueno Vinni Hall
Mahalia Ann Hines Laura Holland Yonghee Hong Benjamin Horowitz Ruthann Johnson
Peter Joseph Mike Harmon Susan Holtzclaw Shihkuan Hsu Mary Ann Ludwig
David Marcovitz Van Mathews Joshiah Maynard Kevin McDonough Tami McDougal
Andy Metcalf Patricia Mizerka Louise Monegain Carmen Palmer Dorothy Parker
June Pembroke Carol Perry Candace Pontbriant David Rein Kam Richter Mary Rose
Ninnart Sathissaras Mike Schroeder Virginia Selmon Jonghee Shim Joe Shively
Diane Simpson Katherine Smith Tom Solon Clarence Starling Siew Sze Tho
Sandra Trabaek Hsueh-yin Ting Philistine Tweedle Shu-Feng Tzeng Andrew Wadsworth
Ruth Whitelaw Fran Williams Julian Williams Deb Winking **1993:** Lillie Albert
Dyanne Alexander Diana Beck Pamela Brown Leah Buscemi David Claud Sue Dole
Beth Grosshandler Nancy Hertzog Maureen Hogan Chu Chun Huang Ching-Rong Lee
I-Hui Lee Junghee Lee Misook Lee Hui-Fen Lin Maureen Hogan Chu Chun Huang
Sandra Levin Dee McCollum Colleen Medley Lynne Meyer Chris Migotsky
Mindy Miron Sue Williams Suzanne Oliver Aimee Rickman Kyung Joo Roh
Bryan Thalhammer **1994:** Robin Allen Diana Beck Linda Blumenthal John Bruno
Leah Buscemi Robert Chen Nadine Dolby Mary Donegan Carmilva Flores Paula Geigle
Mark Gierl Heriberto Godina Amy Hanson Nancy Hertzog Hui-Ju Huong
Kimberly Kendally Mark Larson Hyun An Lee I-Hui Lee Karen Lee Li-Ching Lin
Dan Linneman Wendy Madden Colleen Medley Chris Migotsky Steven Murray
David Oakes Brenda Page Mike Schroeder Stephanie Tatum Carmina Tolentino
Amy Tseng Mikka Whiteaker Ashley Yang **1995:** Henry Akplu Dolores Appl
Cheryl Baldwin John Bruno Marya Burke Iduina Chaves Christine Chin Edith Cisneros
Deb Daniels Tresa Dunbar Rhoda Feldman Carmilva Flores Heriberto Godina
Matthew Hanson Ann Herda Nancy Hertzog Hui-Ju Huong Mark Larson Hwa Lee
I-Hui Lee Li-Ching Lin Dan Linneman Chris Migotsky Carol Mills Marilyn Murphy
Pat Norris David Oakes Brenda Page William Patterson Tim Pollock Kristin Powell
Mike Schroeder Meera Shin Theresa Souchet Carmina Tolentino Mikka Whiteaker
Ashley Yang Sheri Yarbrough Jane Zander **1996:** Daniella Barroqueiro Joyce Bezdicek
Debbie Bruns Iduina Chaves Edith Cisneros Jamie Daugherty Rita Davis Gary DePaul
Joan Feltovich Carmilva Flores Chris Dunbar Raquel Farmer Carmilva Flores Ina Gabler
Yolanda Garcia Tam Hill Edna Johnson Riyo Kadota Catherine Kirby Claudya Lum
Wendy Madden Sarah McCusker David Metzer Chris Migotsky JoAnna Mills Carol Mills
Darryl Pifer Nicole Roberts Sirpa Tiilikainen Hubert Toney Xiouhui Wang
Brent Williams Sheri Yarbrough Martha Zurita **1997:** Sarah Buila Fred Burrack
Amber Carpenter Edith Cisneros Ann Marie Clark Rita Davis Rhoda Feldman
Janetta Fleming Dean Grosshandler Dan Heck Lisa Henne Richard Henne

Mary Holbrock Trav Johnson Jae Kennedy Pei-Hsuan Lin Sharon Litchfield Claire Lloyd
Cheryl Mitchell Linda Moore Shankar Nair Kathy Norman Paul Obiokor Shireen Pavri
Naj Shaik Pat Steinhaus Carolyn Sullins Lakshmi Tata Susan Van Beaver
Velma Williams Jai-ling Yau Eboni Zamahi Chun Zhang **1998:** Jinny Ahn
Manal Alghazo Alexis Benson Kevin Brady Jim Buell Marya Burke Merrill Chandler
Teresa Chen Beena Choksi Edith Cisneros Bob Ciszek Rob Corso Michelle Hinn
Shwuyi Leu Karla Lewis Pei-Hsuan Lin Claire Lloyd Micheline Magnotta Jennifer Mathis
Erlis Murph Linda Moore Ong Art Naiya-Patana Paul Obiokor George Pavil
George Reece Bari Rothbaum Karl Radnitzer Bari Sanders David Snow Terry Souchet
Lisa Stahurski Ken Strand Jasmine Yang **1999:** Elizabeth Appiah Maureen Banks
Jared Berrett Laurel Borgia Edith Cisneros Laura Dethorne Luke Evans Deb Gilman
Joyce Hwang Hey-Deuk Kim Cari Klecka Jin-Hee Lee Claire Lloyd Jean Mendoza
Linnea Rademaker Shelley Roberts Anne Robertson Lora Schmid-Dolan Andrea Wilson
Ricki Witz Chen Xi **2000:** Joyce Bezdicek Sheryl Bullock Merrill Chandler
Lattrice Eggleston Don Gibson Cari Klecka Dong Dong Zhang **2001:** Jolyn Blank
Brenda Bowen Carey Campbell Ya-Hui Chung Tracie Constantino Deb Fisher
Randy Fletcher Lara Handsfield Catherine Hunter Rita Frerichs Yuqin Gong
Chiron Graves James Irwin Brinda Jegatheesan Yiming Jin Yore Kedem Joyce Lee
Robin Linn Anav Lucia Louro Alisa Lowrey Meng-long Lai Vaughn Page Wee-Hour Pek
Claudia Petty Walenia Silva Phil Silvey Juna Snow Aysel Tufekci Kate Walker
Jerry Wang Yu-Tzwu Wang Guo Yi-Huey **2002:** Issam Abi-El-Mona Junghyan An
Patricia Brady Julia Conner KarenVCummings Khalil Dirani Debra Erickson
Ramon Fernandez Chiming Hsieh Ju-shan Hsieh Kamau LaRaviere Hedda Meadan
Juny Montoya Chryso Mouzourou Grace Msangi Izabela Saviekiene Olga Shinkareva
Yongsook Song Yolanda Sosa-Ortiz Steven Thomas Sara Westjohn Noemi Waight
Phil Wilder Josephine Yambi Jianjun Zheng **2003:** Nesrin Bakir Fortunatus Bijura
Sheelagh Chadwick Donna Charlevoix Yu-Ting Chen Yu-Ming Cheng Yu-Ping Cheng
Soo Joung Choi Lynette Danley Guy Davis Yunus Eryaman Mara Freeman
Minta Gonzales Victoria Hammer Lisa Hood Yu-Lu Hsiung Hui-mei Hsu
Leanne Kallemeyn Rebecca Kellermeyer Alice Kim Dan Kim Irena Kola Nicole Lamers
Hyunju Lee Heather Lee Alexis Lopez Yvonne Lefcourt Philip MacLellan Matt Marvel
Koji Matsunobu Scott McDonald Yasin Ozturk Heekyong Pyon Luisa Rosu
Steve Rutledge Sara Salloum Norma Scagnoli Nathan Schaumleffel Rick Taylor
Qingyan Tian Marilyn Tyus Ava Zeineddin **2004:** Bogani Bantwini Jeana Bracey
Holli Burgon Rong-ji Chen Meng-Fei Cheng Hee Jun Choi Jennifer Chung Laura Engel
Yali Feng Susan Gregson So-Young Hong Hui-mei Hsu May Jadallah Eunok Alice Kim
Sooyoung Kim Serhat Kurt Tony Lee Wonsuk Lee Renee Lemons Rachel Maehr
Martin Maurer Brian McNurlen Sofia Mohammad Cray Mulder Chae Hee Park
Peter Parker Amanda Quesenberry Megan Radek Tania Rempert Jannike Seward
Woochan Shim Pragasit Sitthitikul Jason Sparks Virgil Varvel Kelly Watt Su-Jeong Wee
Yeanme You Miho Young Abdul Zouhir **2005:** Elise Ahn Michelle Bae Nawal Ali
Rod Githens Jesse Helton Eunyoung Jung Eunhyun Kim Eunyoung Kim
Oenardi Lawanto Lisa Park Steve Parris Ellie Ro Libby Roeger Terry Solomonson
Melissa Stephens Jeni Weidenbenner Eun Won Whang

Contents

List of Worksheets, Figures, and Photographs

WORKSHEETS

FIGURES

PHOTOGRAPHS

CHAPTER 1

Single Cases

A multicase study project as a whole will have its plan and organization, and so will the study of each individual case. The director or coordinator will think about all the cases, but a field researcher or data gatherer will concentrate on each single case almost as if it is the only one. (Of course, in some studies such as a doctoral dissertation, the director and field researcher will be the same person, but this person will still have to consider the two responsibilities separately.) A researcher may spend a long or short time on a case, but works vigorously to understand each particular case (one case at a time). During work on the single case, the collection of cases remains mostly at the back of the mind. The target case commands most of the attention. But there is tension: The single case and the collection each vie for more attention. In this book, I call this tension the "case–quintain dilemma."

For multicase research, the cases need to be similar in some ways— perhaps a set of teachers, staff development sessions, clinics, or airport security stations. For the study of a program in many sites, the collection may include all of the cases that exist. But more often it is a selection of cases. For the study of a phenomenon such as "highly centralized management," the cases selected will be many fewer than all cases that exist.

Cases are rather special. A case is a noun, a thing, an entity; it is seldom a verb, a participle, a functioning. Schools may be our cases—real things that are easy to visualize, however hard they may be to understand (Stouffer, 1941). Training modules may be our cases—amorphous and abstract, but still things, whereas "training" is not. Nurses may be our cases; we usually do not define "nursing activity" as the case. "Managing," "becoming effective," "giving birth," and "voting" are examples of functioning, not entities we are likely to identify as cases. For our cases, we may select "managers," "production sites," "labor and delivery rooms," or "training sessions for voters." With these cases we find opportunities to examine functioning, but the functioning is not the case.

Even when our main focus is on a phenomenon that is a function, such as "training," we choose cases that are entities. Functions and general activities lack the specificity, the organic character, to be maximally useful for case study (Stake, 2005). We can use the case as an arena or host or fulcrum to bring many functions and relationships together for study.

To study a case, we carefully examine its functioning and activities, but the first objective of a case study is to understand the case. In time, we may move on to studying its functioning and relating it to other cases. Early on, we need to find out how the case gets things done. By definition, the prime referent in case study is the case, not the methods by which the case operates (Yin, 1994). Some qualitative studies investigate a collection of events or series of instances. Events and instances can be bounded; certainly they are situational, complex, and related to issues; but they often lack the organic systemicity some of us want in case study. Each case is a specific entity.

A national child care program may be a case. A child services agency may be a case. The *reasons* for child abandonment or the *policies* of dealing with foster parents will seldom be considered cases. We think of a reason and a policy more as a generality than as a specific thing. Each of the cases in a multicase project is a specific thing. In the social sciences and human services, the specific case usually has working parts and is purposive. It is an integrated system. Functional or dysfunctional, rational or irrational, the case is a system, in the way that an abandoned child or a foster family or a child services agency is a system.

1.1. SITUATION AND EXPERIENCE

The reason for making a fuss about what is and what is not a case is fundamental to qualitative case study. It is an epistemological reason. Qualitative understanding of cases requires experiencing the activity of the case as it occurs in its contexts and in its particular situation. The situation is expected to shape the activity, as well as the experiencing and the interpretation of the activity. In choosing a case, we almost always choose to study its situation.

Ordinary measurement of the case fails to give adequate attention to the ways the case interacts with fellow cases in its environment, such as its family members or community leaders (Tierney, 2000). The interactions within an entity and across entities help us recognize the case as an integrated system. It is relatively easy to identify the situation of a person or organization; it is more difficult to identify the situation of a functioning or policy. Qualitative case study was developed to study the experience of real cases operating in real situations.

The case has an inside and an outside. Certain components lie within the system, within the boundaries of the case; certain features lie outside. A few of the outside features help define the contexts or environment of the case. The case researcher considers many features of the case. Some are selected to be studied. Only a few can be studied thoroughly. Because much of the important activity of the case is recognizably patterned, both coherence and sequence are sought. The researcher tries to capture the experience of that activity. He or she may be unable to draw a line marking where the case ends and where its environment begins, but boundedness, contexts, and experience are useful concepts for specifying the case (Stake, 1988).

1.2. A TECHNICAL VIEW OF A CASE

The case researcher needs to generate a picture of the case and then produce a portrayal of the case for others to see. In certain ways, the case is dynamic. It operates in real time. It acts purposively, encounters obstacles, and often has a strong sense of self. It interacts with other cases, playing different roles, vying and complying. It has stages of life—only one of which may be observed, but the sense of history and future are part of the picture. How does the case researcher gather data that can come together in a portrayal, perhaps a narrative documentary (Silverman, 2000), for the reader?

Later in this chapter, I take up the matter of *conceptual structure*. Research questions form the kind of conceptual structure suitable for designing and interpreting educational research. Often this is research seeking to understand how educators facilitate the understanding and capability of learners. Where does the researcher look for those questions? And for answers to those questions? For both, the qualitative researcher relies partly on coming to know personally the activity and experience of the case.

For this purpose, the most meaningful data-gathering methods are often observational—both direct observation and learning from the observations of others.[1] The latter, indirect method is necessary for activity at which the researcher is not present; the researcher needs to ask someone who was there, and to find records kept of what happened and artifacts that suggest it. For audiences of the report, it is important to describe what the case's activity is and what its effects seem to be. What it does depends on the situation, so it is also important to describe situations. An outline for gathering data on a case is presented in Worksheet 1. Versions of Worksheets 1, filled in and slightly revised according to the needs of each case study, can be found later in the book as Figures 6.1, 7.1, and 8.1.

Many case studies require a researcher to work half time for half a year. Only a small number of observations, interviews, and document reviews are possible. In many situations, for every hour spent actually gathering data, the typical researcher needs another 6 hours for planning, negotiating, pondering, writing, explaining, and other practical activities. So in Worksheet 1 there are spaces for only three activity sites to be observed, six interviews, and two embedded case studies (mini-cases). More can be added if there is time to process the data. The worksheet needs to be adapted, of course, for each separate situation (which has been done in Figures 6.1, 7.1, and 8.1. Always, there is a ton of information to gather that is not directly related to the research questions. But the most important data will be those driven by research questions.

1.3. THE QUINTAIN

The single case is meaningful, to some extent, in terms of other cases. The researcher and the readers of the case report are acquainted with other cases. Any case would be incomprehensible if other, somewhat similar cases were not already known. So even when there is no attempt to be comparative, the single case is studied with attention to other cases.

In multicase study research, the single case is of interest because it belongs to a particular collection of cases. The individual cases share a common characteristic or condition. The cases in the collection are

---

[1]Egon Guba and Yvonna Lincoln said, "In situations where motives, attitudes, beliefs, and values direct much, if not most of human activity, the most sophisticated instrumentation we possess is still the careful observer—the human being who can watch, see, listen, question, probe, and finally analyze and organize his direct experience" (1981, p. 213).

WORKSHEET 1. Graphic Design of a Case Study

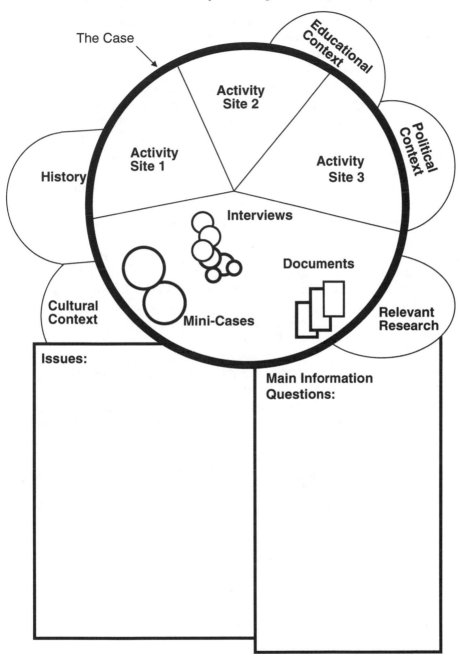

somehow categorically bound together. They may be members of a group or examples of a phenomenon. Let us call this group, category, or phenomenon a "quintain."

A quintain (pronounced kwin′ton) is an object or phenomenon or condition to be studied—a target, but not a bull's eye. In multicase study, it is the target collection. In program evaluation, we may call it an "evaluand"; in music, it may be a "repertoire." For multicase study, however, we have needed a word representing the collective target, whether it is a program, a phenomenon, or a condition. This quintain is the arena or holding company or umbrella for the cases we will study. The word needs to be generic. Neither "program" nor "phenomenon" is a big enough word. An uncommon word, "quintain," may facilitate the dialogue—although I admit that it probably won't catch on. (From here on, I promise to restrain the foray into esoteric vocabulary.)

In this book, the main example of a quintain is the Step by Step early childhood program. For the proverbial blind men describing an elephant, the elephant is the quintain. Some examples of phenomena that could be quintains are "campus support for international students," "agency use of home pages," "parent assistance in the classroom," and "labor and delivery nursing." These quintains are functions or conditions of which we might seek examples to study. (As a program evaluator, I keep thinking quickly of the quintain as a program; we evaluators look for sites in which the program operates in embedded cases.)

Multicase research starts with the quintain. To understand it better, we study some of its single cases—its sites or manifestations. But it is the quintain we seek to understand. We study what is similar and different about the cases in order to understand the quintain better.

Our planning for multicase research will be somewhat different from our planning for a single-case study. The ultimate question shifts from "What helps us understand the case?" toward "What helps us understand the quintain?" It is a move away from holistic viewing of the cases toward constrained viewing of the cases—a viewing constrained by the dominion of the quintain over the cases.

Multicase research of a program can be designed another way. It can be an ordinary case study of the quintain, still with a look at several embedded cases. Each mini-case then will be constrained by its representation of or relationship to the program. But if the study is designed as a qualitative multicase study, then the individual cases should be studied to learn about their self-centering, complexity, and situational uniqueness. Thus each case is to be understood in depth, giving little immediate attention to the quintain. If the purpose of the research is to gain a general picture or to support immediate policy setting, the design may be "formalized" (Firestone & Herriott, 1984), so that most attention is paid to selected variables in each case, not the case as a whole.

To illustrate, if the quintain is an educational program and if a single-case study is designed to study the whole thing, then much case study attention can be given to its central administration; its contexts; and the relationships among its policy makers, funders, partners, distracters, and competitors. If, however, a multicase study is designed, the central organization matters are studied to some extent, but the local administration and operation of the cases are deeply studied. A multicase study of a program is not so much a study of the quintain as it is a study of cases for what they tell us about the quintain. Of course, there is no one right way. Researchers can design a study to give either proportionate or disproportionate attention to the quintain and individual cases.

1.4. THE CASE–QUINTAIN DILEMMA

But even if careful design decisions are made, the researcher is pulled toward attending more to both the pieces and the whole. Both the quintain and the cases become more worthy of study as fast as they are studied. The more a social action becomes understood, the more there is to be understood. What earlier was believed to be dismissable becomes a component when it is better seen. Whether everything actually *is* a part of everything, or whether we have a human capacity for *seeing* everything as a part of everything, it all becomes more complex as it becomes better known, and it cries out for being still better known. It becomes increasingly worthy of being included in the study. Again, this is true for both the quintain and the case.

This is not just a procedural dilemma, but an epistemological one as well. What is more worth knowing? Both the collective and the specific are worth knowing, but what is worth knowing next? What should we think about? The multicase study is about the quintain, but is it the quintain with loose ties to the cases or the quintain with vital ties to the cases? What is more important for understanding the quintain—that one thing is common to the cases or that another is dissimilar among them? In any one study, the strategy may be easy to choose, but not for research as a whole. The pursuit of science seems to place the highest value on the generalizable, and the pursuit of professional work seems to value the particular most, but they both need both. For the multicase researcher, this is a dilemma.

Both case studies and multicase studies are usually studies of particularization more than generalization. One can use a case study or multicase study as a step toward theory, as described by Barney Glaser and Anselm Strauss (1967; see also Ragin & Becker, 1992). But the power of case study is its attention to the local situation, not in how it represents other cases in general. It is true that social scientists seeking generalization attend to both the particular and the general. They often justify the study of the particular as serving grand explanation not so much in a statistical sense as in a conceptual sense. Even with formal experiments and statistical surveys, there is interest in illustrative and deviant cases. But many important groups of researchers—including social workers, historians, program evaluators, institutional researchers, and practitioners in all professions—are deeply interested in the individual case without necessarily caring how it might represent other cases.

There are many purposes for case research, running from the most theoretical to the most practical. When the purpose of case study is to go beyond the case, we call it "instrumental" case study. When the main and enduring interest is in the case itself, we call it "intrinsic" case study (Stake, 1988). With multicase study and its strong interest in the quintain, the interest in the cases will be primarily instrumental.

As you can tell, my emphasis in case study is on the particular and the situational. Even if all case researchers agreed (and they do not), it is true that—as Stephen Kemmis (1980) pointed out—the terms "case" and "study" defy clear definition. A case study is both a process of inquiry about the case and the product of that inquiry. Lawrence Stenhouse (1978) wanted us to call the final report a "case record," but it is usually called a "case study." Here and there, researchers will call anything they please a case study.

For a multicase study, the case records are often presented intact, accompanying a cross-case analysis with some emphasis on the binding concept or idea. As the design is "formalized" (Firestone & Herriott, 1984) more and more, the case reports may become mere synopses or statistical summaries. Sometimes a research question dealing only with the binding concept is developed, with occasional reference to individual cases. Such formalization is likely to waste the special effort that has gone into a contextual, particularistic, and experiential study.

Data from a multicase study usually will come mostly from the cases studied, but the researchers may gather other data than case data. They are likely to rely on what is already known about the quintain, but also may study it further. The more the cases become merely incidental to the study, however, the less appropriate it is to call it a multicase study.

1.5. THE RESEARCH QUESTIONS

A multicase study is organized around at least one research question. It asks what is most important for understanding the quintain. It may focus on the binding concept or idea that holds the cases together. It is a conceptual infrastructure for building the study. The multicase study will probably have several research questions.

In the Step by Step early childhood program, a multicase study was initiated to explore and document not only the breadth of the teaching methods used, but also initiatives in inclusive education, anti-bias education, linkages with institutions for teacher training and retraining, and parent education programs. Exploring the adaptation of core principles in different contexts, the main question was "How are the individual countries carrying out the different initiatives in the Step by Step program?" Six cross-cutting themes were identified that informed additional questions, such as "How does Step by Step promote equal opportunities for each child?" and "What kinds of networks and partnerships are supporting the program at the local, national, regional, and international levels?" The answers were intended to initiate a healthy process of critical reflection within the International Step by Step Association (ISSA) and its member organizations in individual countries on the 10th anniversary of the program's initiation.

Within a multicase project, the study of individual cases will often not be organized around the multicase research question. To some extent, sometimes entirely, each case gets organized and studied separately around research questions of its own. A local orientation, tending carefully to particular sites and activities, risks paying too little attention to what binds the cases together, but it is an important step for relating the quintain to the situationality of the individual cases. For example, in Bosnia and Herzegovina, because of boundary-crossing problems, it was initially challenging to conduct training that included participants from across ethnic areas.

For these individual case studies, I call the deeper research questions "issues." Issues are not information questions, such as "Who organized the assistance to the city's homeless population?" or "In what ways was the Internet used in staff recruitment?" These may be important questions, seeking greatly needed information, but they fall short of tapping into the basic activity and values of the case. Issues are questions such as "In what ways did their changes in recruitment require a change in performance standards?" or "Did this executive development training, originally developed with male executives in mind, need reconceptualization for female executives?" These issue questions might be answered superficially in a few words, but they should serve as prompts to deeper reflection of the operation of the program.

1.6. THE PARTICULAR AND THE GENERAL

Case study issues reflect complex, situated, problematic relationships. They pull attention both to ordinary experience and also to the disciplines of knowledge (e.g., sociology, economics, ethics, literary criticism). Departing greatly from designs of experiments and tests of hypotheses, qualitative case researchers focus on relationships connecting ordinary practice in natural habitats to a few factors and concerns of the academic disciplines. (Issues "brought in" are called "etic" issues; those found in the field are called "emic.") This broader purview of relationships is applied to the particular case. Generalizing (Becker, 1992) remains in the mind of the case researcher. Can we consider a tension between generalization and particularization as a healthy tension?

The two issues two paragraphs back were written for a particular case. If they are important to the multicase study, they should be asked again in a more general way, perhaps as follows: "Does change in recruitment standards away from affirmative action require change in performance standards?" and "Does executive training originally developed for male clients need reconceptualization for women?" Changing "Did" to "Does" changes thinking from the particular to the general.

Whether stated for generalization or for particularization, these organizing questions should serve to deepen understanding of the findings (Polanyi, 1962). Quintains are often better understood by looking at the way problems are handled than by looking at efficiency or productivity outcomes. Starting with a topical concern, case researchers consider the *foreshadowed problems*, concentrate on issue-related observations, interpret patterns of data, and reformulate the issues as findings or assertions.

Similarly, the multicase research director starts with a quintain, arranges to study cases in terms of their own situational issues, interprets patterns within each case, and then analyzes cross-case findings to make assertions about the binding. An example of the way an issue might evolve is illustrated in Figure 1.1. The hypothetical scene is a case study of a music education program.

For both the multicase project and the case studies, the selection of issue questions is crucial. In designing their studies, researchers ask, "Which issue questions bring out our concerns? Which might turn out to

1. *The quintain*: Preparation of music teachers in colleges of education of the American Midwest.

2. *The foreshadowed problem*: School boards that hire music teachers support an emphasis on preparation for band, chorus, and public performances, but a few teachers and most music education leaders advocate for a more intellectual emphasis, including history, literature, and critical study of music.

3. *The issue at some of the campuses*: What are the pros and cons of the teaching faculties' placing higher priority on music theory and music as a discipline in courses for their teacher trainees?

4. *After data analysis, the multicase assertion*: In general, the music departments have aligned with school districts opposing the hiring of teachers with strong inclinations toward intellectually based school music.

FIGURE 1.1. An example of the evolution of a research question.

be the dominant theme for the whole study?" To maximize understanding of each case, they ask, "Which issues seek out compelling uniqueness?" For the multicase study, they ask, "Which issues help our understanding of the quintain?"

The research questions of the more quantitative studies will be "formalized," as described by William Firestone and Robert Herriott (1984); this means that they are expressed in terms of factors or variables, and sometimes as regression equations. Examples of formalized questions include "Does organizational stability depend largely on age, training, and loyalty of the staff?" and "Are breakthroughs in science education a function of the priorities of government and the science community?" Some issue questions imply causality; some do not.

Some researchers consistently raise social justice issues (House & Howe, 1999). Some researchers consistently raise professional development issues (Schön, 1983; Stake, DeStefano, Harnisch, Sloane, & Davis, 1997). But in general, they ask, "Which issues facilitate the planning and activities of inquiry?" Issues are chosen partly in terms of what can be learned within the opportunities for study. They will be chosen differently depending on the purposes of different studies, and differently by different researchers. We might say that a contract is drawn between researcher and quintain. The researcher asks, "What can be learned *here* that a reader needs to know?"

The issues used to organize the multicase study may or may not be the ones used to organize the final report. Some cases will provide particular information and not much else, raising little debate, contributing little to new cross-case understandings. Some cases will provide insights into multicase relationships not yet recognized—for example, "How does the strong support of the local leaders actually diminish public understanding of the program?" Issues at the case level sometimes lead to improvement of generalizations, especially when they are rooted in a situation of stress, teasing out more of the complexity.

1.7. THE CONTEXTS

Each case to be studied is a complex entity located in its own situation. It has its special contexts or backgrounds. Historical context is almost always of interest, but so are cultural and physical contexts. Others that are often of interest are the social, economic, political, ethical, and aesthetic contexts. The program or phenomenon operates in many different situations. One purpose of a multicase study is to illuminate some of these many contexts, especially the problematic ones.

The case is singular, but it has subsections (e.g., the production, marketing, and sales departments); groups (e.g., the patients, nurses, and administrators); occasions (e.g., the work days, paydays, and holidays); and many other dimensions and domains. Many of the subsections are so well populated that they need to be sampled. Each subsection may have its own contexts—contexts that go a long way toward making relationships understandable. Qualitative case study calls for the examination of experience in these situations. Yvonna Lincoln and Egon Guba (1985) pointed out that qualitative research is based on a view that social phenomena, human dilemmas, and the nature of cases are situational. The study of situations reveals *experiential knowledge*, which is important to understanding the quintain.

The search for generalizations usually accompanies a search for causes. In seeking research funding, social policy researchers promise findings that can lead to program improvement (Firestone & Herriott, 1984). They claim or imply that they are dealing with cause-and-effect relationships. But many, perhaps most, qualitative researchers dwell little on causal explanation of events (Becker, 1992). They tend to see the activities as interrelated, but with forces merely interacting rather than determinative. In *War and Peace*, Tolstoy said that the soldier burning his breakfast beans influenced the battle as much as Napoleon did. In modern thinking, that seems far-fetched. Modernists prefer the view that human activity has causes and effects.

But a cautious qualitative researcher sees the quintain as multiply sequenced, multiply contextual, and functioning coincidentally, rather than as causally determined. Many of them find the search for cause as oversimplifying. They describe instead the sequence and coincidence of events, interrelated and contextually bound. Actions are seen as purposive, yes, but underdetermined. They favor research designs that describe the diverse sequential activities of the case. Doing case studies does not require priority on diversity of issues and contexts, but most qualitative researchers carefully study such diversity.

In the earlier example of the training of music teachers (see Figure 1.1), cases were selected on the basis of priority given to training in the teaching of music in the schools. Bound in purpose, the colleges all trained teachers to become "certified" to teach school music. That was their binding concept, but it extended to a concern about narrowness of the training. The context included consideration of communities' expectations for school band and choral programs, with a strong orientation toward sports and holiday performances. The context also included the scarcity of arts-related jobs for new college graduates. Developing these considerations within the study required attention to community values, student aspirations, aesthetic respectability, the economics of employment, and the orientation of the schools to standardized testing. Some of the picture became clearer at the individual sites, but it also became more complicated, such as finding that liberal arts colleges and education colleges placed their music education graduates in rather different schools. This example demonstrates that researchers have some of the influence of contexts in mind at the outset of a study, but they need to be prepared for the subtleties of unexpected influence.

Too much emphasis on original research questions and contexts can distract researchers from recognizing new issues when they emerge. But too little emphasis on research questions can leave researchers unprepared for subtle evidence supporting the most important relationships (Firestone & Herriott, 1984). Many inexperienced case researchers, wanting to be open-minded, seek to avoid forcing the study to be about their own interests, and begin observations without a plan. But to be sensitive to the meanings of activities as perceived by different people, they should anticipate what some of those perspectives might be. It is not easy to find a perfect middle ground between underanticipating and overanticipating, but a new researcher should expect that good hard thinking about the relative importance of research questions will increase the relevance of observations.

1.8. MAKING THE INDIVIDUAL CASE REPORT

Even when the study is well done, the research questions will not be fully answered. Some assertions can be made that partially answer the question, but ways the questions need to be improved will become apparent. And new questions needing to be asked will become apparent. So the case study report is a summary of what has been done to try to get answers, what assertions can be made with some confidence, and what more needs to be studied. This seems like "slim pickings," but the quality of the investigation, the increased familiarity with the program and phenomena, and the new realizations of complexity can make the research community proud.

The aim of multicase research, as presented in this book, is to come to understand the quintain better. The research questions are selected to guide this search for understanding, and the discussion in the interpretation sections will also be guided by research questions. Some of the questions will have dropped out, some may have evolved, and some new questions may have become important enough to deserve review. But the report will be structured, in part, around the research questions.

Planning the Report

The presence of research questions is apparent in Figure 1.2, which presents a completed plan for producing the final report in the Ukraine case study of the Step by Step case project (see Chapter 6). A blank form of this graphic was used early in the planning, and entries were modified slightly by the team in subsequent stages. It is a general plan for reporting, suitable for a variety of case studies. When the time comes for reporting the analysis and interpretations of a multicase study, a different report assembly form is needed. An example is offered in Chapter 4 as Worksheet 7.

In its original format, the Ukraine case report covered 39 pages. An estimate had been made early in the research that 45 pages (standard paper and margins, single spacing) should be the target for the submission. That number appears now at the bottom of the column marked "Pages" in Figure 1.2. Those 45 pages were to be divided into 16 sections, with each topic identified by a short name (see the "Topic section" column). Notice that Liubchyk (the child who was the case for the Ukraine study) was targeted for description in 10 of the pages—some at the beginning, some at the middle, and some at the end. After the report opened

Issues appearing

Insertions	Topic sections	Pages	Pages of context	Questionnaire info	Inclusion	Teacher training	Child-centered educ.	Democratic play	Program sustainability	Choice vs. standard	Minor topics	Quotes, impressions
D,C,3	Liubchyk	5		×		×					1. Teacher selection	A. Black today, green tomorrow
F,1	Oksana	3	1	×	×	×			×		2. Child protection	B. Director, not bureaucrat
4	Tchr. tng., Lviv	3	1	×	×	×					3. Child view of disability	C. L.'s view of time & mgmt.
	Press conf., Lviv	2		×				×			4. Tchr. view of disability	D. Body contact
	Tchr. tng., Kyiv	2			×						5. Nature of disability	E. Tchr. staffing or potholes
	Tchr. tng., Ukr.	2	2	×	×						6. Role of church	F. Oksana's activity centers
3	Liubchyk	3		×	×						7. Teacher unions	G. Parents voted support
	His parents	2		×	×						8. European Union TACIS	H. Psycholog'l assessment
	Parent orgs.	2	2	×							9. Chernobyl effects	I. Aggression, affection
B,9	LEA, Lviv	3	1								10. Special ed. alternatives	
	Ministry	2	2	×			×	×			11. Preparing parents	
2,8	SbS Ukraine	2	2	×			×	×		×		
10	Interpretation: Alt. ed. policy	4					×					
	Interpretation: Teacher training	4		×		×						
E,5	Interpretation: Inclusion	4		×								
A	Liubchyk	2		×								

45 11

FIGURE 1.2. Plan for assembling the final report case study in Ukraine.

with five pages on Liubchyk, his teacher, Oksana, a Step by Step first-grade teacher, was to be presented next.

As this case study evolved, the three most important research questions became those that dealt with alternative education policy (i.e., policy departing somewhat from the state curriculum), Step by Step teacher training, and inclusion of children with disabilities in regular classrooms. Interpretation of what was observed regarding those three questions was scheduled to appear in the three next-to-last sections, each allotted four pages. (See the three "Interpretation" entries in the "Topic sections" column, second, third, and fourth up from the bottom.)

Data and background for the three main questions would not appear only in these interpretation sections, but would be distributed throughout the report. The third, fourth, and fifth columns following the "Pages" column indicate where the researchers expected to provide data on the three main questions. At first, it was a wild guess where things would go, but sequence, names, pages, and placements were modified along the way, and the plan became little changed during the last weeks of the study.

Every day or so, the researchers came up with a minor topic, a quotation, or even an impression that seemed good enough for potential inclusion. These were listed in the last two columns of the matrix by number or letter, and were later located in a suitable section. For example, one day Liubchyk said to his teacher, "Black today, green tomorrow." This was interpreted to mean that he acknowledged the color of the clothing she was wearing, and was suggesting that she wear green the next day. It was decided that this quotation would be saved for the final section (note the letter A in the left column), where it would be placed with observations of the successes and limitations of admitting Liubchyk to this regular classroom.

Much was to be accomplished in these 45 pages. Gaining an understanding of the case and its contexts; raising the research questions; and examining the interaction not only of the children, but of the teachers, parents, teacher trainers, and even school and national education leaders, were the intentions of this case study. The experience with Liubchyk was to illustrate the work of the Step by Step inclusive education initiative in Ukraine, and to contribute to multicase understanding of the several international and local research questions.

CHAPTER 2

The Multicase Study

As indicated in Chapter 1, getting the research question and other content of the study right is as important as getting the methods right—and probably requires greater effort. Teams needs to work through and continue working through these issues for both the multicase study as a whole and the individual case studies.

The main illustration of multicase research in this book is the Step by Step project—a study taking more than a year to complete, with each of the cases requiring at least one person working at least half time at least half a year. I am comfortable with the idea that a good multicase study could be completed much more quickly (even in a few months, perhaps, and often by a single researcher), but I would expect many reviewers of the report to judge it as lacking thoroughness and depth of interpretation. It takes time to do the job well.

To get into the details of multicase methods, let us look at a simpler multicase study—the evaluation of the Veterans Benefits Administration (VBA) program to train its staff to write better letters to veterans (Stake & Davis, 1997). The training program was called Reader Focused Writing (RFW). RFW was the quintain. We had an evaluation staff of four and designed our multicase study to observe and interview at training sites in 5 of the 57 regional offices; thus the quintain had five cases being studied. In addition to the fieldwork (or sometimes as part of it), we planned the following outcome data-gathering activities:

- A "final exam" letter-writing task for each trainee.
- A pre–post comparison of trainee-composed letters to veterans.
- A survey of a sample of trainees for their perspectives on the training.

- A survey of directors of regional offices (approximately one per state).
- Structured interviews of directors of training at sites visited.
- Telephone interview of veterans about strengths and weaknesses of letters received.

The site visits lasted 2–3 days and were written up in four to seven single-spaced pages. As required, the whole study was completed in 2 months. The work was divided up and assigned to team members as shown in Figure 2.1. This graphic was helpful in explaining the study during data gathering and as part of the final multicase report.

This study was about the size of a dissertation research project; the activity and file holdings were sufficiently small to allow a good embrace of the quintain. (Multicase research can be handled well as dissertation research. The doctoral student is the director, data gatherer, and analyst for the study, but with a responsible advisor and committee, he or she gets help in interpreting observations and refining research questions. If the cases are only studied as briefly as in the RFW project, the dissertation probably would be better if a single case were studied rather than multiple cases.)

2.1. STAFFING

maybe all three, most multicase studies are so complex that they almost need to be done by one person! That is, the writing of a good report almost requires all the experience to be squeezed into one head. It is very difficult to transfer to others a full picture of what both researchers and data sources know of experience, interactivity, and context. ("Data sources" are interviewees, people observed, and others directly or indirectly providing data for the research.) Still, this kind of study is so complex that several minds—sometimes many minds—are needed to do the work (Delamont, 1992) and to examine the different interpretations of happenings (Denzin, 2000). Some outstanding multicase studies feature a succession of reviewers interpreting the observations.[1] Each case may be studied by an individual or by a team.

Figure 2.2 is a sketch of a plan for a huge multicase evaluation study in Brazil. The quintain was Escola Ativa, a rural primary school demon-

---

[1]An example is Thomas Seals's counseling dissertation, beginning with the case of a gay partnership (Seals, 1985).

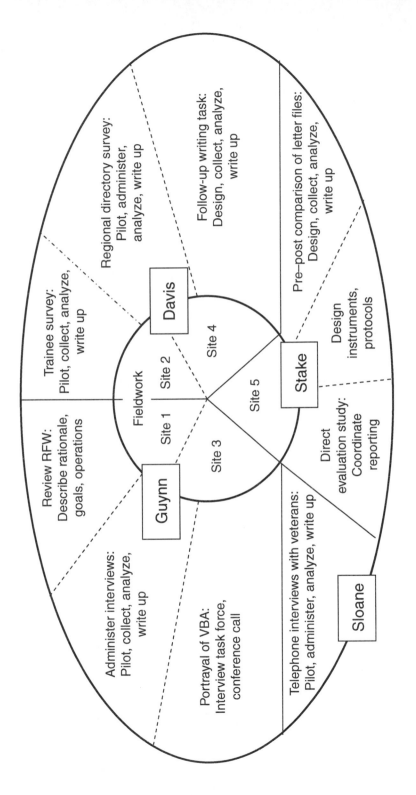

FIGURE 2.1. Division of responsibility among members of the multicase team for Veterans Benefits Administration (VBA) Reader Focused Writing (RFW) evaluation.

19

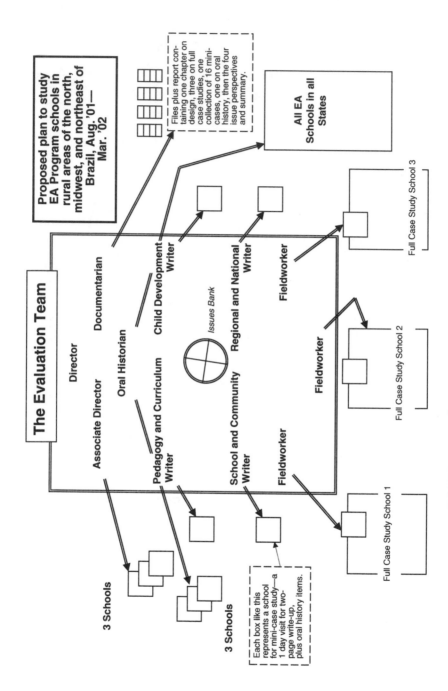

The Evaluation Team

Director

Associate Director   Documentarian

Oral Historian

Pedagogy and Curriculum
Writer

Child Development
Writer

Issues Bank

School and Community   Regional and National
Writer   Writer

Fieldworker

Fieldworker

Fieldworker

Fieldworker

3 Schools

3 Schools

Each box like this
represents a school
for mini-case study—a
1 day visit for two-
page write-up,
plus oral history items.

Proposed plan to study
EA Program schools in
rural areas of the north,
midwest, and northeast of
Brazil, Aug. '01—
Mar. '02

Files plus report con-
taining one chapter on
design, three on full
case studies, one
collection of 16 mini-
cases, one on oral
history, then the four
issue perspectives
and summary.

All EA
Schools in all
States

Full Case Study School 1

Full Case Study School 2

Full Case Study School 3

FIGURE 2.2. Qualitative evaluation design for Escola Ativa.

stration program in several Brazilian states, with children and community members taking much of the responsibility for teaching. A team of 11 was anticipated, with each of the experts doing at least a 1-day mini-study of a school somewhere across the Amazon River watershed. Four of the experts were to make quintain-level interpretations centered around the themes of their expertise in the cross-case analysis. Three schools were to be studied for a longer period, providing elaborate detail on how students and community people took extended teaching responsibilities. The staffing emphasis here was on getting senior scholars out into the schools briefly, having these scholars examine draft reports by other team members, and then having them write thematic chapters.

Other than for a dissertation, a single multicase researcher seldom does all the case studies. But as the analyst, the director or lead researcher needs to study all the case reports thoroughly. All too often, the several researchers on a team will not get well enough acquainted with all the reports. Just dividing duties up within a team, with each person taking certain activities and issues, probably means that the responsibility for synthesizing the findings and writing an integrated report will be underplayed—as might have been the case had the Escola Ativa project been funded. Effective multicase study leadership is usually an exercise in managing team members' minds. A leaderless team may be the most enjoyable and perhaps the most creative, but conducting a really good research study means having a strong leader and a diverse group of help-ers. One of the earliest staffing decisions will be deciding whether or not the research director will also be the analyst for the cross-case analysis and the main writer of the final cross-case report.

As to staffing the case research, it is usually difficult to find case-workers who have both the necessary topical expertise for the research questions and the necessary experience with qualitative field research methods. In *Case Studies in Science Education* (Stake & Easley, 1979), our main cases were studied by nine competent educational researchers: Terry Denny, Jacquetta Hill-Burnett, Alan Peshkin, Rudolfo Serrano, Louis Smith, Mary Lee Smith, Wayne Welch, and Rob Walker. Still, one of the National Science Foundation's reviewers of the final report objected strenuously to the poor qualification of the fieldworkers.

Not every member of the team needs to have both content and method expertise, but much of the work will have to be done without help nearby. Sometimes, for special reasons, the research will be done by nonresearchers. A member who has neither content nor research skills may not make much of a contribution to the enterprise, however. It is not a good idea, for example, to send such a member out to ask people some questions.

People differ greatly in how well they can interview. Asking questions in a way that teases out subtle meanings is a gift that grows with experience and mentoring. Teaming an accomplished content person with an experienced interviewer to do an interview is a great idea, but under time and financial pressure it seems extravagant, because two interviews could be completed separately in the same time. The more standardized the interview protocol (with little expectation of on-the-spot interpretation and probing), the less an expert interviewer is needed.

After the organization of the study, there is preparatory work at the project level. The director needs to develop communication with the fieldworkers—answering the occasional question, giving encouragement. Drafts of a few observations and document reviews need to be read, and revisions suggested as necessary. When a complete case report has been drafted, then other people are needed to review it, partly for commentary on issues and the binding concept as these have been written up. It is desirable for researchers on other cases to read some of these drafts, but they may not find time for it. When most or all of the draft reports are revised, the cross-case analysis can begin. The director usually heads this effort, with help from other members of the team—not in bits and pieces, because it takes long, sustained work to combine the understandings and recognize inconsistencies across cases.

These responsibilities call for concentration, collaborative work, and luck. It is important to find staff members who relish working alone, yet are capable of sharing team responsibility at multiple levels.

2.2. SELECTING CASES

The benefits of multicase study will be limited if fewer than, say, 4 cases are chosen, or more than 10. Two or three cases do not show enough of the interactivity between programs and their situations, whereas 15 or 30 cases provide more uniqueness of interactivity than the research team and readers can come to understand. But for good reason, many multicase studies have fewer than 4 or more than 15 cases.

One of the unusual tasks of multicase study in the social sciences and human services is the selection of cases to study. The selection process regularly begins with cases already at least partially identified. Sometimes all the cases for a multicase study are known in advance; sometimes all are chosen by the director or research team. Sometimes all existing cases are studied; sometimes only the volunteers are studied; sometimes the cases are selected by a third party (the funding agency, perhaps). But it is common for the research director to have something—sometimes everything—to say about choosing the cases to be studied.

For the doctor, the social worker, and the program evaluator, their cases are usually known or assigned in advance; they seldom get to choose. Their cases are often of prominent interest to them before any formal examination begins. For education and social science researchers, multicase designs usually require cases to be chosen. Understanding the critical phenomena depends on choosing the cases well (Creswell, 1998; Patton, 1990; Vaughan, 1992; Yin, 1994).

Suppose we are trying to understand the behavior of people who falsify student testing records, and we decide to probe the phenomenon with a multicase study. This quintain could be the phenomenon "falsification of records," or "that group of people who falsify records." Intentional falsification of records apparently does not happen often, at least verifiable cases are few and far between. Let us imagine that we can identify no more than seven cases we might conveniently study. Four are high school counselors, one a dean of students, one a student (hacker), and one a political candidate who falsified his own credentials. We want to generalize about record falsification; however, we realize that our primary interest is in educational institutions and is not general enough to include the hacker and the candidate for office. So we narrow the quintain and design the study to include only the other five.

As a general rule, there are three main criteria for selecting cases:

- Is the case relevant to the quintain?
- Do the cases provide diversity across contexts?
- Do the cases provide good opportunities to learn about complexity and contexts?

As indicated earlier, a multicase study starts with recognizing what concept or idea binds the cases together. Sometimes this concept needs to be targeted; usually we target the quintain that provides the binding concept. The cases to be studied may each have a different relationship with the quintain. Some may be model cases, and others may have only an incidental relationship. If other considerations are satisfied, cases will be selected because they represent the program or phenomenon.

An important reason for doing the multicase study is to examine how the program or phenomenon performs in different environments. This often means that cases in both typical and atypical settings should be selected. When cases are selected carefully, the design of a study can incorporate a diversity of contexts.

Miles and Huberman stated in their classic methodology book, *Qualitative Data Analysis* (1994), that it is important to obtain a representative sample of all the cases to which users may generalize. From their scientific perspective, statistical sampling is greatly preferred. (Here I am contrasting science with professional services. Science is a search for generalizable knowledge. Professional services, such as teaching, nursing, counseling, consulting, and program evaluation, are efforts to help people and organizations function better. Science is also different from the field of organizational management (Bolman & Deal, 2003).

Contrary to the positions of Lawrence Stenhouse (1978) and myself (Stake, 2005), statistical or science-based cases are expected to represent a population of cases. The binding concept, the phenomenon of interest in the case, needs to be prominent in these cases. Here, as described also by Bronislav Malinowski (1922/1984), Charles Ragin and Howard Becker (1992), and Robert Yin (1992), the main work is science—an enterprise to gain the best possible explanations of phenomena.

At the outset of such a multicase study, the phenomenon is identified. The cases are opportunities to study it. Even in the larger multicase studies, the sample size is often much too small to warrant random selection. For qualitative fieldwork, we will usually draw a purposive sample of cases, a sample tailored to our study; this will build in variety and create opportunities for intensive study.

Just above, I introduced the phenomenon of falsification of records as an example. Let us say we want to improve our understanding of falsification, to fit it into what we know about ethics, organizational management, and human relations—that is, to learn about various "abstract dimensions." What some (Vispoel, Schmitz, Samarapungavan, & Boerger, 1987) call "abstract dimensions," I am calling "issues" in this book. They are relevant topics or areas of concern. Mary Kennedy (1979) called them "relevant attributes." Malinowski (1922/1984) called them "theories." Issues include the topics not only of main research questions, but of potential or latent research questions as well.

We recognize a possibly large population of cases of falsification, but a rather small group of accessible cases. We want to generalize about falsification of student records; we have little interest in any of the particular cases. As for *representation* of the population, the opportunity from these five cases seems small, but we are optimistic that we can learn some important things from almost any case. We will choose a small number of falsifiers of records who are staff members of an educational institution. As indicated above, we have ruled out studying applicants and aspirants who falsify their credentials. Such falsification may be more common, but we will save them for another study.

We are now more interested in records falsification by an institutional staff member—perhaps someone protecting something or trying to gain an advantage. What are the criteria for choosing cases?[2] We examine various manifestations of the phenomenon, thinking to some extent of how typical the cases are, but focusing more closely on cases that seem to offer the opportunity to learn a lot. Usually I favor cases from which we can learn about their activity and situation. This may mean taking the ones that are most accessible, the ones we can spend the most time with. There may be a tradeoff between potential for learning and representativeness. Sometimes it is possible to get special insights from examining atypical cases—more so even than from examining less accessible typical cases.

Here is another illustration: Suppose we are interested in museum education—particularly in interactive displays, where the visitor manipulates some exhibit and gets feedback. We propose a multicase study of four museums. We might set up a typology, perhaps of (1) museum types (namely, art, science, and history museums); (2) city size (perhaps medium and very large); and (3) educational philosophy (namely, exhibitory or participative). That makes a typology of 12 cells. Examples of museums probably cannot be found for all 12 cells; given our resources, it probably would be better to study four museums. Having decided this, we might start by thinking we should have one art, one history, and two science museums, two because interactive displays have been more fully developed in science museums. Three of the four might characterize the interactivist educational philosophy. We might choose two in medium-sized and two in very large cities, still seeking accessibility more than randomization or geographical diversity.

We would extend our acquaintance with the potential cases, considering logistics, the museums' disposition to allow the study, and our resources. We would take note of the range of interactive displays used at the possible sites. Falling short of structured representation, we would look for four museums that differ across the three attributes. We might end up choosing the four that give us the best opportunities to learn about interactive displays, even if they are all in middle-sized cities. Any best possible selection of four museums from a balanced design would not give us a compelling representation of museums as a whole. With so small a sample, randomization would give us little statistical basis for generalizing about interactions between interactivity and context. Several desirable types usually have to be omitted. For multicase studies, selection by

---

[2]William Firestone (1993) proposed two criteria: maximizing diversity in the cases, and representing the population as much as possible.

sampling of attributes should not be the highest priority. Balance and variety are important; relevance to the quintain and opportunity to learn are usually of greater importance.

A similar selection process will occur within an individual case study. Even when the case was decided upon in advance, the researchers need to select persons, places, and events to observe. A few may become embedded cases (mini-cases)—cases within the case. Appearing in Figure 6.1 (which illustrates the Ukraine study of Liubchyk) are two mini-cases—one of Liubchyk's teacher, Oksana, and one of his mother. Later, a third mini-case was added to provide observations at a health improvement center created by a parents' organization. Here again, our own training, experience, and intuition help us make a good selection. The Step by Step early childhood program in Ukraine aimed to get children with disabilities included in regular classrooms, and to avoid segregated special education (the usual practice in Ukraine). The sponsors of the Ukraine case study chose to study a child in the school with the most developed inclusion efforts. Selection of the child was influenced by the vigorous activity of his parents, two teachers, a social worker, and the principal. In a short time, the researchers needed to select other parents, teachers, and community leaders to interview. They asked themselves which people's activities and perceptions would add most to the portrayal. There is no mechanical way of selecting data sources.

Once, as part of the evaluation of Indiana Bell Telephone's Buddy Program (Quinn & Quinn, 1992), a research team was studying the placement of computers in the homes of fourth graders for scholastic purposes. The telephone company intended it to be a pilot study for public school reform in that state. The cases (i.e., the school sites) had been previously selected to receive computers, and the innovation was underway. In the multicase evaluation directed by William Quinn, his team of five worked collaboratively, but each field researcher had one case study to develop more or less alone. A principal issue had to do with impact on the students' families. Clear rules had to be set for computer use by other family members; that is, the computer was to be available for word processing, record keeping, and games by other family members, but certain times were to be set aside for fourth-grade homework. At one site, 50 homes had computers. The researcher got a small amount of information from every home, but observation in the home occurred only in a small number. Which homes were selected for visits? Here again, the field researcher noted attributes of interest: gender of the fourth grader, number and gender of siblings, family structure, home discipline, previous use of computers and other technology in the homes, and so on. Here, the researchers discussed such case characteristics with informants, got recommendations, visited several homes, and got attribute data. Too little could be learned from inhospitable parents. The choice of homes was made[3]—assuring variety but not necessarily representativeness, without strong argument for typicality, and again weighted by considerations of access and even of hospitality (for the time was short). In evaluating the Buddy Program, the researchers were seeking assurance of relevance and variety; but the primary criterion for selection of cases and of homes within each case was opportunity to learn.

2.3. ACTIVITY IN ITS SITUATION

One primary focus within the case studies that make up a multicase study will be the characterization of the program or phenomenon. That is, we seek a better description of the quintain. But the characterization will be seen differently in different situations. Therefore, one of the most important tasks for the multicase researcher is to show how the program or phenomenon appears in different contexts. The more the study is a qualitative study, the more emphasis will be placed on the experience of people in the program or with the phenomenon.

What are the researchers looking for? Usually they need to find out firsthand what each individual case does—its activity, its functioning. Sometimes the most direct answers come from observing the activity. The researchers will observe as much as they can themselves, ask others for their observations, study the records of what has happened, and gather artifacts of those happenings. For example, a department of an organization being studied provides services, manages itself and responds to micromanagement by external authorities, observes rules, adapts to constraints, seeks opportunities, changes staffing, and so on. Describing and interpreting these activities constitute a large part of many case studies. Putting them together, in context, constitutes the central findings of the multicase study.

The case's activities are expected to be influenced by contexts, so contexts need to be studied and described, whether or not evidence of influence is found. Staffing, for example, may be affected by the political context, particularly by union activity and some form of "old-boy network." Public announcement of services may be affected by historical and physical contexts. Budgets have an economic context. Qualitative re-

---

[3]William Firestone (1993), Michael Patton (1990), and Ansel Strauss and Juliet Corbin (1990) have discussed successive case selection over time.

searchers have strong expectations that the reality perceived by people inside and outside the case will be social, cultural, situational, and contextual—and they want the interactivity of functions and contexts described as well as possible.

With analysis of variance and causal modeling, quantitative researchers study criterion differences attributable to main effects (i.e., to influences of interest). They look for differences among "treatments," and for effects of gender, time, and location. For instance, they look for different influences of rural and urban settings, and for the different performances of boys and girls (and of other subpopulations). Demographics and programmatic treatment are common main effects. In an experimental study, quantitative researchers may compare subsequent performance of those receiving different kinds or levels of services. Even if many, many comparisons are made, however, some performance differences remain unexplained. In a business setting, a typical treatment would be personally tailored work conditions. Suppose urban females respond differently to such a treatment. The difference would show up in the analysis as an interaction effect. But suppose Carmen, a city girl, consistently responds differently from other city girls. Researchers want to understand what is common and what is unusual about Carmen's response pattern. This is unlikely to be discerned by quantitative analysis, yet it may be easily spotted by a case study of Carmen. And on further analysis, her pattern of behavior may be useful for interpreting the functioning of several subgroups. When individual cases respond differently in complex situations, the interactivity of main effects and settings can be expected to require the particularistic scrutiny of case study.

For a number of years, psychologists Lee Cronbach and Richard Snow (1977) studied aptitude–treatment interactions. They hoped to find general rules by which teachers could adapt instruction to personal learning styles. At deeper and deeper levels of interaction, they found significance. This did not lead to prespecifying teaching methods for individuals, but it supported the conclusion that differentiated consistencies of response by individuals are to be expected in complex situations.

People simultaneously experience many things. In qualitative case study, a researcher has certain possible influences in mind—but, sweeping widely, the researcher lets his or her mind and eye scan a large number of happenings, variables, and contexts. He or she examines different activity in different settings, looking for "correspondence." Correspondence means patterns of covariation. It is correlation. It means that things are happening together. When we experience repetitious correspondence, we usually think we understand some of the "interactivity" of the case—that is, some ways in which the activity of the case interacts with its contexts.

In a three-case dissertation study, Brinda Jegatheesan (2005) studied three central Asian families living in Chicago, each having a child with autism. She gathered many observations of the families in their homes, where these children were not treated as children with a disability, although they needed special help to live what were, for them, ordinary lives. Much of the activity was rooted in teachings of the Koran. Even though the family spoke Urdu, Hindi, Bangla, and English, Arabic was the primary language of home instruction, because Arabic is the language of the Koran. Public schooling was treated as essential for social and economic reasons, but communication was being taught closely through religious text.

Activity is generally seen to be at least somewhat determined by the situation. For Barry MacDonald, Clement Adelman, Saville Kushner, and Rob Walker (1982), the situation was school desegregation. For Alan Peshkin (1986), it was a fundamentalist Christian school. Here are some other situations expected to influence program activity and social phenomena: an accountability climate, a commitment to inclusion, a laissez-faire policy, a period of reconciliation, a free-trade environment, and a flu epidemic. Dominance of any of these eight may be rare, but some social tension shapes every situation. The multicase research team tries to tease out how the situation at each of several different sites influences program activity or the phenomena.

2.4. DATA GATHERING ACROSS CASES

Researchers in the field seek the *ordinary* happenings for each case. They investigate settings, and follow the range of value commitments. Herbert Blumer (1969, p. 149) urged accepting, developing, and using the distinctive expressions found in order to study what is ordinary for the particular case. The details of life that the researcher is unable to see for him- or herself are found by interviewing people who did see it or by finding documents recording it. For single-case and multicase studies, the most common methods of case study are observation, interview, coding, data management, and interpretation.[4] They are described in the primary sources for research methods (see Gall, Gall, & Borg, 2003; Gomm, 2004; Denzin & Lincoln,

---

[4]Focus groups appear attractive to new case researchers, because so many people can be questioned simultaneously. I have sometimes found focus groups useful when I am in a time bind, and they sometimes develop unexpected revelations, but they seldom provide good evidence for the issues the researcher wants to talk about. Naturally occurring narratives are likely to be better (Clandenin & Connelly, 1999).

2005; Erickson, 1986; and Bickman & Rog, 1998). The methods actually used in the cases may be quite similar from case to case, or may be quite different. The more the multicase analysis is to be quantitative, the more useful it may be to use the same methods for all cases.

The team needs data to document both the unusual and the ordinary. The workload is heavy—not only for the actual data gathering, but for arrangements, analysis, and write-up as well. We sometimes speak of the stages of a research study, but issue development continues from beginning to end. And some write-up begins after the first contact with people. A speculative, page-allocating outline or graphic (such as that shown in Figure 1.2) helps anticipate how themes and situations will be worked together and how the case will become gradually better understood. I would say that starting without a plan—in other words, anticipating an unstructured, open-ended study—is a road to failure.

A good organization plan for the case study is essential, but it should not be too constraining. Experienced caseworkers know that there will be late-emerging issues; often these will be subtle, will need to be watched for. We can distinguish, according to Malinowski, between arriving with minds closed and arriving with an eye for what to look for. He also said:

> Good training in theory, and acquaintance with its latest results, is not identical with being burdened with "preconceived ideas." If a man sets out on an expedition, determined to prove certain hypotheses, if he is incapable of changing his views constantly and casting them off ungrudgingly under the pressure of evidence, needless to say his work will be worthless. But the more problems he brings with him into the field, the more he is in the habit of molding his theories according to facts, and of seeing facts in their bearing upon theory, the better he is equipped for the work. Preconceived ideas are pernicious in any scientific work, but *foreshadowed problems* are the main endowment of a scientific thinker, and these problems are first revealed to the observer by his theoretical studies. (1922/1961/1984, p. 9; italics in original)

As an example, after becoming acquainted with parent volunteers in classrooms, the researcher may find that some parents use intimidation to control students' behavior, and the researcher may divert some attention to observing it. Moreover, some issues need quantitative observation or questioning. Still, many qualitative fieldworkers spend little of their resources constructing instruments—partly because, the way they do research, non-standardized questions are needed with most data sources. A meager budget may be consumed too quickly by devising and pilot-testing instruments. There are too many foreshadowing problems, with some maturing, some dying, some ever advancing in complexity. Even the ordinary may be too complicated to be mastered with the resources at hand.

Is the case *embraceable*? If a case is too large for a single person to know experientially, and/or if a multicase study is too diverse for a small team to know experientially, the research methods shift toward the quantitative. Good case research requires integrated, holistic comprehension of the case, but when the cases are not embraceable, measurement and statistical analysis are the main tools.

A good coding system can be valuable when the team members are experienced with the system and with each other. But learning a detailed analytic coding system within the study period often causes more trouble than it is worth (Smith & Dwyer, 1979). Codes sometimes start too early to reduce complex phenomena to simple categories. Certain sites, actors, or issues that are hard to capture or characterize should be assigned to a single team member—perhaps a junior member. Case complexity may have to be diminished to what can be comprehended by the team. The members negotiate the parts and issues to be studied, leaving the rest to brief mentions. Team members should write up their own parts, signing up others as critical friends. Usually the project director will carry out the cross-site analysis and write the synthesis, getting critiques from the team, people in the field, and (again) their critical friends.

If there is not a saying that "Content trumps method," there should be. In Figure 2.3 is a presentation of a number of questions typifying those in a case study interview. One of the most important things to notice is the prominence of the substance of research questions. An interview should be less about the interviewee than about the case. Of course, the way the interviewee sees the case operating is essential knowledge, and the researcher needs to find out a little about the interviewee to understand his or her interpretations.

The questions in the box in Figure 2.3 are examples of research questions most suitable (as to generality and specificity) for designing a case study. Such questions are good for interviewing too, but other questions more general and specific should also be used. Some of the most effective interviewing is "probe-based," meaning that certain materials (texts, videos, or other artifacts) are used as probes to evoke interviewee comment or interpretation. The probe materials give focus and scope to topics of interest, as well as motivate participation. For example, Terry Souchet, Merrill Chandler, David Snow, Marya Burke, and I (1999) made three 90-second tapes showing a trio of Chicago principals discussing such matters as instructional leadership and effects of student testing on curricula. In a 90-minute individualized interview, the researchers showed each tape to each interviewee and asked questions structured around it. (For another example, see Stake, 1984, pp. 4.1–4.58.) This can be an effective way of focusing respondents on situations they have observed.

Examples of basic research questions

- What is the nature of community support for child-oriented strategies?
- How can reading be taught more effectively?
- Are the concepts of "open society" and "inclusion" fundamentally interdependent?
- How are authority and decision making distributed in philanthropic foundations?

These are also open-ended interview questions—sometimes useful for obtaining quotations, but difficult to code and aggregate.

Examples of questions for zeroing in on a main research issue

- Now that the classrooms here have an inclusion policy and a second teacher, is more being learned?
- Is the emphasis on parent assistance in your classroom impeding the child's independent learning?
- Does requiring these teachers to pay themselves for their staff development change participation?
- Do conditions facilitate or even allow Anna, your department head, to be an instructional leader?

These questions are pointed toward understanding of a particular situation, rather than toward generalizing about situations everywhere. They draw attention to specific happenings or problems in that situation. It is important to have good descriptions of that particular situation to make responses meaningful to a distant reader.

Examples of questions to obtain measurment data

- How effective is the regional director?
- How well do your students understand the concept of negotiation?
- What portion of the class period is primarily conceptual education time?
- Was there correlation between teaching quality and participation in annual planning?
- How have student enrollment loads increased or decreased in the last 2 years?

Responses to these questions can be scaled or categorized for aggregation over a large number of cases, and can then be statistically analyzed. They may not be very good for generating stories or quotations.

Examples of questions about immediate problems

- What software should we buy?
- How will the business manager's work get done if that position is eliminated?
- Should we have intelligence testing in the second grade?
- Is there an issue of nepotism in the appointment of the mayor's cousin as director?
- Is it time to change team leaders?

(continued)

FIGURE 2.3. An overview of interview questions for case studies.

These questions are situational, suitable for large numbers of respondents who share or know about the particular situation. They are good for aggregation and statistical analysis, but also good for quotations and stories.

Note: All four of these types of interview questions may be needed in a research study. It is important to have questions directly asking for experiential descriptions related to the main research question.

Examples of questions to ask yourself in designing an interview

- Does the interviewee know information you need, or do you expect to create that knowledge by putting together answers from quite a few interviewees?
- Are you deeply interested in this particular case, or more interested in generalizing to a population of cases?
- Do you have enough information about the interviewee's own situation?
- Should the interviewee be aware of your main research question?
- Are you dealing with a relevant, weighty matter that justifies this interviewee's time?
- Are you searching for a causal implication that the interviewee knows?

You need to scrutinize your questions to see whether they sufficiently fit your intentions.

FIGURE 2.3. *(continued)*

Finally, a system for documentation and storage of data is necessary. Some tips on setting up a system are included in Figure 2.4. Much more can be found in Huberman and Miles (1994).

2.5. TRIANGULATION WITHIN CASES

Researchers in social situations deal a lot with impressions—their own, as well as those of others. Impressions can be good data, but good researchers want assurance of what they are seeing and hearing. They want assurance that they are not oversimplifying the situation. They worry that they are perhaps reading too much into what they see. They want assurance that most of the meaning gained by a reader from their interpretations is the meaning they intended to convey. The process of gaining these assurances is called "triangulation." Each important finding needs to have at least three (often more) confirmations and assurances that key meanings are not being overlooked. Each important interpretation needs assurance that it is supported by the data gathered and not easily misinterpreted by readers of the report.

- Keep a personal log as a back-up to data storage.
- Link document storage to data gathering and writing. The main documents are the ones the research team creates, including designs, sketches, notes, tallies, photos, analyses, and interpretations.
- A researcher probably should make a mock-up of the final report early, with tentative page allocations. If it is a team, writing tasks should be assigned then, too.
- Put the writer of a topic in charge of document storage for that topic.
- Too few files and too many files are both mistakes. There should be a file at least for each issue, activity site, data source (person), context, and section of the final report.
- Usually, a researcher gathering data should prepare a statement of those data suitable for the first draft of the report, and should provide a copy of that statement to other team members, if any. (Some progress on report writing should occur almost every day.)
- Researchers accustomed to working with computer storage of ongoing research can make their main files electronic. All others should make their main files paper files.
- Major data records should be routinely duplicated and stored in more than one file.
- Records and statements needing discussion with other team members should be marked with a red star (or some other symbol). Regularly scheduled data discussions are desirable for clarification and triangulation.
- Because of the shortage of time, audio- and videotapes should be used and transcribed only when it is clear that they are vital to the final report.
- Found documents should be numbered and stored, and brief information about them should be placed in appropriate files.
- Personal memory will be an important storage for writing the final report. One way to make memory more reliable is to keep a good log, including names, telephone numbers, addresses, dates and times, and musings.

FIGURE 2.4. Documentation and storage tips.

We researchers want our descriptions to be accurate. We know that our perceptions are subject to different interpretations—which is all the more reason for wanting to record those perceptions with precision. We know that what appears real to one person will not seem real to another; we want these multiple realities to be recognized. It is the process by which we mean to keep misunderstandings to a minimum. Triangulation is mostly a process of repetitious data gathering and critical review of what is being said.[5]

---

[5]Statistician R. C. Lewontin (1995) said, "It is frightening to think that social science is in the hands of professionals who are so deaf to human nuance that they believe that people do not lie to themselves (and to others) about the most freighted aspects of their own lives" (p. 28).

Both report writers and report readers have to deal with *ill-structured* knowledge. The quintain, contexts, narratives, and understandings are nuanced, internally contradictory, time-bound, and defying easy conceptualization. Often the report carries a *constructivist* philosophy (Schwandt, 2000). It is not unusual to find writers expecting their readers to be tolerant of ambiguity and to have an appetite for multiple perspectives. Still, I have yet to meet case writers who are unconcerned about the clarity of their own perception and the validity of their own communication. (Methodologist Joseph Maxwell [1992] has spoken of the need for thinking of validity separately for descriptions, interpretations, theories, generalizations, and evaluative judgments.) Meanings often do not emerge with integrity. They must be squeezed into the reader's conceptual space. Still, there is an urgent need for researchers to assure that their sense of situation, their observations, their reporting, and their writing have an "accurate" aim. However accuracy is construed, researchers do not want to be inaccurate. They do not want to find themselves lacking in confirmation.

It may seem implausible, but the author has partial responsibility for the validity of the readers' interpretations. When he spoke of validity in standardized testing, Samuel Messick (1989) called this "consequential validity." The author needs to repeat key assertions in several ways. He or she needs to give illustrations. He or she will leave some of the work for the readers to do, but should give them the makings of understanding. Even when authors recognize that their evidence is weak, leaving them on the speculative side, they will identify the guesses they have hazarded, and they should (though all too few authors do) indicate their efforts to triangulate.

To reduce the likelihood of misinterpretation, various strategies are employed; two of the most common are redundancy of data gathering and procedural challenges to explanations (Denzin, 1989; Goetz & LeCompte, 1984). When making observations or listening to tapes, we see and hear not once, but again and again. Getting another person to watch and hear is routine, especially a person from another point of view. The observer/reviewer can role-play another point of view, that perhaps of an administrator, a visitor from far away, or someone with a contrary philosophy, maybe all three, to challenge the meaning of a critical episode. Some understandings will converge, whereas others will break into separate perceptions, leaving both to be reported with lower confidence that the meaning has been reached.

What needs triangulation? Triangulation is an effort to assure that the right information and interpretations have been obtained. Triangulation is expected to lead either to confirmation that the observation means what we think it means or to ideas about how the observation would be interpreted differently by different people.

Here are some statements that might be reported:

1. "The children all sat at tables."
2. "The children sat at tables close by; the minority children sat farther away."
3. "Some children disregarded what the teacher asked them to do."

Here are some rules. Which applies to each of the three statements above?

a. If the description is trivial or beyond question, there is little need to triangulate.
b. If the description is relevant and debatable, there is some need to triangulate.
c. If the data are critical to a main assertion, there is much need to triangulate.
d. If the data are evidence for a controversial finding, there is much need to triangulate.
e. If a statement is clearly a speaker's interpretation, there is little need to triangulate the quotation but not its content.

Here are some additional observations for possible inclusion in the report:

4. "The teacher was irritated."
5. "The seating reflected institutional approval: Sitting close to the teacher was a reward."
6. "The teacher said she was making children comfortable, seating them by those they liked."

(Most readers would concede that Statements 1 and 6 do not need verification.)

If Statement 5 is important to the findings of the study, the interpretation needs more evidence than a single quotation or correlation. Several teachers could be asked. Evidence that students with low institutional approval were sometimes are seated close to the teacher would undercut the assertion. Triangulation sometimes helps the researcher recognize that the situation is more complex than it was thought to be.

As Norman Denzin (1989) once pointed out, there are several kinds of triangulation, leading to advisories such as these:

- Find ways to use multiple rather than single observers of the same thing.
- Use second and third perspectives, or even more (e.g., the views of parents and kids as well as teachers).
- Use more than one research method on the same thing (e.g., document review and interview).
- Check carefully to decide how much the total description warrants generalization:
  - Do your conclusions generalize across other times of day, other times of the year, other years?
  - Do your conclusions generalize to other places?
  - Do your conclusions about the aggregate of these persons generalize to individuals?
  - Do findings of the interaction among individuals in this group pertain to other groups?
  - Do findings of the aggregate of these persons here generalize to a population?

When knowledge is being constructed, no two observers construct it exactly the same way. Complete confirmation is not possible; views are partly agreed upon, partly not. To the extent that what is not agreed upon is unimportant, what is agreed upon is confirmed. When what is not agreed upon *is* important, the different views should be reported.

"Member checking" is a vital technique for field researchers. After gathering data and drafting a report—possibly even thinking that the report may be part of the cumulative rough draft—the researcher asks the main actor or interviewee to read it for accuracy and possible misrepresentation. A similar account is sometimes responded to by a focus group. Both of these provide new data for the study, as well as contribute to the revision and improved interpretation of the reporting.

All these procedures are called "triangulation." (Laurel Richardson and Elizabeth St. Pierre [2005] have called this gaining of assurance "crystallization.") Triangulation has been generally considered a process of using multiple perceptions to clarify meaning, but it is also verifying the repeatability of an observation or interpretation. But, because it is acknowledged that no observations or interpretations are perfectly repeatable, triangulation serves also to clarify meaning by identifying different ways the case is being seen (Flick, 1998; Silverman, 1993; Smith,

1994). The qualitative researcher is interested in diversity of perception, even the multiple realities within which people live. Triangulation helps to identify these different realities.

I have been speaking here about triangulation within a case study. We are also concerned about triangulation *across* case studies—that is, about the *credibility* (Lincoln & Guba, 1985) of descriptions and findings in the multicase study as a whole. That discussion will be saved for the next chapter.

CHAPTER 3

Cross-Case Analysis

It is common for the individual case reports, sometimes abbreviated, to be included in the multicase report. Of course, the sponsor of the project and most readers want more than that: They want cross-case analysis. They want the benefit of the team's understanding of the aggregate. Given the binding concept—a theme, issue, phenomenon, or functional relationship that strings the cases together—the researchers have an obligation to provide interpretation across the cases. Often the cross-case analysis comes to dominate the report.

There is a problem with this, however: The main reason for doing single-case study research often gets mangled in a cross-case analysis. The case researcher has tried to display the unique vitality of each case, noting its particular situation and how the context influences the experience of the program or phenomenon. Many readers look to the cross-case analysis to find what is common across the cases, not what is unique to each. I generally find that researchers doing cross-case analysis are emphasizing the common relationships across cases. The work has been long and laborious, and the team may hurry to that culmination. (Sharan Merriam [1998], a leading case study methodologist, emphasizes the similarity between single-case analysis and multicase analysis. There is much similarity, but I tend to emphasize the difference.) Unlike the single-case analysis, the cross-case analysis needs to deal with what I have described in Chapter 1 as the "case–quintain dilemma," perhaps by invoking a "case–quintain dialectic."

The dialectic works like this. (Note that the terms Cases, Findings, Factors, Themes, Assertions, the Quintain, and the Analyst will be capitalized from now on in this chapter to draw attention to their technical roles in the cross-case analysis and the planning of the report.) The Themes originated with people planning to study the Quintain. The

Findings originated with people studying the Cases. These are two conceptual orientations, not independent but different. To treat them both as forces for understanding the Quintain, the Analyst keeps them both alive even as he or she is writing the Assertions of the final report. The Themes preserve the main research questions for the overall study. The Findings preserve certain activity (belonging to Case and Quintain alike) found in the special circumstances of the Cases. When the Themes and Factors meet, they appear to the Analyst as both consolidation and extension of understanding.

3.1. RATIONALE

The study was undertaken to understand the Quintain (i.e., the program or phenomenon)—both its commonality and its differences across manifestations. Each Case is studied to gain understanding of that particular entity as it is situated. The Quintain is studied in some of its situations. It is supposed that the complex meanings of the Quintain are understood differently and better because of the particular activity and contexts of each Case.

For example, it is supposed that the meaning of a policy change toward inclusion and away from exclusion of certain people from participation is influenced differentially by the particular history and the political and economic conditions of the Case. Although any one Case will be similar to other Cases in many respects, it will have unusual features; perhaps this one has charismatic leadership, media coverage, and public hostility because a notable person was once excluded there. Comprehension of the phenomenon of inclusion requires knowing not only how it works and does not work in general, independent of local conditions, but how it works under various local conditions.

After cross-case analysis, the researchers will make Assertions about the Quintain. They will take evidence from the case studies to show how uniformity or disparity characterizes the Quintain. Often the Quintain will appear increasingly less a coordinated system and more a loose confederation, or less a simple pattern and more a mosaic. With deep study, the differences among the Cases often seem to grow.

The researchers work to understand the program or to explain the phenomenon as it appears in the several Cases studied. Some of the outstanding differences across Cases can be identified, but usually it is not possible to catch a fuller meaning of the Quintain without careful review of the details of the Cases. In the final report, the section reporting the cross-case analysis is expected to be shorter than the sum of the case

studies, yet it should convey the most important Findings from each—
somehow combined as Assertions. Some of the important findings from
the Cases will be context-bound. Given the load, some oversimplifica-
tion is likely and perhaps inevitable.

If the situationality of the individual Cases is much less important to
the researchers than general understanding of the Quintain, then multicase research is perhaps the wrong design. Cases can be measured and
described without the kind of situational case study defined in this book.
A correlational study might do better to seek out the influences of certain Factors on educational outcomes. Much qualitative and quantitative
research is intended to study phenomena or policies manifested in large
numbers of Cases. Some of the data gathering for case study, such as
unstructured interview or document review, can be applied to dozens of
Cases, even hundreds, with relatively small examination of the complex
experience at those sites. The emphasis in this book is on scrutinizing
site-specific experiences.

The Assertions in a cross-case report are the researchers' Findings
about the Quintain. For example, the Assertion might be "This training
program has concentrated on [meeting] new requirements and fixing
problems and has not been developed individualistically and comprehensively to serve the professional development needs of the trainees"
(Stake, Platt, Davis, Vanderveen, & Dirani, 2003). The Assertion needs
to be based on evidence. The evidence that persuaded the researchers
needs to accompany each Assertion. It is not evidence for a court of law
or geometric proof. It is persuasion, logical persuasion, that the Assertion
is credible. Such presentation takes careful thinking and writing.

Researchers usually do not consider their Assertions to be beyond
dispute. Research has sometimes been sold as providing conclusions that
trump opinion. But social scientists know that social and educational
research findings carry opinion and authenticated findings together in a
package (Schwandt, 2000). Evidence in multicase studies will not win
over every critic, but it does need to be persuasive to critical friends. The
reader should have the opportunity to learn the reasons behind each
Assertion.

3.2. READING THE COLLECTED REPORTS

If a researcher has acquaintance with only one or a few Cases, the simple
approach is just to apply each Case's Findings to a Theme-based description of the Quintain. But relying on such researchers for cross-site findings is seldom good enough. Most of them have not studied the program

as a whole and do not sufficiently understand its purview, history, complexity, challenges, and so forth. And often some of the fieldworkers get "burned out" on this particular study and beg out of the cross-case analysis. A better approach is for the analysis to be done by the project director or a designated author—someone who will work at understanding the program or phenomenon as a whole and will examine all the case reports closely. If the synthesis and writing must be divided up among team members, each should take one or two themes, read all the case reports, and follow a procedure something like that described below. But I think the analysis is a job for just one person, who gets assistance as needed from discussions with team members and critical friends. Let us call this person Anna Lee, the Analyst.

While reading the Cases, Anna Lee has at her fingertips a copy of the research questions. These are called Themes in Worksheet 2. The Themes were initially identified in the project proposal, were sometimes modified as the research began, and were modified some more as the research progressed. Anna Lee decides to forgo the initial numbering of the Themes, instead numbering them in the order of her anticipation of their value in adding to the understanding of the Quintain. The first listed will get first (and perhaps best) attention in the cross-case procedure, and resource depletion and deadlines may hurry the drafting of the report. Into Worksheet 2, Anna Lee inserts these Themes. They should be in words suitable for a rough draft of the final cross-site report. She doesn't want her thinking about the Cases to be overly influenced by the Themes, but neither does she wish to ignore them.

During her study of the Cases, Anna Lee reads some of the related literature, gets briefed, and (if possible) reads a draft of each final case report. Important changes are made to these reports late, and Anna Lee should read the whole collection "at a sitting"—keeping in mind the project as a whole, but mostly concentrating on each Case's activity in its situation. Most Analysts will keep systematic notes, often making marginal comments and adding Post-it Notes on special pages of the report. The larger the number of Cases, the more valuable such note keeping will be. From her underlining, color coding, marginal notes, and Analyst's Log, Anna Lee completely fills in Worksheet 3, providing essential information from the Cases for the cross-case analysis.

For most studies, the all-important Case Findings are gathered on copies of Worksheet 3, one for each Case. Anna Lee identifies the Findings specified in the Case reports, but may add one or a few that she feels the report writer has overlooked. Also on Worksheet 3, Anna Lee thinks it potentially useful to identify situational constraints. Case activity or policies may be constrained at some sites by important local limits or

WORKSHEET 2. The Themes (Research Questions) of the Multicase Study

These Themes indicate primary information about the Quintain that the researchers seek. Below are some examples from the Step by Step project:

Theme 1:
Theme 2:
Theme 3:
Theme 4:
Theme 5:
Theme 6:
Theme 7:

Example 1: What are the primary developmental outcomes, but also other costs and benefits, for children enrolled in the Step by Step programs?
Example 2: Public education policy acknowledging the range of community-based early education options.
Example 3: Problems of inclusion of children of disadvantage and disability where there is a strong tradition of segregated special schools for them.
Example 4: Is staff development for teachers seen as serious capacity building and continuing professional education?
Example 5: Do all partners who sign agreements participate substantively in planning, operation, and interpretation?
Example 6: Evidence showing that there is program sustainability.

events, such as "central office reorganization" or "malfunctioning online facilities."

For a more quantitative analysis, space has been provided in Worksheet 3 for identifying Factors from the Case. Many case study research questions include Factors (or influences). Additional space may be needed in Worksheet 3 to list all the Factors. While reading the Cases, Anna Lee thinks of Factors that might be discussed in the forthcoming multicase summary. (A more qualitative study will have less use for such variables or descriptors, but even there designation of Factors may help stimulate interpretation, especially as to what is common and different across Cases. Possible Factors at a site might include "Installation of a new faculty evaluation scheme" or "Aggressiveness of the opponents to traditional schooling." Other examples of Factors are shown in Figures 9.1–9.6 in Chapter 9. We will take up Factors again later in this chapter, when Track III is introduced.)

The main emphasis at this stage is on reading the individual case reports. The multicase procedure will come a little later. For the case report next to be read, it may be useful to have its circle graphic plan (Worksheet 1; see Figures 6.1, 7.1, and 8.1), if one was created by the case researcher, and the empty form for cross-case Assertions (Worksheet 6) close at hand. In her own words, Anna Lee writes a synopsis (in Worksheet 3) of the story told in the case report, identifying the Case, the sites where the Case was observed, and key information sources. She thinks that a few words of context information should also be useful, and a very brief summary of the activity will be equally important. These should help Anna Lee remember the situationality of the Case. She creates the entries in Worksheet 3 rather than copying verbatim from the case report.

An important part of Worksheet 3 is the final section, the one for commentary. Many Analysts will make many of their comments directly on a copy of the case report, but Worksheet 3 can be useful as a directory for returning to the comments. Some of these comments may also be placed in the Analyst's Log.

Anna Lee is beginning the highly reductive process of cross-case analysis. She expects to lose much of the particularity of each Case, but wants to keep the most important experiential knowledge. Anna Lee needs to understand the individual Cases in depth before analyzing the Case Findings and preparing the cross-case report. She reads the Cases one at a time, and then fills out a copy of Worksheet 3 for each one, not in too much detail. She will be examining several of them simultaneously. And the important aspects of each Case will probably be those she recalls from memory and those in the margins. The notes and

WORKSHEET 3. Analyst's Notes While Reading a Case Report

Code Letters for This Case: _____

Case Study Report Title: _____

Author(s):

Analyst's Synopsis (possibly identifying
the case,
the sites,
the activity,
key information sources and
context information):

Situational Constraints:

Uniqueness among Other Cases:

Prominence of Theme 1 in This Case:
Prominence of Theme 2 in This Case:
Prominence of Theme 3 in This Case:
Prominence of Theme 4 in This Case:
Prominence of Theme 5 in This Case:
Prominence of Theme 6 in This Case:

Expected Utility of This Case for Developing Theme 1:
Expected Utility of This Case for Developing Theme 2:
Expected Utility of This Case for Developing Theme 3:
Expected Utility of This Case for Developing Theme 4:
Expected Utility of This Case for Developing Theme 5:
Expected Utility of This Case for Developing Theme 6:

Conceptual Factors (for Track III):

Findings:
   I.
   II.
   III.
   IV.

Possible Excerpts for the Multicase Report (noting case report page number):

Commentary (sometimes noting case report page number):

worksheets do not "remember" enough. The worksheets are intended to help her find needed passages.

Anna Lee allows a few moments to consider how unusual this case situation is for this Quintain. Typical situations probably contribute most to the main descriptions in the final report. The unusual situations probably do most to help limit the generality of the answers to the research questions. A brief indication of the case situation's uniqueness is asked for in Worksheet 3.

An important part of Worksheet 3 is the space for indicating the prominence of each of the cross-case Themes (as identified in Worksheet 2) in each of the Cases. The more the Theme appears in the Case, the more relevant the Case should be; thus prominence can be seen as one indication of the relevance of the Case. Anna Lee describes the prominence of each Theme for each Case briefly in her own words.

For more quantitative work (using Track III), Anna Lee identifies Factors or influences in Worksheet 3. And in the "Possible Excerpts" and "Commentary" sections, the form provides room for notes to remind Anna Lee of quotations, impressions, or incidents that might be useful in preparing the cross-case report.

3.3. CROSS-CASE PROCEDURE[1]

For the cross-case procedure, I offer three alternative tracks. I consider Track I the preferred track, because it best maintains the Case Findings and situationality. It also uses more sources for generating Assertions. But it is the most difficult to do. Track II merges similar Findings, maintaining a little of the situationality. Track III, the most quantitative track, shifts the focus from Findings to Factors.

For grand strategy, I think it is desirable for the analyst to set up a "case–quintain dialectic"—a rhetorical, adversarial procedure, wherein attention to the local situations and attention to the program or phenomenon as a whole contend with each other for emphasis. Each needs to be heard while the other is being analyzed. I think it best that the issues of the individual Cases *not* merge too quickly into the main research questions of the overall multicase study. They need to be heard a while, then put aside a while, then brought out again, and back and forth

---

[1]To make good sense of these procedures, most readers will need simultaneously to be working with actual case studies, filling in worksheets and sorting strips as called for.

(the dialectic). Unlike me, some researchers want minimum attention to the Cases and maximum attention to the Quintain.

The main activity of cross-case analysis is reading the case reports and applying their Findings of situated experience to the research questions of the Quintain. These research questions guide the multicase study of the program or phenomenon. We expect to create and modify general understandings on the basis of the Case's experience. The analysis is not simply a matter of listing the Case Findings pertinent to each research question, because, to some extent, the Findings need to keep their contextual meaning during the authoring of the multicase report. With each of the tracks, the Analyst needs to keep a vast amount of information in mind over a long reading and analysis time.

To facilitate the cross-case analysis, I am offering a set of worksheets in this book as a whole. These worksheets may also be downloaded from www.ed.uiuc.edu/circe/worksheets/worksheet/. Worksheets 2 through 6 are presented in this chapter; Worksheet 1 has been presented in Chapter 1; and Worksheet 7 is offered in Chapter 4. The worksheets are intended to help the Analyst in his or her work, not to present data to readers (Worksheets 4, 5A–5C, and 6 in particular might distract rather than help a reader of the multicase report). Moreover, I am offering three alternative versions of Worksheet 5, one for each of the alternative tracks for the cross-case procedure. You can choose whichever of these is best suited to your particular multicase study and can modify all of the worksheets as needed to fit your own project. The worksheets are titled as follows:

- Worksheet 1. Graphic Design of a Case Study
- Worksheet 2. The Themes (Research Questions) of the Multicase Study
- Worksheet 3. Analyst's Notes While Reading a Case Report
- Worksheet 4. Ratings of Expected Utility of Each Case for Each Theme
- Worksheet 5A. A Matrix for Generating Theme-Based Assertions from Case Findings (Track I)
- Worksheet 5B. A Matrix for Generating Theme-Based Assertions from Merged Findings (Track II)
- Worksheet 5C. A Matrix for Generating Theme-Based Assertions from Important Factor Clusters (Track III)
- Worksheet 6. Multicase Assertions for the Final Report
- Worksheet 7. Planning the Multicase Final Report

While the individual case studies are being done, Anna Lee refines the plan for cross-case analysis of Case Findings. She anticipates a synthesis of Findings; keeps a list of potential cross-case Assertions (Worksheet 6); and visualizes writing the report, including estimating its length and format. She becomes more familiar with the Quintain, reading articles, e-mail correspondence, and other documents beyond those in the case studies. She does some interviewing and finds existing descriptions of the Quintain. She keeps an Analyst's Log for jotting things to remember, from schedules and e-mail addresses to discarded Assertions.

3.4. EXPECTED UTILITY OF CASES AND ORDINARINESS OF SITUATIONS

During or after reading the Cases, Anna Lee made some estimates on Worksheet 3. She noted the prominence of each Theme in each Case report. She also noted how much attention the case researcher paid to each Theme, briefly commenting on this in Worksheet 3. And at that time, also in Worksheet 3, she noted the uniqueness of each Case among the other cases of the Quintain.

Now, having read all the case reports, Anna Lee again considers how unusual each Case was. On rereading the synopses in Worksheets 3 and recalling her previous reading of the case reports, she thinks about whether the atypicality of the Case might extend or limit an Assertion to be made in the final report. For each Case, she comments in the margin of Worksheet 3, confirming the previous note on uniqueness or adding new information about typicality.

Next, taking one Theme at a time, Anna Lee considers the expected utility of each of the case reports for further development of the Theme. For Theme 1, one at a time, she reviews the case synopses and their expected utility for developing this Theme as described in Worksheet 3. She then rates the utility of the Cases as H (high), M (middling), or L (low). She enters the ratings of the Cases for Theme 1 across its row in Worksheet 4. Next, Anna Lee rates the utility of each case for developing Theme 2 and enters the ratings in Worksheet 4. And so on, until all Themes have received ratings of the estimated utility of the Cases.

Anna Lee could have modified these ratings upon discussions with the Case researchers while or after they do their work. But to keep the scales consistent across Cases, the marks should be assigned by Anna Lee, not by the case researchers. When all Cases are rated in Worksheet 4, Anna Lee carefully scans the ratings, noting the highly relevant Cases for each Theme. This step is so important that it will be repeated with fresh

WORKSHEET 4. Ratings of Expected Utility of Each Case for Each Theme

Utility of Cases	Case A	Case B	Case C	Case D	Case E
Original Multicase Themes					
Theme 1					
Theme 2					
Theme 3					
Theme 4					
Theme 5					
Theme 6					
Added Multicase Themes					
Theme 7					
Theme 8					

H = high utility; M = middling utility; L = low utility. High utility means that the Case appears to be one of the most useful for developing this Theme. As indicated, the original Themes can be augmented by additional Themes even as late as the beginning of the cross-case analysis. Descriptions of each Theme can be attached to this worksheet, so that the basis for estimates can be readily examined.

thinking later on. The refinement of each Theme depends on getting useful Findings and supplementary data from the most relevant Cases.

3.5. THE GROUNDS FOR ASSERTIONS

Making Assertions will require rating Findings or Factors. It will simplify the task to have "Theme cards." Anna Lee takes as many blank cards (3″ × 5″ index cards are fine) as there are Themes. From Worksheet 2, she numbers and prints each Theme (probably abbreviating) on a card, printing large enough for it to be read a few feet away. For example, she may write, "Theme 1: Equal opportunity for all children."

Here is where Anna Lee chooses one of the three tracks. The deepest analysis of the Cases almost certainly will come from the first track; if she chooses Track I, she will use Worksheet 5A. But the detail might overwhelm the Analyst. With a large number of Cases and a short amount of time, or with little information about the Quintain, another track may be better. The Merged Finding track (Track II) is identified with Worksheet 5B. And if there is preference for quantitative analyses and little interest in the situationality of the Cases, the Factor track (Track III, for which Worksheet 5C is used) is most likely to be appreciated. Anna Lee selects a track and worksheet. All tracks follow the same strategy. All tracks use Worksheets 4 and 6. All tracks share some of the same language.

Track I: Emphasizing Case Findings

Track I is the track emphasizing the various situations and Findings of the Cases.

Anna Lee has read the final report of each individual Case and has discussed it with the field researcher. She has prepared Worksheets 2, 3, and 4. She once again reviews the display of multicase Themes on Worksheet 2. She visualizes the multicase project as a whole. She is working toward several cross-case Assertions based on the Case evidence gathered. (Remember, Case Findings merge to some extent across Cases, some of them around a framework of proposed multicase Themes. If suitable evidence is anticipated, the Merged Findings can be written up as tentative Assertions in the multicase report. If Merged Findings appear

WORKSHEET 5A. A Matrix for Generating Theme-Based Assertions from Case Findings Rated Important

	Themes							
Case A:	1	2	3	4	5	6	7	8
Finding I								
Finding II								
Finding III								
Finding IV								
Case B:	1	2	3	4	5	6	7	8
Finding I								
Finding II								
Finding III								
Case C:	1	2	3	4	5	6	7	8
Finding I								
Finding II								
Finding III								
Finding IV								
Finding V								
And so on for remaining Cases								

H = high importance; M = middling importance; L = low importance. A high mark means that for this Theme, the Case Finding is of high importance. Parentheses around a Theme number means that it should carry extra weight in drafting an Assertion. The notation " . . . (atypical)" after a case means that its situation might warrant extra caution in drafting an Assertion.

more important than individual Case Findings, Track II is likely to be preferred.)

Anna Lee will record tentative Assertions, perhaps gradually, in Worksheet 6. (Here is an example of a tentative Assertion in the Step by Step multicase report: "With endorsement of child inclusion policies by the European Union, many countries' ministries of education were voicing support for such practices.") Anna Lee may begin listing tentative Assertions at any time during the study; later, she will decide which Assertions to emphasize, which to subordinate, and which to drop. The decision will be facilitated by a sustained look at the matrix to be created in Worksheet 5A, but the main basis of the Assertions will be the reading and review of the case reports.

Anna Lee prepares to rate the Findings from the Cases. She chooses to sort paper strips rather than to rate the Findings directly on a list. (For some of us, it is easier if we actually move the individual Findings around.)

For studies with only a few Cases and with each Case having five or fewer Findings, Anna might rate them on Worksheet 3 and mark the rating on Worksheet 5A. She might mark the rating in the margin of Worksheet 3, but she needs enough space to rate each Finding once for each Theme. Since she will need Findings strips for composing the Assertions statements later, it is better to start with strips than to work directly on the sheets.

Anna Lee places Worksheet 2 next to blank Worksheet 5A to provide a handy reference to the Themes. On Worksheet 5A, she lists the Findings for each Case; each Finding is entered at the far left of its own row. She will enter the ratings for all the Findings of a Case, taking one Theme at a time. If she were using Worksheet 5A just as it is shown here, the first set of cells she would fill would be the four vertical cells for Case A and Theme 1.

Anna will rate each Finding of Case A as to its importance for understanding the Quintain through a particular Theme. She will use a 3-point scale similar to the one described earlier for rating Case utility on Worksheet 4: H (high), M (middling), or L (low). She will try to keep in mind something of the activity and context of the Case. It is the situated meaning of the Finding that is being rated. The question is not "How similar is this Finding to the Theme?" The rating is based on "How important is this Finding (derived from its Case) for understanding the Quintain (with regard to this Theme)?" Anna will move from Case A to Case B, then on through the remaining Cases, until all the cells of Worksheet 5A have an entry. That, in general, is what she will do. Here, in greater detail, is what she does.

Sorting Findings Strips

For sorting the Findings, Anna Lee makes "Findings strips." From a computer form of Worksheet 3, or from scratch, she prints (for each Case) its Findings on blank paper (the heavier the paper, the better). The Findings need to be Case-identified and numbered. (In Figure 3.1, for example, SLO-I refers to Finding I from the Slovakia Case study in the Step by Step project.) After and below each Finding, Anna Lee "pastes in" a row of T-slots for ratings, as shown in Figure 3.1. There should be as many T-slots as there are Themes in Worksheet 2 (six are shown in Figure 3.1). Two inches or so of space are inserted between one Finding (with its T-slots) and the next. The page is then printed, and the Findings are cut into strips of approximately equal size.

Then Anna Lee makes the ratings on the criterion stated above, circling an H, M, or L for each Theme on each Findings strip. She transfers to Worksheet 5A the circled letters on the Case A strips for all the Themes. That is, she enters a letter indicating importance in each of the Case A cells. For a Case Finding rated of middling importance for Theme 3, Anna Lee enters an M in the cell. If there are four Case A Findings, all highly important for Theme 1, she inserts an H in each of the four vertical cells topping the Theme 1 column of Worksheet 5A. Anna Lee fills all the cells for Case A.

Utility and Prominence of Cases

Anna Lee now shifts her attention back to the multicase Themes. She wants to transfer the utility information from Worksheet 4 to Worksheet 5A, answering the question "Which Findings will feed into

> SLO-I. Despite the doubts of many, the mothers of the Roma children have continued the home schooling of their preschool children for more than a year.
>
> T1: H M L T2: H M L T3: H M L T4: H M L T5: H M L T6: H M L

FIGURE 3.1. A strip for rating the importance of a Case Finding for developing each of six Themes (T1–T6). This strip is an example of a possible first Finding from the Slovakia Case report. H = high importance; M = middling importance; L = low importance.

which Themes?" On Worksheet 5A, she locates the row of Theme numbers to the right of the Case A heading. She puts parentheses around each Theme number rated high for Case A, as indicated on Worksheet 4. If, for example, on Worksheet 4 in the first column, the utility of Case A appears high (possibly either high or middling[2]) for Themes 3 and 5, she puts parentheses around the 3 and 5 to the right of the Case A heading of Worksheet 5A. Seeing, for example, on Worksheet 4, Column 2, that Case B has a high expected utility for Themes 1, 3, and 6, Anna Lee places parentheses around the 1, 3, and 6 to the right of the Case B heading of Worksheet 5A. And so on until the Themes with high (or either high or middling) utility are marked for each Case. This is an indication of utility for the Cases for each Theme. (Some of these Theme numbers may get double parentheses in a minute.)

There is still more information to add to Worksheet 5A for developing Assertions from the Themes. Anna Lee adds the information on prominence from the notes (Worksheet 3) she made while reading the Cases. She identifies the Themes that were seen as having high prominence in Case A. For Case A, if Theme 1 appeared prominent, Anna Lee adds parentheses to the numeral 1 in the Case A row of Worksheet 5A. If it already has parentheses, she adds another pair. If Case B was seen to have Theme 5 highly prominent, then Anna Lee puts parentheses around the numeral 5 in the Case B row. Parentheses are not added to the ratings in the cells, just to the numerals to the right of the Case headings. Anna Lee continues the procedure for all the Cases.

Anna Lee gives some thought to the matches among cells and headings—that is, among the parenthetical headings (coming from case reports and through Worksheet 4) and the importance ratings (coming from the Findings strips). She does not expect full agreement, because the information is coming from different sources and is based on somewhat different criteria. If she sees troubling contradictions, she looks for clerical errors. If she finds no such errors, she posts a notice in the Analyst's Log for later pondering.

Atypicality

And there is one last indicator to be marked on Worksheet 5A: the atypicality of any Case. For any Case identified in Worksheet 3 as atypi-

---

[2]Whether to parenthesize the Theme number based on high utility alone or on either high or middling utility will need to be decided partly on the basis of whether it appears that there is a shortage or an abundance of support for the Theme. If there are several highly relevant Cases for a Theme, the middling Cases should not get much attention.

cal (unusual, extraordinary) among the Quintain's Cases, its Case heading in Worksheet 5A should be marked " . . . (atypical)." Its cell entries should be treated with extra thought when the Analyst is generating Assertions. The atypicality may extend or limit the generalizations being expressed in the Assertions.

To repeat, Worksheet 5A should now have at least one mark in each cell of its columns. Some of the numerical column headings may be in parentheses, and some in double parentheses. The data of Worksheet 5A will be the main source of Assertions from the cross-case analysis. These Assertions will be labeled, for example, CCA3-1, the first from Theme 3, on through CCA6-2, the second Assertion from Theme 6. But the Analyst has made tentative Assertions along the way, numbering them simply 1, 2, 3. Next, we will consider one more source of Assertions.

Assertions by Bypass

Anna Lee moves again to the Findings strips.[3] She retrieves the Theme 1 card and makes it easily visible to her on the table. She selects all of the Findings strips with high Theme 1 ratings from all of the Case decks together. She shuffles those selected strips, then ranks the strips from highest to lowest in the Findings' usefulness for adding to understanding of the Quintain, with special attention to Theme 1. Then from the highest end, Anna Lee picks from four to six Findings that seem to contribute the most to the understanding of Theme 1 and to the Quintain as a whole. (They may have little in common; they may even be contradictory.) Anna Lee reads those Findings again and, ignoring some, composes the best Assertion she can to help understand Theme 1. If she is satisfied that there is evidence in the Cases for such an Assertion, she writes this in Worksheet 6, labeling it BYP1-1—the first Theme 1 Assertion from this so-called "bypass" procedure. She then repeats the bypass procedure for each of the other Themes.

Tentative Assertions

It is now time for hard work on the Assertions. Some of the best Assertions will be suggested by the entries of Worksheet 5A, Theme by Theme. The Themes (Worksheet 2) were the original questions for studying the Quintain. Worksheet 5A will identify Case Findings and Themes for making Assertions. (Shifting to Themes again is part of the

---

[3]If strips were not made, meaning that the number of Findings per Case was small, there seems little need for this source of extra Assertions.

dialectic.) Any Assertions that have little relation to Themes will come from the Analyst's sensitivity to the Findings of the Cases.

For Assertions based on a Theme, Anna Lee looks in its column of Worksheet 5A. She first looks for H ratings under double parentheses. Were she working on Theme 3 in Figure 9.8, she would see five such Findings. She would pencil three check marks ($\sqrt{}\ \sqrt{}\ \sqrt{}$) in the left margin for each. She moves onto the same Theme's H entries under single parentheses. There are none in Figure 9.8. She would place two check marks ($\sqrt{}\ \sqrt{}$) in the left margin, had there been any for each of these Findings. Still in the same Theme column of the Worksheet, Anna Lee locates all that have double parentheses and an M. Figure 9.8 has two Theme 3 M's with double parentheses just above them. They also get two check marks ($\sqrt{}\ \sqrt{}$). Finally, she locates all that have an H without any parentheses for their Case and gives each a single check mark ($\sqrt{}$). Figure 9.8 has three of these for Theme 3. Working on Theme 3 in Figure 9.8, Anna Lee has 10 Findings that have been identified as sources for Assertions, some more important than others. Anna Lee locates the Findings strips for these 10 Findings. She records the check marks on each strip, duplicating what she has marked in the left margin of Worksheet 5A.

Anna Lee now reads the 10 Findings again, attending most to the ones with triple checks and least to the single-checked Findings. She looks for a few making the strongest, most relevant combination of Findings, then seeks others supporting that combination. Then she composes a tentative Assertion—"After decades of reasoning that children needing special instruction should attend their own special classrooms and schools, many of the region's country-level educational officials are speaking of the benefits of inclusion, but most local-level officials and citizens are not yet ready to support inclusionary practices." The Assertion should have a single or common focus, a contribution toward understanding the Quintain, and evidence from more than one Case to support it. Anna Lee adds this cross-case Assertion to the list on Worksheet 6 and identifies it with CCA and a number, noting also that it is from Case A. By checking for atypicality in the Case headings, Anna Lee considers whether or not the unusualness of the situation might limit or enhance the Assertion's generalizability. If need be, she modifies the wording of the still tentative Assertion.

Returning to the remainder of the 10 penciled Theme 3 Findings, Anna Lee seeks several that have a different commonality from the Assertion just added. She thinks again about the study as a whole. Then she finds four, and decides that all four share a common concept of the Theme. She composes a tentative Assertion statement, writes it on Worksheet 6, and labels it, noting the Cases.

Anna Lee looks through the remaining Findings, again asking, "Now what is the best combination of ideas for understanding the Quintain?" She finds that the strongest statement occurs in a single Finding, Case C's Finding V. There was some similarity in Case B's Finding II, a Finding used in the first Assertion. That's all right. She makes an Assertion from the two of them, perhaps as follows: "Although the Step by Step program standards and training do not directly call upon teachers to conceptualize what an open society might be, what the teachers are actually doing is creating an open society within their classrooms." She edits it a little to make a better Assertion and gives it a number.

Anna Lee now thinks about the Case–Quintain dilemma. Does the Quintain need to be thought about more in terms of what is happening in the individual Cases separately, or more in terms of what is common across the Cases? Neither is necessarily right. But one probably advances the understanding and utility of the research more than the other.

Anna Lee returns to Theme 3. She considers the match between the Findings and Theme 3. The Case Findings may not lead to much evidence for better understanding the Quintain. Anna Lee has worried about that already. There may be data of relevance to Theme 3 in the Cases that did not contribute to the statement of Findings. It may be important to go back and find it. Or perhaps she concludes that the multicase study did little to educate us further about the Quintain with regard to Theme 3.

A draft of the final report section on Theme 3 probably should be written now, because so much thinking about it has occurred in this handling of Worksheets 5A and 6. For some analysts, however, it will be preferable to process all the Themes before beginning the drafting of the final report. Further discussion of the Assertions continues in Section 3.6.

Sooner or later, Anna Lee goes on to another theme—say, Theme 4 in Figures 9.7 and 9.8. She crosses through the pencil marks on Worksheet 5A and returns to the newly checked Case A strips, this time as to importance for developing Theme 4 in the cross-case report. The procedure described above for Theme 3 is repeated for Theme 4. The weighted Findings are raked through for tentative Assertions. One or more of them are entered on Worksheet 6. The procedure is repeated for the remaining Themes.

To sum up, Anna Lee started with the case reports and identified the prominence of several Themes. Then she took the Themes and looked for utility of the Cases to develop them. Then she took the Findings and described the relevance to each Theme. Then she gathered the high-importance Findings for each Theme. In short, she has taken the Themes one by one to see what the Case Findings have provided, but she has continued to remember the situationality of the Case through its Findings.

The procedure continues as described in Section 3.6, "Cross-Case Assertions."

Track II: Merging Case Findings

Some analysts worry about getting bogged down in Case Findings, preferring to merge Findings across Cases. Their highest priority is not preserving the situationality of the Findings. For these analysts, Worksheet 5A (with its greater situationality) is the long way around. If it seems desirable to reduce the number of Findings to work with—that is, if the analyst wants to move toward generalization—he or she may choose Track II, substituting Merged Findings for individual Case Findings. For that, Worksheet 5B replaces Worksheet 5A.

Now on Track II, Anna Lee (our Analyst) takes from Worksheet 3 each Finding from each Case report and prints each one on its own strip (as was described in Track I). An example of a Finding from the Slovakia Case (see Figure 3.1) is this: "Despite the predictions of many, the parents of the Roma children have continued the home schooling of their preschool children for more than a year."

As she would have in Track I, Anna Lee makes "Findings strips." From a computer file of Worksheet 3, or from scratch, she prints (for each Case) its Findings on blank paper (the heavier the paper, the better). The Findings need to be Case-identified and numbered. Two inches or so of space are inserted between one Finding and the next. She prints the page and cuts the Findings into strips of approximately equal size.

(Each Finding statement here should be no more than a sentence or two. The Case from which the Finding came should be marked on the strip. Anna Lee discusses the Findings with the field researcher. If the deck exceeds five Findings for any one Case, certainly if it exceeds ten, the amount that Anna Lee has to keep in mind may be excessive. Creating the set of Findings should be based on the Cases rather than on the cross-case Themes. With primary attention to the Case research, this results in a very small deck of Findings strips for each Case.)

Again, Anna Lee reviews the multicase Themes on Worksheet 2. She visualizes the multicase project as a whole. She is working toward writing a number of cross-case Assertions based on evidence from the Case reports.

WORKSHEET 5B. A Matrix for Generating Theme-Based Assertions from Merged Findings Rated Important

Merged Findings	From Which Cases?	Themes							
		1	2	3	4	5	6	7	8
Merged Finding I									
Merged Finding II									
Merged Finding III									
Merged Finding IV									
Merged Finding V									
Merged Finding VI									
Merged Finding VII									
Merged Finding VIII									
Merged Finding IX									
Special Finding I									
Special Finding II									
Special Finding III									
Special Finding IV									
And so on									

The Findings are Case-based, not Theme-based. From an entry in a cell at the intersection of a Merged Finding with a Theme comes impetus to compose an Assertion. H = high importance; M = middling importance; L = low importance. A high mark means that for this Theme, the Merged Finding or Special Finding is of high importance. Parentheses around an entry means that it should carry extra weight when Assertions are being drafted. The notation "ATYP" within a cell means that its situation warrants caution in drafting an Assertion.

Sorting and Merging Findings

Anna Lee's task now is to merge Findings across Cases. (An example of a Merged Finding in the Step by Step multicase project is this: "Following exposure to child inclusion policies, several countries' ministries of education were voicing support for such practices.")

For merging Findings into clusters, Anna Lee combines all the decks of Findings strips. She lays out the strips, one by one, placing each according to its similarity to those already on the table. The Case from which the Finding came gets little notice. Findings similar in topic get placed close together; those dissimilar are placed farther apart. Even if Findings are contradictory, any two strips that are on the same topic are placed in the same cluster.

Next Anna Lee studies the content of the clusters. Adding a strip nearby, or dropping a misfitting strip, Anna Lee identifies the most important clusters. She gives each Merged Finding a name that identifies the thrust of the cluster—for example, "Bringing in new blood" and "The role of the churches." She writes the name given each Merged Finding on its own title card. (In naming these Merged Findings, the Analyst should not pay attention to the Themes.) She takes note of the best 4–8, possibly the best 12, Merged Findings title cards.

Anna Lee decides to improve the names she has given the clusters, wanting to represent more of the complexity of each Merged Finding. She changes the title card, "Bringing in new blood" to read, "With high staff turnover and with a preponderance of senior counselors, recruitment has been revised." She sequences the Merged Findings by assigning a roman numeral to each title card. Each Merged Finding, stated in full, is also entered at the far left of each row in Worksheet 5B. From the clusters of original strips, Anna Lee identifies the Cases contributing each Finding to the Merged Findings in the second column of Worksheet 5B. If Case D contributes three Findings to the merge, the Case letter is repeated that many times (DDD).

Some of the Findings will not merge. Anna Lee studies the Findings, which occur in only one Case. A few single Findings judged worth mentioning in the final report may be given title cards and identified in the Special Finding rows of Worksheet 5B. The remaining weak clusters and isolates are put aside.

Anna Lee adds information on the (presumed) utility of the Merged Findings to Worksheet 5B. If any Case has contributed two or more Findings to a Merged Finding (as indicated in the second column), and if, according to Worksheet 3, that theme was rated as prominent in that Case, the entry in the cell at the intersection of that Finding and that Theme is placed in parentheses. For example, if Case A contributed two Findings to the Merged Finding I cluster, and if Case A was described on Worksheet 3 as having Theme 1 prominent, the entry in the cell at the intersection of Merged Finding I and Theme I should be parenthesized. This entry should then carry extra weight in drafting the Assertions.

The uniqueness of Cases was important in Track I. In Track II, the connection between Cases and Merged Findings usually will be less strong. Still, if in Worksheet 5B, Column 2, it is apparent that a Merged Finding comes largely from a single Case, and if that Case is identified in Worksheet 3 as atypical, then it is a good idea to insert the notation "ATYP" in that Case's cell in Worksheet 5B. Cell entries with this "ATYP" notation should be treated with extra thought when the Analyst is generating Assertions. The atypicality may extend or limit any generalization being expressed in an Assertion.

Anna Lee considers the evidence for each Merged Finding, one at a time. For any Finding that she doubts has sufficient evidence, she makes a note at the bottom of Worksheet 6 or in her Analyst's Log. Perhaps it should be discussed speculatively in the final report rather than as an Assertion.

Sorting and Ranking Findings

Anna Lee now shifts attention back to the multicase Themes. Which Merged Findings will feed into which Themes? She places Worksheet 2 next to her Worksheet 5B to provide handy explication of the Themes. Anna Lee goes to Theme 1. (This may be a revised Theme 1. Revisions can be labeled on Worksheet 2 to help the Analyst remember.)

Sorting them, Anna Lee ranks the Merged Findings and Special Findings title cards in order of importance for understanding the Quintain's Theme 1. For each she asks, "How important is this Merged Finding for this Theme?" Then she puts a rating on each of the ranked cards. On each title card (thus for each Merged and Special Finding), Anna Lee marks its rating of importance (High, Middling, or Low, possibly with pluses and minuses) for developing Theme 1. One rating might be T1:M+. The rating M+ should be inserted in its place in the first Theme column of Worksheet 5B. (The rating and ranking are on the same criterion.) With a title card identifying each row, the Theme 1 column should be full when the rating is taken from the last card.

The same thing should be done for Theme 2 and all the remaining Themes. Worksheet 5B should then have at least one mark in each cell of the rows and columns being used. Some of the cell entries may be parenthesized. Some may contain an "ATYP" insertion under the rating.

Tentative Assertions

Anna Lee makes as many copies of Worksheet 5B as there are Themes. In the copy for Theme 1, Anna Lee looks at the entries in the first Theme column of Worksheet 5B. She reorders (rearranges, cuts, and pastes) the Merged Findings so that those with the highest ratings are at the top and the Merged Findings with the lowest ratings are at the bottom, ranked up and down. Merged Findings with ratings in parentheses should rank higher than those with the same ratings but not in parentheses. She expects the Merged Findings now at the top to give rise to the composition of one or a few Assertions.

Anna Lee concentrates on several Merged Findings at the top of the new ordering. She thinks about what can be the most meaningful Assertion to make from these few to contribute to the understanding of the Quintain. Her Assertion may relate to a single Merged Finding or to several. She takes her time. She thinks about the multicase study as a whole. She enters the tentative Assertion in Worksheet 6.

She considers whether or not one or two additional tentative Assertions might come from the Theme 1 ordering. She recognizes that if every Theme were to give rise to several Assertions, she would have too many to discuss in the final report. A lengthy list diminishes the importance of individual Assertions. Still, she wants to have a bunch for selection and discussion with her team, colleagues, project officer, or others. The list shouldn't be too short.

Each Assertion should have a single focus, an orientation for understanding the Quintain, and evidence to support it. A tentative Assertion might be "Within the same classroom, student-initiated themes competed with national curriculum requirements." Composing her own, Anna Lee adds a cross-case Assertion to the list on Worksheet 6 and identifies it with CCA and a number. By checking Worksheet 5B for atypicality flags (ATYP) in the column for that Theme, Anna Lee notes whether or not the unusualness of the situation might limit the Assertion's generalizability. If need be, she modifies its wording.

Anna Lee reads through the top Merged Findings, asking, "Have I left out important contributions from the Cases for understanding the Quintain?" Let us suppose she finds that the strongest potential addition idea occurs in Merged Finding VIII. She composes an Assertion based mainly on VIII. She gives it a number.

Once more she thinks, "Does the Quintain need to be thought about more in terms of what is happening in the individual Cases separately, or more in terms of what is common across the Cases?" Neither is necessarily right. But one of them probably advances the understanding and utility of the research more than the other.

It is time for Anna Lee to think even more deeply about the meaning of Theme 1. She has made one, two, or three tentative Assertions. Does she recall anything from the Cases that might modify those Assertions? Should any other Assertion or a commentary be added? From the Merged Findings and what Anna Lee can remember about the cases, what else will need to be said about Theme 1? In the lower portion of Worksheet 6, Anna Lee writes one or more brief comments extending the understanding of the Quintain as related to Theme 1. She thinks briefly about how a section of the final report might be written on Theme 1.

Anna Lee gets a fresh copy of Worksheet 5B and starts work on Theme 2. She repeats the procedure described above for Theme 1. She orders the Merged Findings and composes more tentative Assertions. The procedure continues until she has some for all or most of the Themes. On Worksheet 6 she labels her rated tentative Assertions CCA1-1, the first from Theme 1, on down perhaps to CCA6-2, the second from Theme 6.

Anna Lee may have been listing tentative Assertions much earlier during the study, numbering them in Worksheet 6 simply 1, 2, 3. To those, she will add Assertions from these rating procedures. Eventually she will decide which Assertions to emphasize, which to subordinate, and which to drop. Her decision will be facilitated by careful study of the matrix created in Worksheet 5B. The main basis for changing Assertions from tentative to final should be her further review of the Cases.

Anna Lee views the data of Worksheet 5B as providing a set of Assertions closely related to the Themes and less closely related to the situationality of the Cases. Anna Lee will need to go behind Worksheet 5B to retrace a few of the Case Findings, sometimes even to reread parts of individual cases to decide how a Merged Finding should be interpreted. The process of Track II is simpler than Track I, but a still simpler one is described next. In Track III, the situations surrounding the Cases become almost entirely lost. The Merged Findings of Track II are complex and not necessarily easy to work with. Analysts using Track II should skip now to Section 3.6.

Track III: Providing Factors for Analysis

A Theme or a Finding, as used here, is a central idea having importance related to its situation. It is at least somewhat context-bound, more local than universal. A Factor, as used here, is a widely found, sometimes influential variable of interest well beyond its situation. For example, we might use "Language spoken in the home" as a Factor. A corresponding Theme, for example, might be "Effects of home language on national standardized test results." More examples of Themes are shown at the bottom of Worksheet 2. Analysts working in a quantitative mode usually convert Themes or Findings into variables or Factors to be measured and compared or correlated.

The second Theme in the examples of Worksheet 2 comes from the Slovakia Case study presented in Chapter 7 of this book. It is "Public education policy acknowledging the range in community-based early education options." Two Factors are mentioned in this statement: "Public policy" and "Community-based." Some people would infer an outcome variable too, such as "Child outcomes." The Analyst expects data for each selected variable from the Case reports. Obviously, the task is less difficult if the Case researchers convert the observations into commitment scales and performance scores, but this may cost the Analyst and the reader understanding about the conditions under which the commitment and performance occurred.

Another example comes from George Stanhope's (2005) doctoral dissertation on schools implementing Illinois Learning Standards (ILS). An adaptation of one of his draft charts is presented in Figure 3.2. In this part of his study, four schools were selected as Cases that had performed well on state reviews of implementation of instruction based on the Illinois State Standards. Of the many Themes and Factors used, only four Themes and six Factors are shown here.

Stanhope found Factors[4] within his Themes and assigned to each Factor a rating of quality for each school. For example, the first Theme identified the principal's support of the implementation. One of its several Factors was "Scheduling." King and Scot Schools got a Factor rating of "High" for Scheduling, whereas James and Crane Schools were rated "Very High." Stanhope used these descriptors in his search for commonality and differences among the schools and for Assertions about the Quintain.

---

[4]Stanhope did not use the term "Factors." Some readers expect that word to mean outcomes of psychometric factor analysis.

It would not be unusual for an Analyst to use Case Findings in part of the cross-site analysis and to use Factors in another part. Obviously, the larger the number of Cases, the more helpful the use of Factors is.

Now on Track III, Anna Lee (our Analyst) takes from Worksheet 3 all the Factors (or influences, or whatever she prefers to call them) for each Case report. She records each Factor in large print on its own 3" × 5" card. Each Factor should be no more than a few words. The Case from which the Factor came should be identified on the card. (The set of Factors can be discussed with the field researcher, but the analyst should feel free to add Factors) If the deck exceeds five Factors for any one Case, certainly if it exceeds ten, the amount the Analyst has to keep in mind may be excessive. (The set of Factors should be based on the Cases rather than on the cross-case Themes. So, with primary attention to the Case research completed, this Factor identification results in a small deck of Factor cards for each Case.)

Anna Lee reviews the multicase Themes of Worksheet 2. As she reads the Themes, she visualizes the multicase project as a whole. She is working toward writing a number of cross-case Assertions based on the evidence gathered from the case reports. It is important that she get the Factors from the Cases, without worrying at this time about individual Themes.

Merging Factors

Anna Lee's task now is to merge Factors into clusters. She takes all the Factor cards and lays them out, one by one, placing each according to its similarity to those already on the table. Similar Factors are placed in the same cluster; dissimilar ones are placed farther apart.

Next, Anna Lee studies the content of the clusters. Adding a card nearby, or dropping a misfit, Anna Lee identifies Factor Clusters likely to be important for describing the Quintain. She gives each Factor cluster a name that identifies the common meaning of its Factors. Two examples from Stanhope's (2005) research are "Vertical teaming" and "Scheduling." Anna Lee settles on 4–15 main Factor Clusters. (Perhaps 10 clusters is the maximum an Analyst will feel can be discussed at length in a comprehensive final report, but more can be worked on during the analysis.)

Anna Lee decides to improve the names she has given the Factor Clusters, wanting to reflect the complexity of each. ("Vertical teaming," for instance, may be changed to "Articulation among administrators and teachers.") She prints the title to be used on a new title card for each Factor Cluster. Her Factor Cluster statements are entered (in small print) at

	"New Testament" School District		"Consolidated" School District	
Theme	King	James	Scot	Crane
The Principal's support of ILS implementation	Expect teachers to work as grade-level teams; use ILS and data to drive instruction	Expect teachers to work as grade-level teams; use ILS and data to drive instruction; meet with adjacent grade levels at the end of the year to review student data	Expect teachers to work as grade-level teams; use ILS to guide instruction; and provide a schedule and copy of meeting minutes	Expect teachers to work as vertical and horizontal teams; use ILS and data to drive curriculum and instruction; collect and respond to meeting minutes
Factor: Vertical teaming	*Above Average*	*High*	*Average*	*Very High*
The Principal's support of ILS implementation	Create times for teachers to discuss data	Create times for teachers to discuss data and times to address team goals	Create times for teachers to discuss data	Create times for teachers to discuss data and times to map curriculum
Factor: Scheduling	*High*	*Very High*	*High*	*Very High*
School Improvement Team (SIT) support of ILS implementation	Monitor progress on building goals monthly, and annually update plans each spring for the next school year, using the plan-on-a-page	Monitor progress on building goals monthly, and annually update plans each spring for the next school year, using internal review and the plan-on-a-page	Monitor progress on building goals monthly, and annually update plans each spring for the next school year	Monitor progress on building goals monthly, and annually update plans each spring for the next school year
Factor: Monitor progress and planning	*High*	*Very High*	*High*	*High*

Factor				
Teacher teams improve instruction	All teachers participate on building teams	All teachers participate on building teams	All teachers participate on building teams	All teachers participate on building teams
Factor: Teacher participation	*Above Average*	*Above Average*	*Above Average*	*Above Average*
Teacher teams improve instruction	Grade-level teams align and integrate curriculum, instruction, and assessment	Grade-level teams align and integrate curriculum, instruction, and assessment	Grade-level teams align curriculum and instruction	Grade-level teams align and integrate curriculum, instruction, and assessment
Factor: Align and integrate	*High*	*High*	*Above Average*	*High*
Changes in cultural norms	Formal, data-driven approach to continuous improvement; previously did not exist	Focused, process-driven, and data-driven approach to continuous improvement; previously did not exist	More formal, data-driven approach to continuous improvement; previously existed as continuous change	More focused, process-driven, and data-driven approach to continuous improvement; previously existed as continuous change
Factor: School improvement	*High*	*Very High*	*High*	*Very High*

FIGURE 3.2. Emergent Themes of Illinois Learning Standards (ILS) implementation at King, James, Scot, and Crane Elementary Schools. Adapted from Stanhope (2005). Used by permission of George R. Stanhope.

the far left of each row in Worksheet 5C. From Worksheet 3, Anna Lee identifies the Cases contributing each Factor to the Factor Clusters in the second column of Worksheet 5C. If a Case contributes more than once to the Factor Cluster, the Case letter is repeated that many times (DDD for three from Case D) in the second column.

Some of the Factors will not cluster with any others. The non-clustering cards (those showing a Factor at only one site) are studied by Anna Lee. Those she judges worth mentioning in the final report are given title cards and are identified in the Special Factor rows of Worksheet 5C. The remaining weak clusters and isolates are put aside.

Anna Lee makes some additional marks in the cells of Worksheet 5C. If a Case contributed two or more Factors to a Factor Cluster (as indicated in Worksheet 5C, Column 2), and if that case was rated in Worksheet 3 as having this Theme highly prominent, the cell entry at the intersection of that Factor Cluster and that Theme is placed in parentheses. For example, if Case A has contributed two Factors to the Factor Cluster III pile, and if Case A is described on Worksheet 3 as having Theme 1 quite prominent, the entry in the third cell down (for Factor Cluster III) of the Theme 1 column should be parenthesized. The entries with parentheses should carry extra weight in drafting Assertions.

As to uniqueness, if any Case contributes two or more Factors to a Factor Cluster, and if that Case is rated in Worksheet 3 as atypical among the Quintain's Cases, then the notation "ATYP" should be inserted in that Case's cell in Worksheet 5C. The rating should be treated with extra thought. The situation of this Case as described in its Case report should be given extra attention, possibly leading to modification of an Assertion constructed around this Theme.

Sorting and Ranking Factors

Anna Lee's attention shifts back to the multicase Themes. She asks, "Which Factor Clusters will feed into which Themes?" She places Worksheet 2 next to blank Worksheet 5C to provide handy reference to the Themes. Anna Lee goes to Theme 1. (This may be a revised Theme 1. Revisions can be labeled on Worksheet 2 to help the Analyst remember.)

Sorting them, Anna Lee next ranks the Factor Clusters and Special Factors title cards in order of importance for understanding the Quintain's Theme 1. For each, she asks, "How important is this Factor Cluster (or Special Factor) for this Theme?" After the cards are in order, writing on each title card (thus for each Factor Cluster and Special Factor), she writes a rating of importance: "High," "Middling," or "Low," (possibly with pluses and minuses), such as T1:M+. Anna Lee also inserts the rat-

WORKSHEET 5C. A Matrix for Generating Theme-Based Assertions from Important Factor Clusters

Ratings of Importance	From Which Cases?	Themes						
		1	2	3	4	5	6	7
Factor Cluster I								
Factor Cluster II								
Factor Cluster III								
Factor Cluster IV								
Factor Cluster V								
Factor Cluster VI								
Factor Cluster VII								
Factor Cluster VIII								
Special Factor IX								
Special Factor X								
And so on								

H = high importance; M = middling importance; L = low importance. A high mark means that for this Theme, the Factor Cluster is of high importance. Parentheses around an entry means that it should carry extra weight when Assertions are being drafted. The notation "ATYP" after a Case means that its situation might warrant caution in drafting an Assertion.

ing M+ (meaning slightly better than middling importance) in its place in the Theme 1 column of Worksheet 5C. (The rating and ranking are on the same criterion.) With a title card for each row, the column for Theme 1 should be full after the rating is taken from the last card.

Anna Lee does the same thing for Theme 2 and each of the remaining Themes. Worksheet 5C should have a rating in each cell of its columns. Some of these cell entries may be parenthesized. Some may contain an "ATYP" indication of atypicality under the rating.

Tentative Assertions

Anna Lee makes as many copies of Worksheet 5C as there are Themes. In a copy for Theme 1, Anna Lee looks at the entries in the first Theme column of Worksheet 5C. She reorders the Factor Clusters so that those with the highest ratings are at the top and those with the lowest ratings are at the bottom (ranked in order all the way down). Factor clusters with ratings in parentheses should rank higher than those with the same ratings but not in parenthesizes. She expects the Factor Clusters now at the top to give rise to the composition of one or a few Assertions.

Anna Lee concentrates on a few Factor Clusters at the top of the ordering. When these Factor Clusters and this Theme are considered, what do the Cases have to say about the Quintain? Anna Lee may have a strong impression of how a Factor Cluster and Theme fit together in the case reports. If she cannot remember enough about the individual Factors, she looks into (in each Worksheet 3) the Cases that contributed the Factors to the Factor Cluster. Several references to the Factors are apparent there. She thinks about what can be the most meaningful Assertion. What says something different about the Quintain? The Assertion may relate to a single Factor Cluster or to several. She reflects on what the multicase study has accomplished. Thinking of all that, she decides on the next tentative Assertion and enters it in Worksheet 6. (If the highest Factor Clusters do not warrant an Assertion related to Theme 1, then of course it does not get one.)

Anna Lee recognizes that two or three Assertions for the Theme do not contain all the good information in several Factor Clusters, but the final multicase report will concentrate on only several of the most important Assertions. For example, an important Assertion for the Stanhope (2005) study might be this: "The Illinois Learning Standards were less rigidly and more adaptively followed when the school principal took part in the staff development.") Information from other clusters may get a mention as the Assertions are being discussed.

Anna Lee decides whether or not one or two additional tentative Assertions might come from the Theme 1 ordering. She recognizes that if every Theme were to initiate several Assertions, she would have too many to discuss in the final report. Still, she needs more now than she will end up including in the report. She will be talking with people about what is most important to include.

Each Assertion should have a single focus, an orientation for understanding the Quintain, and evidence to support it. A tentative Assertion for the Step by Step project might be "Within the same classroom, student-initiated themes competed with national curriculum requirements." Anna Lee composes such an Assertion for Worksheet 6 and identifies it with CCA and a numeral. By checking Worksheet 5C for atypicality flags in the column for that theme, Anna Lee notes whether or not the atypicality of the situation might limit the Assertion's generalizability. If need be, she modifies its wording.

Once more she thinks, "Does the Quintain need to be thought about more in terms of what is happening in the individual Cases, or more in terms of what is common across the Cases?" It's the Case–Quintain dilemma again.

It is time for Anna Lee to think even more deeply about the meaning of Theme 1. She has one or more tentative Assertions based on it. Is there anything she recalls from the Cases that might cause her to change them? What else needs to be said? In the lower half of Worksheet 6, Anna Lee may write one or more additional brief comments extending the understanding of the Quintain as related to Theme 1. She thinks briefly about how a section of the final report might be written on Theme 1. In fact, she may decide to set the analysis aside while she writes on it.

Anna Lee gets a fresh copy of Worksheet 5C for working on Theme 2. She repeats the Theme 1 procedure for Theme 2: She rank-orders the Factor Clusters and Special Factors, and composes more tentative Assertions. She continues the procedure until she has Assertions for all the Themes. She will label her rated Assertions CCA1-1, the first from Theme 1, on down perhaps to CCA6-2, the second from Theme 6.

Anna Lee may have been listing tentative Assertions from the beginning of the analysis, numbering them in Worksheet 6 simply 1, 2, 3. To those, she will add Assertions from these rating procedures. Eventually she will decide which Assertions to emphasize, which to subordinate, and which to drop. Her decision will be facilitated by careful study of the reordered columns of Worksheet 5C. The main basis for changing Assertions from tentative to final should be her further review of the Cases.

(Not every final report author will have the patience of Anna Lee. Some will want to start writing immediately about the Themes and Assertions as they come to mind, perhaps using blank Worksheets 1–7 more reflectively than procedurally.)

That is enough for now for Theme 1. Anna Lee goes on to Theme 2. She starts sorting and searching for one or two Assertions, maybe three, for Theme 2. Again, she is asking, "How important is each Factor Cluster (or Special Factor) for this Theme?" The procedure described above for Theme 1 is repeated for Theme 2. New Assertions (and comments) for Theme 2 are entered on Worksheet 6. And then the procedure is repeated for the remaining Themes. Anna Lee takes the Themes one by one to see what the Factor Clusters can contribute to the understanding of the Quintain.

Anna Lee has drafted several Assertions for the most promising Factor Clusters and has entered each Assertion in Worksheet 6. The Factor Clusters and the Theme did not dictate the content of the Assertion. Anna Lee had to know the Findings and the Case Studies well enough to decide what actually should be said. The procedure gave her hints and reminders of the coverage needed, but the new understanding of the Quintain depends on her interpretation of the case reports.

The process of Track III should be easier than those of Tracks I and II. In Track III, the situations surrounding the Cases become blurred. The Factor Clusters of Track III may sound simple, but they are abstract, complex, and not easy to relate to the Cases. Anna Lee needed to go behind Worksheet 5C to retrace a few of the Case Factors, sometimes even to reread parts of individual Cases to decide how a Factor Cluster should be interpreted. The analysis procedure now continues in Section 3.6.

3.6. CROSS-CASE ASSERTIONS

The three tracks offer technical procedures moving through ratings of prominence, ordinariness, utility, and importance, to tentative Assertions. Now comes an interpretive process common to all three tracks. We expect that the heart of the final report will be the Assertions about the Quintain. From the work so far, our analyst Anna Lee has good ideas of what needs to be said, but the Assertions of Worksheet 6 will help her visualize reporting the cross-case analysis. It should also help her structure and allocate pages for the final report. Anna Lee will indicate this allocation graphically in Worksheet 7 (see Chapter 4) after the final cross-case Assertions in Worksheet 6 have been composed.

WORKSHEET 6. Multicase Assertions for the Final Report

Designator	Assertions	Related to Which Themes or Factors?	Evidence, Persuasions, Reference in Which Cases?
	Commentary (other important points to make about the Quintain, possibly regarding a finding from a single case)		

Assertions designated with simple numbers are direct (nonrating) entries by the analyst. Assertions designated with CCA are from the regular cross-case rating procedure. Assertions designated with BYP are from the special ("bypass") cross-case rating procedure.

It is time to go back to work on the tentative Assertions. Anna Lee finds some quiet and thinks hard about the Quintain, the Cases, and the Assertions. On Worksheet 6, she studies the list of tentative Assertions and the commentary. How much can the tentative Assertions still be modified? Should other Assertions be added, and if so, from where? From the Findings or Factors and from what Anna Lee remembers about the Cases, what else will need to be said about them? Could the Assertions be seen as a hatchet job, or, conversely, as a whitewash? In the lower part of Worksheet 6, Anna Lee writes additional comments pondering her questions, seeking understanding of the Quintain. For each Theme, she thinks briefly about how a section of the final report could be written. It is a good time for Anna Lee to scan the Analyst's Log, but it is also not too late to add to it.

Anna Lee looks at the number of tentative Assertions. She has over twice the number she considers ideal for the report. She recognizes some overlap, some need for rewriting, an immediate need for arranging their order. What better order? She decides not to use the order of the original or revised Themes, or of the Cases or Factors, at least not now; instead, she decides to list the Assertions first, with the ones that are now most important. She wants help from other people in thinking through the meaning and importance of the Assertions, but she wants to have a working package for them to consider. She spends more than an hour reordering, combining, and editing the Assertions. She demotes a few—the ones least important, those with least evidence, and those that are out of harmony with the study. She lists them in a new, expanded copy of Worksheet 6, with lots of room in the "Evidence . . . " column (possibly numbering them differently to keep the new Assertion statements separate from the old). She marks the old Worksheet 6 "superseded," but keeps it. She transfers Theme and Case evidence information from old Worksheet 6.

Anna Lee takes up new **Assertion 1**. (Here and hereafter, the new Assertion numbers are given in boldface.) This is the one she now considers most important for the final report. She thinks of its meaning carefully. How could it be differently interpreted? How could it be misinterpreted? She restates it a bit, with words crossed out and added in brackets, to keep track of the changes. If she is feeling compulsive about its appearance, she crosses out all the old statement and leaves it preceding the revised one.

Next Anna Lee considers the evidence identified. She rereads the Findings or Factors that fed into this Assertion. She tries to think of the situation of the Case from which they emerged. Was it an unusual case, so identified in Worksheet 3? Were there Cases in which the related

Theme was prominent but failed to provide support for the Assertion? Does all this call for further restatement of the Assertion? These considerations need hours, not just minutes.

Some of the ingredient Case Findings or Factors cannot be expected to provide evidence for the Assertion. All through the analysis, Anna Lee has thought about the quality of the evidence and has not felt comfortable about it. She knows it is rare to find strong evidence for an Assertion. Most Assertions are based on compelling persuasion—at least, compelling to the researcher. Compelling persuasion is called "evidence" here. There usually will be data of relevance, some of it perhaps compelling, in the Cases that did not contribute to the statement of Findings. Somehow the case researchers or Anna Lee became persuaded this Assertion is warranted. On what grounds did that persuasion occur?

Anna Lee adds a few more remarks to the "Evidence . . . " column. It may be important to go back and seek further reasoning, but it might be better to do this during the writing of the report. A draft of the final report on **Assertion 1** could be written now. For some Analysts, it will be better to compose all the final Assertion statements before drafting the final report. You can see that a grasp of other Assertions may affect how Anna Lee writes about this one.

Anna Lee moves from **Assertion 1** to **Assertion 2**. Again she scrutinizes the content and form of the **Assertion**, somewhat reworking it, pondering the evidence. Then she does this once again for each of the remaining **Assertions**. There they are, the final **Assertions**. Now she is feeling that the list is too long—not just for the final report, but for her sanity.

It is perhaps time for Anna Lee to review all the Themes (or Merged Findings or Factors), to boost her confidence in what has been accomplished. She examines both how they fit together and how they fit the most important Assertions; she relates them to the changes the multicase researchers are trying to make in the meaning of the Quintain. If she is troubled by the lack of fit or the lack of change in meaning, then that could be the most important Assertion. Even so, it will be important to tell what was done throughout the generation of Assertions. But the lack of coherence of the Cases, or the sturdy durability of the image of the Quintain, may itself be the message.

As to the number of Assertions, Anna Lee perhaps should find more satisfaction in the quality and complexity of a few Assertions than in the coverage of many. She needs advice from her team, colleagues, or committee; ideally, this will give her strength for the writing soon to come.

The cross-case Themes (Worksheet 2) usually will be apparent in the conceptual structure of the final report. They tell us what we were looking for in studying the Cases. Some individual Findings or Factors may be so powerful that they lead the way to repicturing the Quintain, but usually the Theme structure is only modified a little by the Case insights. In Worksheet 6, we have the final **Assertions** (or at least a few of them) that will be the heart of the report.

To close the interpretive cross-site process, Anna Lee studies Worksheet 6. She may decide that the arrangement of the now fewer Assertions needs to be changed some more. It may also be useful to rearrange the comments, underlining and asterisking, so that they will be of more help in writing the report. Another Worksheet 6 could be filled out with another renumbering of Assertions and comments. In the vision of the final report outlined in Worksheet 7, the Assertions are planned to follow a section describing this multicase study.

As the analysis ends, Anna Lee decides immediately to write such a section about the cross-case analysis—mentioning the Quintain and its Themes, then briefly saying something about the Cases and their Findings, and then listing the Assertions as a whole. This sketch not only will get her final report writing going, but will express her view of what the analysis has been all about.

The task has shifted from analysis to synthesis. Putting the Assertions together is not like assembling a jigsaw puzzle, for the pieces lack shape. This is less a time of following procedures and more a time of interpretation and composition. Anna Lee drafts paragraphs and rewrites them. The famous journalist James Reston once said, "How can I know what I think until I read what I write?" But reading them invites rewriting them. Today's computer generously provides an edit function. In my time we had erasers, crumpled pages around the wastebasket, and a shield for erasing the carbon copies when we changed a word. It may be easier now to give birth to an Assertion, and to its environment of reason and circumstance, but it is also more dangerous. Editing is *too* easy. An elegant correction may not have been sufficiently thought through. It is good to think of asserting as something gradual and (breaking again the Chapter 1 pledge) pulsatile.

Anna Lee goes to the most critically needed Cases, the evidence-bearing Cases. She reads pertinent pages again, noting marginal comments. She may find a forgotten connection, a new angle, a quotation. Just handling the documents themselves influences her thinking. She looks particularly for experience described that indicates that an Assertion accurately describes the Quintain.

How should she try to spell out the evidentiary reasoning? Is there reason to doubt that a Case belongs to the Quintain? Is she missing some bigger picture? Are there new meanings of the Quintain emerging? Even at this late moment, Anna Lee stops to think, "What Assertions should have been on this list?"

3.7. TRIANGULATION ACROSS CASES

Triangulation for a multicase study serves the same purpose as in a single-case study: to assure that we have the picture as clear and suitably meaningful as we can get it, relatively free of our own biases, and not likely to mislead the reader greatly. Triangulation occurs along the way. Some of it will be done while organizing and writing the final report.

Getting the picture right results from assertions that are rooted in the Case Findings or Factors, even providing evidence of newly understood relationships. The picture is the picture of the Quintain, which was not studied directly, and its Cases, which were. The activity and contexts of the Cases were examined, but they were only sampled, leaving room for failing to see important facets and nuances. Chapter 2 included a few paragraphs about Case triangulation, partly raising the question of how complete the picture of an individual Case is.

As a form of validation, triangulation follows a classical strategy—seeing whether the new views are consistent with what is already well known about the Case, and now about the Quintain. Nobody may know more about both than the researcher, but many people will know more about some things. During the cross-site procedure, there should have been continuing discussions with team members, colleagues, and other people close by. Triangulation also requires going further afield, checking with people who know some of the Quintain or related activity. We learn many things from knowledgeable people, but we need also to know what they can see is wrong with the views we are reporting. We need to get almost as many of them as we can find time for to have them read all or parts of our manuscript, urging them to find fault, obligating them to say what the conclusions mean to them.

The process of triangulation occurs throughout the fieldwork and analysis. It means being redundant and skeptical in seeing, hearing, coding, analyzing, and writing. It benefits from discussion with both critical insiders and outsiders. The exchanges should be both routinized and spontaneous. Mature is the researcher who rejoices in finding a big mistake.

CHAPTER 4

The Report

The findings of the study will be reported to several audiences, and more than a single report may be needed. Often a different cover letter or oral explanation alerts particular readers to the findings. (In studies of public programs or publicly financed activities, care should be taken not to provide better information to some groups than to others. Usually all information should be accessible to the public. What is deemed inappropriate information for the public should not be available to funding agencies or authorities.)

During the cross-case analysis, the imagination of the analyst grows as to what the final report will look like. Certain story lines and impressions guide his or her thoughts as to what can be said about the quintain. Such hunches are important in all research work, but the conclusions to be drawn need to be based on evidence, and they need to survive critical challenges. An evidentiary discipline cannot be ensured by rubric or guideline. Strategic thinking needs to be a part of the ethic and experience of the research team.

In the following section, a worksheet and guidelines for planning the report are presented. For a small multicase study, these are probably not needed. For a larger study, some system other than personal memory is needed. But the system can be used as a support or as a recipe. The analyst needs to find what works for each individual study. Sticking close to the qualitative tradition, the analyst will rely as much as possible on keeping everything in mind, relying on the worksheet as little as possible, changing it as often as needed. But the more other members of the team or outsiders such as draft reviewers or editors need to have a matrix to go by, the more such a guide as Worksheet 7 needs to be developed and kept up to date. (The similarity to the Figure 1.2 guide for writing up the report of a single case is apparent.) Yours need not look like Worksheet 7, and Worksheet 7 (like all the other worksheets) can be adapted and modified to suit your own purposes.

The actual writing of the report will be a combination of the researchers' intuition and the evidence from the cross-case analysis. The analyst uses the worksheets to help keep track of all the data available and to transform the most prominent relationships into assertions. Usually the assertions are the conceptual structure of the final report.

4.1. PLANNING THE MULTICASE REPORT

Organizing the final multicase report works better if you have a plan. Worksheet 7 is a diagram for planning the writing and assembly of such a report. A single person or a group can develop the plan. Hereafter we will refer to the planner as a woman and again will call her the analyst. Of course this analyst does not have to be the same person doing the multicase analysis, but much of the same familiarity with research questions and casework is needed by both.

The analyst first estimates the number of pages in the report, anticipating allocating those pages to the several topics and cases and placing them in order. There is no one right order for the sections, but the report usually goes from explanation of the research and background ideas to a description of the research, an interpretation, and a summary.

In particular, the analyst has to decide whether or not to have a summary. This is sometimes called an "executive summary," implying that executives won't read very much, so this summary should be quite short. The executive summary can be placed at either the beginning or the end of the report. Sometimes it is published separately from the rest of the report. Separate care needs to go into the organization of the executive summary.

The wide column at the left in Worksheet 7, the one headed "Main Topics (Sections)," is used to indicate the content of the report, including the order of topics. Page allocations are to be estimated in the next column. The next 10 columns, as indicated by column headings to be modified by the analyst, tell where important information is to be placed. The two larger columns at the right are for listing and designating important but small pieces of information, with the designation numbers and letters later placed in the left margin adjacent to the topical section where each bit will be best located.

The worksheet may be enlarged to permit entry of the section headings actually to be used, abbreviated, in the "Main topics" column. Con-

WORKSHEET 7. Planning the Multicase Final Report

Anticipated appearances of reappearing topics across the sections of the report

Main topics (Sections)	Pages	Case A	Case C	Case E	Theme 3	Theme 5	Factor 1	Quintain Staff	Future									Single-Mention Topics	Quotes Impressions
The Study																	1.	a.
Quintain																	2.	b.
Themes																	3.	c.
Assertion 1																	4.	d.
Assertion 2																	5.	e.
Assertion 3																	6.	f.
Assertion 4																	7.	g.
Assertion 5																		h.
Assertion 6																		
Main Finding																		
Main Finding																		
Lesser Findings																		
New View																		
Methods																		
Lit. Review																		
Summary																		

tent-free titles (such as shown here) are often used but I prefer more informative headings, such as "The Urban Case" or "The Rise in Community Interaction." Description of the study with a statement of the research questions and cases selected usually comes first, but often after a formal introductory section mentioning the programmatic and personal circumstances of starting the study. The section about the quintain may come next—describing the way it was seen at the outset, identifying the cases, and perhaps discussing the binding concept that holds the cases together. Theoretical background for the quintain may be presented here or later in the report, sometimes as an appendix.

The presentation of assertions and findings or conclusions may be presented next. Because the cases are usually long, it may be rather chancy to imply that the reader will read them before learning what was learned in the project. The main findings or conclusions should be described in some detail in their own sections, but lesser conclusions can be grouped into a single section. The case reports, in full or abbreviated, can be presented in the main body of the report or in the appendix. Sometimes the case reports are bound separately (Stake & Easley, 1979).

After the case report sections, the analyst may insert a section to show how the quintain is newly conceptualized as a result of the study.

Somewhere in the report, the methods used in the multicase study should be presented. Many analysts prefer to present the methods early in the study, but that may give an undesirable emphasis of method over substance. A section on methods can appear in the appendix. Similarly, a section reviewing the most relevant literature can be placed early in the report, toward the end, or in the appendix; alternatively, previous studies and interpretations may appear throughout the report without having a special section.

In Worksheet 7, the last section listed is the summary. (If very brief, this can be called an executive summary, as noted above). It can appear as either the first or last few pages of the final report, or elsewhere.

These main topics are likely to change somewhat after the matrix is first filled in, and more rows may need to be added. But if the number of rows exceeds 15 or 20, the procedure may become too unwieldy to be of much help to the analyst. The first two columns here contain more or less the same information as the table of contents. The total number of pages should be indicated at the bottom of the "Pages" column.

With the main topics all identified, the analyst will show in which sections important information can be placed. The analyst should label the 10 column headings on Worksheet 7 between "Pages" and "Single-Mention Topics" to identify the cases, themes, factors, and so forth that will appear again and again in the report and that cross-case analysis has

shown to be of particular importance for this study. For instance, the analyst may have concluded that Case A is an especially significant one, so
the first column after "Pages" could be headed "Case A." The analyst may
simply make checkmarks in the "Case A" column indicating where that
case contributes in important ways to each of the main topic sections, or
a more sophisticated symbol system set up. It is common for some or all of
the case reports to be included in the multicase report. For example, Case
A of course is about Case A, so a row for Case A will be added to
Worksheet 7, and the cell at the intersection of that row and the column
for Case A will be checked. In addition, Case A may contribute quite a
bit to Assertion 1 (as finalized) and to two of the other assertions, so
those three cells will be checked also. If Case A provides an unusual situation for locating the quintain, as indicated in Worksheets 3 and 4, that
information should be noted in the row for the "New View" of the quintain. Or if Case A is making any other contribution to the new view of
the quintain or to the literature review, those cells should be checked off
as well.

The writer of each main topic will use these check marks as a
reminder of what needs to be included in the section. Or, to put it the
other way around, this procedure is to give some assurance that important information about cases, themes, factors, and so forth is not inadver-
tently omitted.

For example, Case A might give focus to the involvement of parents,
and that also might be the content of Assertion 2 (which is perhaps even
named "Involvement of parents"). So in the column for Case A, a
checkmark would be made for Assertion 2. Involvement of parents will,
of course, show up in other sections as well. In the instance of the Step by
Step quintain, we just cannot talk at length about classrooms without
talking about involvement of parents. If the original Theme 3 is particularly pertinent to involvement of parents, then the cell at the intersection of the "Case A" column and the "Themes" row (or the "Theme 3"
row, if a special one has been created for it) should also be checked.

4.2. COMPARING CASES

Comparison is a search for similarity and difference in cases. There is
comparison in all inquiry and all discourse, but comparison has only a
minor role to play in individual case studies. Comparative studies—
whether of quantitative or qualitative design—seek similarities and differences among cases on a relatively few specified attributes. The purpose

of the those studies is to make some grand comparison rather than to increase understanding of individual cases.

Multicase study is not a design for comparing cases. The cases studied are a selected group of instances chosen for better understanding of the quintain. Most case researchers report each case as a case, knowing that this case will be compared to others, but not giving emphasis to attributes for comparison. A few researchers take responsibility for setting up comparative cases for the reader or acknowledging reference cases that readers have in mind.

Naturalistic, ethnographic, and phenomenological researchers try to describe the several cases in sufficient detail for the reader to make comparisons if he or she needs or wishes to do so. Sometimes they point out comparisons that might be made. In contrast, quantitative and program evaluation case researchers do try to provide comparisons—sometimes by presenting one or more reference cases, sometimes by providing statistical norms for reference groups from which a hypothetical reference case can be projected. Both quantitative and qualitative researchers provide a rather narrow basis for comparison of cases. Still, clearly, a tradition of grand comparison exists within comparative anthropology and sister disciplines (Ragin, 1987; Raisin & Britton, 1997; Sjoberg, Williams, Vaughan, & Sjoberg, 1991; Tobin, 1989; Yin, 1992).

Comparison is a competitor to probing study of a case. It is a grand research strategy, a powerful conceptualization, usually fixing attention on one or a few variables. In so doing, it obscures the situationality and complex interaction of case knowledge. Comparative description usually is simplistic, greatly unlike what Clifford Geertz (1973) called "thick description." Thick description of a nursing education program, for example, might include multiple perceptions of the faculty, curricular changes, the charisma of the clinical director, the working relationships with a community health organization, the multiple realities of the executive committee, and the lack of student interest in government policy. In such particularities lie the vitality, trauma, and uniqueness of the case. Comparison might be made on any of these characteristics but tends to be made on variables traditionally noted in the description of nursing programs (e.g., staffing, practicum opportunities, employment opportunities for graduates, and institutional donors). Illustration of how a phenomenon occurs in the circumstances of a quintain can provide valued and trustworthy knowledge (Vaughan, 1992), but this is not what we usually mean by "comparison."

We conceptualize the case in various ways to facilitate learning about the quintain. The quintain is something that functions, that operates, that has life. The multicase study is the observation of that life in multiple situations (Kemmis, 1980). The quintain is something to be described and interpreted. The ideal for most naturalistic, holistic, ethnographic, and phenomenological case studies is to provide description: subjective, potentially disciplined interpretation; a respect and curiosity for culturally different perceptions of phenomena; and empathic representation of local settings. Avoiding stereotypes is part of the ethic. Direct comparison is somewhat out of place in such a mix.

4.3. ADVOCACY

There was a time when most researchers claimed that their studies were value-free. They meant that they did not take sides as to what the world should be like. They meant that they resisted pressures to tilt their findings toward any client or theory or ideology. They meant that their reports would not treat supporters with favor and antagonists with disfavor. They held up an ideal of science as impersonal and value-neutral.

Today most researchers acknowledge that they themselves and their reports cannot be value-neutral, however much they might wish them to be. They acknowledge that, like everyone else's, their observations and interpretations are shaped by personal experience, culture, and coterie. They find themselves reluctant to see or say something that might jeopardize a worthy case. And they are not unaware that certain findings can influence their chances of future research support.

Their advocacy is usually the program's. Multicase studies are sometimes created at least partly to promote the quintain or to advocate the spread of its policies and practices. The rhetoric is likely to emphasize the need to understand it in its far-flung locations, and possibly to facilitate staff members' reflections on what they are doing; however, if the study is done without external requirements from a central office or funding source, it almost can be assumed that the program is healthy and will be shown to advantage.

Such semipromotional studies should not be left to true believers, people with an ax to grind, mercenaries, and would-be value-free scientists. In the spirit of action research (Carr & Kemmis, 1986; Elliott, 1991; Holly, Arhar, & Kasten, 2005; Noffke, 1997), they can be done by members of an organization. Whoever they are, the researchers should seek evidence of the complexities of what the program is and is not, and work to prevent the findings' being read simply as a verdict of "good" or "bad."

The presence of values is particularly acute in qualitative research, because of the intent to come to a better understanding of personal and political issues.[1] A teacher's teaching or an institution's policies are supposed to be examined with ideology in mind. A study may not be intentionally evaluative, but if it digs into the intention and implication of action, it will be evaluative. Even straightforward descriptions will be something of an expression of values, partly through what they reveal and partly through what they omit. Qualitative studies are intentionally value-laden. Their credibility and utility will be influenced more by even-handed treatment (can that be defined?) than by statements or implications that the report is free of advocacy.

Most favoritism in research is to be found in what is *not* said—in underplaying a negative side of the picture. The reader wants a full account, as well as accountability, but the report writer cannot help being selective, for there is more to be said than can be said. What he or she selects to say will be based on the research question and the utility of alternative explanations; however, it will also be based partly on what the report writer cares about, partly on what is deemed important to know, and partly on what effects the findings might have. There is no value-free science in this world.

And let us not presume that there is a bustling market for value-free studies. For every reader who would like maximum removal from value judgments—a freedom from considering what the world should be—there are at least 20 and maybe 100 who would have the study leaning toward support of their particular causes. Knowledge and understanding are promised by researchers (and on earlier pages of this book), but promotion, deterrence, and reform are what most people want. They may say that they want the action to be based on facts, but, knowing that the facts will be incomplete and debatable, they are impatient. On with action! The urge for action is common to all advocacies, good and bad. Strivings for human rights and self-aggrandizement ride the same train. Research is valued if it makes people powerful, not because it makes them wise.

In the intensity of writing the report, we case researchers usually reflect something of the value-free ideology. At that moment, we see ourselves dispassionately refining assertions to answer the research ques-

---

[1]The distinguished measurement psychologist Lee Cronbach (1977) was speaking about program evaluation, but his words pertain to multicase studies as well. At the charter meeting of the Evaluation Research Society, he said, "If [this research] is not primarily a scientific activity, what is it? It is first and foremost a political activity, a function performed within a social system" (p. 1).

tions. We take a disdainful view of advocacy and promotion. Yet as we step away from the keyboard, we recognize again that we have strong feelings about certain matters, and that we have painted some of them into our work. Here are six advocacies common in qualitative case studies:

1. We care about the case or quintain being studied. Often we believe in it. Sometimes we are studying a part of our own organization. Seldom do we have a large conflict of interest, but we often have a *confluence* of interest. We *hope* to find the program working. We are disposed to see evidence of success.

2. We care about case research. We want to see others care about it. We want to encourage them to do it. We promote case studies—our own and those of our colleagues. We favor methods that enable us to do fieldwork well, and encourage others to use them too.

3. We advocate rationality. We would like to be clear, logical, and even-handed, and we would like our sponsors and other stakeholders, our colleagues, and our department heads to do the same. We often pause in our data gathering or reporting to point out a way that the case could have behaved more rationally.

4. We care to be heard. We are troubled if our studies are not used. We feel that case reports are more useful if program participants get involved in the study.

5. We are distressed by underprivilege. We see gaps between privileged patrons and managers on the one hand, and staff members, underprivileged participants, and communities on the other. We sometimes organize some of the study around issues of privilege, conceptualizing issues that might illuminate or alleviate underprivilege, and attempting to assure a wider distribution of findings.

6. We are advocates of a democratic society. We see democracies as depending on the exchange of good information, which our studies can provide. But we also see democracies as needing the exercise of public expression, dialogue, and collective action. Most educational researchers try to create reports that stimulate action.

These six advocacies are easy to find in case reports. You may think that these are not advocacies—merely aspects the culture of research communities. You may think that these are values to which all researchers should aspire. Yes, they are commendable, and yes, they are value commitments. They are also biases. The point is that biases can be good, bad, or some of each. We should consider the argument of Jennifer

Greene (1995, 2000) that research should contribute to advancing the higher values of society.

It is nearly impossible for us as human beings to change our personalities. Some of our research training tries to get us to eliminate our offensive biases, and we should take steps in that direction (Scriven, 1998), but such biases will remain. We sometimes only succeed in driving our biases deeper into the shadows.

It is an ethical responsibility for us as case researchers to identify affiliations and ideological commitments that might influence our interpretations—not only for the contracting parties but for the readers of reports, and, of course, for ourselves. But there is no way for us as evaluators to identify all relevant predispositions, or even to *know* them. We can reveal ourselves a little through self-references, biographical notes, curricula vitae, previous reports, acknowledgments of preference and alliance, and even (indirectly) the ways we write—but an entire list of possible influences would be arbitrary, unhelpful, ever incomplete, and always out of date. Still, it is possible to help readers realize some of the biases, good and bad, to be found in our work.

We sometimes aspire to a professional practice by which—hypothetically—all researchers studying a single quintain would produce largely the same assertions. But that aspiration cannot be fulfilled, and efforts to make it happen would move us toward simplification and trivialization of the quintain. Different researchers may get the same measurements, but they cannot help interpreting things differently. Their findings will be different (though, ideally, not often completely at odds). In the complex representation of program operation and accomplishment, there is no single reality we can capture. The only realities are the ones constructed by people, and people differ (Schwandt, 2000). Were we to agree completely on what we see, we would presume that we are seeing correctly—and often we are not.

We have a case study practice that is influenced by the value commitments of many different people, yet a set of methodological standards implying that we can attain widely agreed-upon portrayals of a quintain. Something needs to give. Perhaps we should more effectively constrain our value commitments and search harder for metaevaluation consensus; however; we clearly should develop our standards and principles so that they deal better with the uncertainty and individuality of qualitative study. Researchers should be encouraged to "have a life" and to "have a dream," so their interpretations are enriched by personal experience. Comprehensive, idiosyncratic, irreproducible interpretations are a contribution to understanding and action.

4.4. GENERALIZATION

Even if the main assertions are clearly stated, the multicase report will say different things to different audiences, accommodating and eluding various expectations. Among the expectations are (1) that the multicase report will be a guide to setting policy for a population of cases such as those studied; and (2) that the report will provide people with the vicarious experience useful for transferring assertions from those cases to others. Those two expectations may sound similar, but since ancient Greece, scholars have debated the worth of general and particular knowledge.

Socrates and Plato pursued the grand meanings of worldly affairs. That is, they sought generalizations to summarize the laws, communications, and customs of people collectively, and also possibly to improve them. As the physical and social sciences subsequently developed, and as they still do today, they followed a similar epistemological aim—elevating grand theory, and holding personal, professional, and public experience regarding individual cases at a subordinate level of knowing.

Aristotle acknowledged that grand, collective, impersonal knowledge is part of dealing with worldly affairs, but he also recognized that people absolutely need to engage the knowledge of past experience. Any prudent handling of life will be attendant to the particular values of each situation, and to relationships between past and present situations. The roots of generalization need to be nourished by detail and context. Just as much as abstract generalization, and maybe more, experiential knowing is critical to the epistemology of individual people and agencies. The study of human activity loses too much if it reports primarily what is common among the several, and universal across the many. Aristotle's term for prudent knowledge, purposive knowledge, and experiential knowing was *phronesis*.

In criticizing Socratic social science and researchers' quest for epistemic laws to guide human affairs, philosopher of science Bent Flyvbjerg (2001, p. 2) said:

> *Phronesis* goes beyond both analytical, scientific knowledge (*episteme*) and technical knowledge or know-how (*techne*) and involves judgments and decisions made in the manner of a virtuoso social and political actor. I will argue that *phronesis* is commonly involved in social practice, and that therefore, attempts to reduce social science and theory to *episteme* or *techne*, or to comprehend them in those terms is misguided.

In Flyvbjerg's view, the more epistemic generalizations have often been misleading and of little operational value.

But even if Flyvbjerg's dismay with social science is warranted, there will continue to be expectations that multicase research should provide formal generalizations for guiding policy and collective practice. When this is so, multicase analysis can be facilitated by placing greater emphasis on "factors" and by adjusting the procedures of Worksheets 1–7 to substitute expeditiously the structural thinking[2] of sociology, economics, and education in the review of individual cases (Gobo, 2004). At an even earlier stage, it will help to have the case researchers facilitate multicase analysis by sharing descriptors and highlighting common research questions. As indicated repeatedly in this book, this approach demotes the understanding of the cases as unique and situated. Even when we are approximating a truth (which we never know), epistemic generalizations will be overly abstract guides to practice.

Because it is assumed that such generalizations are based on enduring relationships and can be used to predict the effects of change, they continue to be respected in research communities and administrative circles. They are problematic because they lead to expectations that they will optimally facilitate professional practice, which they will not. It is true that useful limits of practice may be established and that help may be given, but the essential determination of professional action will regularly come from custom and advocacy, not from science (Flyvbjerg, 2004).

Still, such formal generalizations make an important contribution to debate and deliberation of social policy. When recognized for what they are—that is, hypotheses and working positions—they provide valuable counterpositions to experience and convention. Note the reversal of the roles played by the particular versus the general in this definition of "case study" from the more common "but [case study] may be useful in the preliminary stages of an investigation since it provides hypotheses which may be tested . . . " (Abercrombie, Hill, & Turner, 1984, p. 46). Both the particular and the general are grist for deliberation and debate (House & Howe, 1999). *Phronesis, episteme,* and *techne* all make their contributions to the discourse (and, sometimes, to the row and calumny).

Following Mary Kennedy (1979), Lee Ruddin (2005) has claimed that "One serious drawback in the single case study methodology that has prevented it from being widely accepted is the lack of generally accepted rules for drawing causations and generalization inference from the data." It seems more likely to me that the act of generalizing is deeply set in the human repertoire and that it will continue to operate largely without

---

[2]Structural thinking is found as rules and statements of likelihood, functional relationships, and categorical comparisons.

protocol. Still, protocol may sometimes help; with that in mind, I have provided the worksheets for this book.

What multicase studies have most to offer is a collection of situated case activities in a binding of larger research questions. However, the generalizations are of a different sort. Such studies abstain from formal projection to cases that are not examined; rather, they show how a variety of components and constraints lead to a partly irreducible individualism among the cases. The common and the unusual are both portrayed, and both are situated in a complex of experience against a local and diverse background. Worksheets 1–7, however epistemic in appearance, can be made instruments for maintaining respect for the individual cases.

What readers can learn from a human affairs study is related to the five levels of learning identified by Hubert and Stuart Dreyfus (1986). Only at the lowest level, the novice level, is there concentration on epistemic generalizations, rule-bound and context-free. As readers advance up the steps, it is expected that their learning will increasingly involve situational elements, virtues, goals, plans, and the experience of the readers themselves, through the highest level, as described by Flyvbjerg (2001): " . . . experts' behavior is intuitive, holistic, and synchronic, understood in the way that a given situation releases a picture of problem, goal, plan, decision and action in one instant and with no division into phases" (p. 21). Competent performers, experts, and virtuosos need case-based contextual understanding to add to their own direct and vicarious experience. There is a widespread belief that what leaders want is statistical conclusions, but for problem solving, what they need more is experience. Being a leader requires making complex judgments, and the securest position is that of reflected experience (Foucault, 1980; Schön, 1983).

It would be a mistake if a multicase researcher fails to disclose whatever generalizations appear evident from the data, in a tentative way. In the obligation to be useful to society and to the individual reader (whether this is a policy maker, another researcher, or a practitioner), the researcher should talk briefly or at length about individual cases. He or she should enrich the reader's experiential knowing with as much of the action and context of the cases as possible. Because the reader knows the situations to which the assertions might apply, the responsibility of making generalizations should be more the reader's than the writer's.

CHAPTER 5

The Step by Step
Multicase Study Project[1]

The Step by Step early childhood multicase project was selected to provide an example of the methods described in this book. Because the full range of multicase studies—for example, dissertations, internal studies, monitoring studies, comparative research, and national program portrayals—is so great, no one type of study can be considered a good representation of the others. Differences in design, issues, and multicase analysis are large. But the methods and issues developed in each type of study are in some ways similar, and so despite its huge scope and uniqueness, this ongoing Step by Step project provides a valuable resource for contemplating the work of multicase researchers.

A still-developing rationalization for applicability is fundamental to all learning from case studies. In many ways, a single case is not representative of other cases, but the interactions and operational responses in its situations are so frequently found in dissimilar cases that they are seen as relevant by readers (scholars and novices alike). This reasoning extends to multicase studies. Whatever the number of cases studied, the findings from the individual cases and the commonalities among the cases are weak representations of the complete population of cases, but those findings can be useful for understanding the population and still unstudied individual cases (Flyvbjerg, 2001).[2]

---

[1]Information for this chapter is taken from descriptive materials prepared by Sarah Klaus and Cassie Landers as part of the Step by Step Multicase Study Project.

[2]This is not a denial of the case–quintain dilemma. However different a case may be from its quintain, the study of cases can help both.

5.1. THE OPEN SOCIETY INSTITUTE
AND THE INTERNATIONAL STEP BY STEP ASSOCIATION

For 20 years, as much as any other individual, philanthropist George Soros has worked to promote democracy in his own native Hungary and in other former Soviet bloc countries. In 1994, the Open Society Institute (OSI) and its international network of Soros Foundations embarked on what was intended to be a 2-year project to introduce child-centered methodologies and family/community engagement practices in preschools and institutions providing in-service teacher training in 15 countries in Central and Eastern Europe. Now, over 10 years later, the project has expanded greatly. New goals and objectives have been introduced during this decade:

- The target age group has been extended. Step by Step now serves children 0–10 years of age; that is, it reaches up to include the first 4 years of primary school and down to include infant/toddler programs.
- Multiple new program areas have been added. These include whole-school improvement; inclusion of children with disabilities in mainstream classes; community-based child development programs for children and families; educating for social justice (anti-bias training for professionals); publication of developmentally appropriate children's literature; and initiatives to transform preservice teacher and caregiver education.
- Establishment in each country of a nongovernmental organization (NGO) or professional association, which provides high-quality services to professionals and serves as an independent voice in national educational reform and policy development.
- An international professional association has been created—the International Step by Step Association (ISSA), which is independent of OSI. ISSA is a network of the NGOs described in the preceding paragraph, which are engaged in large-scale national reform and regional advocacy initiatives. ISSA offers a network of services to national Step by Step NGOs, as well as to professionals, organizations, and new countries seeking support from the Step by Step program.

At the end of 2004, Step by Step was being implemented in 30 countries in cooperation with their ministries of education, and was serving over 1 million children and their families. By the end of 2004, more than 220,000 educators had participated in professional training, and

1,400 preservice and in-service faculty members at more than 700 institutions had started to teach such methods in their courses.

5.2. THE STEP BY STEP APPROACH

Step by Step is a comprehensive child-centered approach that serves families with children from birth through age 10. The philosophy has been summed up by two child development specialists as follows:

> Through every experience, young children learn that they are worthy, valued, and respected. They know that their rights will be protected. At the same time, they are learning to expand their concerns and give up some of the egocentrism for the good of others and the group. As members of a democratic community, children develop a sense of shared concern, recognizing that their interests overlap with the interests of others and that their welfare is inextricably entwined with the welfare of others. (Seefeldt & Barbour, 1994, p. 584.)

In the introduction to a supplementary Step by Step guide for teachers, *Education and the Culture of Democracy: Early Childhood Practice* (Hansen, Kaufmann, & Saifer, n.d.), Vaclav Havel writes:

> The most important thing is a new concept of education. At all levels, schools must cultivate a spirit of free and independent thinking in the students. . . . The schools must also lead young people to become self-confident, participating citizens; if everyone doesn't take an interest in politics, it will become the domain of those least suited to it. (p. v)

Thus, at its core, the Step by Step Program aims to:

- Promote development of democratic, open societies by introducing educational methodologies that promote critical thinking, respect for differences, choice, and responsibility.
- Improve opportunities for minority, at-risk, impoverished, disabled children and their families, through anti-bias initiatives and other educational interventions that promote school success in inclusive, integrated settings that value diversity.

At the classroom level, Step by Step integrates international practices and standards of early childhood and primary education with a commitment to working with families and communities. Step by Step's child-centered education is built around two core beliefs:

- Children create their own knowledge from their experience and interaction with the world around them.
- Teachers and parents foster children's growth and development by building on the children's interests, needs, and strengths.

A thematic approach is employed, in which classrooms are organized around developmentally appropriate learning and activity centers. A priority is placed on peer learning. Activity centers are shaped to the interests and learning level of each age group, and contain a variety of materials to meet the learning needs of individual children. Step by Step classrooms encourage children to (1) make choices and accept responsibility, (2) learn independently as well as cooperatively, and (3) be tolerant and respectful of differences.

Step by Step teachers facilitate children's learning and focus on creating a community of learners. Highly valued student skills include intellectual curiosity, independent learning, enthusiasm, empathy, and caring. Strong family and community participation is essential to long-term sustainability. Families' active participation in the school community is welcomed. Parents are encouraged to join in the classroom activities, to share their talents, to create learning materials, and to attend parent meetings.

In order to achieve deep systemic reform, the program operates at three levels:

- Introducing new models of teaching practice in each country, first in pilot sites and then extensively throughout each country.
- Reforming teacher-training systems (preservice and in-service) to incorporate these new models.
- Securing official (ministry of education) endorsement and support for these new approaches, which in many cases requires introduction of new policies.

The core activity of the Step by Step program is providing training for educators (teachers, teacher assistants, teaching methods specialists, psychologists, administrators) engaged in preschools and primary schools. ISSA's commitment is long-term and offers ongoing technical assistance and professional development. The Step by Step training cycle begins by creating model classrooms in several preschools and primary schools.

Core training is provided to a team of child education experts responsible for developing the program.

The Step by Step program in the individual countries is mentored by ISSA's extensive network of international professionals. Through visits to each country and ongoing communication, the ISSA professionals and the personnel in the different countries work together as teams to design effective implementation strategies and maintain quality. As the programs expand, quality is assessed using ISSA standards and the certification process. Certification is dependent on actual classroom practice and assesses teachers on the following dimensions: individualization, learning environment, family participation, teaching strategies for meaningful learning, planning and assessment, professional development, and social inclusion.

Exemplary Step by Step classrooms can become training centers. These centers provide cost-effective, comprehensive training for teachers through classroom observations and training courses. Many training centers are accredited by the countries' ministries of education and formally linked to teacher-training institutions and universities. Step by Step also forms partnerships with existing pedagogical institutes, universities, and teacher-training institutes. Full courses on early childhood and interactive teaching methods have been developed.

Policy reform is critical to sustaining educational innovations. In an effort to influence policy, Step by Step works in collaboration with each country's ministry of education and other relevant agencies. Strategies to encourage the participation of local and national policy makers in all aspects of program design and implementation have regularly been reworked.

The degree and rate of the program's expansion in a particular country depends on many factors, including resource availability and the commitment of the ministry of education. Ultimately the goal is to establish high-quality, sustainable training programs, officially accredited by the ministry and available to all interested teachers, schools, and communities.

Since its inception in 1994, Step by Step developed a range of initiatives to support the ever-expanding facets of school reform, minority education, and community outreach. (See Figure 5.1.) These initiatives share the following common principles:

- Equal access to education and development opportunities.
- Child-centered, individualized teaching and learning.
- Development of skills for lifelong participation in a democracy.
- Teachers as facilitators.

Within the context of child-centered learning and family participation, ISSA supports a wide range of programs. When implemented together, these initiatives provide a comprehensive foundation for reform of education and care for children from birth through age 10. Programs can also be implemented individually.

Early Childhood (Birth to Age 6)

- Parent education programs
- Early childhood development community centers
- Preschool
- Center-based infant and toddler programs

Primary School (Grades 1–4)

- Creating democratic classrooms and schools
- Community education
- Transition to middle school

Equal Access

- Education for social justice
- Inclusive education
- Minority education

Teacher Education

- Courses for teacher-training/retraining institutions
- Student practica
- Training for adult trainers
- Teacher certification

Civic Participation in Education

- Parent advocacy
- Organizational development for educational NGOs

Professional Standards and Assessment Instruments

- Program and teacher standards
- Trainer standards
- Child observation and assessment instruments (preschool and primary)

FIGURE 5.1. International Step by Step Association (ISSA) initiatives.

- Family involvement.
- Community engagement in public education.
- Culturally appropriate learning environments.
- Ongoing professional development.

Each country adapts the Step by Step interventions to its national educational standards and local culture. The program in each country works in partnership with communities, kindergartens, primary schools, retraining institutes, pedagogical institutes, and universities, as well as national and local governments. The three case studies presented in this volume (see Chapters 6–8) focus on several of these initiatives in depth, exploring adaptations made at the national and local levels. Two of them deal with specific initiatives in the area of equal access (Ukraine and Slovakia), and one explores Step by Step teacher education (Romania).

In the Ukraine case study (see Chapter 6), the researchers explore Step by Step's inclusive education initiative. In Ukraine, as in many of the countries where Step by Step is active, only children with very mild disabilities are typically included in regular classrooms. In response, Step by Step has initiated extensive programs in these regions to train and retrain teachers of mainstream classrooms in the inclusion of children with mild and moderate special needs. Step by Step inclusive education programs also engage in development of fiscal and administrative procedures to sustain these programs; dissemination of best practices for children with different types of disabilities; restructuring social, educational, and health systems in inclusive settings; and development of advocacy and community awareness programs.

The Slovakia case study (see Chapter 7) addresses another education access issue addressed by the Step by Step program: school success for Roma children. Availability and accessibility of high-quality education for minority children are priorities for ISSA and its network. The Roma are the largest ethnic minority in Europe.[3] The majority of Roma children do not have access to good-quality education, and one third of these children are assigned to "special schools" on the basis of culturally biased testing. Step by Step seeks to create innovative solutions backed by sustained policy reform. For example, Roma teaching assistants are placed in classrooms to facilitate majority-language learning and to serve as a bridge between the school and the Roma community. The challenges are great, but the commitment to achieving acceptable alternatives is a driving force for Step by Step efforts.

---

[3]"Roma" have often been commonly known as "gypsies." As the identity of the ethnic group has evolved, use of "Roma" has been preferred.

In the Romania case study (see Chapter 8), the researcher explores the nature of Step by Step's decentralized teacher-training approach. As mentioned earlier, Step by Step seeks to establish training centers at the best program preschools and primary schools. These training centers provide both training and mentoring to interested preschool and primary school educators in their areas. Step by Step uses a system of pedagogical quality standards for teachers to guide professional development. The Step by Step program in each country is adapted to the context of that country's professional development system in order to ensure sustainability.

Although much has changed since 1994, by the start of the case study project, all Step by Step initiatives continued to have at their core a focus on helping children. It is hoped that children in these parts of the world will become self-motivated learners and creative, critically thinking, and tolerant adults—people who will help create a more open society, where active citizen participation and appreciation for differences and multiple views are widely valued. The Step by Step program continues to promote the right of all children to a high-quality education. Special efforts are made to reach out to children of minority families, children with disabilities, refugee children, and children in poverty. Programmatic emphasis is being placed on tailoring services to these groups.

5.3. PREVIOUS STEP BY STEP EVALUATIONS

Due to the intensity of the program's implementation and its rapid growth, the Step by Step staff launched a comprehensive longitudinal self-study, but did not complete it. This was not thought to be a serious problem when the decision was made, since the project was initially intended as a 2-year initiative. Nonetheless, attempts have been made to capture the impact of the program on children and families in the intervening years. These efforts include the following:

• *Studies carried out nationally in cooperation with pedagogical institutes, universities, and ministries of education in individual countries.* These studies have been a critical step in acceptance of the Step by Step methods by the ministries of education in participating countries. Some of these studies indicate that Step by Step programs promote social and emotional development, as well as helping children in the programs score higher on tests measuring cooperation, leadership, self-esteem, problem solving, and perseverance. Studies also show consistently that Step by Step children score as high as or higher than children in other programs in core academic areas. A collection of national studies focusing on child outcomes is in progress.

• A *four-country independent evaluation of Step by Step, conducted in 1999 with funding from USAID (U.S. Agency for International Development)*. This evaluation demonstrated impact on children's democratic behaviors, ideas, and values—including making choices, taking initiatives, valuing individual expression, and contributing as members of a learning community. It provided the first evidence that Step by Step provides real support to children who enter with less developed academic skills, supporting the view that the Step by Step child-centered approach enables teachers to respond to children's individual needs.

• *Studies in Macedonia, Serbia, and Slovakia*. These studies demonstrated that Roma children who attend Step by Step preschool programs are now, unlike before, prepared to enter first grade. They had significantly lower dropout rates in primary school and scored significantly higher on national standardized academic tests.

• *The Roma Special Schools Project*. This was a pilot project to challenge the inordinate number of Roma children in the region assigned to special schools and remedial classrooms. It showed that 62% of these supposedly intellectually challenged children could reach grade-level expectations within 3 years when provided with a supportive, child-centered environment—one valuing the students' culture and including their language in the curriculum. In addition to core Step by Step teacher training, this program also provided Roma teaching assistants and a Roma family coordinator for participating schools, as well as teacher training in anti-bias education and second language-learning.

• *Four-country study on Step by Step NGO sustainability*. Initial sustainability studies in four countries, conducted in 2000, by pairs of independent evaluators yielded positive results, showing that the established Step by Step NGOs in the study had the capacity to carry out their program activities and had laid the groundwork for long-term sustainability.

It seemed important to Step by Step leaders not just to continue the inquiry as to the suitability of Step by Step for support by ministries of education, but to undertake research to learn more from the experience and reflect on how to improve implementation. To advance this research orientation, the leaders of the Step by Step program decided to conduct a multicase study. They invited the Step by Step organization in each country to participate, and 28 of the national Step by Step programs accepted this invitation.

5.4. AIMS OF THE STEP BY STEP MULTICASE PROJECT

OSI sought to build reflective practice (within both the Step by Step program and ISSA) to inform future practice and activity. In particular, as the 10th anniversary of Step by Step approached, many participants expressed interest in reflecting on and documenting the decade of experience, to synthesize for broad circulation the outcomes and learning points. Building on this interest and opportunity, OSI decided to engage in a 1- to 2-year process of documenting insights from the Step by Step program, through a case study project.

OSI hoped to gain a body of knowledge to contribute to the early childhood development field, drawing upon the diversity, complexity, and richness of the 30-country experience. Over the longer term, information from the study could strengthen and inform the commitment (especially at the national government level, as well as between and within international organizations and in all efforts to achieve global, sustainable social progress and development) to improving program implementation, advocacy, and policy affecting young children. The knowledge gleaned through the collection of Step by Step case studies had the potential to be OSI's main contribution to this interagency process.

An equally important aim was to provide Step by Step professionals across the project countries with an opportunity to develop and practice the skills of case research. Case study, an important qualitative research method, had not been widely used by educational professionals and researchers in the regions where Step by Step was active. It was seen as a useful complement to the developmental philosophy of Step by Step and to its emphasis on the uniqueness of every individual, classroom, school, community, and country. The design of the case study project, therefore, was an opportunity to offer country case study teams multiple learning experiences and ongoing mentoring as they developed their cases. It was expected that each of the 28 countries participating in the study would contribute a case study to the collection, and that the project would contribute to the development of capacity in case study research in the early childhood field in these regions.

5.5. DEVELOPING CASE TOPICS

All Step by Step country-based programs were organized initially to focus on reform of preschool and primary school education systems. Each participating country also had opportunities to engage in a multitude of additional initiatives, such as anti-bias education, school improvement, inclusive education, education of Roma and other minority children, parent education, infant/toddler programs, and so on. In order to ensure a balance of topics across the case studies, participating countries were asked to indicate their preferred topics as part of the application process. Some countries suggested additional topics. Final topic assignments were negotiated with the OSI office in Budapest. While offering some level of choice, this process also ensured that all topics were represented in the final compilation of cases. Luckily, teams were interested in a variety of topics, and it was easy to organize a balanced multicase study.

Within each topic over the course of the project, each team worked with an international mentor to further select study sites, identify key research questions, and develop field research plans and instruments.

5.6. ACTION RESEARCH

The motivation for the multicase project is worth further reflection here. The study was complex. Clearly, the intention to better understand and reflect on the work in the separate countries, as well as on the international level, was strong. Internally, the project was anticipated as a kind of "action research" (Elliott, 1991)—an effort at self-study, for purposes of both understanding and improvement. But it was also anticipated that the study would reinforce the participants' perception of the worth of their work, and that it would be useful in maintaining support for Step by Step internationally, expanding programs in existing countries, and drawing additional countries into alliance. The two purposes—research and promotion—were acknowledged to be somewhat at odds. A good look at weak spots was a basis for program improvement, but not necessarily a means of attracting new partners. Surely there would be differences among countries in how much they would expose themselves to an international audience.

One of the greatest talents within the teams was promotional writing skill. Their national duties required preparation of many proposals. Soliciting support from funding agencies was almost a daily task. Much had to be written, and much of it needed to put the applicants in the best possible light. So Step by Step had a team from each country with considerable experience in the writing of applications for funding for projects, but with less experience in writing critically about what was happening within the country. This was further complicated by the fact that under the former education systems in most participating countries, students were not trained to develop critical, evidence-based writing skills. The first drafts of the reports showed competing tendencies toward overinterpretation (claims not based on evidence) and lack of interpretation (presentation of evidence without cause). The training modules made a stab at building self-criticism, but the field notes and report drafts continued to feature strong claims of effectiveness and productivity.

5.7. THEMES FOR CROSS-CASE ANALYSIS

The Step by Step case studies were to describe the work within individual countries as well as commonalities of the Step by Step program across countries.[4] Although there would be greater creative freedom for country research teams if thematic possibilities were left completely in their hands, the need for collective portrayal required examination of a complex and multilayered program, assuring inclusion of the most important content and experiences. The original aims of the Step by Step program and the anticipation of the 10th-anniversary retrospective suggested six cross-cutting thematic areas:

- Children's outcomes.
- Family and community engagement.
- Equal opportunities for each child to develop his or her potential.
- Teacher professional development.
- Enabling networks and partnerships.
- Program sustainability.

Although this was far from an exhaustive list of the participants' common interests, it was formalized to guide the thinking for a final matrix to be developed for the case study project. Once a cross-cutting theme matrix was developed (as part of the design), these themes could be addressed to some extent in each case study. For instance, in Skopje, Macedonia, the Foundation for Education and Cultural Initiatives developed a Children's Creative Center (an "interactive museum"), with full support of the local government. Examining children's outcomes within

---

[4]The case–quintain dilemma has been identified earlier in this chapter, as well as throughout this book.

this case study involved interviewing children and parents to learn about the experience of the children coming to the museum. In each country, and within the agreed-upon topic, a case was identified that reflected some or all of the themes and illuminated some of the long-term efforts of Step by Step in that country. The cases and principal issues are indicated for each of 28 participating countries in Figure 5.2.

Huge differences exist among the Step by Step countries. Many are extremely poor. Kyrgyzstan, Uzbekistan, and Tajikistan gained worldwide attention because of military action in nearby Afghanistan. Seven of the participating countries (Estonia, Latvia, Lithuania, Slovakia, Czech Republic, Slovenia, Hungary) became full members of the European Union during the course of the case study project and many others are seeking membership. As a result, education policies in these countries are being revised to conform to EU standards. Teacher training in many countries of the former Yugoslavia as well as in Tajikistan, Azerbaijan, Armenia, and Haiti continue to be constrained by slow recovery following wars. The situations across these countries have common elements, but diversity as well. The Step by Step cases were to provide a good opportunity to learn about developments in early childhood education policy and practice in these regions.

As the project leaders reviewed the drafts of the case study reports, they modified the six cross-cutting themes. It was more of a rearranging than a change of content, but case study attention to children's outcomes and program sustainability was seen as less prominent, and the following eight themes were seen as more fully covered:

- Promoting high-quality child-centered teaching, ISSA standards, and certification.
- Family and community engagement.
- Creating child-centered environments and learning opportunities.
- Reforming and decentralizing teacher professional development.
- Reaching children outside preschools.
- Social inclusion and access to high-quality education for Roma children.
- Inclusion of children with disabilities.
- Building a network of networks, particularly Step by Step NGOs and the ISSA network.

For the illustration of cross-case analysis in Chapter 9, one theme will be identified as "Equal opportunity," combining three of the themes above, and the second as "Teacher professional development," drawing

COUNTRY	TOPIC	AUTHORS
Albania	Infant and toddler programs (the crèche)	Gerda Sula, Milika Dhamo
Armenia	Parent education program	Gayane Terzyan, Luiza Militosyan
Azerbaijan	Mentoring	Mehriban Ahmadova, Sanubar Mammadova
Belarus	Step by Step—Ministry relations	Steffen Saifer, Iryna Lapitskaya
Bosnia	Establishing a national professional network (postwar)	Radmila Rangelov-Jusovic, Elvira Ramcilovic
Bulgaria	Implementing Education for Social Justice, an anti-bias program, to support Roma integration	Dimitar Dimitrov, Yoana Tsvetkova
Croatia	Professional journals	Boris Jokic, Zrinka Ristic Dedic
Czech Rep.	The role of Step by Step teacher certifiers	Lenka Frankova
Estonia	Democratic values in the classroom	Meeli Pandis, Kristel Pau, Judit Strompl, Maili Vesiko
Georgia	Thematic instruction in preschools	Mariam Shonia, Marine Japaridze, Mariam Goguadze
Haiti	Community engagement in one school	Caroline Hudicourt, Dominique Hudicourt
Hungary	Study of family–school partnerships for a Roma and non-Roma family	Attila Pappa, Silvia Nemeth
Kazakhstan	Preschool-based community center	Zhumagul Taszhurekova
Kosovo	Implementing reforms in a primary school (postwar)	Dasamir Berxulli, Ganimete Kulinxha, Eda Vula
Kyrgyzstan	Teacher-training center network (primary)	Anara Tentimisheva, Alima Abdyvasieva
Latvia	Role of parents in inclusive education	Elfrida Krastina, Zenija Berzina, Daiga Zake, Sandra Kraukel
Lithuania	Impact of teacher-training center (primary)	Antanas Valantinas, Regina Sabaliauskiene, Regina Rimkiene
Macedonia	The Children's Creative Center	Suzana Kirandziska, Atina Tasevska, Darko Marchevski
Moldova	Partnerships to support democratic changes in rural schools	Cornelia Cincilei, Valentina Pritcan
Mongolia	Introducing inclusive education in teacher preservice education	Dari Jigjidsouren, Narrantuya Sodnomjav
Montenegro	Reading and writing in a primary classroom	Milja Vujacic, Dussanka Popovic

FIGURE 5.2. Individual country assignment in the Step by Step case study project.

Romania	Teacher training center (preschool)	Catalina Ulrich, Ioana Herseni, Luciana Terente
Russia	Family participation (preschool)	Elena Yudina, Alina Kulikova
Serbia	Ministry impact on the implementation of Step by Step in primary schools	Aleksandar Stojanovi, Dino Pasalic, Vesna Zlatarovi, Milena Mihajlovic
Slovakia	Step by Step Programs in a Roma Community (Jarovnice)	Eva Konçoková, Jana Handzelova
Slovenia	Experience of a teacher undergoing Step by Step certification	Mojca Jurisevic, Mateja Rezek, Sonja Rutar
Tajikistan	Family participation in primary schools	Nurali Salikhov, Zarina Bazidova
Ukraine	Inclusive education in Ukraine	Natalia Sofiy, Svitlana Efimova

FIGURE 5.2. *(continued)*

on the first and fourth. For a full cross-case analysis, all eight would probably be used.

5.8. THE TEAMS AND THE STEERING GROUP

It was intended that each country's Step by Step organization would work with OSI to appoint a research team of up to four people. About half of the selected researchers were drawn from universities and pedagogic institutes, while the other half came from within the Step by Step organizations. An international mentor was to be assigned to each research team by OSI. Each Step by Step organization would identify a case, possibly the organization itself, but more likely a program initiative, a teacher-training center, a teacher, or a child. Whatever was chosen as the focus, it would permit illumination of the experience of Step by Step locally. This would be "the case" for that country. But, as indicated above, the research and the report were also intended to provide a platform for describing the work of the organization in that country, and collectively of the international work of the Step by Step program.

The cross-cutting information was to be important internally for furthering the scope and quality of the program, but externally as well, for early childhood education professionals and policy setters around the world. Equally important, perhaps, was the extension and cultivation of an informal network of field researchers using a variety of approaches to study an underappreciated commonplace: the organization of early childhood education.

A research steering committee was appointed—a group of mentors and training associates. It consisted of eight persons,[5] several of them active as officers or consultants in Step by Step country programs. It provided a variety of expertise in early childhood and primary education, educational reform, and qualitative case study methods. The group worked closely with Sarah Klaus, Director of OSI's Step by Step program, and Hugh McLean, the OSI's evaluation specialist. McLean was the primary designer of the multicase study and the training modules.

5.9. TRAINING THE CASE RESEARCHERS

In the fall of 2003, OSI engaged members of the steering committee to conduct two pilot cases,[6] then to conduct an online training course. The course would be the major means of educating the in-country researchers in the methods of conducting case studies. The steering committee began meeting in December 2003 to assist OSI in further developing the content matrix for the studies, and to consider collecting copies of existing research and statistics. In addition to holding face-to-face discussions, members of the steering group became heavy users of Blackboard, an online communication system made available by OSI. Together they developed ways of training and facilitating the case study work. They discussed at length the competition between the research questions of the individual studies and the six cross-cutting themes. Each steering group member was a mentor to several in-country case study teams, mostly via Blackboard and regular e-mail. In cases where additional support was needed, the mentors made brief visits to the countries to observe and assist in refining the research design.

Few of the country case study team members were experienced case study researchers. Most had done some educational research, most commonly for doctoral dissertations. Several were confused by the dissimilar-

---

[5]The group consisted of Larry Bremner and Linda Lee of Canada; Hugh McLean of South Africa; Teresa Vasconcelos of Portugal; Tatjana Vonta of Slovenia; and Cassie Landers, Steffen Saifer, and Robert E. Stake of the United States. Occasional assistance was provided by Nurbek Teleshaliyev of Kyrgyzstan, and by Henriette Heimgaertner and Nico Van Oudenhoven of the Netherlands.

[6]The pilot case reports were useful for raising issues about the conduct of the research, but did not prove to be exemplary models for the country teams.

ity of case research to the statistical studies and implementation studies they knew. Different definitions of "case study" emerged during the discussions. The plan was to have each team member participate for 6 weeks in online instruction on case study methods. The training materials had been developed in English and Russian by Hugh McLean as part of his program evaluation duties for OSI. There were six modules:

Module 1. Introduction and research plan.
Module 2. What is case study?
Module 3. Designing a case study.
Module 4. Site research preparation.
Module 5. Seminar and site research.
Module 6. Writing up the case.

The content of the course emphasized definition of "case study," the relationship of program action to social science, the need for evidence for assertions, and the importance of context in interpreting a case. The members submitted context summaries and sketches of data-gathering plans for the review of their mentors. In late February 2004, after 4 weeks, almost 100 team members gathered at the Central European University Conference Center in Budapest for interactive training and discussions.

In Budapest, the 2 days of training and activities were run by the steering group and translated into Russian and English by two able translators. Many of the researchers already knew each other and looked forward to working together on the project. But most still had doubts about what they were supposed to do and what they could do. They met with their mentors and tried to work out plans for further specifying the case and identifying the data-gathering methods. In perhaps half of the countries, the mentors spent a few days on site, discussing plans and assisting with the interviewing. A deadline for first drafts of reports was set for May 1, only a little more than 2 months after the training in Budapest.

First drafts slowly converged on Budapest. The main writer of each country's team was invited to meet in late May at Visegrad, Hungary, at a country hotel along the Danube. Questions of interpretation and formatting were discussed in large and small groups. Each writer was reminded of the importance of the six cross-cutting themes, and these were discussed in small groups, but most writers seemed to be concentrating on developing their own country's issues. Assignments were distributed to each team to collect statistics for the cross-cutting research.

After all the case reports are written, the work of expert child study researchers may be needed to help country teams contribute to the cross-cutting report, addressing those issues most important for under-standing Step by Step as a whole. The format of the country reports was purposely left unspecified, to allow the best presentation of each country's own story. It was suggested that the body of the report might be 30% context, 50% evidence, and 20% discussion. Attention was given to handling the research question, use of instruments, use of documents, and triangulation. Ethical guidelines were raised. By the time of the 10th anniversary, however, the multicase analysis was started but much work remained to be done.

Three Step by Step Case Studies

As illustrations of multicase methods and of the Step by Step case study project, three of the country case studies are presented in Chapters 6–8. They illustrate the good fieldwork and reporting that can be done by program staffers with little experience as qualitative researchers—a not uncommon situation. The following briefing is intended to help the novice multicase researcher realize what to look for in the individual cases.

The formats of these three reports differ, because they reflect the differing topics and approaches to data collection chosen by these three research teams. However, the three studies are alike in this respect: Each research team took the opportunity to illustrate the work and aspiration of both the individual country's Step by Step activities and the multinational Step by Step program by taking a small entity as the case and moving outward into community and institutional partnerships. The Ukrainian case is a primary school student with a disability. The Slovak case is a miniature school system for Roma children in an impoverished, segregated, small Roma settlement across the river from an even smaller village. And the Romanian case is a model teacher-training center based at a kindergarten. Each of the investigations yielded a "thick-description" scene (Geertz, 1973), providing readers with a vicarious experience of teaching and learning in this child-centered education program. Each of them also involved a struggle experienced by most case study researchers: making smooth transitions between micro- and macroanalysis. It is common for a person to think of society and individuals in the same breath, but putting the two together in a case report often makes a bumpy track for the reader.

Are the reports credible? As usual, the reader will find little trace of triangulation to assure that what was told was what was there. Like most writers of all kinds these report writers are weak in describing their commitment to providing verification for what they write. Too often, they hope that the facts will speak for themselves. The aim here was not the aim of social science or journalism; the intention was to facilitate greater insights. Good art does that, and good case research does it as well.

ADDRESSING THE SIX CROSS-CASE THEMES

Sarah Klaus and Hugh McLean at Step by Step headquarters often reminded the fieldworkers that each case study needed to contribute to the understanding of six cross-case themes:

- Children's outcomes.
- Family and community engagement.
- Equal opportunities for each child to develop his or her potential.
- Teacher professional development.
- Enabling networks and partnerships.
- Program sustainability.

I would say that the general attitude among the fieldworkers was that these six matters needed only to have a *place* in the study. There was only small expectation that these matters needed to be studied to demonstrate how they were shaped by the life and context of that country. The eight mentors for the case study teams (see footnote 5 to Chapter 5) did not press for such demonstration, probably thinking that just getting the story of each case told was difficult enough. Cassie Landers, the project cross-case analyst, was not commissioned to exhort the mentors to raise the likelihood that her analysis would receive all the input that it should.

The first of the cross-case themes was children's outcomes. There was not much reason to expect that substantive data on children's outcomes would be presented in the cases (Graue & Walsh, 1998). Quite a bit of perspectival and anecdotal evidence of positive effects on children was presented, but most of it was testimony from people who would like the program to be seen in a positive light. The initial call for case study research made it clear that the purpose of the study was not outcome evaluation. The shared concept paper for the case study project made it clear that the purpose of the study was not outcome evaluation. But the main reason for scarce data on children's outcomes, as I saw it, was that efforts to understand what the teachers were doing, and particularly what the teacher trainers were doing, were not expected to include assessment of what the children were doing. To accompany the case studies, Sarah Klaus hired a researcher to collect all available information from existing national studies on outcomes of children in the individual countries' Step by Step programs, to learn what comparative analysis would be possible with existing data. In the process of implementing the program, the ministry of education in many countries had required a formal, comparative child outcome study as a prerequisite for approval of the program.

The second cross-case theme, family and community engagement, was a major story line in many of the case studies. And this engagement is a strong presence in the three case studies presented in Chapters 6–8. The families of Step by Step students were almost unanimously supportive of the child-centered approach, and family participation in school activities was found to be substantial although there was little historical precedent for such participation.

Equal educational opportunity for all children is a hallmark of OSI's approach in many countries. The Step by Step case studies gave high attention to opportunity for Roma children and for children with disabilities, as well as for the most impoverished children, who have no access to preschool education. The teams did not develop the equal opportunity theme in the case research designs as much as they could have, however. Perhaps equal opportunity was (and is) such ordinary thinking for the team members that they did not recognize how it needed to be developed for readers more accustomed to the socialization and academic aspects of kindergarten.

One of the small visible mismatches between Step by Step rhetoric and practice had to do with the concept of a child's "full potential." The teachers and administrators of Step by Step mentioned those words, but seemed only to mean that children should have continuing choices and opportunities matching their developmental levels. There was essentially no operationalization of the idea that teachers or anyone else can see what a child's "full potential" is. Generally, the development and use of appropriate child-centered assessment methods are less explored in the studies than one might have expected, given the orientation of the program toward individualized learning for each child. Furthermore, in the case studies one can find a tension between providing such learning for children and ensuring that national curriculum requirements are met. These challenges to educational planning are present and are not easily resolved by less experienced teachers.

The coursework of teacher training is well inventoried in the case studies. It was seen as more important for the researchers to list the range of "trainings" for teachers developed in their particular countries than to examine the experience of any one offering. The idea that in-service training should be carried out by practitioners in their own classrooms and with real children was a key idea—colleagues teaching colleagues. The bonding of teacher trainees among themselves, as well as with their colleague trainers, was an important portrayal in the case reports.

A risk in all training is that it is too abstract, too theoretical. The case studies here measure well the extent to which Step by Step has oriented its training toward the practical. Step by Step's standards are emphasized, to be sure, and the dangers of theory and abstraction are present, but the definition of child-centered education is spelled out with pictures, stories, and face-to-face encounters. Mentoring—the practice of sending experienced professionals to observe and support new teachers—is less well documented in the studies, though visible. Some studies also address issues of professional literature (journals and manuals) and the influence that teachers working in the same sites have on each other. These scenes are important for the readers of all the case studies. They depict action-oriented professional development.

Still, the multicase project did not move toward action research on teacher training to the extent that was hoped for. Rather than team's saying, "Let's use this opportunity to learn more about how we do our work," they more often said, "How can we show the achievements of the program?" The shortchanging of self-study was probably attributable to the mentors. Certainly an action research component was emphasized in the training and was voiced strongly in steering group meetings by Hugh McLean, but the ever-looming job of describing and interpreting the Step by Step work for a case report elbowed aside most action research efforts.

Networking was closely linked to training. The primary form of networking that was observed (and hoped for) was networking among teachers, but there were important communication links as well among trainers, administrators, and committee members. Some of the networking extended across national borders, particularly the networking between Step by Step organizations in different countries. The case studies brought to light some of that networking, but probably not as much as the cross-case analyst needed.

Partnering was evident in institutional relations as well as in personal relations. Joint efforts with local, regional, and national offices of education as well as with other nongovernmental organizations and international donor organizations, were prominent in the case descriptions. Partnering was also brought to light as networking, collaborative learning, and mentoring. In each country, these collective actions could have been the focus of a whole study alone. Here, as in much of the case presentation, the team described what existed but often provided too few details about the professional experience of working together. It seemed difficult for the field researchers to make the common collaborative action of Step by Step come to life. Again, it may have been that they were too close to that action to feel the need for writing vividly about it.

Program sustainability was one of the hardest themes to submit to research attention. It was relatively easy for the researchers to get quotes about developing good personal relations with officials or parents, but much more difficult to show how those relationships became valuable when needed. In these three examples, the reader can see again and again that long-term relations appeared to be getting established with important partners, but that it was very difficult to test the sustainability of these relations. Still, it was important to acknowledge that sustainability is a critical matter, because resources (however generously given) will not be forthcoming forever.

Sustainability does not just happen; it is pursued, striven for, heralded. These researchers are dispassionate observers some of the time, but they are program advocates around the clock. Most of the words they write in the course of their overall work are intended to provide for, protect, preserve, and extend their programs. In the case studies, Hugh McLean urged them to hold back assertions until the evidence was substantial. In some sections of the reports they did, but not always. These are important distinctions for those who anticipate designing their own multicase studies. Many such researchers will rely on advocates; they will work with advocates; at times, they will be advocates themselves. The value of their work in case reports depends not on making their quintain look good, but on whether they give the readers of their reports a sufficient view of the realities (both long suits and shortfalls), to permit them to understand the complexity of the cases.

A thematic overview is similar to what science offers in its reports on natural phenomena. The overview from a scientist organizes the most important meanings from a study. Here were six cross-country themes. Additional country and local themes will appear in the three case studies. It is not unreasonable to think that this sweeping purview is the most important contribution of a multicase study. Most of these ideas have been a part of the Step by Step program since its inception, but the grand mosaic has often been missing. Here, in these case studies, the themes are brought together to frame the routine work, the aspiration, and the struggle—of each of the countries and all of them together—to educate their children better.

At this writing, the Step by Step case study project is in the process of delving into and writing up the cross-cutting issues identified for the multicase study. Also in development is a series of theme-specific papers that will explore important issues such as "reforming and decentralizing teacher training" and "reaching children outside of preschool" across small groupings of cases. The cases offered in this book provide a glimpse of this work.

THE EXPERIENCE OF THE CASE RESEARCHERS AND MENTORS

The authors of these three cases—Natalia Sofiy and Svitlana Efimova in Ukraine (Chapter 6), Eva Koncoková and Jana Handzelová in Slovakia (Chapter 7), and Catalina Ulrich in Romania (Chapter 8)—worked with their own country teams, worked with me as a mentoring group, and worked with their colleagues from the other 25 countries. It was a very special personal experience.

Just the fact that about 100 early childhood educators were joining together from the far corners of the world to be a case study research community was breathtaking. Most of them had been halfway around the world to professional meetings and had collaborated in Step by Step professional development. But this was something really new.

As they first signed in at the online course website, these team members expressed both greetings and apprehensions. They said they did not know how to do a case study. So, much as the children in their kindergartens began each morning with a Morning Meeting, sitting in a circle to talk about the coming day, these women and a few men looked into the "circle" of the case study community through their computers and wondered what the weeks ahead would bring. Gerda Sula in Albania, Mehriban Ahmadova in Azerbaijan, Kristel Pau in Estonia, Suzana Kirandziska in Macedonia, and many, many more.

Online, Sarah Klaus and Hugh McLean began to tell them about the new assignment. Both collectively and country by country, they were going to tell the story of Step by Step. They already knew much of the story, but this was to be *case study research*, so they were going to need to take a deeper look at the teaching, training, and partnering in their respective countries. To help them do that, the researchers would get a little coaching. The next 4 months would be an adventure and a load.

Even at Step by Step offices in Budapest, few realized that the adventure was not just for a few months, but for most of them would roll on for much longer—possibly for the rest of their lives. It was a bit of a dream, but it was possible that they would engage in a more disciplined, experiential study of their work. It was different from program evaluation. Some suggested that it would be "action research"—the study of themselves as professionals, and the study of them all as an organization.

Klaus and McLean called it "case study," emphasizing the up-close examination of the activities and relationships of each country's program—showing its uniqueness in more detail, showing its travail with more candor. The researchers would look for experiences that revealed the complexities of Step by Step. The big emphasis was on Step by Step as they knew it individually, not Step by Step as they knew it collectively. There was mention of the special nature of a multicase study, capturing the themes of the Step by Step world, but the case researchers were asked mostly to concentrate on what they were experiencing in their own countries.

In Ukraine, Sofiy, and Efimova would observe 8-year-old Liubchyk, diagnosed with autism, and in doing so would capture the issues of inclusion in a regular first grade: "Liubchyk chooses a picture among those offered by Halyna, the assistant teacher, but he refuses to join a group. He is not pressed to do so. 'What is this bird?' she asks. Liubchyk spreads his arms and says, 'A swallow.'"

Before long, in Tajikistan, Nurali Salikhov would be interviewing mothers in traditional dress and headscarves, trying to learn how much they assist the classroom teacher. In Slovakia, Eva Koncoková would return to the Roma settlement in Jarovnice to observe home schooling (as shown on the cover of this book). In Haiti, Caroline Hudicourt and Dominique Hudicourt would hover close to home as insurgents overran the schools and countryside.

McLean coached the team members to generate a report of the experience of Step by Step in each country. He saw them joining together as a new force, a troupe of child study researchers—observers, interviewers, and interpreters of education. This troupe was to constitute a self-auditing mechanism to inform, reflect on, and strengthen the Step by Step program.

For 6 weeks of training, the researchers interacted via a distance-learning platform comprising six modules designed to support case research and write-up. To the surprise of the steering group, it did not become a chat line. When team members talked to each other, they usually stuck with e-mail, telephone, and conversations at work. They were surprised by the training emphasis on describing the context of Step by Step activity, particularly the national context. But this was the easy part, because many of them were administrators and organizers who already had much experience in describing what their programs were doing, with what groups of people, with what challenges. The hard part was changing from talking about Step by Step as they would do in a proposal for funding to talking about Step by Step as an experience for teachers, children, and others.

In late February 2004, the researchers came—from the steppes, from the Baltic and the Balkans, from near and far, intrigued and skeptical—to the first training conference in Budapest. Around the big tables at the high-rise Central European University Conference Center, research teams from several countries sat together with their mentor, discussing methods to obtain data and ways to report their cases. The full group of participants is shown in Photo 1.

Gradually, most of the researchers came to understand that as each country's team told a separate story, the collection of stories would provide an accumulation of understanding of common topics: teacher professional development; involvement of parents; impact on children; inclusion of minorities, at-risk children, and those with disability; and program sustainability. To many, this was clearly overwhelming. A miracle seemed called for—as if to include all the details of Tolstoy's *War and Peace* in a 20-page report.

Although some refinement was expected, the designation of the countries' cases did not change much. In Romania, Catalina Ulrich studied a Danube Delta kindergarten that provided training to teachers. In Latvia, Zenija Berzina studied two children with disabilities. Several of the research teams studied the education of Roma children. Some studies

PHOTO 1. Step by Step case study researchers at Central European University Conference Center, February 2004. Photo courtesy of Open Society Institute. Used by permission.

were less personal, such as the development of a journal for teachers in Croatia and the refinement of Step by Step teacher certification in the Czech Republic.

Each study was to expand the context and complexity of its immediate case to show Step by Step working to increase the commitment of the whole country to child-centered, culture-sensitive, educational policies. On a few occasions, a research mentor went into the field with a team, but mostly the team members did the work by themselves. These researchers were busy people. They already had full-time jobs: training teachers, writing proposals, having babies, writing dissertations, and running offices. But they dug in. They observed training sessions and classrooms. They studied documents. They found sources of oral history. They interviewed partners.

Perhaps the hardest work was taking a big issue, such as partnering with a country's ministry of education, and bringing out the issue through the light of personal experience. Not many of the researchers managed to capture the experiential moment when a partnership changed from possibility to actuality. It was easier just to say that it happened than to show the problematic and conditional way in which it happened.

And it was hard for these researchers to be modest about Step by Step. They knew their accomplishments and were reluctant to question them. Rarely did they seek out a teacher or official who thought poorly of these accomplishments.

As indicated earlier, the camaraderie among researchers, and between researchers and mentors, was important for nourishing thinking and writing. Face-to-face meetings were much more valuable than e-mail for getting problems solved, but also for building relationships among researchers across national borders.

All during the spring of 2004, far more communicative than the research teams was the project's steering group. The group members kept the interactive platform hot for several months. Discussing early reports from one of the sites, one mentor said to the others, "But what is the evidence the children changed?" Others answered, "It's more important to show what the teachers did." "It seems from the report that the teachers are perfect. They don't make mistakes." "You don't expect their trainers to report their mistakes, do you?" "If all through the observations, you don't see children squabbling, that has to be evidence of good teaching." And so on.

Rough drafts from most of the countries were piling up in Budapest by early June 2004. A few were nearly finished; most were not. Expectations of having a published collection by November started to wane. Most of the teams were committed to continuing, but the summer passed with few completions. The process of capacity building went on, however. Elfrida Krastina of Latvia spoke of the experience of doing the case study: "I am a mathematician. When I started this, it was all Greek to me. I have learned so much."

To celebrate the 10th anniversary of the Step by Step program, 180 of its people gathered in Budapest early in November 2004. George Soros attended this meeting. In the plenary sessions, there were presentations by early childhood researchers and expressions of congratulation. In breakout sessions, a representative from each country briefly summarized its case study; here again, however, general acclamations of accomplishment overrode efforts to present the personal experience of Step by Step children, parents, and educators. The studies sparked a few deep discussions (for which there was not enough time) about program implementation strategies and ideas for future research.

While this multicase project progressed, the world moved along. Old hostilities among people continued, and new ones emerged—not only in Iraq, the Gaza Strip, Colombia, and Thailand (all beyond the touch, so far, of Step by Step), but even in the 28 countries involved in the project, in Russia at Beslan, in Georgia, in Haiti. The most common government response was retaliation: more terror, more war on terror. It seems impossible for the love of parents, the wisdom of teachers, and the trust and friendliness of children to restrain the thrust of revenge. But the case studies indicate that the first 10 years of Step by Step have nourished optimism, the dedication of teachers, and commitments from ministries of education. Each case was different, but together they illuminated a step forward for 28 countries and the world.

CHAPTER 6

The Ukraine Case Study

When Step by Step began its work in Ukraine and in many other former Soviet bloc countries, there was a political commitment to fully supporting care for all children. It was believed that certain children, particularly orphans, displaced children, and those with disabilities, would be able to receive appropriate services only if they were enrolled in special schools, not in the regular schools. Separate institutions were developed for different categories of children. No formal system of foster care existed, so children whose parents were not deemed fit (for example, parents who were accused of abusing their children, were alcoholics, or who lived in extreme poverty) were institutionalized. Likewise, parents of children with special needs were encouraged to enroll their children in special schools, many of which were internats, or boarding facilities. As a result, they lived in isolation from more typical children and from society at large. Even children with only physical disabilities were provided with the special education curriculum and a lower-prestige diploma.

The 2005 revolution in Ukraine and new aspirations for membership in the EU were generating increasing interest in programs like the Step by Step program with its ethics of inclusion and social justice. A history of special schools for children with disabilities was slowly but strongly being brought to an end. The ultimate goal of education was increasingly viewed as maximizing achievement for all. All six of the cross-case themes were important in Ukraine, but inclusion and equality of opportunity, stood above the rest.

With Natalia Sofiy, director of the USSF, Ukraine was one of the leaders in the international Step by Step program. One thing to watch for in its story is the role of parents, not only as supporters but also as demanders. Romanna, the mother of Liubchyk, is a hero of Step by Step as much as any of its teachers, teacher trainers, or staff. The board meeting of the health improvement center is a story of parliamentary futility, but also of parental dedication to the care and education of children with special needs in Kyiv Oblast. The research team members have a sensitivity to experiential knowledge and have told their story in such a way that all readers get a vicarious experience of Step by Step in Ukraine.

The plan for the Ukraine study is shown in Figure 6.1. Liubchyk is the case represented by the bold circle. The main observations of him were made in his first-grade classroom in Maliuk School. The researchers describe his socialization, sense of membership in the class, pride in his work, and low distraction from class instruction, as well as his progress in

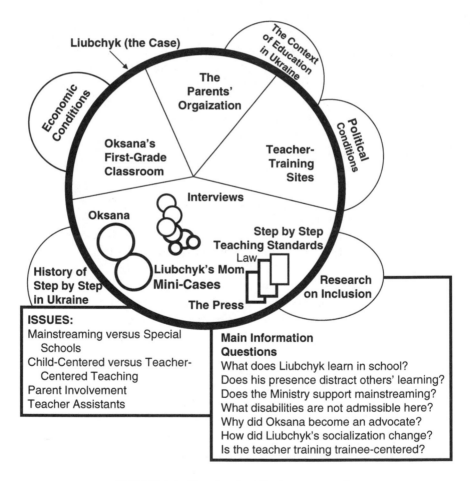

FIGURE 6.1. Plan for the Ukraine case study.

reading and arithmetic. The embedded mini-cases of his mother and his teacher Oksana are important components. And the use of role-playing as a key experiential part of the teacher training is nicely illustrated. The contexts of Ukraine as related to the Soviet educational system and the EU were part of the original plan shown in Figure 6.1.

The plan for writing up the Ukraine report has been shown in Chapter 1 as Figure 1.2. To personalize the portrayal of Liubchyk, the authors decided to open and close with detailed descriptions of him in the classroom.—R. E. S.

Inclusive Education: The Step by Step Program Influencing Children, Teachers, Parents, and State Policies in Ukraine[1]

SVITLANA EFIMOVA and NATALIA SOFIY

LIST OF CHARACTERS

Liubchyk[2]—a child with special needs
Romanna—mother of Liubchyk
Oksana—teacher of Liubchyk and trainer of the Ukrainian Step by
    Step program
Halyna—teacher assistant
Vika—teacher of music
Marianna—social worker
Katrusia, Olenka, Anychka, Hanusia, Oleg, Mykolka—children in
    Liubchyk's class
Hrystyna Matskiv—director of the Maliuk School in Lviv
Natalia Sofiy—director of the Ukrainian Step by Step Foundation
Julia Kavun—training coordinator of the Ukrainian Step by Step
    Foundation

---

[1]Copyright 2004 by the Open Society Institute. Adapted by permission.
[2]The names of Liubchyk and the other children, as well as Liubchyk's mother and teachers were changed.

Ira, Oksana, and Olga—trainers in the Ukrainian Step by Step
Foundation

Volodymyr Kryzhanivskiy—director of Shans, a health improvement
center in Bila Tservka

Tamara Lutsenko—vice-director for education, Shans

Victor Ogneviuk—vice-minister, Ministry of Education and Science
of Ukraine

Vyatcheslav Zasenko—vice-director, Institute of Special Pedagogy,
Academy of Pedagogical Sciences of Ukraine

Ailsa Cregan (Great Britain)—mentor to the Ukrainian Step by
Step Foundation on inclusive education within the project *Cre-
ating Centers of Excellence for Inclusive Education*, supported by the
Technical Aid to the Commonwealth of Independent States
(TACIS), Institution Building Partnership Programme (IBPP)

Primary and preschool teachers in the cities of Kyiv, Lviv, and Bila
Tserkva; parents of children with special needs; and representatives of the mass media in Lviv

LIUBCHYK

This was the first-grade room of the "Children of the Sun." The children
had chosen this title jointly. They liked to say that they were the
Children of the Sun. On the classroom door were this title and individual
photos of all the children. To enter the room, a person needed to slip first
through two small rooms, a lobby and a bedroom.

It is 10:50 A.M. on a day in March 2004. Liubchyk is just coming in
with his mom. She helps him take off his coat. Liubchyk is a slender
boy, a tall boy, with fair hair and grey eyes. He is 8, a child with special needs. He first started kindergarten in Maliuk School back in
2000.

Liubchyk goes immediately to the Reading Center, stays maybe
3 seconds, then comes to the teacher's table. Ms. Halyna, the
teaching assistant, comes across and greets him, "Good morning,
Liubchyk!"

He cheerfully replies, "Halyna, at seven!" (which seems to mean
that Ms. Halyna should remember to return home from work at
7:00). He takes several photos from the teacher's table and starts
looking through them. Pointing to a picture, Halyna asks, "Who's
that?" "Adij [Andrew]," Liubchyk answers. He starts saying the
names of all the persons in the pictures. Then he puts the pictures

back in the envelope and returns them to their place on the table. "Halyna, lunch toowelve," he says, pointing to the clock. "Yes, lunch is at twelve," Halyna answers.

The classroom teacher, Ms. Oksana, is working on mathematics with the group as a whole. The children saw Liubchyk come in, but were not distracted from their tasks. After Oksana gives the children small individual tasks, she approaches Liubchyk to greet him, "Good morning, Liubchyk." "Oksana, at seven!" he replies. "Please say, 'Good morning.' " He does. "Liubchyk, will you work here with us?" He says, "No," and goes to the Reading Center and starts turning the pages of the mathematics textbook. The group lesson goes on.

As a rule, Liubchyk worked with the other students only when he wanted to.

In a few minutes, he takes notebooks from his bag and shows Ms. Halyna some printed and outlined letters he has penciled. He then shows her his coloring book, the pages diligently colored. "You have done good work. You get 2 points. One goes on your notebook—the other, stick it to your diary," Ms. Halyna tells him.

A bookcase served as a partial wall between the study area with individual tables and the free area, the Morning Meeting area. Against the bookcase were photos of all the children, each one pasted on a sheet of colored paper. These sheets served as "diaries." At the top of each sheet was written, in the child's hand: "I, [name], was, am, and will be a diligent [boy/girl]." On this sheet, they attached stickers received for special achievement.

Liubchyk takes a glittering heart, goes to the bookcase, and sticks it by the photo closest to him. Ms. Halyna observes him. "Is this really your photo? This is Marjann, isn't it? Watch carefully and put the award on your place." With little enthusiasm, Liubchyk corrects his mistake.

The group lesson continues, now with the children lining up in two rows in the free area. They will work in two teams. Ms. Oksana says, "Liubchyk, you could join any of the teams," but he refuses. He edges closer to Ms. Marianna, the social pedagogue assigned primarily to him.

Oksana addresses a child from the first team: "Hanusia, chose a number from 1 to 10." "Five." "Oleg, what is the next number?" "Six." "And the previous?" "Seven." "Team, please help." "Four." "Good." "Katrusia, give me an even number from 1 to 10!" From the other team, Katrusia says, "Three." "Team, help." This work moves along quickly. Its objective is repetition and mastering of already learned material in math. After observing the children for some time, Liubchyk touches Marianna with his finger, smiles, says "Lunch," and leaves the room. Marianna follows him. Ms. Halyna says to me (Svitlana Efimova), "They left to read the menu."

When Liubchyk and Marianna return, the children are back at their tables. Liubchyk approaches Ms. Halyna, takes the table calendar and starts to turn over its pages, reciting the numbers shown in the corners corresponding to the number of the month (thus his mathematics lesson continues). Ms. Halyna calls them out, and Liubchyk repeats them.

The break starts; the children begin to relax. One boy goes to the Reading Center, takes a book from the shelf, and sprawls on the large, flat, soft, mouse-shaped rug to read. Three boys start playing with cars. Some girls play a running game. One girl, Anychka, approaches Liubchyk and reaches up to embrace him. He does not resist, but as soon as she takes her hands away, he hides behind Ms. Marianna. Another girl approaches. It is Hanusia. "Liubchyk, please come with me," she says. He grasps Marianna more firmly and hides his face. The two girls play by themselves. Liubchyk picks up the photos again, looks through them briefly and puts them back in their place.

After the break, Ms. Halyna starts the reading lesson. Liubchyk goes to the blackboard and stands in front of Ms. Halyna. She suggests he sit down. He takes a place with a boy at the closest table. He sits for 10 minutes, with Marianna nearby. He turns over his notebook and writes something. Ms. Oksana brings his reading notebook. Liubchyk moves toward her and takes the notebook. She embraces him, then tries to move to the other children, but Liubchyk starts showing her one of the pages of letters he has written. Oksana indicates that he did it nicely but did not finish it. "The work needs to be finished." She proposes that Liubchyk do it now, but he says, "No!" During the rest of the lesson, Liubchyk plays with a chain—first putting blue and yellow links together, and then pulling them apart and putting them in a basket.

Then came lunchtime. The children lined up in pairs. A girl approaches Liubchyk, taking him by the hand. He did not resist. All went to the lunchroom and sit at a long table. Liubchyk had his favorite place at the table, a corner near the entrance. (If the place were occupied, he would fight to get it.) They had soup, bread, and a carrot.

After the meal, Liubchyk and the rest of the children brought their plates to the kitchen table. He thus helped the assistants who looked after the children while they ate. He thanked them with a deliberate touch. The children walked back from the lunchroom again in pairs. Liubchyk paired with a girl; then two more girls gathered around him, embracing him. He did not seek escape.

Next is the music lesson, divided into two halves. First, in the music room, the children sing to musical accompaniment. The second half, in their own classroom, has them listening to music and drawing their feelings on paper—their free association with the music. As a rule, Liubchyk does not visit the music room, and he does not now. For the part in their own room, he willingly puts sheets of white paper on the tables to get himself prepared and to help the other children get ready for listening and drawing. It turns out that Ms. Oksana has given him insufficient paper. Liubchyk says, "Too little!" Engaging him in the management, Ms. Oksana says, "Should I give you more?" "Yes." "How many should I give you? Please count." Liubchyk counts and says, " Two tables. Four." He distributes sheets for everyone and approaches Oksana, possibly for acknowledgment.

The children come from the music room. Liubchyk sits at the table with them. The music teacher, Ms. Vika, tells the children about the character and mood of the music. She draws a parallel to the character and moods of people. For this second task, the children are to listen to two music fragments, each with a different mood, and then to draw them. Each sheet of paper is to be divided into two halves. On one side, they should put the date and draw the first impression (a sad passage); on the other, they should sign it and draw the other impression (a happy one). Ms. Vika says, "First listen to the music. Then I will play it once again, and you will draw."

All during the directions, Liubchyk is vigorously drawing something with cross-hatches. It seems that he listens neither to the teacher nor to the music. He is excited, and it is clear why later. He does the drawing very well, but he does not sign it. When Ms. Vika asks him to sign the sheet and to add the date, he does so with pleasure, writing "MARCH 15" and "LIUBCHYK" in block letters. Vika asks him to comment on his picture: "What is it?" He explains that on the right side is the sun, nearly hidden by clouds from which the rain is falling. On the left is a bright car driving at high speed. He also explains which of the pictures is the sad one and which the happy one. He has drawn with some precision. Vika tells me, "Liubchyk especially likes listening to the music and then drawing it."

The children passed their work to Ms. Vika. Later an exhibition would be made. Liubchyk passed in his work and was awarded with a token. Happily, he went to his portrait and stuck the token to it—already the third today. (The tokens were not part of Step by Step teaching, but there are many influences on what happens in any classroom.)

LIUBCHYK'S TEACHER

Ms. Oksana was the lead teacher of this first-grade room. She was helped daily by Ms. Halyna and Ms. Marianna and by an out-of-the-room activities teacher, Ms. Lilia. Still other teachers taught religion, English, and music on scheduled days.

Ms. Oksana had been working at Maliuk School since 1998, having won a competition for a primary-grade vacancy at that time. Last year (2003), her first students at this primary school graduated. Oksana regularly worked to upgrade her professional competence and standing, extending particularly her knowledge of the Step by Step program. She participated in training seminars organized by the Ukrainian Step by Step Foundation. She had taken part in the *Program for the Primary School* in 1999, *Training for Trainers* in 2001, *Training for Advocacy and Lobbying* in 2002, and *Training for Social Support to Families* in 2003. She had also been invited to participate in the upcoming *Advanced Training for Trainers* in Kyiv in July 2004. Oksana was herself a trainer in the Ukrainian Step by Step Program.

Active in public work, Oksana was cofounder of the nongovernmental organization (NGO), Lad, which assisted families in the protection of children's rights. She was also chair of the widely recognized group, Ukraine 11, a part of the Ukrainian Amnesty International Association. Oksana conducted training on civic education in these organizations.

Oksana's teaching experience had now run to 16 years, but she had only recently begun working with children with special needs. She worked first in Maliuk with a girl having disordered reception of cerebral signals. The child stayed for just 1 year; then her parents found an opportunity for treatments in the United States and they emigrated.

As we know, Oksana was Liubchyk's current classroom teacher. Oksana told us that each experience of working with children with special needs was unique. "It always means new discoveries and meeting new challenges. It invariably requires a different approach and a customized organization of the environment for each case."

Having had the opportunity of getting to know her current students during their kindergarten year, Oksana had found it difficult to imagine Liubchyk still among them in the first grade. To her he had been rather uncontrollable, and in ways he still was. It was difficult to involve him in studying. She remained strongly convinced that "the problems of one child cannot be solved by generating problems for other children." She was well aware of her responsibility to all the children and their parents.

Before this academic year began, there was a meeting to discuss the question of Liubchyk's education. Attending were Liubchyk's parents; Ms. Oksana and Ms. Halyna, the upcoming teachers of the first grade; Liubchyk's kindergarten teacher, Ms. Natalia; and the Maliuk School director, Ms. Hrystyna Matskiv. Ms. Natalia started the meeting by predicting that further interaction between Liubchyk and the same group of children, his group-mates, would be very beneficial for him. She said that the other children treated him well and that he did not distract them. With emotion, Liubchyk's parents identified what their child was capable of doing. They called him in and asked him some difficult questions. Oksana had some trouble understanding Liubchyk's language, but since his parents interpreted for him, she saw that he was correct. She had the impression that they would have demonstrated all that Liubchyk could do, and she did not want to "harass" the child any longer. At the end of the meeting, everyone agreed that Liubchyk should attend first grade on "probation" status for 3 months, with the assistance of a social worker (Ms. Marianna). It was also decided that Ms. Halyna, with experience in special education, should be Liubchyk's academic teacher.

The beginning of the school year was difficult. Ms. Oksana said that she was very cautious. Liubchyk's parents were heard asking Ms. Natalia (a former preschool teacher) to assure the teachers that he worked well when encouraged. Oksana was upset by the implication. But soon things changed. Oksana said,

> "There were many reasons. First, thank God, I started seeing the child with different eyes. I understood his parents' worries and concerns, their earnest desire to see Liubchyk attending this very class. Second, his intellectual level proved to be much higher than I had imagined. In time, the 'ice of mistrust' [between his parents and me] melted. They understood my insistance on protecting the academic conditions of the other children and my striving to create a friendly atmosphere for Liubchyk's interaction with others."

Resisting to a small degree the advice of a consultant, Oksana gave Liubchyk considerable freedom to join and withdraw from activities at his choosing.

There at Maliuk School, Oksana conducted a training seminar, *Developing a Caring Community and Believing in One's Abilities*, for parents of children with special needs, representatives of NGOs, and school and kindergarten teachers working with such children. It enhanced her relationship with Liubchyk's mother, Romanna, who was among the invited parents. During the 3-day seminar, Ms. Oksana and Ms. Romanna had a good opportunity to get to know each other better. Oksana said, "The training required groups to do specific tasks that gave us opportunity for better analyzing ourselves and getting to know each other."

The training module included a discussion of how communities develop. Some of the parents revealed their feelings when they first heard their child's diagnosis of disability. Liubchyk's mother said that she perceived the situation as a personal tragedy and did not think that a community could give support. The possibility of such support came to her as a revelation. Ms. Oksana said,

> "This helped me to understand Romanna as a person and to see the situation through her eyes. I began to understand her problems and what motivated her to act as she did. The informal communication during breaks also fostered trust. Romanna expressed confidence that the information shared about her child would not be used against him, but would facilitate work in the future. Thus it became somewhat easier for me [Oksana] to understand the problems of this child, the peculiarities of his personality, and his developmental stage."

Ms. Oksana said that Liubchyk's parents had expressed much gratitude to the teachers: "During these 6 months, Liubchyk has made significant steps in his development. Unlike at the beginning of the academic year, when he experienced a certain discomfort, now he goes off to school in high spirits." Liubchyk's grandmother, also involved in his upbringing, put it this way: "We can thank the atmosphere of this place."

It was apparent that Oksana strove to create a positive atmosphere for the Children of the Sun. She worked to assure that all the children treated Liubchyk right. She said that by observing how adults treat Liubchyk, the children had the opportunity to learn how to interact with him, to rejoice in his successes, and to acquire the experience of communicating and caring for people with special needs.

Oksana attributed much of Liubchyk's academic understanding to regular communication between his parents and his teachers.[3] Almost daily they analyzed his difficulties and successes. And there were longer meetings. Once a quarter, one of the parents (usually his mother), Ms. Oksana, Ms. Halyna, and Ms. Marianna met to reflect upon and plan their assistance to Liubchyk.

---

[3]Much of this case study report is devoted to portrayal of the training of teachers in the Step by Step approach in Ukraine—not only to issues of inclusion, but to child-centered and democratic teaching and to parent and community involvement.

Ms. Oksana applied her personal experience with children with special needs to her work as a trainer. She told other teachers,

> "Just like every teacher, I had my notions of how to organize education for children with special needs placed in a general education classroom. But when I was faced with the problem myself, it proved much more difficult. When we meet a child like that, we understand that he or she needs help, but we don't know much about how to help. Then when we see that the child is achieving something with our help, we start having feelings that this is more valuable than giving knowledge to other children—although undoubtedly that is also very important.
>
> "The neglect of children with disabilities will always echo back. But it is not the fear of punishment that compels us! I simply remember this: Inclusion is an idea implemented by people. It can either be credited or discredited. Life changes, and people's attitude toward inclusion changes. The philosophy of our program is that all children who can be involved in regular classroom experience should be given the chance. I have become deeply convinced that only when working directly with a specific child, and not merely through his or her diagnosis, only then can conclusions as to the potential benefit of enrollment in a general education school be drawn."

TEACHER TRAINING IN LVIV

A training session on *Step by Step Program and Teacher Standards* was held at the Maliuk Kindergarten–Primary School on April 15–16, 2004, for the teachers at that school.

> It is April 15, 1:30 P.M. Four tables are put one against another in the spacious auditorium. A blackboard is on the wall; a flip chart stands at the side. Piles of books—*Step by Step Program and Teacher Standards* (five copies)—and sheets of paper are on the table.
>
> Ms. Oksana, the Step by Step program mentor from the city of Ivano Frankivsk, is the trainer for this session. She greets the 14 participants who are entering the room and sitting down at the tables. Oksana informs them about the topic and the objectives of the training: "Your Maliuk School is one of the best in Ukraine. You are experienced Step by Step teachers. By using Step by Step standards, you can improve your work even more. There is more to be learned about how what you do with your children is correlated with the

Standards." A short introduction of the participants follows, each teacher making a self-presentation. On the flip chart, the participants write a few words about their expectations of the training. The teachers say they want to learn something new, to enhance their knowledge, and to communicate with colleagues.

For the first activity, Oksana used the KWL model: "Know–Want to Know–Learned." During brainstorming, on the right side of the blackboard, Oksana wrote the answers of the participants to the question: "What is a standard?" On the left, "What would you like to learn about Step by Step standards?" During the brainstorming, four persons spoke. Oksana said, "Our colleagues can tell us about our objectives."

One of the participants says, "We can improve our work with the help of standards." Olena proposes the following task: "There are six standards for teachers, for each of which there are quality indicators. Let us consider all of them and see to what extent they are already present in our practice."

The first standard, *Individualization*, had three quality indicators. Oksana pointed to three groups of participants: two groups of five and one group of four. Each group was to work on one indicator. "Read your indicator, find its manifestation in your practice, and give an example." The groups read the standard, *Individualization*, and its indicators. They discussed them quietly—increasingly, it seemed, with self-assurance.

Ms. Oksana says, "Please read about your indicator and give an example." Here is a fragment of an answer from one of the groups: "Our indicator is 1.2: 'Teachers understand that young children vary considerably in the pattern and pace of their growth, thinking, language, and social capacities due to individual differences and cultural persuasions.' I have a boy with special needs in my class. In my opinion, he is treated with more tolerance now because of the children observing how we treat him."

Oksana asked the participants to work individually on the indicators for the second standard, *Learning Environment*. After discussion of the indicators, there was a short break during which Oksana led the participants in physical exercise.

The next standard, *Family Participation*, has six indicators. This standard was discussed in pairs. During discussion of the fourth standard, *Teaching Strategies for Meaningful Learning*, Oksana asked, "How would you create groups in such a situation?" "Inclusive children are so flighty!"

one participant said. "Yes, yes," others said. The groups formed as proposed and worked at their assignment.

After some time Oksana asks about indicator 4.1, which is "Teachers recognize the need for a variety of teaching approaches to accommodate the different learning styles, temperaments, and personalities of individual children." (This includes adaptation of materials and teaching approaches and the possibility of children's choice during the work.) "Yes, we have it," one of the participants answers. "We prepare at least five types of individual cards with the tasks. Some children do them quickly and need more tasks. Some are slower. Natalia, a girl with cerebral palsy, has writing difficulties, so we prepare task cards with underlined options for her. As to choice, giving a full choice is difficult. All depends upon the lesson objectives. A lot of the choice occurs in the lessons on drawing and handicrafts: clay, mosaics, appliqué work, and grains. Children write on paper, in advance, the materials they choose to use."

The fifth standard, *Planning and Assessment*, has seven indicators, and the sixth standard, *Professional Development*, has four. Oksana asks the four groups to think about real situations from their experience and to role-play a presentation of their standard to each other. So the first two groups do the fifth standard, and the other two do the sixth. After discussing the role play, Oksana thanks them for "fruitful, wonderful" work and asks them each to make one comment about today's activity. The comments include "Interesting," "Productive," "Learned a lot new," "Joyful," "I made sure that I work by the program and I'm doing it fine!", and "We were convinced that we know more than just a little!"

"Thank you. Tomorrow we shall discuss two topics in depth. First, individualization; the second will be your choice. Before we start, with your permission, I will observe some of your classes. So what shall we have as the second topic of the day?" "We would like to speak about the selection of tasks and theme planning," a participant answers. Others agree. "Good. See you tomorrow."

April 16, 1:30 P.M. Oksana distributes the study materials, waiting for the participants. The teachers come, and the training starts. Oksana says, "Friends! I have prepared some materials for you on theme planning, organization of study space, portfolios, work with parents, and determination of the types of intelligence of a child. You know part of it, and some of this will supplement your knowledge. I have visited some of your classes. I saw that you implement many of the Step by Step practices successfully. Let us make our second day of training a question-and-answer session. What about that?" The participants agree.

The first question is this: "For teaching several themes simultaneously, I propose several tasks. The objective is to complete all of them. The sequence is arbitrary. Sometimes a child will work only on one thing. He or she does not want to move to something different. What can we do?"

Oksana answers, "We select tasks depending on the child's intellectual capabilities. The plan may include several tasks at different levels of difficulty. Each is to be appropriately scored. Although each task may earn certain points, the children have to be oriented to earning the score for performing all the tasks. The children should do an equal number of tasks, some needing more time to complete. Together, the tasks have to evoke the feeling of success, not of failure."

Individualization was seen as setting the task appropriate to the child's developmental level. With the type of task the same for all, there was less segregation of children, one from another. The teachers were to recognize and develop multiple competencies in all the children, not only one main line of intellect. If a child with a certain type of intellect always selected a certain type of task, the teacher had to be clever in enticing him or her to work on other types.

The next topic dealt with obtaining a balance among individual work, teacher-led instruction, and group work. Oksana expressed the thought that group work was more efficient than teacher-based instruction, and that individual work resulted in child separation. Also, Oksana claimed that a child's individual strengths are more evident during small-group work than during teacher–child work.

One teacher asks, "How can we get a child with special needs involved in group work when he or she prefers individual activity?" Oksana answers, "You should use every small opportunity to encourage the child to do something in common with the others; however, this should not become coercive. If an activity makes the child happy to go to school every morning, this is a breakthrough." The training session comes to an end. Oksana asks the participants to fill in the evaluation questionnaire.

A PRESS CONFERENCE IN LVIV

Friday, April 2, 2004. It is a beautiful spring day. At 10:00 A.M., Maliuk School is holding a press conference on the issue of child care for children with special needs. In the conference hall, tables are arranged in the shape of rectangle. A large TV has been placed to the side. Gradually the room fills with people. The media representatives are setting up their cameras. Ms. Hrystyna, Maliuk School's director, and Julia Kavun, training coordinator of the Ukranian Step by Step Foundation, are distributing papers, pens, and folders containing materials on inclusion of children into a mainstreamed school system. A working atmosphere reigns. Some media representatives are going through registration. Others are making themselves comfortable at the tables. The mothers of Liubchyk, in the first grade, and of Natalia, the child with cerebral palsy in the third grade, sit with the teachers of their children in quiet conversation. Hrystyna and Julia are at the head of the table. Some of the journalists place microphones and tape recorders in front of them.

At 10:05, Julia starts the event with greetings. She introduces Ms. Hrystyna and identifies the goal of the meeting: to present the inclusive educational model followed in Maliuk School. Hrystyna makes a brief presentation of her school within the *Inclusion of Children with Special Needs* initiative:

> "At Maliuk we have 205 pupils, from the age of 2 to Grade 4. We have been working with the Step by Step child-centered program since 1994. In 1996 we started to include children with special needs. In 2001 we became part of a national experiment, *Social Adaptation and Integration of Children with Special Needs in Psycho-Physical Development by Inclusion in the Mainstream School System*. It was an initiative of the Ministry of Education. The experiment was organized by the Ukrainian Step by Step Foundation and the Institute of Special Pedagogy of Ukraine. At this time, we have eight children with special needs studying in various grades."

After other introductions, Ms. Hrystyna invites the journalists to watch a film, *Children with Special Needs: Step by Step in Ukraine*, which "will help you understand the issue better." The 20-minute film shows regular schools in Kyiv and Lviv in which children with special needs are enrolled. It has interviews with the teachers, the Ukranian Step by Step Foundation's director, and a representative of the Parents' Association. The film includes an interview with Hrystyna. While watching the film, the reporters make notes, smiling as they see Natalia, the "heroine" with cerebral palsy, play with other children and tell why she likes her school. Natalia's mother, present at the press conference, is shown in the film as well. She smiles shyly and whispers something to Liubchyk's mother. When the film is over, Julia opens the session to reporters' questions.

A REPORTER: Are you planning to increase the number of children with special needs here?

MS. HRYSTYNA: Our experience has been that everything depends on the child's development, but the number of such children should not be over two or three in one class or in a group. Our teachers have little special education expertise, because the universities did not include this specialization in their curricula. The Step by Step Foundation has been the only organization providing us such assistance. Most of our teachers have taken part in workshops on the subject of child care for children with special needs. They were organized and carried out by the foundation.

MS. JULIA: With the modern practice of inclusive education, in a single class there can be from two to four children with special needs. But, of course, it depends on many factors: the severity of the child's disability, the availability of teacher assistants, and so on. We are carrying out the Ukraine experiment in such a way that an experimental class might have various numbers of children with special needs. Some classes have up to six pupils. During 2003–2004, we have been conducting research to see in what ways inclusive education influences all the participants in the process.

MS. HRYSTYNA: We receive substantial assistance from social pedagogues working at our school, thanks to the Step by Step Foundation.

MS. JULIA: That assistance was possible through the project, *Creating Centres of Excellence*, created by the Step by Step Foundation in partnership with the International Step by Step Association and the EveryChild organization. It was supported by the TACIS Program of the European Commission.

TETYANA MESHKO (a reporter for the newspaper *Moloda Halychyna*): I have a question for the mothers. How did you end up at Maliuk?

MOTHER OF NATALIA: Mr. Nikolaev, director of the training and rehabilitation center Dzherelo, recommended Maliuk to me. The preschool program was not all that my daughter needed. She needed continuing communication with other children. Dzherelo already had quite a large group, some 16 kids. So Mr. Nikolaev referred me to Maliuk.

MS. JULIA: We collaborate with the Psychological–Medical–Pedagogic Consultation (PMPC). It informs parents of the possibility of their children enrolling in inclusive schools. It provides them with addresses and contacts.

MS. HRYSTYNA: Two years ago our PMPC was opposed to the process of inclusion, but now we have close cooperation. We often ask for their help. [Note: For a fuller description of the traditional role of the PMPC, see the "National Context" section, later in this report.]

LARYSA POPROTSKA (a reporter for the newspaper *Vysokyj Zamok*): In terms of further education, what happens next after the children graduate from Maliuk?

MS. HRYSTYNA: That is a very troubling issue. Yesterday we went to the PMPC with one of our graduates to look for a school he can attend next. We have identified a school for children with speaking problems. This pupil also has mild mental retardation. We are going to ask the school to take the boy.

MS. JULIA: The Step by Step Foundation is planning to work closer with middle schools. The first step is to design and implement programs aimed at transition from the elementary to the middle school level. Other steps involve meetings with teachers, visits of children with special needs to mainstream schools, and orientation seminars for teaching personnel.

MAKSYM OSCHIPKO (a reporter for MIST, a television and radio station): How long did it take, and how costly was it, to reequip and rehabilitate the building?

MS. HRYSTYNA: It was done with funds allotted for the project. It should have been a government responsibility—if we aspire to true democracy. Altogether, it is seldom a huge amount. Only installation of an elevator requires a large expenditure, and that is only needed for schools having two or three floors.

MAKSYM OSCHIPKO: May we see these children in their classes?

MS. HRYSTYNA: Yes, certainly.

MS. JULIA: If you have no other questions, you may visit the classrooms. Thank you for your time and participation. We will be looking forward to seeing your stories!

Ms. Hrystyna asked the teachers to help the reporters find the classrooms with children with special needs. The cameramen collected their equipment and followed the teachers and journalists. The group visited the primary classrooms first. Some of them, together with Natalia's mother, visited Natalia's classroom. Some of them went with Oksana to her first-grade room. Another group followed Natalia, the preschool teacher. They spent about 20 minutes in the classrooms, taking photos and talking to the children and teachers. When two reporters came to the room where Liubchyk was, he was looking at a book with Marianna. In a while, he put the book down and left the classroom. Marianna followed him. Liubchyk's mother gave an interview to one reporter in the room of the press conference. The journalists also interviewed the teachers and Ms. Hrystyna.

12:50 P.M. The press conference continued in one of the halls of the Lviv Oblast State Administration Building. (The city of Lviv is the capital of Lviv Oblast.) This was a two-story building, located near the boarding school for orphaned children and children whose parents have lost parental rights.

> The room is on the second floor, a large and well-lighted room. The tables are arranged in a rectangle. On the wall behind the table are pictures of children, a flag of the Ukranian Step by Step Foundation, and some written materials. Close to the entrance door is a table with a list of participants and pens, folders of information, and leaflets. At the main table is Ms. Tatiana Khimchenko, vice-director of the Center for Strategic Support, which helped organize this event. Also at the table are Julia Kavun, training coordinator of the Step by Step Foundation, and Natalia Pastushenko, vice-director of the Lviv Oblast Scientific–Methodological Institute of Education. (It was hoped that Mr. Lazarko, chief of the Department of Education of the Lviv City Council, and Mr. Kashuba, chief of the Central Department of Youth Policy of the Lviv Oblast State Administration, would attend, but they are unable to.)
>
> Some journalists who did not attend the morning session at Maliuk School and some who did come into the room. They set up their cameras, pass through the registration procedure, and make themselves comfortable at the table. Tatiana greets the participants and announces again the goal of the meeting. She then introduces Julia and Natalia and passes the floor to Julia. Julia starts the press conference by introducing statistics on the education of children with special needs:

>> "According to the *National Report of Ukraine* on implementing the 2003 recommendations of the World Bank on the interests of children, the number of children with disabilities in Ukraine had increased to 28,500. The overall population of 1.4 million children had been decreasing. Since 1993, the proportion of children with disabilities increased from 1.1% to 1.6%. Approximately 65% of these children were assigned to boarding schools. The rest were assigned to mainstream schools, but with little expectation of participation in the school life and learning process. Specialized schools were aggravating the consequences

of deficiencies in child development. The children felt isolated from the world and unprepared to live independently."

Then she again presents the project:

"In 2003–2004, the Lviv City Council, together with the Lviv Oblast State Administration and the Ukrainian Step by Step Foundation, are working in partnership with the International Step by Step Association (Netherlands) and the international charitable organization EveryChild (Ukrainian branch). They have been introducing a model of inclusive education at the educational complex Maliuk and in School 15 (Bila Tserkva, Kyiv Oblast). The tasks of the project are the following:

- Preparing teachers to work with children with disabilities in mainstream school environments.
- Partially redesigning educational institutions to provide children with special needs access to the school's resources.
- Creating learning resource and training centers as these pertain to inclusive education.
- Establishing interdepartmental cooperation among local administration offices to facilitate implementation of the inclusive education model.
- Holding a series of interdepartmental workshops for the oblast and local department representatives responsible for issues of guardianship, care, and education in respect to children with special needs.

"We are proud of our achievements: Eight children—six of whom under former conditions would have been assigned to a special educational institution—attend Maliuk. They are learning in accordance with the program of the regular school, modified to suit their learning abilities. The parents take active part in the inclusion process. One mother told us, 'When our child was born, we felt that she was loved only by the family. Now our girl enjoys an active social life, learning, and eagerly anticipating her future.' By the way, this year this mother started working at a job again for the first time since the child's birth.

"Presently, lobbying for the children's interests is underway. We are expecting endorsement in the *Provision on Inclusive Education* by the Ministry of Science and Education of Ukraine."

To Julia's presentation, Natalia adds:

Ms. Natalia: "Today, numerous documents promote equal access to quality education. Statistics show an increase in the number of children with special needs. There is a need for funds to improve their education. We are grateful to those who help us. The current experiment, underway since 2001, and the Creating Centres of Excellence fully support our institute. Within the framework of the experiment, we regularly provide teacher training and methodological support. We have positive results from the research on adaptation of children with special needs to mainstream schools, results supporting inclusion. This practice has two advantages. First, able-bodied children learn to be tolerant, even to appreciate the importance of their neighbors. Second, children with special needs get a greater sense of themselves as people. And the parents of these children become more optimistic. They are in better humor, with a different attitude toward their jobs. The country thus gets better workers. The institute will keep providing support. We are hoping for government financial support."

The session was then opened to reporters' questions.

VIRA KARPINSKA (a reporter for the newspaper *Lvivska Gazeta*): How many children with disabilities are there in Lviv Oblast?

MS. NATALIA: Unfortunately, I don't have this information.

TETYANA MESHKO (a reporter for the newspaper *Moloda Halychyna*): What other schools are using the inclusive model?

MS. JULIA: At the present moment, 27 educational establishments in seven oblasts in Ukraine use the inclusive educational model.

MARICHKA KRYZHANIVKSA (a reporter for the radio station *Radio-Lux*): What schools in Lviv use the inclusive program?

MS. NATALIA: Right now, six schools. They are listed in your folder. And there are additional schools in Lviv and Lviv Oblast interested in this program.

DANA KOVALENKO (a reporter for the newspaper *Subotnia Poshta*): What is expected after 2004?

MS. JULIA: We shall continue lobbying for this model.

VIKTORIA PRYKHID (a reporter for the newspaper *Postup u Lvovi*): Can you speak of the concrete achievement of the children?

MS. JULIA: For example, a third-grade pupil with cerebral palsy is a very popular person in her class. Diagnostic methods have confirmed her status as a "star." And a boy who came into first grade at Maliuk 3 years ago, with mild mental retardation and a strong speech deficiency, now has very good pronunciation and has found new friends. Another boy with an autistic syndrome is no longer sitting in a corner, but is having good social experiences.

Had Ms. Julia needed to clarify her answer to this last question further, she might have said that the achievements of these three children did not imply that they were cured of disability. Instead, a social environment had been established so that education and maturation could proceed in spite of the disability. Liubchyk was not brought into a remedial place as much as he was accepted in a place for social and academic experience. The program provided him with appropriate opportunities to learn.

After thanking everyone for participating, Tatiana closed the press conference. Unhurriedly, the journalists left the room. They were asked when they might have their stories finished.

That evening, two news releases covered the press conference. Later, three newspaper articles appeared: "Friendship Offered by a Child Is the Best Medicine" (by Tetyana Meshko, *Moloda Halychyna*, April 15), "The Right to a Decent Life" (by Lidia Lozynska, *For Free Ukraine*, April 8), and "The School for Every Child" (by Viktoria Prykhid, *Postup u Lvovi*, April 5). Copies were posted on bulletin boards by the Maliuk staff with great satisfaction. They said that the material in print reflected their achievements, as well as the problems of working with children with special needs. They continued to hope for more support from the authorities.

TEACHER TRAINING IN KYIV

A Step by Step training program, *Children with Special Needs in Regular Preschool and Primary School Classrooms*, was scheduled in Kyiv for April 21–23, 2004. This was introductory training for deputy principals and teachers of the regular schools of the Holosiivky District of Kyiv. It would occur at Barvinok, a Step by Step training center and kindergarten–primary school. The school occupied a two-story building with 14 classrooms. The sessions were held in the special training room.

April 21, 2004. The first day of training starts at 10:00 A.M.—a bit later than usual, because some participants have to come to Kyiv on suburban trains from across the oblast.

The spring sun shines joyfully through the window, causing many participants to anticipate happy completion of the school year, summer holidays coming soon, and the beginning of planning for the next school year. All the participants in the session are women. They enter the training room where tables and chairs are grouped, matching the number of trainees: 28. Notebooks, pens, and small badges are at the tables, plus crayons and markers of various colors. At the front of the room is a table for the two trainers. A flip chart is at the side. To the right is a table with an overhead projector; nearby is the screen. The trainers greet the persons entering and ask them to take places at the tables.

Ira, a woman, the trainer at this center, asks the participants to put their names on the badges as they like to be addressed. Some start to write their names in pen, but after seeing others take crayons or markers, they turn the cards over and put their names boldly in color, decorating them with flowers and other ornamentation. Ira asks the participants to present themselves and to tell the reasons they came to the training. Some of the reasons:

- "Each child is special, so he has special needs. I would like to learn about various approaches to working with these children."
- "The topic is of great interest for me, because I have such children in my class."
- "I am familiar with the Step by Step program, but I would like to learn more about working with children with special needs."
- "I would like to hear more about the experience of other teachers in working with children with special needs."
- "I would like to learn how to work with such children. I feel that they have the right to study at mainstream schools, but I am afraid I may do them harm."
- "Frankly speaking, I came because my principal told me that beginning next year, we are to work with this program."
- "I have a friend, the mother of a child with Down's syndrome. She is unwilling to give the child to a special school. At this training, I think I will hear more about institutions accepting such children. I need to learn more myself."

Ira told the participants the objectives of the training and asked them to work out some work rules for the session. Ira indicated that the participants should feel free to express their wishes. Olga, the second trainer, stood ready to put their words on the flip chart. Silence. It seemed that the participants were ready to keep on listening, even as they were encouraged to speak. It is not easy to create your own government.

Then someone says, "Don't criticize." Ira thinks, then tells them that in their classrooms when teachers ask the children to set rules, they often start with "No": "No shouting" or "No fighting." Why do they start with "No?" Obviously, they are used to associating rules with prohibitions. Ira tells them that she always suggests that the children think about rules that are affirming, as encouragement to doing good. And she urges the participants to do the same.

Anna, who has just offered the rule not to criticize, changes it to "Express yourself constructively." Other participants come forward with their ideas, trying to avoid saying "No." Olga writes the rules on the flip chart with green and blue markers. Upon completion, Ira asks, "Are all the rules clear? Do you have any questions?" Hearing none, she proposes her own rule: "The rule of the raised hand," which means "a call for silence." After that, Ira asks, "Does anybody object to these rules? Silence. Taking that as agreement, she says, "We are going to revise them on a daily basis, making changes as needed."

After this, the trainers introduce the "four corners" exercise. A sign is placed in each corner of the room. The signs read:

1. "Children with special needs must attend the same classes with other children if they are capable of mastering the same material."
2. "Children with special needs must attend special schools that provide for their specific educational and medical needs."
3. "All children, regardless of their abilities, must attend regular classes."
4. "The parents of children with special needs must decide which school each child will attend."

Olga asked the participants to walk around and read the signs, then go to the sign that best expressed their own opinion. With the other participants there, they were to select five reasons why this statement should be supported. One person from each group was to be selected to present the collective opinion. Olga set a limit of 15 minutes for all presentations.

The participants move about, reading the statements. Sign 1 draws the largest group, and Sign 2 the smallest. The discussions are based mostly on personal experience: "My neighbors have a child like that, and they do not want to send her to the boarding school, and the regular school refuses to accept her. The parents' hearts are broken. They want their child in a more stimulating environment." "I have a child in my mainstream class, but the parents do not pay appropriate attention to the child." Some participants say that if they could, they would go to the middle of the room to reflect how they feel. Some participants change their minds, leaving to continue discussion with a new group.

Olga rings a small bell and says that they have 4 minutes remaining. When time is up, she invites the spokespersons to take the floor. After each presentation, Olga applauds and explains that the issues raised will be covered during the training. At the workshop's end, they will be asked to review their opinions and see whether there are changes. Their thoughts are to be noted in a special Reflections Notebook.

Olga read out the standard on *Objectives and Tasks*. She defined the concept of "inclusion" with transparencies and handouts, and identified the benefits of inclusion programs. Olga asked the participants to prepare to discuss these issues with people outside the training, and to write down questions and answers to them in the Notebook. "It is important to indicate what type of information is relevant, in order for us to explain the issue to others."

April 22, 2:05 P.M. On the second day, the participants have lunch in an adjacent room. The food is cooked by those working in the kindergarten's kitchen: soup with meatballs, mashed potatoes with cutlets, fresh vegetable salads, and a fruit compote.

They return to the meeting room. A few participants make new badges, marking their names in color. The trainers, who have finished their lunch earlier, greet the participants. Ira stands in the center, Olga by the table. Ira asks the participants not to sit down, but to make a circle, then to turn right. She says, "Today, in the morning, the sun was shining, but now the clouds have come. What will be next? During lunch Olga and I listened to the weather forecast." At the same time, Ira, who is in the circle with everyone else, starts massaging the shoulders of the participant in front of her. The participants follow suit. "So a bright sun shone in the morning, but suddenly the clouds came, and the rain started to fall. It turned into a heavy shower, then into hail, and then suddenly turned into light rain. The wind came up and it blew away the clouds, and the sun shone again."

The participants giggle. One says, "The message and the massage are straight to the point. They take the place of the after-lunch nap." Ira asks the participants to turn around and repeat the massage, and to tell their partners a new forecast. Two minutes later, Ira says, "You can do such an exercise with your children, encouraging them to invent new stories."

Ira reminded the participants then that before lunch they had had the opportunity to learn about the significance of teamwork in the inclusive classroom. Next they discussed working with families as main partners and team members. Ira said that it was only possible to understand parents when you understand their values: "For understanding other people's values, it is important to realize your own values." She said, "Understanding the values of others depends on conviction in the values of our own lives."

Ira proposes that each participant write, on each of five cards, a value that is important for her. Three minutes later, she asks participants to name some of them, while Olga puts them on the flip chart. The participants call out: "Health," "Love," "Mutual assistance," "Family relations," "Faith," and "Family." Ira adds two more: "Freedom of choice" and "Freedom of conscience." She comments, "Remember, just as your values differed, the values of different families will vary. And sometimes the values of members of the same family will vary."

Next Ira asks them to leave only two cards on the table and to put the other three under their chair. The participants seem dismayed, as if reluctant to give up any, even just to put them under the chair. Maria laughs and says, "So, if I need to reject any of my values, let it be love, but it's a pity." The participants are having a hard time making the choice. "But all of them are closely interrelated. How could I live without a thirst for life, without health or love?" Then Ira proposes, "Now I want you to exchange one of two values on the table for one under your chair." This causes another storm of emotions. But some of the participants feel relief as they come to realize what the point is: "You cannot know any person simply by a value or two."

Ira projected a transparency titled "Establishing Ties with Families." She asked the participants to read the statements, taking turns.

During the coffee break, Ira asks four participants to help with the next task. Among the four is Sasha, a young teacher who has just completed her study at Kyiv Pedagogical University, specializing in the topic of "The Primary School Teacher." Sasha is dressed in trousers, a light shirt, and a man's tie. Ira chooses Sasha to play the father's role. (Regretably, there are no men among the participants.) Ira asks Alla and Svitlana, deputy principals, and Nadia, a primary school teacher, to play other roles to start a discussion. Ira appears cautious in choosing a participant for the role of a child with special needs. Although everyone understands the issues, a fear exists in even imagining oneself as such a child. For this role, Ira chooses Nadia, who yesterday, during the "Four Corners" exercise, vigorously spoke out for protection of the rights of children with special needs to study together with their "coevals." Maybe Nadia, being a teacher, will play the role of such a child with more ease. In addition, Nadia has in her class Olia, a girl with cerebral palsy. Ira tells the four of them about the scenario she wants them to act out.

After the break, Ira invited the participants to return to the room and told them that this afternoon they had the opportunity to understand better the feelings of a family having a child with special needs. This may help them become better able to help such a family. Ira also said that first of all, the participants needed to get acquainted with the family, as played by Sasha, Alla, Svitlana, and Nadia. The participants applauded the actors.

Ira reads: "I want to present a young couple: Alexander [Sasha comes to the center of the room] and his wife Ann [Alla comes forward]." Sasha and Alla hold hands (as scripted) and walk around the room. Ira continues to read: "Alexander and Ann have just married, and they are very happy. They have started to furnish their home, and during the second year of their marriage, Ann joyfully tells Alexander that she is pregnant." At that moment, Sasha and Alla walk slower. Ira reads: "With great pleasure, the young parents inform their relatives about the birth of their daughter, whom they name Maria." Ira invites Svitlana to the center of the room, where the action continues. Svitlana approaches her parents, takes their hands in her right hand, trying to coordinate her steps with them. They slowly walk around the room together.

Ira continues: "After 2 years, the young couple decides to have another child. The father wants a boy, but when asked which he wants, he answers, 'It is unimportant. Just let the child be healthy!' Finally, the long-expected boy is born. But the mother sees the worried faces of the doctors discussing something." Ira raises her voice, distinctly pronouncing every word: "Their child is born with disabilities! Relatives and friends do not know whether to congratulate the parents or to express regret."

At that moment, Nadia comes toward the center of the room, slowly approaching her family, taking their joined hands with her right hand. To help her play the part of this child more realistically, Nadia has put two small balls under her arms, restricting their movement, and tied her knees with a band. Nadia has asked Natalia, the mentor of the senior preschool group, standing at the door watching the role play, about the balls and band. Behind Natalia stands a kitchen worker, Ms. Nina, who is also interested in the role play. Ira reads the text seriously, making appropriate pauses, raising and lowering her voice. Silence comes over the room. In the beginning the participants were watching "the young couple" with jokes and laughter, but now everybody solemnly watches the participants moving around the circle.

Ira continues: "The parents remember their dreams. Like all parents, they had dreamed of healthy, beautiful children. But now, they face the fact that for their son, this dream will never come true." At that moment, Olga, the cotrainer, approaches the father and mother and slips wooden blocks (from the blocks set) over their arms, burdening them. She "beads" the blocks on their free arms.

Ira continues to read. Olga adds more blocks to the members of the family, little by little. Many participants have tears in their eyes. Nina, watching this role play from behind the door, says, "Oh, I cannot look," and retreats to the kitchen. Ira finishes: "What a change in the life of the family! It will never be the same as before!" The role play ends. Ira says to them all: "These are the members of our family. How can we help them?"

Ira thanked the actors and asked them to rejoin the group for discussion. As the role play ended there was none of the usual applause. In addition, the participants appeared unready to start a discussion. They were all wrapped in the enormity of disability.

Then one participant who watched the role play breaks the silence: "You know, my friend was in the same situation. Their second child was born with disabilities. One thing was different: The husband left them immediately."

Ira says, "Let's applaud our actors and try to define the possible ways to help such a family in our community." The participants applaud. Olga is at the flip chart, ready to write ideas. For some participants, a change back into a rational training routine appears a relief. But some participants want to share their emotions.

Natalia, the mentor, who has watched the role play from the door, turns to leave. In the corridor, she meets Nina, who asks, "How did the situation end?" Natalia answers, "Life goes on." Nina answers, "Lord willing, I'll never see it happen again."

TEACHER TRAINING IN UKRAINE

Qualified and motivated teachers are among the most important indicators of the quality of education. However, according to the Ukranian statistics for 2001, with the number of primary teachers less than 360,000, almost 50,000 of them left their jobs. That is 14% of the total. A little over 11% of these 50,000 left on their own. (These come from Chapter 8 of the cumulative report on labor issues in Ukraine in 2001, *Flow of the Work Force*, State Committee of Statistics.) Such a loss occurs for several reasons. Among them is a worsening of the financial conditions for teachers during the years 1996–2000. In 2000, a teacher's salary was 50% of the wages paid in the industrial sphere—despite the fact that according to a law of Ukraine, *On Education*, the average salary of pedagogical workers is not to be lower than the average salary of industrial workers. The statistics also indicated that the age of pedagogues in general was increasing. The number of retiring teachers grew slightly, from 10% in 1999 to 11% in 2001. In recent years, Ukraine has also experienced a series of strikes among educators. According to the State Committee of Statistics, of the 76 striking organizations in 2000, 27 were in education. In 2001, 13 educational strikes were included in the 31 overall.

The system of teacher training included 26 classical, pedagogical universities and institutes, as well as 45 pedagogical high schools and colleges (much like U.S. vocational schools). For teacher retraining, the system included 25 oblast institutes of postgraduate pedagogical education and two city institutes of postgraduate pedagogical education, one in Kyiv and one in Sevastopol. As indicated in the quotation below, the Ministry of Education and Science controlled the content of the programs of teacher training:

> "So far, teacher training is centralized. That is not always good. Some first attempts to decentralize are being made. For example, teacher preparation in the new specializations [is to be started] at the National Pedagogical University and at Kamyanets Podilsky Pedagogical Institute. They will teach the new specializations, 'Teachers for Inclusive Classrooms' and 'Social Pedagogues.' The list of these specializations is not approved yet. As soon as the list is approved by the Ministry, the appropriate programs will be developed. We continue to have centralized preparation of teachers of other specializations. Nongovernment higher education institutes have expanded their list of specializations, but they also have to be approved by the

Ministry of Education. The situation is that the laws on education exist, and the Ministry of Education is responsible for them. I think the Ministry is coping with it successfully." (From an interview with Vyatcheslav Zasenko, vice-director of the Institute of Special Pedagogy, Academy of Pedagogical Sciences of Ukraine, Kyiv)

Professional development, recertification, and advancement for teachers was conducted in accordance with the Statement on Attestation of the Pedagogues of Ukraine (by Order 419 of the Ministry of Education and Science of Ukraine, dated December 1, 1998),[4] also in accordance with the law *On Education* (Article 54). Its purpose was "initiation [of] teachers' creative professional activities, stimulation [of] on-going professional and general education, qualitative work, raising the responsibility for the results of learning and upbringing, providing for social protection of the competence of pedagogical work."

Most teachers chose among courses provided by the local oblast's institutes of postgraduate pedagogical education. The local state administrations provided financing only to cover the cost of the courses themselves, and did not cover expenses connected with travel and accommodation. So few teachers chose courses offered at other institutions in other cities.

Such was the situation faced by the Ukrainian Step by Step Foundation. In 2003, it obtained a license from the Ministry of Education and Science for providing teacher courses in the sphere of innovative education. Teachers who wanted to take the Step by Step courses had to cover the expenses themselves. Still, the Ukrainian Step by Step Foundation conducted teacher courses every month for the minimum of 72 hours required by the state. The teachers could choose to participate in a 72-hour program based at the training site or choose the long-distance program, which involved 48 hours of program at the site and 24 hours of distance learning. Enough teachers took the Step by Step courses to keep the trainers (who were all regular teachers as well) overworked.

---

[4]In Ukraine and many other countries of the region, teachers undergo "attestation" to renew their credentials every 5 years. In the prior period, all teachers must enroll in some continuing professional education. If one's professional development is seen as outstanding during the review, he or she can be moved to a higher standing and receive a pay raise. Teachers can also opt to undergo this "attestation" more frequently than every 5 years.

LIUBCHYK

April 26, 2004, 11:00 A.M. After playing "Little Balls," a game of repeating and memorizing numbers, the children break into four groups. Each group selects its own math game: "Math Dominos," "Math Lotto," "Geometric Lotto," or "Voyage around the World." Ms. Halyna encourages Liubchyk to join the group choosing "Geometric Lotto." She says, "I will be there with you." He acquiesces. There are eight children in the group. They pick the geometrical chips. Sofiyka makes the first move. She puts forward a small blue quadrangle saying, "Color!" Oleg puts down a blue triangle and says, "Thickness!" It is now Liubchyk's turn. Halyna tells him, "Liubchyk, what chip will you choose? Look how thick the figure should be." She takes one of his fingers letting him feel the thickness of the blue triangle, then suggests he feel his chips. Liubchyk chooses a rectangle with the same thickness. "What task will you give to Oleg? Color? Thickness? Size? Shape?" He chooses color. The game continues. When it is Liubchyk's turn again, with the help of his assistant he puts forward a required figure. But almost at once he gets up and goes to Ms. Marianna, who is sitting at the teachers' desk. He sits near her, takes a piece of paper that shows letters and syllables written in dots, and starts drawing lines to connect the dots and form the letters and syllables. The rest of his group finish the "Geometric Lotto" game.

Ms. Oksana then says, "Children, form a circle. Liubchyk, come be with us." "No," he says. "Will you join us later? Okay?" Oksana gives out instructions for the next task. They are to break into groups and select a certain geometrical shape of a certain color. Every group is to solve a "Hungarian Crossword" that hides the main characters of the fairy tale *Thumbelina*. Marianna retells Liubchyk everything the teacher says. Oksana asks Liubchyk also to select a certain geometrical shape. He chooses a little green circle. She gives him the same paper as the rest of the children, but this time the task is somewhat different: Each child has to read and write down names of the fairy tale's characters, and to make a drawing of one of them. Liubchyk starts work at the teachers' desk. Marianna suggests that he join the group. Liubchyk reluctantly approaches his peers and continues his task. Having quickly completed the task, the children gather in a circle. They analyze the results of their activities with the teacher. Liubchyk remains at the table.

Their next task is to read passages from the fairy tale. Every child selects a passage, identifies the number of words it contains, then goes to a place affording a comfortable posture and reads it aloud. Liubchyk gets up abruptly, walks through the reading group, takes a book, and leaves the classroom. Ms. Marianna follows him and brings him back to the classroom. Liubchyk then walks up to Oksana, touches her, and points at the clock, saying, "Oksana! It's time for lunch!" The clock does show 12:00 sharp, lunchtime. "Yes, Liubchyk, but we have a few minutes more, because the clock is 5 minutes fast. Look here, I still have 5 minutes." Ms. Oksana shows her watch. "Let Katrusia read her passage to you. Is that all right? Katrusia, come here." Katrusia comes eagerly and takes Liubchyk by the hand, and they go to the corridor to read.

Observations by Ailsa Cregan, Mentor

April 29, 2004. Liubchyk is a quiet and gentle boy. I have heard him described as "autistic" by his mother, but pronounced autistic characteristics are absent. He does not resort to stereotypical movements. He is not obsessive about routine. He does not deliberately avoid eye contact. And he does make relationships with people. His use of language appears no more significantly delayed than his overall cognitive development is delayed. And his understanding of what is said to him is not typical of an autistic child.

While Liubchyk, when allowed, spends much time playing on his own in an abstract or dreamy kind of way, he is not obsessive about the play objects. For example, I observed him picking up and putting down logiblocks [Legos], sometimes fitting them into a box, but he did not object when interrupted. He cooperated, taking up a teacher-directed task of choosing a crayon and coloring items as suggested. This he did at his own leisurely pace and for a limited length of time, but with reasonable care. After such "interruptions," he likes to return to his previous occupation or drift off to another part of the room.

Liubchyk is often helped by a girl in his class, who willingly and spontaneously takes responsibility for him. For example, she took Liubchyk to a quiet corner to read to him. She prompted him to pay attention, and he obediently looked and listened, even though the language was probably beyond him. This is an extremely productive relationship, not only from an "academic" point of view but socially; it is very important for Liubchyk. More such interactions with his peers will help bring him out of his dream world. I understand that he often rejects the advances of children other than his special friend by turning away or pushing them away. However, I suggest that teachers enlist the help of another relatively mature child, to approach him regularly despite rejection, so that step-by-step peer interaction becomes wider and more customary.

Activities undertaken by the class may often be beyond Liubchyk's capability, inappropriate for his level of development, and outside his conceptual grasp. However, I observed him being given tasks at a manageable level, which did relate to what other children were doing. In this way he participated in their kind of overall understanding, even when physically apart from them. I suggest that Liubchyk might regularly sit together with a special group—say, with his special friend and one other—and his participation be directed by the children, who could be specially instructed in advance as necessary. When sitting nicely, Liubchyk should receive regular social rewards.

At other times, Liubchyk receives individual teaching from an adult assistant. Careful monitoring of the program is important to ensure that the activities are geared to incremental goals leading to more advanced objectives in different areas of development.

One vital area is self-help, including feeding, toileting, washing, and dressing. Goals should be drawn up to be achieved in just a week or so. The goal should be discussed with Liubchyk's grandmother, who hopefully will work along the same lines as the school, on one small specific task at a time. The small steps should be recorded and checked off carefully.

I was impressed by the affection shown Liubchyk. He is often stroked, hugged, or talked to by the adults around him, and sometimes by the children. He responds well to this and will put his arms around people or rest his head against them. In this respect, he definitely seems to have made progress since my last visit 6 months ago. Therefore, the beginning of next term, after he has had time to settle in, would be a good time to make a regular new demand on him. For example, after a break, his teacher might insist that he physically join the group as a whole, sitting or standing with them, even if he doesn't want to. I would think Liubchyk is capable of understanding "When you've done . . ., then you can do . . . " (something he likes). Learning to acquiesce to this type of demand will be a good basis for further extension of demands.

A Step by Step educator realizes that the child's original diagnosis—autism—would not be what other doctors might say. But Step by Step can work with the situation. It does not consider its views the only possible perspectives on growth and maturation. Step by Step is a partner with parents, schools, and agencies, trying to work together for the best interests of each child.

LIUBCHYK'S MOTHER

My (Svitlana Efimova's) first meeting with Romanna, Liubchyk's mother, took place during the training session *Development of a Caring Community and Believing in One's Abilities*, at Maliuk. Because of my job situation at the time, I was able to attend this session for only 1 day. But I was in the same group with her during the activity. Our task was to identify and discuss problems in working with "difficult audiences." Romanna was the leader of our team, actively participating, and she made the presentation of results.

We met a second time at Maliuk when Romanna came to take Liubchyk home. I asked her for permission to observe Liubchyk—hoping that our previous acquaintance would lead to a positive answer, but knowing that the opposite was possible. After we made ourselves comfortable in the conference room (although I was a bit anxious), I disclosed my intentions to Romanna. She listened attentively, then said that she didn't mind, and yes, more than that, she was pleased with the proposal. I asked if I could visit her at home; again she said, "Yes." On Wednesday, April 7, 2004, at 3:00 P.M., Romanna, Liubchyk, and I went to their home. Despite the fact that previously he had not minded my presence, he closed the front door on me. "Liubchyk, you did let me come to your home, didn't you?" I asked. Romanna said, "My son, a true man, first promises something to a woman, and then is afraid of keeping the promise." She opened the door, and we went in.

We came to the room Liubchyk shared with his sister, Dana. She also attends Maliuk and was in a group supervised by a teacher who had previously worked with Liubchyk. In the room there were many toys, a bookshelf, two beds, and a large furry cat in an easy chair. "Liubchyk, who is this?" I said. "Musia," he replied. Romanna said, "Musia is our best psychiatrist. Musia senses Liubchyk's moods well and often helps him feel better." We left Liubchyk in his room to explore the presents I had brought, and we went to a more comfortable place for motherly conversation, the kitchen. Romanna made coffee and started telling her story:

> "Liubchyk is our first child. My husband and I waited eagerly for him and were very happy finally to have him. He was an absolutely healthy and beautiful child. He quickly learned to communicate, but things changed rapidly. The problems started when Liubchyk was about 2 years old. For a long time, we couldn't comprehend why it occurred and how we could mend it. The doctors gave us contradictory information. Some said they saw no problem; others said the child was extremely ill and nothing would help. My husband and I made a decision: If there were even one chance, we would fight for it. We didn't 'close up,' to be left alone facing our problem. We started looking for support from around the world—one way or another!
>
> "Our relatives, friends, and friends of friends did everything they could to help. Once someone mentioned a certain school where an

interesting methodology of child care was implemented. Much earlier, even before we saw that there was something wrong with Liubchyk, we had spoken of sending our Liubchyk there. But somehow we forgot about it. When he turned 4 and required an environment of children his age, we visited a specialized kindergarten for children with speech problems. The principal of the kindergarten didn't object, but the teacher and methodologist were apprehensive about our Liubchyk. They said he was not 'one of theirs.'

"The PMPC recommended educating the boy at home. Then we remembered *that* extraordinary school. By then, it had moved to another place and was called Maliuk. The director of this school, Ms. Hrystyna, signed us in, and Liubchyk started to attend the preschool together with other children his age.

"Liubchyk is a very interesting child. He has unique skills. For example, when he was only 2½, I showed him puzzles containing 15 pieces in a frame. He saw the way I was piecing them together and immediately put it together—but in a different way. He would take a piece and place it in a certain spot that later proved to be its exact place. At the age of 5, Liubchyk started telling time by the position of the hands of the clock. He had other skills oriented to space. When I was at work, he would come to me, unmistakably finding the office. He is amused when people lose their bearings. Once his grandmother and I went to the wrong bus. He showed us where we really should go and laughed. When later we sat in the kitchen, we said, 'Do you remember, son, how we almost got on the wrong bus?' He only laughed.

"He also likes mechanical things, especially trains. Thanks to them, he learned to count. Liubchyk keeps a keen eye for things related to time. He counts everything and gets agitated about days until holidays, hours until feeding the animals, the times I am supposed to take my medicine.

"He likes verses very much. He is particularly fond of the book *Journey to Vice Versa Country* by Symonenko. It is a story in verse where things are mixed up. It amuses him very much when I read it to him. He also loves to study the children's encyclopedia. We travel a lot, learning about our land. We have a lot of photographs. Let me show you some. [We paged through several albums of beautiful pictures with views and with smiling and serious faces of the family.]

"We deeply hope that with time everything will be all right. I take him as a normal person, all together, with whom I have a common language—a language I understand completely. However, I also understand that Liubchyk has to become more adapted to life in the future. I think that together we will be able to solve all problems."

Much of what I had learned, Oksana had learned before me. The 2 hours passed quickly. Then Romanna and Liubchyk had to pick up Liubchyk's younger sister from the kindergarten. He himself reminded his mother of it several times. We left the house together and bade each other a warm farewell.

SHANS, A PARENT NGO

Shans was a non-governmental organization established by a group of parents. With the permission of the local education authority, they had established a rehabilitation center called "Health Improvement Center" in Bila Tserkva in Kyiv Oblast. Later they established the NGO called "Shans" at the center. The LEA provided the Center space in a preschool that had been closed. At first, they accepted only children with cerebral palsy but later opened it to children with other disabilities and provided a preschool-type setting. Later, they linked with a primary school so the children could continue their education in the mainstream system.

It is the evening of an April day (2004) when I (Natalia Sofiy) arrive at the Health Improvement Center. It is my first visit although I have long been acquainted with Volodymyr Kryzhanivskiy, the director of the center, and his deputy for education, Tamara Lutsenko. We had been drawn together by our common work with children having special needs, helping them get to mainstream classrooms. We had worked on many projects together.

I am hurrying to find the center. The time of the center's board meeting is getting close and I want to take photographs. I approach a typical two-story kindergarten building, surrounded by a courtyard, with trees and grass already turning green. Clearly, spring is coming. On an asphalt walk are two children, a boy and a girl in her wheelchair, between the ages of 9 and 10 years. I call to them and ask where to find the entrance to the center. The boy explains that I should pass the center and find a dark blue gate. Soon I see that gate, and behind it was Tamara, approaching to meet me. We greet each other, and Tamara hastens to take me to Mr. Volodymyr. They have both just returned from Kharkiv for the board meeting which is to be at 2:00. Inside the center, I see its bright and clean spaces, which seem especially bright and clean because of the sunny day, and probably because the center is soon going to be visited by the Commission of the Cabinet of the Supreme Rada—or simply because that is the way it is. In the corridor are wheelchairs, but no children. "Our children have just gone with their teachers for classes," Tamara says, as if having read my mind.

We reach the study of Mr. Volodymyr, who cheerfully greets us and presents Mr. Valery, the manager of the center. Volodymyr asks what I want to do. I say I would like to interview him and Tamara, and I ask permission to attend the board meeting. I take the opportunity to give them the newsletters of the International Step by Step Association and a copy of the *Step by Step Program and Teacher Standards*—publications Tamara had asked about. Volodymyr agrees and suggests that we go to one of the activity areas of the center for the interview.

Interview with Mr. Volodymyr and Ms. Tamara

The interview with Volodymyr Kryzhanivskiy, director of the health improvement center Shans, and Tamara Lutsenko, the deputy director for education, follows.

MS. NATALIA: Volodymyr, please tell me about the Belotserkivske Society for Children with Special Needs and Their Parents. When was it created, and what was the reason for its creation?

MR. VOLODYMYR: Our organization was founded in February 1995, but of course it was not created in a day. Many events came earlier. Before the Soviet Union collapsed, parents of children with special needs, like myself, had an opportunity to go for treatment wherever they liked. After the collapse, the opportunities diminished. In 1993, I saw a TV program about a new way of treating children with cerebral palsy, using special suits. As you know, when parents hear something new they immediately want it, and I am one of those. So I went to Moscow and talked with Professor Semenova, the creator of this method. But I could not afford to send my child there for the treatment. It would have been expensive, even though we had relatives with whom we could stay.

One of the ideas Semenova told me about was of parents establishing Hospital 18 in Moscow. She advised me to establish something similar in Ukraine. I did not think then of an organization. I took the documents about her method, came home, and met with the director of the City Health Department. She told me that it would be possible to create such a center as one of the branches of a children's hospital, which at that time was under construction. My desire was to create a center, not an NGO. But time passed and nothing happened. I went to the executive committee, where I was told, "If you want to make something happen, first establish an NGO. An NGO has more legal power and more opportunities." I met with the heads of all the NGOs in Bila Tserkva: the Children's Fund; the NGO for disabled persons, Phoenix; the Red Cross. I thought the existing organizations could take on this responsibility. However, each of them had their own directions of work, and they did not want to draw energy away from them. So I went out to gather parents. There were not so many, maybe 15 persons. And we all said, "Let's do something!"

MS. NATALIA: How did you locate the other parents?

MR. VOLODYMYR: Through NGOs. At the Children's Hospital Department of Statistics, all children with cerebral palsy up to the age of 14 are registered. It is confidential information, but I got it. Working in this hospital is a neurologist friend of mine, whose son has cerebral palsy. She helped me. Then I called the parents. The parents have supported me since 1994. In February 1995, we held an assembly. By then there were close to 40 parents. We organized around the statutes of Phoenix.

MS. NATALIA: So the prime reason for the association of parents was the continuing need for treatment?

MR. VOLODYMYR: Yes. For example, if a child does not move, that child could be cured, and she could be taken care of, and go to school on her own. The primary aim was to cure a child. However, at that time, I had no ideas about any organizations. I did not see what the tasks of our center could be, nor from where funding could come.

MS. NATALIA: What is your background?

MR. VOLODYMYR: An engineer. Later I met Tamara. We demanded that the city council make a decision about opening our center. We met with the parent organization Dzherelo, from Lviv. They had already begun their activity. We went to Lviv, to learn their experience. We came to the conclusion that we cannot resolve this question simply from a medical point of view. It is a complex problem and needs a complex approach. As a model, we took Lviv's Dzherelo, but with our own approach.

MS. NATALIA: And what was the difference?

MR. VOLODYMYR: The difference was that they had powerful sponsors from Canada. We had to rely on our own resources. I think it was the right step, because now we have more guaranteed funding.

MS. NATALIA: What about other differences?

MR. VOLODYMYR: The specificity of work of the center is also different. A child when born may have a special need, which is not always obvious. We emphasized early diagnosis and intervention. A child should be diagnosed early so as not to miss the right moment. We have ways that help determine this disease from the very beginning. One uniqueness of our center is that we render services not only to the children who visit the center, but also to newborns.

MS. TAMARA: From the pedagogical standpoint, we differ from the Lviv Center in that we set educational standards. At the very first, we made a strong request of the local education authorities that our children be involved with the children of a certain school, and with teachers who will abide by state curricular standards in a framework of individualized instruction. We already have two graduates. Andrey Tkachenko continues his training at PTU [a technical training college]. Unfortunately, because of the state of her health, Galja cannot continue in school, but she has the certificate of incomplete secondary education.

MS. NATALIA: So you chose to teach using individualized programs at home, didn't you?

MS. TAMARA: We chose that way, having no dependable idea how else it could be done. In 1995 we founded the organization, and in 1996 we established the center. And then we had to set up a link with Education. Thanks to the Department of Education and the city administration, we got authorized to provide training to teachers of primary classes in their free time. These were teachers working in our center, being paid by the state. The children were officially enrolled in school. However, when our children grew older, we faced the problem of preparation for the subject-matter system. For just five children, we could not employ teachers of physics, chemistry, biology, and so on. As our children passed to the fifth grade (a part of middle school) the teachers of the school where our children had been placed started to visit our center to get training. However, now we have changed premises, so we cooperate with School 20, which is nearby. Since November of this school year, we have been bringing children to this school for their lessons.

MR. VOLODYMYR: We are speaking about integrated training, inclusive schooling. Since 1996, we have been acquainted with the activity of the Ukrainian Step by Step Foundation. We became convinced that such training is optimal for our children. It is the best form of training. First, we observed a big difference between training of children at home and in the center. The overwhelming advantage was that children learned to communicate better while studying at the center.

Ms. TAMARA: We saw all the advantages and all the restrictions of [doing the] training at the center. The advantage of the center was that children had started to communicate socially here, with words and gestures. Those children had different levels of special need, but they all had clever eyes looking at the world and perceiving it. But we also understood that we cannot do it all within the center. For example, the teacher of physics cannot bring all equipment necessary for experiments to the center; the teacher of chemistry will not bring the reagents; the teacher of biology will not create a herbarium; and so forth. We want to thank the collectives of Schools 5 and 20 for creating the conditions for inclusion of our children in the schools. The regular pupils of these schools had the opportunity to come to our center and to communicate with our children. The children worked on computers; they drew together. A children's community formed. Integration occurred rather easily. The teachers were ready; so were the children and the parents of the healthy children. There was no rejection of our children. The teachers report that this condition exists in their classrooms: If the healthy children have completed their assignment, they are allowed to work with the child from the rehabilitation center!

Ms. NATALIA: And do you recall the first children going to a mainstream school from the center? What were their emotions?

MR. VOLODYMYR: As for the children going to school, we don't have any problems. The problems occur when children come from home to the center. They are not included immediately into the collective. They do not know yet how to behave. One boy from Fastiv was intelligent enough, and he went into the preschool group. There was a special celebration. He rushed from his place, not knowing how to behave. After their experience at the center, the children go to a regular school without apparent anxiety. Probably inside themselves there is a little worry, but from the outside it can't be seen.

Ms. TAMARA: But they get prepared here for school. Our children have rituals at the first and last bells, and larger celebrations. We are always invited. The senior pupils help get our children to the assembly hall. The problems are with the parents. Parents differently perceive the levels of development and abilities of the children. We try to convince them that it is best for them to send them to school.

Ms. NATALIA: That means the parents did not want their children to attend a mainstream school?

MR. VOLODYMYR: They were afraid. Some parents felt that their children would be lost in a regular school. Some parents were afraid to have their children exposed: "People will point fingers at my child." It was a stage at which they wanted to hide the children and not to show it. The children were persuading the parents, saying, "Daddy, Mummy, I want to go to a regular school." Because children were ready for that, they communicated with other children.

MS. NATALIA: Tell me, please, at the very beginning of the center, did you group parents according to diagnosis of the child? And do you now?

MS. TAMARA: We cannot be limited to the category of children with cerebral palsy. We now work with parents whose children have epilepsy and Down's syndrome. These children belong to "nowhere." So we made changes in our charter, and now we accept all children. A reason for not having two or three centers in one city is to better accumulate human and other resources at one place.

We had to stop at this point. It was time for the board meeting.

Board Meeting of the Center

The board meeting of Shans took place in one of the conference spaces of the center.

At the table are the nine members of the board; six mothers of children with special needs; and Tamara, Volodymyr, and Valery. On the table are cups, cookies, and coffee. Mr. Volodymyr notices that "somehow you are not so cheerful today." "We do not have enough time," someone replies. "But this is great," says Volodymyr, "It means that we are doing something!" After election of a secretary, Volodymyr identifies issues he hopes they will discuss:

- Training that has taken place.
- The organization of "Khodoton."
- The organization of a children's trip to Poland.
- Other.

Ms. Valia, supervisor of the senior youth, reports first on training. Briefly, she tells about training for the development of leadership skills that has been carried out for the children. She notes that parents, as well as 13 children of the center, took part in the training. Ms. Valia says, "Some of the trainers were puzzled at meeting such an audience, though it told them much about the children."

Ms. Marina, a young mother sitting beside her, says, "Children with cerebral palsy have a different way of thinking. It is necessary to specially prepare trainers to work with such children." Marina smiles cheerfully, saying, "The younger children were so active!"

Ms. Valia continues to speak about training that occurred recently, including some by Swedish trainers (in which, Valia remarks sadly, only five parents took part). Ms. Ljuda, another mother who took part in that training, says that she came to the conclusion concerning her own daughter Anyuta, "It is impossible to keep them from achieving." "So this is very good," Ms. Olga says in a loud voice, "but did the trainers offer any particular techniques for work with such children?" "Certainly," Valia says, and speaks of concrete ways of training children with mental needs how to use public transport, and to do other things.

Ms. Marina comments, "We have to give more attention to developing the habits of self-service. We should enable a child to learn household things—how to cut, how to use the phone, things like that." Marina recalls the last trip to Germany, where they saw children with mental needs taken shopping, in order to buy products to prepare dinner themselves. Then together they decided on a menu, prepared it, and had dinner together. Marina adds, "We need also to equip the center with a household room where we teach children household habits."

Ms. LJUDA: So, we parents strongly want to "hypercare." I understand it. I struggle with it. I go to a neighbor and sit there for 30 minutes, with my child being left at home.

Ms. MARINA: . . . I had no alternative with my child on crutches. I said, "If he wants to survive, he will survive!" In fact, I need to earn my living! I was leaving him with my small daughter, 18-month-old Dimka. But I knew that my daughter is responsible!

The mums started exchanging similar experiences, but other people said, "Talk faster. Time flies!" Volodymyr sought a summation: "So let us see if we agree. We continue the training. We work with the trainers and the parents to get parents to participate more actively." Tamara then spoke about training for the development of lobbying skills, which was planned for May as participation in Step by Step training.

MR. VOLODYMYR: Let's talk about the visit of the Committee of the Supreme Rada, scheduled to take place on May 17–22. This visit can be very important for the center. The Supreme Rada sets the budget. It is important to identify all our needs right now. And some other organizations have started to show interest in us.

Recently, representatives of the Women's Club came here. They would like to help us too. We need to do a lot of work in the center, but it is so hard, for some reason, to involve parents in that!

MS. IRA: Let's give the parents a choice, a choice of days, to work for the May holidays, or to compensate in money so we could employ someone else. Let's call them all and ask once again.

MS. MARINA: That is correct, but it all depends on having a database! We need to finish it!

MR. VOLODYMYR: We shall speak about that, but now let's come back to the first question. Let us listen to Mr. Valery, who took part in two training sessions. One was training on the removal of barriers, and the second training was on the issues of fund raising.

MR. VALERY: The Lviv people have developed a technique of auditing availability, which can be used by us in Bila Tserkva.

MS. MARINA: What are we talking about? We do not even have toilets in the public spaces!

MR. VOLODYMYR: I have an idea about the removal of barriers. I recently met Tanya Manilova, who uses a wheelchair. She can talk about barriers. Such a committee is being created in the city. It should include one representative from the NGOs. Tanya could join this committee. In this city, the situation is critical. For the whole city, there are only two traffic lights with a sound signal!

MR. VALERY: Concerning the fund-raising training. It was led by experts from the United States, using the American experience. In many ways, this experience is inappropriate for us with a different economy and laws, but for myself I have drawn this conclusion: If the administration worries about such people, it can be trusted. Another conclusion I have drawn: In the United States, it looks like they have adopted our experience of creating young pioneer organizations. I have in mind the experience of volunteers. Up to 70% of the young people take part in such programs, but we, unfortunately, have lost it. In addition, this phrase comes from an American trainer: "A revolution is likely to begin with a few not indifferent patriots." What is the result of our participation in this training program? We are now preparing two projects. The first project is to create a mechanism of cooperation among businesses, the administration, and NGOs to resolve social issues. The project provides for creation of a model of cooperation among these three sectors, making it possible to define common problems and to unite efforts and resources for the resolving of these problems. The second project provides Internet support for the exchange of experience and information. But certainly, first of all, we need to have a computer and access to the Internet.

At this point, a 20-year-old woman appears at the door and asks, "Who is Olja?" "I am Olja," one of the mums answers. Olja cheerily tells the others, "She is a new member, a mother whom I have recently met. Please have a seat with us. Listen, we will finish soon, and then we can speak with you." The mother joins the group and listens to the conversation, which turns to the list of children for the trip to Poland for the Sport Games. Again, there is a question about the creation of a database, the absence of which is complicating arrangements. People are now hurrying a little. The session has already lasted nearly an hour.

MR. VOLODYMYR: And, on the last item, what shall we do with Khodoton? Shall we organize it this year or not? I do understand that we are in a hurry, but let us resolve this question essentially, and if "yes," we shall consider this question in more detail at the next board meeting.

MS. MARINA: I think it is necessary to do it! Last year, one mum of a 16-year-old boy with cerebral palsy said that her son was waiting for this event for the whole year. For some children, it is the only chance to go into the street and to be with other people!

They agreed about the date of the next board meeting. Ms. Marina was very upset that she could not be present, but the others said, "One missed meeting is not the end of the world!" Ms. Tamara went to talk with the young mother.

NATIONAL CONTEXT

In 2002, the number of children with disabilities in Ukraine of school age (6–17 years) was about 110,000 (according to different sources). The existing system of special schools provided for the needs of only 20% of these children. The children with special needs who received formal education fell into the following groups:

- About 7,200 (about 7%) were enrolled in special classrooms at regular (ordinary) schools, with about 500 regular school teachers working with them.
- About 60,500 children with disabilities (55%) were enrolled at 393 special schools ("internats") of different types, with about 10,900 special teachers ("defectologists") working with them.
- About 40,000 (35%) were enrolled in regular classrooms in regular

schools, most without adequate correction and rehabilitation assistance. The majority of these children had mental retardation and psychological delays.

No information could be found on the number of children with disabilities who did not receive any formal education in Ukraine. It was supposed that the majority of school age children with disabilities were receiving some formal education. There were 16,000 children with disabilities in 179 compensatory kindergartens, and 60,000 children with disabilities attending special classrooms in 1,400 regular kindergartens. This provided a starting point for their integration into mainstream education. It was a unique feature of the special education system in Ukraine's preschool education.

Legislation

No Ukrainian legislation provided direct support of inclusive education. Only recently had the need for inclusion of children with disabilities begun to draw public attention. The *National Doctrine of Education Development in Ukraine in Century XXI* provided perspectives on the development of all forms of education for children with disabilities, including the inclusion option. Equal access for these children and youth to a high-quality education was declared one of the priorities in the *National Doctrine*. In the section *Equal Access to Quality Education*, there was a part devoted to the education of children with special needs, with the following principles declared:

- Accessible, free education for children with disabilities.
- Identification and diagnosis of children with disabilities.
- Different forms of education for children with disabilities.
- Development of support systems for parents.
- Development of a network of educational–rehabilitation centers.

Among the main state policy documents confirming the right of education for all were the following:

- The Constitution of Ukraine (adopted June 28, 1996), Article 53: "Everyone has a right to education. General comprehensive education is obligatory." This article also requires the state to provide free and accessible education at all levels: preschool, primary, secondary, and higher education.

- The Ukrainian law *On Education* (adopted June 4, 1991), especially Article 51, *On the Rights of Students*, and Article 60, *On the Rights of Parents*. Here it is declared that students and parents of children under 17 years of age have the right to choose their educational establishment.
- The state national program *Education/Ukraine in Century XXI* (adopted in 1991), within its *Priorities of the Secondary Education Reforms*, calling for the "improvement of education for children with special needs at different kinds of educational establishments."
- The Ukrainian law *On Comprehensive Secondary Education* (1999), which guarantees secondary education for all children and recognizes both group and individual instruction. As for the education of children with special needs, the law identifies the Psychological–Medical–Pedagogic Consultations (PMPCs, mentioned earlier in the section "A Press Conference in Lviv") as in charge of assigning children to regular or special educational settings.

There were also several instructions of the Ministry of Education and Science of Ukraine and regional educational authorities for conducting experimental studies on aspects of inclusive education of children with disabilities. Recently the work on development of a package of necessary legislative documents was started (*Document on Inclusive Classrooms*, *Document on Inclusive Schools*, etc.)

Treatment of Children with Disabilities

One could not find a child with a disability anywhere in the regular schools in Ukraine during the Soviet period. The fate of these children was simply either to remain at home with the parents or to be sent to the "internats" (a term used for various types of boarding schools for orphaned children or children with disabilities, where they lived and received basic education and vocational training), which was often recommended to the parents as soon as a child was diagnosed as "defective." Those infants given up by their parents under pressure from the professionals went to orphanages that were under the administration of the Ministry of Health and Social Security. They housed children from birth to 4 years of age. The fact that even in 1999, 38 of the 45 orphanages in Ukraine were specialized for children with disabilities of various types was evidence of the continuing propensity of parental abandonment of these children (*State Report on the Condition of Children in Ukraine*, 1999). Despite the name "specialized orphanages," little early special development care was provided to infants or very young children with disabilities. A physical therapist described her visit to a special internat:

> "Children with cerebral palsy were severely disabled, all lying in one big crib. You'd have four or five children lying together. That's what they do. They live there, so they just lie there. You can imagine, the more severely disabled kids. By 4 years old, they probably died. There was no nurturing."

At the age of 4, all children were (and still are) evaluated by a team of specialists for determinating placement. Orphaned children without disabilities got transferred to a regular school internat. Two other types of internats were options: (1) special schools for those deemed educable (children with deafness or other hearing impairments, blind or other visual impairments, severe speech deficits, problems in motor development, orthopedic disabilities, or mild intellectual delays) under the auspices of the Ministry of Education and Science; or (2) social services internats for children deemed uneducable (children with severe intellectual delays, severe mental retardation, or multiple disabilities), under the auspices of the Ministry of Health and Social Security.

The children remaining in the care of their parents through the preschool years were, at age 6, evaluated by the Psychological–Medical–Pedagogic Consultations regarding their overall development. The first diagnosis and determination of where a particular child was to receive his or her education were made then.

In the Soviet Union, where standardized intelligence testing was completely rejected and not available to psychologists and teachers, children were assessed for the presence of a disability through a clinical diagnostic procedure. The diagnostic teams Psychological–Medical–Pedagogic Consultations were generally composed of a psychoneurologist, teachers, a speech therapist, and an administrator of a special school. The PMPC's job was to establish the organic etiology of the disability through qualitative means. Because of the lack of normed references for developmental indices, each professional had to rely on his or her clinical experience in making decisions on disability. Although there are errors in all measurement, this kind of assessment easily allowed personal bias and human error. A parent of a child with cerebral palsy described her experience with this evaluation process:

> "No one introduces themselves. I am at this commission. I came in. There is a bunch of people by the table. Who is who, I have no clue.

They take my child. We went recently . . . obviously I don't know anything, I'm confused . . . and the child . . . what can you say? Besides, he gets scared. He doesn't say anything to anybody. They ask him this question: 'What is the weather today?' It's sunny outside; the sun is bright; there are clouds, like today—but very cold. Yarik says, 'Cold.' And they go, 'Oh, Yarik, how could it be cold? Look, the sun is shining, the sky is clear,' and he says, 'It's cold.' So they want to get him to say that it is spring now, May, warm . . . as it should be. And they ask what the weather is like; he answers, 'Cold.' Maybe he should say, 'It's bright.' Then they start asking the seasons. They ask, 'Do you know the seasons?' He says, 'Yes,' and lists them in order. 'What season comes after autumn?' He answers. 'What about before autumn?' He doesn't answer that. That's it. And when you show him some shapes . . . he is stiff . . . he determines the shapes, but he cannot place them properly. He puts one out, then brushes it off with his elbow. I know that he knows it. But they don't care about it. And this takes exactly 2 minutes. That's it. 'Mom, we are setting up the specialized school for you. Your child . . .' —they said 'retard' or something like that, and 'Go outside and wait for the documents.' That is the whole conversation."

During the Soviet period, such a diagnosis was usually final. The higher-level PMPCs would support the lower-level ones. One parent described the typical response of the zone PMPCs when parents, unsatisfied with the diagnosis and unwilling to send their child "300 kilometers away from our house into some jail," came to request reevaluation: "There is no reason for reevaluation. The diagnosis is correct."

In general, both during the Soviet period and today, childhood disabilities in Ukraine were classified into eight categories: deafness, impaired hearing, blindness, impaired sight, impaired speech, delayed psychological development (emotional disturbance? autism?), intellectual delays, and physical disabilities. Great attention was given to the origins of disability and classification of children according to etiology. The organic etiology of the disability was important, because each separate category of disability meant, to a Soviet defectologist, a unique personality development of children and the need for methods of instruction specially tailored to the defect. This concept led to the development of separate schools for each category of disability with its own standard curriculum, as well as to the training of teachers in special methods of instruction at Departments of Defectology at the major pedagogical institutes in Ukraine. "Defectology" was the Soviet discipline that studied the development of children with disabilities. The educational research in this field was the development of special program content for children with a specific disability type. In addition, textbooks were developed for children, as well as methods books for the teachers who would work with them in the internats.

During the Soviet period, everything revolved around trying to prove to the world that the Soviet Union was a real "superpower." This needed to be instilled in the minds of the citizens. The educational system served as a method of ideological inculcation. Teachers taught what was dictated by the Communist Party. In a sense, this made the teaching job easier: Teachers did not have to think themselves, or prompt the students to think, evaluate, and critique. Moreover, there were several positive things the Soviet Union brought to its republics. Raising the education level of the people was one of them. Standards were set by the government for all students to meet. The national curriculum, with corresponding texts for each subject, was developed and approved by the central government. The goal of the Soviet system—to bring at least a minimum education to all citizens—was admirable. However, a single, blanket curriculum and one set of standards for all led to uniformity as a norm. It also led to exclusion of those who could not live up to the standard, particularly children with disabilities. They were pushed out of the regular schools on the principle that they would distract the teachers from instructing the other students. These children were ignored and avoided, and often forgotten by the internat staff, the general population, and sometimes the parents themselves.

As with any system, the internat system had negative and positive aspects. One overwhelming problem of Ukrainian society, then and now, was the economic struggle of the high majority of its citizens. Families having children with disabilities were under even more stress and financial burden than others. A positive aspect was that these families had a way to alleviate some of their financial stress by delivering their children, some of whom they were not able to care for adequately, into the care of the government. This was especially true for people in rural villages. The professional expertise was to be concentrated in the special institutions where the children could receive appropriate help.

Unfortunately, the special internats were closed institutions. They could not be freely visited, even by parents. Most of the time, the children came home on weekends if the internat was in the parents' city of residence. Rural parents visited the children a few times a year.

On the other hand, refusing to give up a child into the internat system meant that parents were sentencing their children to home imprisonment. Due to myths about disability and the shame parents felt, they sometimes kept their children hidden at home. These myths included notions that children with disabilities were born only to parents who abused alcohol and other drugs. Sending disabled children into special internats or keeping them at home served the same purpose—isolation from society.

The fact that these children were hidden from view promoted ignorance and perpetuated myths about disability. From the Soviet time and continuing into the present, signs in public transportation announce: "These seats are reserved for invalids, elderly persons, and passengers with children." Nothing was constructed for assisting an individual in a wheelchair. There were no people with disabilities in the subways or on any public transportation. An illusion was created that the government would be caring for and accommodating the needs of disabled persons—if, indeed, such persons existed at all.

During one of our interviews, a regular school principal observed:

> "We were quiet about this much too long. We were trying to look like we didn't have this problem. For a long time, nobody talked about it. There were special kindergartens, special schools, where those children were. They were isolated from society. Society was not interested in disability. The government allocated money for it and dealt with it."

The separation and isolation of children with disabilities was damaging to the families, as one parent noted:

> "The knowledge that my child is away somewhere in the internat puts a barrier between the parents of healthy children and the parents of children with disabilities. . . . A difference is felt. The parent feels not only his child's disability, but his own too. And the feelings of guilt."

One mother of a child with cerebral palsy described the traumatic impact on her of learning about her son's disability: She spent the next 2 years in depression, too ashamed to leave her apartment.

The society's ignorance of issues of disability was directly linked to the politics of the country. A physical therapist expressed her views:

> "The Soviet Union always was a perfect country. They never permitted imperfection. If children were imperfections, they were hidden in the internats or at home."

However, by closing their eyes, by being unconscious of the existence and the needs of children with disabilities, the country itself became disabled—blind and deaf to the voices of those who live in it, who are also its citizens.

As a result of these exclusionary practices, the training of the specialists was very limited. Impaired, too, were other professionals—the psychologists, physical therapists, and social pedagogues who might have identified, diagnosed, and provided high-quality assistance to the individuals with special needs; the teachers who might have helped them to acquire functional and academic skills and to be included in the life of the society. During an interview, a group of physical therapists and special education teachers in a new rehabilitation center commented on their training: "They did not introduce us to a single serious speech problem, because 'You will not see this anywhere anyway!' " Physical therapy, special education, social work, and occupational therapy began to appear as real professions only after the fall of the Soviet Union. "During the Soviet Union, we didn't have invalids. As soon as we became independent, we got people with disabilities." As a consequence, there were people trained to work with specific types of disabilities in separate institutions, but a great dearth of professionals skilled in promoting the integration of people with disabilities into society.

Providing separate special schools for children with disabilities was driven by good intentions. But, on the whole, separating children with disabilities from their families and peers and sending them to special schools caused more damage than good to the Ukrainian society. It created myths about disabilities and fears of those who had them. It put a simplistic, demeaning label on a child with a disability, as well as the family. "To mend these injuries will take a long time and a great effort, but it has begun in Ukraine."

Interview with Victor Ogneviuk

It took me (Natalia Sofiy) a long time to obtain a meeting with Victor Ogneviuk, the vice-minister of the Ukraine Ministry of Education and Science—almost 2 months. The circumstances changed every time, and I almost gave up. It was at a time of many religious holidays (Easter, then Trinity), as well as two national holidays, May Day (May 1) and Victory Day (May 9). And people were hard pressed to do all their regular work. In addition, the building of the Ministry of Education and Science was being renovated, which caused additional problems: difficulty in reaching persons by phone, moving to other rooms, and so on. I got permission to do the interview, but the problem was to get a specific date and time. Finally, after Trinity, I was told it would be better just to come to the

Ministry and try to catch Mr. Ogneviuk. The first time wasn't successful. When I went the next afternoon, I expected to fail again, but I decided, "I will just keep going until I get in." However, he was there this time and agreed to meet with me. He was not in his own office because of the renovation; he and his secretary were in the same room. I introduced myself and reminded him of our agreement. Mr. Ogneviuk said, "Yes, I remember, and I will answer your questions with pleasure, but unfortunately I have very little time."

I asked Mr. Ogneviuk this question:

> "Mr. Ogneviuk, in 2001 you signed an instruction to start a pedagogical experiment, *Social Adaptation and Integration of Children with Special Needs into Regular Classrooms*. It was initiated by the Ukrainian Step by Step Foundation, together with the Institute of Special Pedagogy of the Academy of Pedagogical Sciences of Ukraine. What factors influenced your decision at that time?"

Mr. Ogneviuk replied:

> "It is not easy to recall what I felt at the exact moment of signing the document. In my mind, it is absolutely wrong when, using specialized boarding schools or other institutions, we create reservations for children, preventing them from seeing life in all of its forms, manifestations, complexity, and so forth. And this is true not only for children with disabilities. The healthy children have to see that within human society, alongside the healthy ones with able minds, hands, and legs, live children who require their help and compassion. Understanding this problem should become a motivating factor for us.
>
> "You are not unaware that 20 years ago we had an ideal of the 'harmonized, developed personality.' It suggested that people with deficiencies were to be considered inferior. It applied a totally different attitude to them. Today we must understand that we have to resist this ill mentality. We must be governed by humanistic values of a completely different sort. We can't measure everything with a single yardstick and should refrain from absolutisms. The idea of the all-round developed man itself seems to be a good one; however, with that in mind, the society had to conceal those who bore deficiencies.
>
> "They did exist somewhere. They even received some help, and some of the disabled had even a better life then than they do today. It would be true to say that this problem was unknown for most of

the population, hidden from concrete individuals. That is the reason why today when a child who requires specialized help enters a regular class, some parents raise a question, 'How come? Why is a child requiring special help studying with my child?' The community has stereotypes that have to be challenged.

"Today, it is not uncommon for these individuals to join classes in regular schools. However, we have yet to complete a tall order: preparing teaching and mentoring personnel, equipping learning facilities. All the schools were built in such a way that it was made impossible for an exceptional child to enter them without help of others. The schools are not accommodated for these children, and colleges are not either. However, gradually, the situation is improving.

"At the moment, by instruction of the Cabinet of Ministers, a program is being developed with the aim of accommodating the students with special needs in regular schools, colleges, and universities. It envisages inclusion where possible. We have to keep in mind a different situation—when such measures will require special equipment or some extraordinary conditions to provide the required learning environment. It is impossible to educate some children with cerebral palsy in regular schools. On the other hand, there are different forms of this disease, and for some cases we are able to create adjusted conditions. These children require special physical exercise, massage, and other correctional activities.

"The idea of having teacher assistants is thoughtful, even for regular schools, since children differ in their nature and in the quality of their perception. In certain cases, a child requires individual attention, and this is where the teacher assistant can help. The idea is wonderful. Unfortunately, financial difficulties stop it from being implemented. Possibly one day this dream will come true.

"Costwise, it is cheaper to educate a child in a regular school than in a specialized one. The only problem is that today we cannot guarantee that the required conditions will be provided for every school, because of the same infamous impediment, the lack of funds.

"We must admit that it is impossible to do without the boarding schools, for we have orphaned children without families or custodians. There are still many unwanted children, especially the victims of AIDS and other diseases. Some boarding schools will remain active. But it is our preference to have most physically impaired children attend the regular schools, giving them the opportunity to experience the life of the society.

"Today, the most important issue is preparation of a new generation of teachers capable of helping children with special needs. Without well-prepared teachers and mentors, our talk is in vain."

Interview with Vyatcheslav Zasenko

I (Svitlana Efimova) conducted an interview with Vyatcheslav Zasenko, deputy director of the Institute of Special Pedagogy, Academy of Pedagogical Sciences of Ukraine.

MS. SVITLANA: As you know, Dr. Alla Kolupayeva carried out a survey among teachers in mainstreaming schools and those in specialized schools to identify their views of the inclusion of children with special needs in conventional schools. The results of this survey showed that 57% of the regular school teachers and only 10% of the specialist teachers supported inclusion. Can you comment on this?

MR. ZASENKO: The representatives of specialized institutions foresee the threat of competition from an inclusive model for exceptional children. In addition, the specialist teachers are of the opinion that the mainstream schools are not capable of providing a correctional program for the children with special needs.

Teachers from mainstream schools, on the other hand, base their argument on their current practice. Many have already been working with children with special needs. They claim that the methods they are using are quite adequate for effective development and social adaptation of children with exceptional needs. At the same time, some of them realize the complexity of this work and acknowledge that they lack some of the appropriate skills. The training of specialized teachers to implement inclusion is still in its infancy. An attitude factor is also very important. It is inherent in Ukrainian culture to be sympathetic toward pupils with special needs.

MS. SVITLANA: What is your opinion of any existing competition between specialized institutions and schools practicing inclusion?

MR. ZASENKO: Competition can exist only as a subjective feeling, because, objectively, competition simply does not exist. Inclusion is not in any way aimed at getting rid of the specialized education system. There is a wide range of reasons for this. The most important one is that some categories of children with certain types of physical/psychological developmental deficiencies are unable to be students in the mainstream schools, due to their health condition or their specific behavior. Inclusive education can only exist in combination with specialized education, opening up opportunities for children with special needs and satisfying their constitutional right of equal access to quality education. It is important to develop public awareness of the issue, since collisions of polarized points of view are commonplace. In our opinion, inclusive education should not involve 100% of the children with special needs. Nor should all children be placed in specialized institutions. A compromise is needed. With time, the proportion of children in inclusive education will increase.

THE UKRAINIAN STEP BY STEP FOUNDATION

The Ukrainian Step by Step Foundation (abbreviated in this section as USSF) is an NGO established in Ukraine in 1999. At this writing, USSF is an active network of 182 kindergartens, 164 schools, and 33 higher pedagogical institutions in 17 oblasts across Ukraine. The mission of USSF is to serve the educational system of Ukraine, primarily by promoting open society values:

- Equal access to high-quality education for all children.
- Strong family involvement.
- Community participation to help every child reach his or her full potential.
- School improvement operationalized as a center of community development and change agentry.

The mission is pursued, first, by providing training for preschool, primary, and secondary school teachers, as well as for pedagogical university teachers, school administrators, parents, and NGOs; second, by lobbying and advocacy practices; and third, by research and development of educational materials.

Within the framework of reforming processes in the educational system of Ukraine, the mission of USSF is pursued through the following programs:

- Teacher-Training Program.
- Inclusion of Children with Disabilities.
- Education of Minorities.
- Community School Development Program.
- Publishing Program.
- Development of Model Centers for Inclusive Education

Brief History

USSF was established to extend the sustainability of Step by Step activities and to collaborate in efforts toward democratization and rebuilding of the civic society in Ukraine.

1994

The Step by Step project started as a regional project of the International Renaissance Foundation (also known as the National Soros Foundation), with the support of the Open Society Institute (NY, USA) and Children's Resources International (Washington, DC). Since 1994, the Step by Step Project has been involved in transforming the preschool curriculum to provide children education for active participation in humanistic social changes and democracy.

1996

Based on positive findings from evaluation of the impact of the preschool Step by Step methodology on children's development as fulfilling the requirements of parents and teachers, Step by Step was extended to the primary level and to kindergartens in additional oblasts of Ukraine.

With an ultimate goal of transforming the process and content of teacher training, specialized courses based on Step by Step methods were developed and included in the curricula of pedagogical institutes for training both new and experienced teachers. A network of training centers was established across Ukraine to reach all Step by Step educational establishments. At the centers, training and opportunities for supervised practice in classrooms continue to be provided.

Based on core Step by Step principles (especially individualized teaching, developmentally appropriate practices, and parent involvement), a new initiative, *Inclusion of Children with Disabilities into the Regular Schools*, was introduced to the schools using the Step by Step methodology.

1999

After a 3-year transitional period, the Step by Step project in Ukraine established itself as independent from the International Renaissance Foundation, and became the Ukrainian Step by Step Foundation.

2000

Both preschool and primary Step by Step methodologies were approved by the Ministry of Education and Science of Ukraine, authorizing them for choice by any kindergarten or primary school in Ukraine.

After positive evaluation of the primary Step by Step methodology by the Ministry of Education and Science of Ukraine and the Institute of Psychology of the Academy of Pedagogical Sciences of Ukraine, the Step by Step methodology was authorized for use at the secondary school level.

2001

To support the work of teachers in the inclusion of children with disabilities in regular classrooms, and to lobby for corresponding changes in educational policy, USSF further developed its experimental pedagogical program, *Inclusion of Children with Disabilities into Regular School*, jointly with the Ministry of Education and Science and the Institute of Special Pedagogy. The experiment was now to be conducted over 6 years in 27 schools in seven oblasts in Ukraine.

2003

USSF designed and implemented the *Community School Development Program*, which aimed to have the school improvement process serve as change agentry for community development and community education.

USSF also designed and implemented the project *Creating Centres of Excellence*, in partnership with the International Step by Step Association (NL) and the EveryChild Organization (UK), and with the support of the TACIS Program of the European Commission.

USSF was accredited by the Ministry of Education and Science of Ukraine to provide courses for preschool, primary, and secondary teachers, as well as school administrators and university teachers, in the specialization of innovative education. This provided additional motivation for teachers to choose the Step by Step courses as staff development for official consideration in the teacher attestation process.

Capacity of the Ukrainian Step by Step Foundation

USSF is an organization with "all-Ukrainian" status. This means that it is officially represented across the country—specifically, in 17 oblasts, more than half of the oblasts in Ukraine. With the support of membership fees,

USSF publishes and sends a newsletter for all members and other stake-holders. In 2003 (noted above), USSF was licensed by the Ministry of Education and Science to provide in-service courses for preschool, primary, and secondary teachers, as well as school directors and university faculty members, in the field of innovative education. This means that Ukrainian teachers facing attestation (required by the state every 5 years) and needing to complete education courses (also a requirement) can choose USSF courses. USSF provides a team of trainers at or near the training centers, allowing convenient access.

The Ministry of Education and Science and Other Partners

In order to consolidate efforts and to be more efficient in accomplishing its mission, USSF develops partnerships with various governmental organizations and NGOs, at the local, national, and international levels.

1. In general, partnership with the state educational authorities is pursued through offers of consultative support (round table discussion is an example) and joint activities (using joint resources and efforts, and making joint decisions).

   • The Ministry of Education of Ukraine is an important partner of the USSF. All educational innovations introduced in the country need the Ministry's approval. The Ministry's provides support for USSF's activities by developing and adopting instruction, which provides a legitimizing status for USSF initiatives.
   • Local educational authorities provide organizational and financial support to USSF activities. USSF collaborates with local authorities partly by providing information via USSF newsletters.

2. Partnerships with educational institutions take the following forms:

   • Regional treachers-retraining institutions provide organizational and methodological support for USSF initiatives within the regions by offering Step by Step courses, developing the educational materials, and providing methodological guidance for the teachers in the regions.
   • Educational institutions are major partners for USSF, since

they implement instructional initiatives and provide feedback; as members of the USSF, they also participate in its decision making on strategic issues.

3. Relationships with NGOs take these two forms:

   - USSF develops partnerships with NGOs at the national and international levels to combine efforts in implementing changes: initiating and implementing joint projects; providing services (trainings, consultations) to other organizations; and taking advantage of their services.
   - USSF is also an affiliate of such international organizations as the International Step by Step Foundation (NL), the Council for Exceptional Children (USA), National Association for the Education of Young Children (NAEYC) (USA), and the National Staff Development Council (USA). These organizations provide professional development for the USSF and its network.

Interview with Natalia Sofiy

I (Svetlana Efimova) interviewed Natalia Sofiy, the director of USSF, on May 31, 2004. The USSF office was located in a large and well-lit office with several rooms. The one we were in had three desks, one occupied by Natalia. Her working place, just to the right of the window, was equipped with a computer and surrounded by documents. Several pictures were on the nearest wall; one of them Princess Diana. It crossed my mind that a mentor at Maliuk had told me that Natalia reminded her of Diana. "Natalia," the lady said, has the charisma of Princess Diana. They even look alike." Natalia welcomes me with a warm smile and we are ready to begin.

MS. SVITLANA: Natalia, in 2001, the Ministry of Education and Science signed an instruction initiated by the USSF together with its partner, the Institute of Special Pedagogy of the Academy of Pedagogical Sciences, to conduct a pedagogical experiment called *Social Adaptation and Integration of Physically and Mentally Impaired Children into the Regular School System*. It was to take place in 27 schools. Could you shed light on how this experiment was carried out? On what criteria were the schools selected?

MS. NATALIA: It all started in 1996 during the international outreach meeting of Step by Step in Prague, where the initiative on inclusion of children was announced. After that meeting, we met with school principals who had been working since 1994 with the Step by Step program—first in kindergarten and day care, and by that time, at newly formed kindergartens and school structures in Ukraine. (Such meetings took place annually following international events.) The principals welcomed this idea with enthusiasm and were ready to implement it in their practice. There was support neither from the government nor from regulatory authorities at that time.

In the summer of 1997, we held our first training on the growing issue. We invited officers from the Ministry of Education and Science, and representatives of the regional education administrations. It was difficult for them to understand and accept the idea of inclusion. They saw risks to the existing system of specialized institutions. I can safely say that our teachers began to work in spite of rather than thanks to the state. Still, we understood that the initiative would go nowhere without understanding and support from the Ministry of Education and Science. The institutions we worked with belonged to the state. Their officers reported to governmental officials. We also understood that we could achieve substantial change only with action at both levels: administrative and practical.

In 2000, we completed our experiment on the Step by Step program in the elementary schools. The Ministry of Education and Science carried out the evaluation. We met with Ms. Liudmyla Kormilitsyna, head of the Preschool and Specialized Education Department at the Ministry, to discuss the results. Based on our experience that all initiatives have a better chance of survival, provided they remain within the frames of experiment, we agreed to launch another experiment. For this, we had to register all documents according to the effective rules and regulations, and develop an experimental program with involvement of the Institute of Special Pedagogy as our principal partner. Unfortunately, the registration of the program took a year to complete.

Speaking of criteria for school selection, I should say that we did not develop any specific ones at that time. The schools selected for the experiment were those that had already worked with Step by Step and had started to include children with special needs in their classes; we also selected experimental schools as recommended by the Ministry of Education and Science. Thus we selected 27 institutions, of which 20 were the Step by Step schools.

MS. SVITLANA: Did you feel the need for additional funding for the teachers?

MS. NATALIA: The issue of additional funding for teachers was not raised.

However, there was a need for new financing for teacher assistants. During this experiment, the Ministry did not provide funds.

MS. SVITLANA: What strategies did you use to resolve this problem?

MS. NATALIA: We had the instruction from the Ministry, and that made our actions legitimate. Some school directors succeeded in getting additional funding from local budgets to finance the positions of psychologists and social pedagogues. Those additional specialists were able to help both children and teachers. At Maliuk, the kindergarten managed to obtain additional salary money even before the experiment began. That money came from parent donations. The parents admired the Step by Step methodology being used at Maliuk, and they agreed to finance teacher assistants.

Another strategy was the development of projects for which we sought donors. In a TACIS project, *Development of Model Centers for Inclusive Education*, operating in two schools, we partners paid for teacher assistants during the initial year, hoping to attract state funding later. This took place in the city of Bila Tserkva, where we signed an agreement with five participating sponsors. This agreement opened doors for state funding to establish the needed positions.

MS. SVITLANA: Why wasn't the agreement signed in Lviv?

MS. NATALIA: In Bila Tserkva, we had to involve every stakeholder from the very beginning, starting at the school level and working up the administrative structures. Using the local media, we would regularly raise inclusion issues. The Ministry's instruction could not be ignored. It required immediate response from the parties involved. The positive experience of EveryChild in Bila Tserkva helped us immensely.

In November 2003—taking advantage of a visit from David Roels (Council for Exceptional Children), the man who helped us develop and implement the evaluation—we managed to organize a meeting with the Bila Tserkva deputy mayor. Mr. Volodymyr Kuzminskyy, director of EveryChild, helped as well.

The signing wasn't in Lviv because the battle seemed nearly won there. In Lviv we had set our hopes high, with reason to expect that our issues would be understood. There the inclusion initiative had started a long time ago, and we already had the support of local officials. There the head of Education and Science, Mr. P. Khobzei, and his deputy, Ms. K. Horokhovska, shared our views. That experiment seemed over, at least until they relinquished their positions and we had to start all over. We wanted an experiment that showed how official positions on inclusion could be changed.

Some schools agreeing to inclusion of exceptional children began forming separate classes for them, explaining that in this way the children would be better integrated over time. At first, I thought that we could accept this as a transitional step toward true inclusion. When I talked about it with Deborah Ziegler of the Council for Exceptional Children, she said, "Is it right to settle for a compromise? You know what is right. You should keep your vision and not compromise. Otherwise, you can lose your vision. It makes more sense to attempt to persuade the schools to do things right from the beginning. That means include the children in regular classes, not forming isolated classes."

Often we encounter problems because people resist new ideas. In this situation, we had to try to understand why they behaved the way they did. It was possible to reduce their resistance by showing advantages for everyone involved in implementing inclusion.

MS. SVITLANA: Can you remember visiting a Step by Step school and seeing that its personnel were not doing a good job? What did you do to improve the situation?

MS. NATALIA: This is a rather painful question. Improvement requires time and consideration of many factors. Among these factors are people's attitudes and their knowledge. As experience shows, quality is lost where the teachers are changing often. New teachers require time to be trained and to get appropriate experience. It is important to use the experience and assistance of those who know the program well and can help the new teachers. The support of such people as school methodologists, vice-directors, and methodologists from in-service institutes is very important. It is also important to get the support of more experienced teachers from neighboring schools.

MS. SVITLANA: You've been director of USSF for a considerable time. If you could divide your work into three periods, what would they be? What happened during these stages?

MS. NATALIA: The first period was up until 2000. I became the director in 1999. We had been working for 5 years as one of the regional programs of the International Renaissance Foundation, and we still lacked experience as to how an organization should be staffed, develop its operating procedures, do the accounting, and so on. We had to deal with a lot of "housekeeping" matters that seemed not very important and that occupied a lot of our time.

The second period I would call "survival." We had to change our "habits" of receiving more or less systematic financing and start looking for resources to keep our organization alive. It was important to preserve our authenticity and develop projects that corresponded to our organizational mission, but we had to consider activities that did not seem closely related to our mission.

The third period was the further development of the organization as a highly professional unit—not enchanted by its own ability, but busy helping others, reflecting on existing polices and practices, and lobbying and otherwise influencing the policy of the state. A joint program, *Special Child*, was taking shape in Kyiv Oblast because of our activities and cooperation with the educational authorities there. This program works for an increment to the salaries of teachers teaching in inclusive classes. It promises funding for additional positions of teacher assistants in Kyiv Oblast as well. Another example is the state experimental inclusion program recently launched in partnership with the Institute of Special Pedagogy and supported by the Ministry of Education and Science.

We saw our contribution and influence even in the appearance of the term *inkluzia*. It had not existed in Ukraine. We looked hard to find an appropriate word for the concept of inclusion in the Ukrainian language. And despite the fact that Ukraine lacks appropriate regulations for *inkluzia*, one now often hears talk about inclusive education and about the necessity to carry out related changes in the schools, in the environment, the syllabus, and the regulations.

OUR INTERPRETATION OF EDUCATIONAL POLICY

More than 10 years have passed since Ukraine chose to transform itself into an independent democratic society. A series of important policy changes have occurred during that time. The state national program *Education Ukraine in Century XXI*, the *National Doctrine of Education Development in Ukraine in Century XXI*, the program *Children of Ukraine*, and the law *On Comprehensive Secondary Education* have been developed and approved. During the interview with Vyatcheslav Zasenko (see the "National Context" section, above), I (Svitlana Efimova) had asked him how these changes have affected Ukrainian education.

"New forms of educational establishments have appeared: nongovernmental organizations, complexes, kindergarten–primary schools, lyceums, colleges, and rehabilitation centers for children with special needs. Now another new type of educational establishment, the 'specialized school–vocational college," is under development. It is important for people to select the educational and/or vocational level they want."

Supporting integration of Ukraine into the European Community were the Ministry of Education and Science and the Academy of Pedagogical Sciences—the two main authors and developers of national educational policy, including educational policy for children with special needs, and in particular the Step by Step approach. They saw it necessary to depart from the existing system of closed special schools, internats, and specialized residential schools, inherited as part of the Soviet social ideology. Ukraine turned to a more humanistic system of inclusive education. Nevertheless, the inclusive model of education has not widely been considered a serious alternative to special education. (In fact, there is some pressure to increase the number of specialized schools and internats.) Mr. Zasenko emphasized the continuing presence of special education in his interview:

"Inclusive education is not aimed at the ruination of the special education system. . . . Inclusive education can exist only in parallel, providing opportunity for the children with disabilities to realize their constitutional right for equality in education."

We see compromise in many programs. In 2001, the Ministry of Education and Science endorsed a 7-year experimental program on inclusion developed by the Ukrainian Step by Step Foundation jointly with the Academy of Pedagogical Sciences' Institute of Special Pedagogy. And in 2004, a state standard on special education was drafted. Its progressive slant is seen in the fact that it was based on the standard for general education, and thus is to be used by both specialized and regular schools. Setting a single standard, though, does not set reasonable expectations for children with disabilities.

By upholding equal access to quality education and the right of parents to choose the educational establishment, the Ministry of Education and Science and the Academy of Pedagogical Sciences have acknowledged the importance of cooperation between the specialized schools and rehabilitation centers on the one hand, and the regular schools on the other. At the same time, they recognize that such cooperation has not been common and needs to be developed. Such cooperation can take different forms: temporary stays of children from the rehabilitation centers in regular classrooms; attendance in the regular schools with a correctional component at the rehabilitation centers;

attendance at the specialized schools with further education at the vocational colleges.

The Ministry of Education and Science recognizes other important factors in inclusion, such as the preparation of teachers to work in an inclusive learning environment and the provision of physical accommodations in the regular schools. Vice-Minister Victor Ogneviuk stated during his interview:

> "Today, the most important issue is the preparation of a new generation of teachers for helping children with special needs. Without well-prepared teachers and mentors, our talk [about inclusion] is in vain."

Whatever the complexity of educating children with disabilities in the regular schools, the Ministry of Education and Science and the Academy of Pedagogical Sciences were not objecting to trying out alternative educational programs. Ms. Zasenko noted this, although he also stressed the need to adapt such programs to the Ukrainian context:

> "Such programs have a positive rationale. Although the difference between offered and existing programs is never 100%, there are some very important differences here. Different countries have come different ways into their development. They have different values. It can even be harmful simply to transfer them into the national context without review and modification."

Conditionally accepting the alternative programs, the Ministry projects a rise in the quality of education, because, as Mr. Ogneviuk stated,

> " . . . the Ministry and the Academy are not afraid of failing to fulfill the state educational standards. There was no such precedent the last time. There are laws, and the Ministry takes the responsibility for their fulfillment, and it does it well."

OUR INTERPRETATION OF THE TEACHER TRAINING

In the world around Liubchyk, Step by Step teacher training, through inclusivity, has emphasized ways to make the classroom as much a social and experiential learning opportunity for children with disabilities as for other children. Other Step by Step standards (e.g., those on child-centered education, parent and community involvement, and democratic education) have also been stressed, but the greatest emphasis has been on inclusion. The primary schools and educational authorities of Ukraine are moving in this direction, but much remains to be done. The burden of improved teaching is still borne largely by the teachers themselves.

To attain substantial positive change in the system of education is only possible with significant raises in teacher compensation and assurance of their essential social status. These are the most challenging issues today in Ukraine. The actual average salary for teachers is two and a half times less than specified under current regulatory requirements. At the same time, the teacher force has been aging. The number of teachers reaching retirement age is increasing dramatically. Lack of compliance with Article 57 (the state guarantees to pedagogical specialists) of the law of Ukraine *On Education* stirs the threat of massive strikes. The state program *The Teacher* indicates that the "teaching profession has been losing its prestige. There is a gap between the social role of teachers and their social status."

In this context, raising the issue of teacher training primarily means first focusing on their motivation. What benefits can they receive from Step by Step training? It hardly needs saying that teacher qualification courses held at oblast postgraduate institutes are both mandatory and important for teacher attestations. These take place regularly every 5 years; they either allow a teacher to receive a new classification or just confirm the existing one, and also permit a nominal raise in pay. There is no doubt, however, that teachers receive most of their motivation for attending Step by Step training from a natural desire to learn. During an interview after a training session in Kyiv, one teacher said, "This training opened the door to a different world for us. I had fun working and receiving strength for my mind and soul."

The Ukrainian Step by Step Foundation organizes monthly courses for teachers offered at the Central Postgraduate Institute and through the network of training centers. Currently, about 1,200 Ukrainian teachers have completed in-service training courses organized by the foundation. In 2003, partly to bring the Step by Step training certificates up to the status of official certificates issued by oblast postgraduate institutes, the foundation was licensed by the Ministry of Education and Science of Ukraine to train teachers in the area of innovational education. Thus the Ukrainian Step by Step Foundation attained the status of the teacher-training institutes, with one exception: The state does not finance the foundation training. The foundation director has said that this might change when a new law on social services comes into effect. This law states that NGOs can provide services to the government for a fee, although no formal mechanism has been proposed.

Besides the fact that trainees receive from the Ukrainian Step by Step Foundation official state-approved graduation certificates (which become an influential factor during teacher attestation), additional personal motivation comes from the felt necessity to learn new things. It is true for the teachers, as well as for parents and representatives of NGOs. This special training helps in various ways: The specialists receive new knowledge. They activate their own experience and use it more effectively. The courses also bring professionals and others closer together, cultivating partnerships and developing the feeling of community. After attending a training module with Romanna, Liubchyk's mother, his teacher, Oksana, said:

> "[The training session] helped me to understand Romanna as a person and to see the situation through her eyes. I began to understand her problems and what motivated her to act as she did. The informal communication during breaks also fostered trust. Romanna expressed confidence that the information shared about her child would not be used against him, but would facilitate work in the future. Thus it became somewhat easier for me [Oksana] to understand the problems of this child, the peculiarities of his personality, and his developmental stage."

Step by Step training methods are based on common principles of adult education, where it is important to take into account their previous experiences, learn about their expectations, and use proactive learning methods. The Step by Step training in Lviv and Kyiv was centered on the participants, not on the trainers. This approach enhances subsequent opportunities to transfer the received experience into real classroom situations and to make it more child-oriented than teacher-oriented. The teacher is not viewed as the only one possessing important knowledge.

We saw these principles at work in the "Four Corners" exercise, conducted during a training session for school teachers and managers of the Holosiivky District of Kyiv, which took place in Kyiv on April 21–23, 2004 (as described earlier).

A sign is placed in each corner of the room. The signs read:

1. "Children with special needs must attend the same classes with other children if they are capable of mastering the same material."

2. "Children with special needs must attend special schools that provide for their specific educational and medical needs."
3. "All children, regardless of their abilities, must attend regular classes."
4. "The parents of children with special needs will decide which school each child will attend." . . .

The participants move about, reading the statements. Sign 1 draws the largest group, and Sign 2 the smallest. The discussions are based mostly on personal experience: "My neighbors have a child like that, and they do not want to send her to the boarding school . . . " Some participants say that if they could, they would go to the middle of the room to reflect how they feel. Some participants change their minds. . . .

Olga reads out the standards on *Objectives and Tasks*. She defines the concept of "inclusion" with transparencies and handouts, and identifies the benefits of inclusion programs. Olga asks the participants to discuss these issues with people outside the training, and to write down questions and answers to them in the Notebook.

One of the fundamental techniques used by Step by Step is that the training methodology is based partly on the existing experience of participants, which means that both trainers and newcomers are invaluable sources of knowledge. Every training reinforces some participant skills, but at the same time, it induces changes in teaching habits and practice.

The first training in the Step by Step program in 1994 showed that the impact of such experiences can be very different—sometimes very helpful, sometimes rather painful, sometimes both. Imagine teachers who have worked almost 30 years in a kindergarten, and who until now have been totally sure that teaching children to obey, to accept every adult's word, to be like everyone else are the important qualities in adult life, and that the school (from kindergarten to secondary school) is the only preparation for this life. They have been trained according to the existing values of that time, when families were excluded from actively participating in their children's education; when individual differences were not tolerated, and disabilities were reviled; when creativity was sacrificed to uniformity, individual voices to conformity, understanding to knowledge, and flexibility to rigor.

Very often such an experience has been helpful. The teachers of Maliuk School were excited about the Step by Step program in 1994. One of the reasons was that since 1993 they had worked on an innovative educational program, *Facing the Child*, introduced and supported by the Canadian Bureau for International Education. The program was based on principles close to those of the Step by Step program: an individualized approach to each child, developmentally appropriate practices, observation as the main tool of knowing the child, and so on. Being already trained in that program, the teachers accepted Step by Step enthusiastically. But of course they continued some orientation to their previous teaching, such as making a fuss about "correct" responses. One of the teachers said, "We had developed the new system of assessment. Every child chooses a logo (a cloud, a sun, a star), [and when the teacher gives points] sticks one on his or her paper. The child receives this as a signal to celebrate. The children are very excited."

So sometimes trainees and even trainers have methods that work for them, but that are not in the repertoire of Step by Step teaching. This was the case with the use of tokens of reinforcement in Oksana's class. A behaviorist approach to teaching has long been common in Ukraine, and it remains useful for some situations in the eyes of parents and teachers, including Oksana herself. As noted in this report, she heard behaviorist advice on ways to help Liubchyk when a certain desired achievement is sought. In a child-centered situation, the child chooses many of the activities and achievements. So there is opportunity for compromise.

The teacher trainees who realize the importance of Step by Step's central values go back to their classrooms to implement new methods. Although children do not have pedagogical repertoires, they are also sources of explanation and support for each other. This is important for inclusive classes in particular, since the children with special needs must receive deliberate support not only from teachers, but from their classmates as well. Oksana demonstrated this very principle, using Liubchyk as an example of one who cannot do some ordinary things well unless helped out.

[The children are] to read passages from a fairy tale. Every child selects a passage to read, choosing a comfortable place and posture. Liubchyk gets up abruptly, walks to the center of the reading circle, takes the book, and leaves the classroom. Ms. Mariana follows him, takes him by the hand, and brings him back to the classroom. Liubchyk comes up to Ms. Oksana, pulls her by the hand, and shows her the clock, saying, "Oksana, it's time for lunch!" The clock shows 12:00 sharp, lunchtime. "Yes, Liubchyk, but we still have a few more minutes. This clock is a bit fast. Look. (She shows him her watch.) We still have a few minutes here. Let's have Katrusia read you a passage from the fairy tale. All right? Katrusia, come here, please." Katrusia eagerly comes up to Liubchyk, takes him by the hand, and they go to a place in the corridor where they can read.

Another strategy follows the principle that if you want to learn something well, you have to teach someone. Oksana told us,

> "Officially, we do not really have home assignments in our classes. However, the children do receive a sort of homework. For example, sometimes they are assigned to teach their parents something they have learned in class. For example, one day at home they taught their families to make paper fish. These fish now decorate their rooms. One girl brought to 'show and tell' the fish made by her mother and granny. The children had an opportunity to see themselves as 'good teachers.' "

This method helps Step by Step incorporate an important principle of learning—that children learn more effectively when they are getting ready to teach it themselves.

OUR INTERPRETATION OF INCLUSION

"Inclusion" is a human value, a philosophy, and a new educational model. We found it to be demonstrated in the support system for Maliuk School, and to be increasingly discussed both near and far, including among scientists, civic organizations, teachers, and school administrators. However, in Ukraine, a different term is more frequently used: "integration." Integration is the melding of dissimilar people. Inclusion is the melding of dissimilar people in ways that assure the sharing of benefits. Only a few people understand the difference, largely due to lack of experience with the implementation of *inclusion*. In Ukraine, inclusion counters long-standing official policy, and it is only now that initial steps are being taken toward implementing and understanding this movement.

Interestingly, an adequate Ukrainian word has not been found for the practice of inclusion in schools; thus the English word has simply been transliterated into Ukrainian. Changes *have* taken place in terms of the way the issue is approached, however. The concept began its evolution from complete nonacceptance to acceptance in statements by state education administrative officers supporting universal and equal access to high-quality education. Increasingly, as indicated in the previous section, the practice of isolating all children with exceptional needs in specialized boarding schools was condemned.

Whatever wording we use to point out the dissimilarity of inclusion to integration (such as adaptation and adjustment of children to life in our social environment), we must not forget that we are dealing with particular children, parents, teachers who work with these children, school administrators, and many other people. It is important to initiate changes in society that will lead to new opportunities for these children, especially opportunities of access to what they need to be successful children and adults. What is inclusion for them?

Most people say that, at its simplest, inclusion means "an opportunity for a child to spend time with other children in an ordinary environment." This much would be a substantial achievement for Ukraine. However, by accentuating the social aspect of inclusion, we might underestimate the importance of access to high-quality education. Effective discussion needs to involve both those with expertise who advocate mainstreaming and those with expertise who advocate placement in specialized classes and institutions. Most of the latter are convinced that children with developmental disabilities receive better education when placed in smaller classes under the care of specialists. A mainstream class may have up to 30 children, as opposed to 6–12 in a class in a specialized logopedic school. Of course, it is true that teachers with special education training will work with some children toward some goals more effectively. As Mr. Zasenko noted during his interview, "the specialist teachers are of the opinion that the mainstream schools are not capable of providing a correctional program for the children with special needs."

It is difficult for us advocates of inclusion to express validly the position of those who represent the specialized institutions. Indeed, a teacher of a classroom of children who all have mild mental disability may not have a heavier teaching load than a teacher of a regular class that includes one child with significant mental disability.

We get a better understanding of the problem when we differentiate between specialized institutions and mainstream schools developing a new system aiming to foster social values. Ukraine's choice of the path to democracy and an open society suggests that the school system should also be fair and accessible, and not only in the sense of physical accessibility (e.g., ramps, elevators, adapted toilets). Children with special needs should have equal access to the state school curriculum. This is carried out through adaptation of academic tasks, evaluation methods, study content, and the classroom environment.

Ms. Oksana gives out instructions for the next task. They are to break into groups and select a certain geometrical shape of a certain color. Every group is to solve a "Hungarian Crossword" that hides the main characters of the fairy tale *Thumbelina*. Ms. Marianna retells Liubchyk everything the teacher says. Oksana asks Liubchyk also to select a geometrical shape. He chooses a little green circle. She gives him the same paper as the rest of the children, but this time the task is somewhat different: Each child has to read and write down the names of the fairy tale's characters, and to make a drawing of one of them. Liubchyk starts working at the teacher's desk.

The new vision of schooling requires a new vision of the teacher's role. One fear is that teachers will lack the necessary skills to work with these children. A second fear is that the children with special needs will fall short of the curriculum requirements. This leads to two basic conclusions. First, the teachers need to be trained in utilizing special methods for achieving individualization. This requires adaptation of various existing methods of teaching. For example, instead of having a student with special needs do a mathematics task in a copybook, he or she cam be asked to complete a similar exercise using real objects. And it requires seeking out alternative methods of evaluation as well. Second, the teachers need to increase their ability to perceive what each child can do particularly well in life, in order to become successful and independent. Whether or not inclusion should require the teachers to do other parts of a specialist's job is a separate issue.

Once a teacher has taken steps toward inclusion, the issue of support for that teacher becomes crucial. It is important for schools to provide support for the teacher's experimentation, to assign teaching assistance for giving individual attention to the child, and to extend salary support. Mr. Ogneviuk commented on these issues in his interview:

> "The idea of having teacher assistants is thoughtful, even for regular schools, since children differ in their nature and in the quality of their perception. In certain cases, a child requires individual attention, and this is where the teacher assistant can help. The idea is wonderful. Unfortunately, financial difficulties stop it from being implemented. Possibly one day this dream will come true.
>
> "Costwise, it is cheaper to educate a child in a regular school than in a specialized one. The only problem is that today we cannot guarantee that at least minimum support will be provided in every school, because of the infamous impediment, the lack of funds."

But let's come back to the main heroes of our research. For Liubchyk's mother, the opportunity to bring her son to Maliuk School gave her great relief. It strengthened her belief that everything with Liubchyk could be worked out. Clearly, it was an alternative to the decision of the PMPC to send the child to a specialized institution. As Romanna noted, "Liubchyk is a very interesting child. He has unique skills." Hearing her words brings out a picture of a gifted child, a very special child indeed. But this is the essence of inclusive education. Each is skilled. Each is special. Education is available for everyone, including those with gifts of every kind! The desire of parents to see their kids treated like others is one of the most important things for them. Activities like the Khodoton, entitled *We Are No Different from Anyone Else!*, and many other public awareness events organized by parents demonstrate this. It is quite possible that parents will look more carefully at the experiences of their children and at broadening these experiences further to enhance their lives. The question "What sort of a person do you see your child becoming in the future?" can remain largely unanswered. In spite of this, the issue is not any less significant. And it will be important to ask Liubchyk himself from time to time about how he sees his future.

Liubchyk seldom communicated with other children. Perhaps immersion in his own world was the main reason some people saw him as an "autistic child." Still, Liubchyk had his own special friends: Anychka, whom he knew from preschool, and Katrusia. These girls possessed qualities that would be less developed without Liubchyk—a readiness to help and a sense of responsibility to others. When the children who attended preschool with Liubchyk witnessed his unusual behavior, they asked the teacher about it; as a result, they started to understand how children differ and that they too were different. But, at the same time, the children were learning that everyone should have equal access to all the benefits of school. In a nearby Grade 3 class, it was considered a special privilege to be little Natalia's assistant (Natalia was the child with cerebral palsy) on the stairs. The teachers used this as a motivating tool, and the children felt the joy of being helpful.

Having gained this rich experience, it is likely that these children will be willing to use it in their adulthood. How much more difficult this can be for adults who lack such experience! During a Grade 1 parents' meeting, when inclusion of Liubchyk was being discussed, the parents agreed to support it on condition that an extra person (for Liubchyk, it was Ms. Marianna) would assist with the class. The parents themselves came to fully finance these additional teacher assistants. One of the mothers even helped Natalia's mother find a job. Such deeds give financial support to families in a difficult situation. And this allows many of us Ukrainian adults to feel something of which we were deprived when we were young—an opportunity to see and comprehend great personal differences, to help those who are in need, and simply to be happy to be able to help. This feeling can help us understand that children with special needs also should have their fair share of it! However, to achieve this aim, we need to take many steps further.

LIUBCHYK

April 27, 2004, 11:00 A.M. It is the beginning of the final lesson on *Thumberlina*. The first graders sit in a circle with Ms. Oksana. They pose questions to one another on the subject of the fairy tale. Liubchyk and Ms. Halyna are in the center of the reading corner. He is sitting with his back to the children, laying out geometrical shapes in front of him. Ms. Oksana says, "Children, let us spread our circle out a bit wider to include Liubchyk, shall we?" The children move, and Liubchyk gets in the circle, but he continues to sit with his back to the others.

The teacher asks the following question: "What did Thumberlina call the mole?" Hanusia says, "The blind." "Is that what we call someone who can't see?" asks the teacher. The children say, "He didn't like the sun." "He used to say that the birds were fools." "He only counted on his wealth." Oksana says, "Perhaps he was shallow-minded and refused to acknowledge and understand things because he couldn't see them. However, he can't be blamed for how well he can see. All living creatures have their purpose, and the moles play their important role as well." Meanwhile, Ms. Halyna asks Liubchyk to say the names of the children answering the questions. He turns around whenever he hears an answer and faultlessly says their names.

"Now we are going to work in pairs. The boys will be turned into elves and the girls into Thumberlinas. Liubchyk, come, you will play with me," says Oksana. Liubchyk comes to her and hugs her. The task for every pair is to measure various objects in inches ("thumbs"). The teachers have made special measuring sticks of headless match sticks and have provided pieces of paper for each pair to pick up. The children scatter out around the classroom. Oksana sits down with Liubchyk in his favorite place, the center, and calls for Olenka. They begin to measure the geometrical shapes that Liubchyk had laid out earlier. They start with the quadrangle. Ms. Oksana puts down one match at the side of the quadrangle, and then another; now Liubchyk puts down a third one. "Olenka, take note of the measurement. Write down the number of inches." She writes "3." "What shall we measure next, Liubchyk?" asks the teacher. He points at the pen. Now Olenka places matches and Liubchyk counts them, "O-o-ne, two, three, four," and registers the answer on the paper. The next object they measure together by taking turns—one match by Olenka, another by Liubchyk, then Olenka again, and then Liubchyk. Soon the time for the task is up and the children put the results on the blackboard. They get into a circle for active relaxation. They imitate various characters from *Thumberlina*. Liubchyk watches.

The next assignment for each child is to color a scene from the fairy tale and place them in the order the scenes appear in the story. The children work in groups. Liubchyk chooses a picture among those offered by Ms. Halyna, the assistant teacher, but he refuses to join a group. He is not pressed to do so. "What is this bird?" she asks. Liubchyk spreads his arms and says, "A swallow." "Very good," says Halyna, and pats him on the shoulder. The children work on their scenes. When the coloring is completed, the children gather, and the scenes are laid out in order. "Liubchyk, come here, we are missing your picture," says his friend Anychka. Liubchyk gives her his neatly colored swallow, but continues to stay close to Halyna.

"Children! You have done a very good job today. Let us finish our task in song. Let's take each other by the hand and sing our favorite song," says Oksana. Liubchyk is holding Halyna by one hand and Anychka by another. The children sing gaily. Liubchyk puts his head on Halyna's shoulder. "Lunchtime," he says, pointing at the clock.

CHAPTER 7

The Slovakia Case Study

The Slovak case research team wanted to interview Marian Kyjovský, the mayor of Jarovnice, but failed to arrange a meeting. From the data they were collecting, there seemed to be little expression of opposition to the idea of Roma children's attending the regular village school. Perhaps the most dubious person was the principal of the primary school for Roma children. It was widely believed that if the Roma children had had sufficient mastery of preschool concepts and sufficient competence in the Slovak language, they would have been admitted to the village school. But until recently, many had been found intellectually unready and had been placed in special education.

Step by Step people had taken on the task of getting these Roma children ready for regular school. Now some were being admitted to the regular school. What did Mayor Kyjovský think? Did he welcome the rescue effort being performed by Step by Step? The team speculated about what he would say. The researchers never had that conversation. They did talk to Zdena Semanitová, the assistant to the mayor. What she said is included in the report.

Many of the stories the Slovak team encountered were heartwarming. Eva Koncoková had organized her team to study the support given the Roma settlement at Jarovnice. In 2001, for the Roma, Slovakia's Wide Open School Foundation had introduced Step by Step preschool teaching methods, with both children and their parents in community-based settings. Most mothers agreed to continue the schooling at home—counting, telling stories, guiding each child's hand and marker to make circles and letters (see the photo on this book's cover). Social worker

Mária Lichvárová made daily rounds to the homes to see that the week-long activity plans were working.

But for the purposes of this book, we want to look mostly at the researchers. How did they imagine the case and invent the study (Kemmis, 1980)? It wasn't easy for me, their mentor, to know, because the Slovaks operated pretty much incommunicado. I met Eva and others at that first visit to Jarovnice. And I did more than my share of the talking during two training weekends in Budapest. The countenance of the first draft came pretty much as a surprise, and the revised draft as another. The revision met the deadline, and I took the signals to mean that the team had completed its work.

The Slovak researchers fixed their eyes mostly on the situation of the Roma settlement in Jarovnice—its shanty homes, its makeshift

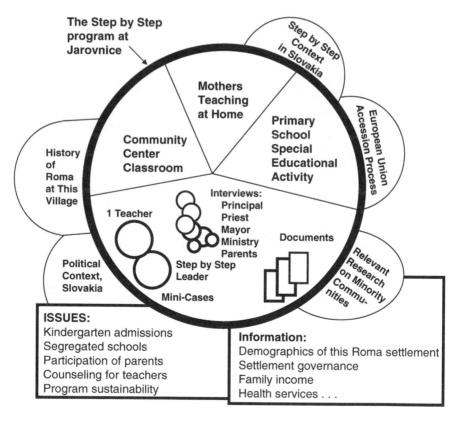

FIGURE 7.1. Plan for the Slovakia case study.

schools, its memorial church. They watched the way the Step by Step teachers countered the children's impoverished experience. And they posted photographs in the report, so that readers would get a visual impression of the community's impoverishment and yet the vitality of the people.

Rather than working from general research questions, or even from national priorities, the team worked from local activities. The local activities identified in the planning graphic (Figure 7.1) were teaching at the Community Center, home teaching coordinated through the Pastoral Center, and special education at the Special Primary School. The issues of equity, discrimination, and unemployment were never far from view, but voicing them was not the work style of this team. Jarovnice is a small village, so the study could cover most of the educational programs, and the researchers had little problem choosing which classrooms or local historians to visit. Of course, some stories were neglected—those of village residents, farmers, employers, and county officials, for example. Never can all be told.—R. E. S.

Impact of Step by Step at the Roma Settlement Jarovnice–Karice: Slovakia Community Resource Mobilization[1]

EVA KONCOKOVÁ and JANA HANDZELOVÁ

SUMMARY

Encouragement and motivation of individuals and communities to create anti-bias and multicultural atmospheres in the process of lifelong learning were the key values of the mission of the Wide Open School Foundation.

All projects, programs, and activities implementing Step by Step methods were committed to the process of developing and improving the

---

[1]Copyright 2004 by the Open Society Institute. Used by permission.

learning environments of children, their families and their communities, thus empowering them to reach their individual potentials and using existing opportunities in a wider context as integrated members of society.

The immediate goal of the Wide Open School Foundation was to help the segregated, disadvantaged Roma community gain acknowledgment across the Slovak society and improve their social status. This was to be accomplished partly by opposing stereotypes and changing interpersonal relationships, by strengthening family participation in the process of education, and by helping the Roma to gain awareness of their own skills. Thus was the quality of their lives to be improved.

With the cooperation of state and local authorities, the foundation implemented supportive programs to develop participatory learning communities. The Roma children were helped to move toward such competencies as critical thinking, teamwork, communication, and living in a multicultural society. At the same time, the children were exploring their own strengths, the depth and breadth of their influence, and their points of vulnerability.

We express our thanks to Mr. Bob Stake, our mentor, and Sarah Klaus, executive director of the International Step by Step Association, for their extraordinary efforts to help us create this case study and to give us the opportunity to show the strength and cultural values of the Roma community. And we express thanks to the persons who collected the data and shared with us their stories:

> Viera Ondercová—field researcher for the case study
> Alena Paniková—executive director of Nadácia otvorenejspoločnosti, Open School Foundation (OSF), Bratislava
> Klára Orgovánová—head of the Plenipotentiary of the Slovak Government for Roma Communities
> Zdeno Krajcir—director of Department of Primary and Preschool Education, Slovak Ministry of Education
> Miroslav Sklenka—project coordinator for nongovernmental organization (NGO) development.

And the following, all from Jarovnice:

> Marian Kyjovský—mayor
> Stanislav Radvanský—parish priest
> Iveta Fabulová—coordinator of the Community Center
> Mária Lichvárová—social worker, Pastoral Center
> Martin Kaleja—Roma teacher assistant at the Community Center

Eva Lukácová—principal of the Special Primary School
Magdalena Safranová—principal of the village Primary School
Jozef Bugna—principal of the Primary School for Roma children
Dezider Lacko—participant in adult literacy training
Peter Repiský—master teacher trainer for the Special Primary School
Vincent Cerven—coordinator of the Roma Initiative
Anton Zboraj—archivist
Karol Conka—representative of the Roma community
Pavlína Baluchová—accountant
Mária Triscová—administrator in the mayor's office
Zdena Semanitová—assistant to the mayor
Jozef Červenak—chronicler

1. THE COMMUNITY CENTER: PREPARATION FOR INCLUSIVE EDUCATION

In 1998, Nadácia Skola dokorán, the Wide Open School Foundation, established a Community Center in the Karice settlement attached to the village of Jarovnice in eastern Slovakia. The aim was to provide space for a variety of educational, community, and cultural opportunities for young children, teenagers, and adults. The Wide Open School Foundation had been created in 1994 with the support of the Step by Step program of the Open Society Institute. Eva Koncoková organized Nadácia Skola dokorán and, as its director, initiated and supervised its work in the Roma settlement of Jarovnice.

At the Community Center, 14 Roma children ages 6 and 7 sit around Iveta Fabulová, their teacher, in the corner of the room, to hear a story about Marika. Their young, blonde-haired teacher has arranged to have nine dark-haired Roma moms join them.

Iveta tells them all a story about Marika, a Roma blacksmith's wife. "She had too many children, and they didn't have enough to eat. One day her husband put shoes on a horse for a farmer, and the farmer paid him with a sack of flour. Marika took the flour, added water and baking soda, and made dough. She slapped the dough into a flat, round shape. She baked it over the fire. The delicious smell of the bread went out to the whole settlement. It smelled so good that everyone came to Marika's house. She fed everyone. Because her name was Marika, they called the bread 'marikle.' Ever since that time, long ago, Roma people have been baking marikle to remember the generosity of Marika."

The children and their moms listen to Iveta quietly. "What do you think about this story?" Her question is addressed to a mom sitting next to her. "She was a good person." "Yes," replies Iveta, "She was generous. She shared bread with other poor people."

"Children, what was the shape of the bread? Was it like this one?" Iveta takes a round loaf from a bag. "Look, its shape is a circle. Try to draw a circle in the air. And repeat after me, 'Circle.'" The children draw circles in the air and shout, "Circle!" in chorus.

"In Presov, people buy garlic bread shaped like this." Iveta points to a yellow triangle on the blackboard. "I want you to draw this triangle and repeat after me, 'Triangle.' And soon we are going to make bread in these two shapes."

Iveta invites them to choose their activity center. The children quickly move to the centers where material has been prepared (clay, paper, pencils, pens). Some choose clay, others paper and pencil, to make these shapes. Olga, a Roma woman, the teacher assistant, helps divide the clay. The mothers move their chairs to join each group. Iveta asks them to help the children name each shape. Later, Iveta says, "Do you know the names of the shapes you made? What is this, Dusan?" Dusan has drawn circles and triangles of different colors and sizes. He answers without hesitation. Many children need the teacher's help to pronounce the Slovak word for "triangle."

The program for the week was posted on the wall. On this day, the activity was baking. The mothers were to bake loaves of bread from raised dough. The program also noted that Iveta and a colleague from the Special Primary School were scheduled to lecture on adult literacy, in a program organized by Civic Association ASAL. (The efforts of the civic associations are described more fully in a later section.)

There were 25 children, 3- to 6-year-olds, enrolled in this preschool program. As indicated earlier, the goal was to prepare the Roma children for admission to regular school—not an easy task—and thus to end their segregation into special education. The staff had implemented both center-based and home-based comprehensive preschool curricular programs. The neediest children attended half-day classes in the Community Center building. Other children participated in a preschool program mainly implemented in the children's homes; it had some 30 Roma volunteers working with 42 children and their families. In preparing the children for primary school, these preschool programs had radically changed the learning environments both in the homes and in the community.

The basis of instruction at the Community Center was a half-day educational program that enabled children to acquire basic academic skills and social skills. It attended to the instructional language (Slovak) of the public school system which differs from the Romani language spoken by Roma families at home. Attendance provided pupils with opportunities for development through both alternative and nontraditional teaching methods. It encouraged a more positive attitude toward school and education. A key part of the educational process was a Roma teaching assistant, who helped the teacher overcome language barriers and create an appropriate cultural environment.

Again, this was a special education prevention program focused on improving the social and cognitive skills of a high-risk group of Roma children. It was intended to provide these children with adequate preparation for school, according to the criteria identified by public school authorities.

Teachers, Roma assistants, and parents were involved. The teachers worked directly with the children, focusing on Slovak language and mathematics. Emphasis was placed on the "whole-language" approach (language experience) for developing prereading and prewriting skills, providing context and meaning. The teachers assessed the developmental level of each individual child in terms of performance. Instruction was individualized by using different kinds of observation and creating portfolios.

The Roma teacher assistants contributed to the whole-day program by supporting the activities planned by the teachers. They helped children in the process of learning, as well as in gaining meaningful involvement of the parents. They helped increase proficiencies in first-language usage, facilitated development of second-language skills, and raised the cultural relevance of the content.

Iveta described the situation in her classroom:

"The Roma children used to arrive in first grade from a family atmosphere that denied them success in primary school. Most of them did not speak [Slovak] properly because of limited interaction with the majority population and because of lack of knowledge of the culture. Their level of socialization was low. At the beginning of the school year, some of the children had problems practicing expected hygienic routines. At home they lived in terrible conditions, without running water and electricity. It was clear that the children came from a disadvantaged family environment, that they lacked skills, and that they were not ready for school. They had a lot of difficulty concentrating and following instructions in Slovak.

"A couple of months ago, these children were not able to hold a pencil in their hands. Now they are able to draw trees, bodies, and animals. They are able to throw a ball. They can concentrate on their work, reach agreement with a friend, and plan their own activity."

Iveta also described her own changes as a Step by Step teacher:

"For the Roma, I had to change my whole strategy—my behavior and communication style. I had to learn more of their culture in order to be comprehended by the children and by their parents. The first lesson in the Step by Step *Anti-Bias Education* training turned me toward overcoming my own professional stereotypes. I needed not to blame the children, but to work to help them reach their potential—which is really great.

"I devoted my personal and professional life to the children. Maybe it is because of my family background. My parents are teachers. All my memories from childhood are connected with teaching. I used to imitate my mom as a teacher. My stuffed toys were my first pupils.

"During my study at secondary school, I often visited the special primary school in Jarovnice. My mom worked there, and I helped to organize trips and summer camps for her students. I was strongly motivated to know more about Roma children. They were called 'mentally handicapped.' I tried to immerse myself in the children's world—to understand their personalities, perceptions, their ways of communication.

"I decided to study special education and school *logopedics*, with the intent to know more about these children. I studied many interesting methodologies. I read the opinions of various experts on work with handicapped children. Afterwards, I worked with children from the less supportive family environments in Bratislava. Later, I moved to Jarovnice to work here.

"In Jarovnice, I enriched my professional work with the ideas of Step by Step methodology. These methods changed my way of working with students and their parents. I myself was changed too.

"I work with children. They happen to be Roma. They take me as a friend. They open up. They share their hopes and dreams. They show me their ways of thinking and living—and I reward them with love and help.

"Involvement of parents in the process of instruction was not easy. Traditional teaching came easily enough. It took a long time to acquaint them with teaching for the individual development of each student."

The parents in Iveta's program had an interest in the early learning efforts to prepare children for primary school. Forty family members were involved as volunteers. They were a heterogeneous group from the community working together on a shared task—the enhancement of child development. They also participated in the cooperative learning for an additional reason—for personal self-improvement. In the community, one could now see varied evidence of interpersonal assistance and cooperation: greater interaction, mutual linking, and effective communication; more effective use of natural resources; greater emotional involvement of all; greater coordination of effort; higher divergent thinking; and specific self–other comparisons.

2. THE COMMUNITY CENTER: A PLACE FOR LIFELONG LEARNING

A long-term goal of the Community Center was its establishment as an informal institution that accepts differences, specific characteristics, and needs of community members, and offers various activities for a range of age categories. The Community Center strove to change interethnic relations and to improve life in a multicultural environment. Its aims included the following:

- Facilitating the personal development of the Roma children, to help them reach their potential.
- Creating equal chances for education through activities promoting the development of critical thinking and problem-solving skills, with follow-up motivation toward learning.
- Support of young families in the areas of health care, early childhood development, housing, and parenting.

The Community Center created an operational framework through different partners and different programs/activities to provide dialogue and communication on the local, national, and international levels. It did so by raising the capacity of the Roma community. Its objectives were pursued by undertaking a comprehensive community approach, emphasizing the local needs of the Karice settlement.

The contents of the educational initiatives were based on Step by Step programming, including the following:

- Early childhood development.
- Infant and toddler (home-based).
- Intensive preschool program to prevent placement in special education.
- Second-language approach.
- Antibias and intercultural education.
- Family and community involvement.

The Community Center offered these programs for mothers:

- Teen pregnancy prevention.
- Family and parenting support.
- Attitudes toward motherhood.
- The Mothers and Children Club.

Members of the community could also take part in the following activities:

- Social programs (social inclusion—desegregation, institutional support).
- Health programs (early childhood care, accidents, illnesses, first aid, immunization).
- Adult literacy (including computer skills development, tutoring, and mentoring).
- Vocational training (marketable skills, computers, English, life skills).

One participant in the adult literacy training, Dezider Lacko, offered the following opinion of the role of the Community Center:

"When the Foundation started to build the Community Center, we did not believe it would be useful for anyone. I am glad that our people have learned to read and write, because some of them are really talented. I think that the people who visit the Community Center share their knowledge with others.

"For example, my wife was not able to read and write. When we went to the Labor Office, my wife's registry was signed with crosses only. When my wife wrote her full name for the first time, the woman said: 'What's that, Ms. Lacková? You can write your name!' My wife was a bit timid, so I said, 'My wife attends a school for parents. There is a center in the settlement. People who cannot write and read go there and learn. And the woman answered, 'It is good that you now understand the importance of learning. You have to encourage the other people in the settlement as well.' "

The team of the Community Center included assistants, mentors, volunteers, and family members. Iveta, the coordinator of the Community Center, had dual roles as teacher and facilitator. She worked with the foundation, facilitating the day-to-day circulation of information and supervising the Roma teacher assistants. With their help, she coordinated the after-school activities. With the help of volunteers, she encouraged parents to carry out activities for the children and organized opportunities at the Community Center for all generations to meet and learn.

2.1. The Community Center: A Place of Community Development

The purpose of community development in Karice was to create programs upgrading human capacity. Many people helped guide community members to appropriate programs. These goals were pursued through projects such as these:

- After-school activities.
- Community-based management.
- The Teens and Technology Program.
- The School and Job Program.
- A community-advisory center.

A large number of settlement members were engaged in community development training provided by the Wide Open School Foundation. The trainers focused on the following:

- Understanding and sharing of their cultural heritage.
- Understanding of Slovak cultural diversity.
- The ability to raise questions and make judgments on cultural issues.
- Participation in school affairs—in decision making, as well as classroom activities and school–community initiatives.

To work to solve social problems, parents, teachers, Roma teacher assistants, and members of the community participated in the training program *Social Assistance*. This training was based on intercultural communication and community management.

2.2. Civic Associations

In the Roma settlement at Jarovnice, two Civic Associations were promoting the work of the Community Center. One such association, Sakoneske Mistes, had been established with the Wide Open School Foundation as its sponsor in 2002. Earlier, in 2001, Civic Association ASAL had been organized. The leaders of ASAL were the first volunteers in the activities and programs of the foundation.

Among the activities promoted by Wide Open School Foundation in cooperation with ASAL, the Pastoral Center, the Special Primary School, and the foundation were the following:

- Parenting and child care.
- Tutoring and mentoring.
- Needlework, cooking, and sewing.
- programs for Roma youth: Teens and Technology, Hygiene and Health in Pubescence.
- Training oriented to the development and improvement of moral and ethical skills.
- Oral history.

Over time, in a few of the activities, non-Roma inhabitants of the village participated with the Roma from the settlement. This wide variety of civic activities helped create closer relationships between Roma and non-Roma inhabitants.

The Special Primary School in Jarovnice helped ASAL provide common activities for children, such as carnivals, sport activities, competitions, and trips. It was also responsible for arranging all the courses provided by ASAL.

3. LIFE IN THE ROMA SETTLEMENT OF JAROVNICE

According to the census of 2002, the village of Jarovnice had 4,008 inhabitants. The number of Roma was 2,936, with 1,473 of them women; thus, in 2002 in Jarovnice, 73% of the inhabitants were Roma. The average age of the village was very young—23 years. In the Karice settlement lived 1,566 children between the ages of 0 and 15 years. The growth of the Roma population continues: In 1977, 64 children were born; in 1987, 100 children; and in 1997, 130 children. One of the most painful facts was that many women becoming mothers were not mature, but were girls as young as 12 or 13, who were unable to take care of their children.

The registry of dwellings in the settlement showed 115 houses, 230 hovels, and 30 barracks. Many were in the worst possible condition. Many had poor sanitary facilities, lacked toilets, and were too small for the number of people living there. Most settlement dwellings were made of wood, sheet metal, and cardboard, minimally furbished. It was even worse in the shanties than in the regular houses, because the windows in winter had to be stuffed with cloth, plastics, and cardboard. Many of the hovels were not approved dwellings and did not have a registry number. In 1999, the settlement church was built. The church's construction was the result of a tragedy—a flood of the small stream running through Karice, the Malá Svinka (the flood is described more fully later).

The village and settlement had plans for construction of 20 flats in the settlement, a bridge over the Malá Svinka, construction of a local road, a wastewater treatment plant, a sewer system, and employment of Roma by the public utility services.

We visited the mayor's office and talked with Assistant Mayor Zdena Semanitová. She said:

> "Jarovnice lies here in this small valley, surrounded by woods and hay fields. A hundred years ago, this was the home of Zigmund Karolyi. His art portrays our pride, our attachment to the land. Karolyi lived in the manor house. Most of the villagers were poor, and still are. There is little work here. Our young people leave for jobs in Malmac; many spend hours and hours driving there and back.
>
> "There are more Roma in the settlement than villagers in the village. They too repeat the lives of their grandparents. Most of them have no work, no cars, no woods of their own. They live by the welfare payments they receive twice a month at the post office. They have not heard of Zigmund Karolyi."

3.1. Education

Formal education among the Roma here was very low. Some of them, especially the older people, were completely illiterate. Many of the younger had become secondarily illiterate because of unemployment and limited opportunity for reading and writing.

At one time prior to Slovak independence, there had been only one village primary school and one special school. In the early 1990s the village built a new primary school and non-Roma moved into the new premises. Thus, in 2004 there were two primary schools in the village and one special school for children with disabilities. Statistics from 2001 show that in the regular (i.e., not the special school) primary school for Roma there were 600 pupils, although the maximum capacity of the building was 300. It was one of the largest Roma schools in Slovakia.

Back in 1932, the first municipality school in Jarovnice was established by the state school administration. It included a special class for Roma children. The teacher for this class was Jozef Hiznay. In 1934, after a year's instruction, 51 Roma children had no higher grade to which to move. A parallel first-grade class was set up for them. The teacher of this class was Ladislav Snidiak.

In 1946, as part of an extension of the Szinaya manor house, a State Children's Nursing Home was established. In 1976, a separate kindergarten for Roma children was set up at the manor house. This kindergarten was attended by 48 preschool children. The number of children increased, and in 1978, three more classes were set up in the former manor barn. In 1987, a building for a kindergarten and day care center was constructed and put into operation. Both Roma and non-Roma children attended. This new building was said to be one of the most modern buildings in Europe at the time.

After the change of political systems in 1989, Roma participation in preschool education diminished. The number of children decreased dramatically. In 2004, there were three classes for non-Roma and Roma children in the kindergarten. Sixteen Roma preschool children attended.

The Wide Open School Foundation worked at moving pupils from the special schools into the mainstream Roma primary school. With all-day assistance, six pupils out of eight had managed to do it. In 2004 they were in sixth grade in the mainstream primary school, from which they had a real chance to continue toward secondary schools and employment.

In 1998, the Wide Open School Foundation established a Community Center and set up a school for parents, the School for Dalodaj. It provided courses for people without a basic education. In 2000, the foundation built the settlement's Community Center building. Among its many programs, it provided preschool education of Roma children for entrance to primary school, as described earlier.

3.2. Employment

In 2000, the unemployment rate among Roma in Jarovnice was 96%. This was attributable in part to the ongoing rapid social and economic change. Through a public benefits work program, 42 Roma (4% of the local residents) were employed. But on January 1, 2001, the unemployment rate of Roma in Jarovnice reached 100%. Then Civic Association ASAL and the Wide Open School Foundation started employing Roma teacher assistants and solicited the active involvement of Roma volunteers in public benefits work through various projects.

3.3. The First Roma People in the Village

No mention of a first arrival of the Roma in Jarovnice was found by us in a municipal chronicle. From an accountant in a local office, Pavlína Baluchová, born in 1944, we heard that the original chronicle of the municipality of Jarovnice did report the arrival of Roma. However, the record was not preserved; from people's stories, we heard that the chronicle was burned. It seems that a personal argument between a teacher named Kiralý and a parish administrator named Jancarý occurred regarding the keeping of the chronicle. They did not reach an agreement, and it was said that one of them threw it into a fire. In the current municipal office of Jarovnice, there was a chronicle containing records of events since December 12, 1957.

We were helped in the search for the first arrival of the Roma by the oral history of Anton Zboraj. He was born in 1926. Since 1960 he had been chairman of the United Farming Cooperative, and since 1972 he had been chairman of the Local National Committee. His information about the Roma was respected, because he frequently came into contact with those who lived in the settlement. He said:

> "Nobody knows exactly, but as far as I know from my parents and grandparents, it happened about the year 1880. The Roma used to live in huts made from earth, unbaked bricks, and wood. They earned their living by doing occasional jobs for farmers, mainly picking potatoes. The farmers gave them a portion of the potatoes they had dug. They lived on the potatoes for the whole winter. They lived also on other food that the farmers gave them for their work. They were very shy in their manners. A very strong feature of their life was the fact that they did not steal from the local inhabitants. Since they had no money, their clothes were very poor. They often wore ragged

clothes. Instead of footwear, they used to wear rags wound up around their feet—so-called 'footrags.'

"Life in the settlement, where they stayed most of the time, was up and down. They used to spent most of their time by the fire, where women prepared food. In the evenings they sang and danced around the fire. Young Roma played the violin. They had their Roma band, which used to play at dances and weddings.

"The local inhabitants attempted to relocate the Roma, but failed. Some Roma tried to adjust their lifestyle to the life of the local inhabitants."

From the chronicle of the municipality of Jarovnice, quoted by Mária Triscová (an administrator in the mayor's office), we learned that from 1900 to 1920, about 70–80 Roma lived in the municipality. They worked for the farmers, made unbaked bricks, and did other small jobs. According to the village's chronicler, Jozef Červenák, other Roma came to Jarovnice in 1942. Some earned their living by quarrying stone, and others continued the practice of making unbaked bricks.

From other information, we learned that they had fewer children than the residents of Karice today—on average, two or three children per family. Some Roma of that time married Slovak inhabitants.

Zboraj's story emphasized that the lifestyle of the Roma was based on strong moral principles—principles of course influenced by the larger community in which they lived. It also pointed out their early cooperation and communication with the majority (Slovak) community. From oral history, we understood that the majority community tried to solve the "increasing problem" of the Roma population by appointing one person from the Roma settlement to act as leader, but this initiative failed. It was said that the Roma community ignored this person or did not trust him.

We also learned about efforts to solve the "Roma problem" through assimilation. The high number of Roma resulted in the settlement's expansion. Some inhabitants sold parts of their fields, and Roma built houses on them. A few employers for whom Roma worked built them simple four-room houses. To occupy these houses, the Roma had to take loans. Since in Socialism all Roma had to be employed, they had the financial means of making their living and paying off their loans.

3.4. Religious Life in the Community

In the Jarovnice settlement in 2004, the only formal religion was Roman Catholicism. Although nowadays the majority of the Roma are said to be deep believers, evangelization was difficult here. A few years ago, nuns from an order called the Little Sisters of Jesus came to Jarovnice. Despite fear and worry, they accommodated themselves in a small trailer in the middle of the settlement and gradually gained the trust of the Roma. Holy Mass for the Roma used to take place only several times a year in the House of Culture, and the number of attendants was small. Now the situation is completely different. In the settlement stands the newly built church consecrated to the Virgin Mary of Fatima, whom the Roma in Jarovnice have long worshipped. Holy Mass takes place three times a week. And every Thursday, Father Peter Beseney of the Salesian order comes to the Roma from Bardejov Postárka, the national director and secretary of the Roma Pastorat Commission in the Conference of Bishops of Slovakia.

In the care of Father Peter, many Roma accepted belief in Christ, learned to pray, and practiced the sacrament. Some of them visibly changed their attitudes toward the majority, and vice versa. Father Peter was popular in the settlement, respected for his open attitude. He tried to understand the Roma and their problems. He presented the tenets of belief simply and clearly, and did not avoid contact with the people. He claimed that one part of the "solution" of the "Roma problem" was development of effective cooperation among the school, the church, the municipal office, and the police.

3.5. A Visit to the Parish Priest

Viera Ondercová went to visit the parish priest for Jarovnice as a whole, Father Stanislav Radvansky, to ask why segregation exists—not only in the area of education, but in religion as well—and to learn more about the local Roma.

> I come to a big house standing near the main Jarovnice church. I can't open the door, so I ring a bell. A voice answers, pleasant, male, and young. Then a young priest appears, welcoming me. This is Father Stanislav Radvanský. The reception room is furnished with old but good furniture. After pleasantries and an exchange of background information, I ask, "Why did they [the Roma] want a church of their own?"
>
> "Some people say it is good, and others not. I think it's a necessity. There are many Roma, and they don't feel comfortable up here [in the village]. And it's true that some people didn´t like to see them in the church. Of course, Christians should love each other, but in our local reality it is . . . [He searches for the right word, as if

he is censoring himself. Later I understand that it is his style of speaking, as if he weighs every word on a pharmacist's scale.] . . . it is difficult to consider it like that, and it would be very simplified. Yesterday we heard a Roma activist say that they want separate municipal authorities, that they will elect their own mayor. That too is unreal—for the time being."

I ask, "Why do the Roma still live in such terrible poverty?"

"The Roma are a completely different nation, with totally different customs and lifestyle. It's a collision of cultures. Perhaps the present time surprises them, with its high speed, its enormous development. They have rarely adapted. Communism was particularly significant, controlling their development artificially. In the West the development was more natural, and the Roma adapted [by withdrawal]. Oh, a few of them appreciate education . . . in fact, they have made their way up, and the others have already forgotten them."

I ask, "Is their belief in God different from the belief of the Slovaks?"

"Their belief is more natural; it includes fear. It is experienced through the heart more than the mind. It is emotional, very stable. Their belief is deep inside."

4. MÁRIA LICHVÁROVÁ

Mária Lichvárová was a social worker. For 2 years, she had worked out of the Pastoral Center. Her task was to assist the life and work of the settlement. Earlier she had taught at the primary school for Roma students only in Jarovnice. Mária devoted her professional life to the Roma. Although she was a contract-based employee, she dedicated even her free time, as well as her professional skills and knowledge, to the Roma children and their parents, relatives, and volunteers. She was deeply involved in the home-based teaching program. She told us:

> "I am a very strong-minded and devoted person. I taught Roma pupils at the primary school. Our school was segregated by communities and families. Mistakes were made on both sides—school and families too. We did not try to find effective ways of communication and cooperation. Traditional ways of thinking influenced our relations, care, and access to Roma pupils. I wanted to change it very much. I carried the idea of change inside me, but we were not prepared to do it."

Her dream of personal and educational change ultimately came to pass. In 2000, Mária became involved in Step by Step training focused on philosophy and methodology; multicultural and anti-bias education; and partnerships and cooperation among school, families, and the Roma community. She received training in ways to change her own teaching practice—only the practice, because her thinking had been already changed.

She started a new phase of her professional career, working with an alternative, inclusive curriculum. With a Roma teacher assistant helping, she developed tools to reach out to the Roma community and make people feel welcome in the school. Mária remembered that her colleagues said, "You must be crazy!", when she told them of her interest and involvement in the integration of Roma children into regular school. "Maybe I was, but I was keen on this new methodology. It brought a new sense to my teaching."

4.1. Gaining Community Acceptance through the Children

The Step by Step team, especially Mária, became accepted by the people in the community. The team members knew them well; they knew their problems; and they understood, from their faces, their feelings, needs, and wishes. When the team started its work in the community, a lot of people from both the settlement and the village did not go along with it. But team members were strongly persuaded that the Roma people needed someone to give them a helping hand. Eva Koncoková, executive director of the Wide Open School Foundation, provided a model for the kind of assistance the settlement needed. She told Mária:

> "They need to feel our love and acknowledgment of their values. I think they are able to feel the difference between true and false love. Love is patience. It does not require immediate results. No miracles. Because love is always in pain, it requires starting again and again."

Mária did love the Roma children. With the results she achieved with them, she gained the support of their parents, relatives, and volunteers at the Pastoral Center. Together they worked to reduce illiteracy among all family members. They also worked to prepare the children for regular school.

As coordinator of the home-teaching volunteers, Mária wrote out the teaching and learning plans. The volunteers learned to rewrite them on the blackboard in the Pastoral Center and to guide the parents through them. By rewriting them, the volunteer parents practiced and continued to improve their own literacy skills. Mária said:

> "It was not easy to enlist them for the long haul. The volunteers had to leave their families several times a month to take part in the training workshops provided by the Wide Open School Foundation. For teaching, we used to use natural materials, such as water, sticks, wood, soil, stones, and so on. Then the foundation supported the educational activities partly by providing other teaching materials, such as paper, exercise books, crayons, fairy tale books, folding picture books, and such."

4.2. The Pastoral Center

The Pastoral Center was established as a part of the newly built Roma church. This center included a long, narrow classroom, visually stimulating, shown in Photo 2. It also had a small, well-equipped social facility with washbasin and toilet, and a room for food preparation. At the entrance to the classroom was a portable blackboard. On the adjacent wall was a weekly thematic plan for work with the children—a plan to be implemented by the parents.

> At the board, a young Roma man is explaining to parents what they are supposed to do with the children. About 20 children are sitting at a long table. Each is holding a marker and has a sheet of paper in front of him or her. The children are imitating the movement of the teacher, using the hand holding the marker. They make circles in the air, then transfer the circles immediately to the paper. A parent standing close to his boy notices that the child is not making the intended arcs. He takes the little hand into his and makes the shapes on the paper. Nobody has to ask him to assist his child. He reacts as soon as he observes his son's difficulties.

Arriving at the Pastoral Center, the parents first got acquainted with the tasks for the day, learned them, and then taught some children (either their own or their neighbors'). On the day of our visit, the working plan looked like this:

> Plan of activities for the month of March:
> Topic: neighborhood, court, meadow, garden

Second week:

1. Model balls from clay—make little animals (chicken, snail, little rabbit).
2. Exercise the voice: what sound does it make?
3. Draw a hole—a lower arc. Number sequence up to 7. Get familiar with the color yellow.
4. Strengthen the knowledge of colors: red, blue, white. Observe domestic animals; talk about the usefulness of domestic animals.

Nursery rhyme:
Pláva kacka po jazere, vo vode si saty perie, rybky sem, rybky tam, ja Vás vsetky pochytám.
[A duck swims on the lake, it washes its clothes in the water, little fish here, little fish there, I'll catch you all.]

More than 100 children and their parents were taking part in home-based school preparation. Since space at the center was quite limited, the children worked in five groups of about 10 children each. One group every day had examples of teaching and learning by Mária or another specially trained professional.

The Pastoral Center contributed to the home-based teaching, providing alternative methods of preschool education for children ages 3–6 years. Currently, coached by Mária Lichvárová, 39 volunteers (parents, grandparents, and neighbors) were working in it 1 day per week, getting training and then teaching children. In other words, each group had 1 day a week participating in preschool activities at the Pastoral Center. On other days, the small-group instruction was at the home of one of the parents. At this time, the home-based instruction had continued for more than a year.

The Pastoral Center was also used for meetings of various groups. Weddings, christenings, and other sacraments were held there. Both young people and adults had group meetings there.

4.3. Home-Based Teaching

The teaching was based on Step by Step methodology. At the Pastoral Center and Community Center, it lasted 4 hours—every day for the teacher, 1 day a week for each child and mom. It respected the personality of each child. The content had been developed and planned for months. The curriculum had been developed according to contemporary

PHOTO 2. Mothers, grandmothers, and children attending the Mothers and Children Club, a community program at the Pastoral Center. Photo copyright Nadácia Skola dokorán. Reproduced by permission.

PHOTO 3. Children learn about shapes by searching for them in the environment. Photo copyright Nadácia Skola dokorán. Reproduced by permission.

PHOTO 4. Parents in the role of teachers improve literacy skills and support their children's personal development. Photo copyright Nadácia Skola dokorán. Reproduced by permission.

PHOTO 5. Children and parents participate in home-based instruction to expand their vocabulary. Photo copyright Nadácia Skola dokorán. Reproduced by permission.

standards for preschool education, with learning units not firmly limited in time.

The assessment of children was verbal, and emphasis was placed on the motivational aspect of assessment. Educational content was divided into weeks, modified to the abilities of individual children, with each of them getting 20 hours per week. In this preparatory stage, the work of the teacher was highly specified. The teaching was not divided into subjects, but into components of education, making up integrated blocks. The components of education were as follows:

- Development of speech, knowledge and the elements of music education, with individualized "logopedic" care (i.e., instruction in pronouncing sounds or words).
- Preparation for writing and the elements of art education.
- Sensory education and elements of mathematical notions.
- Physical education.
- Study skills education.

In the middle of the Roma settlement, among many similar houses, stood a house marked with a picture of a tree symbolizing the Wide Open School Foundation. Other houses and huts in which home-based teaching was carried out were marked in a similar way. The wooden and corrugated iron dwellings looked as if they were all attached together (see Photo 3).

As in nearly all the larger houses here, the center of activity is a room in the middle. In it stands a big table. Over in one corner is a stove; in the other corner is a sofa. Almost every kitchen in this settlement looks the same. It is pleasantly warm here. Some nine children are sitting at the table. Their mothers are crowded closely behind them. It is difficult to estimate the ages of the children, and of the mothers too. Nearly all the mothers are pregnant. The children are a heterogeneous group, ages 2–6. A big sheet of paper with the week's plan written on it is hanging on the door. (It is a copy of the one posted on the notice board at the Pastoral Center.) It also repeats the verse that the children, with help from their mothers, are supposed to learn this week.

Mária, the coordinator, contentedly looking at her charges at work, says, "At one time I taught all the preschool children myself, but as the number of children and parents in the Pastoral Center increased, I could no longer do it. So we gradually involved the family members. Today I only come by each house to check that everybody has copied the learning plan and understands what all they are supposed to teach their children. Then we go out to help other illiterate or half-literate parents fill in forms, so that they are able to claim state benefits."

One of the mothers is holding a big, colored picture book. She reads loudly and clearly a Slovak version of the fairy tale *Cinderella*. She reads one sentence, and immediately another woman says it in the Romani language. The children are listening carefully. They have sheets of paper with a number of circles and lines in front of them. The mother then asks the children about the content of the fairy tale. She checks to see that they understand all the words.

It is both sad and beautiful to see these mostly young women standing near their children, slowly doing what their own mothers were unable to do. Perhaps if Mária or any other person could have shown their mothers the way for their children to get further, then all of them would be further today. Mária keeps reminding us, "We wouldn't accomplish anything if they themselves didn't want it. It all starts with them. They have enough poverty and misunderstanding in their lives. They don't want to be uneducated and incomprehensive of what's going around them any more."

This big, little woman, looking tired but strong, has shown the Roma in the settlement a way to get out of their confinement. Every day she does thousands of little things for them and their children, so that they won't lose hope for a better future.

After reading from the book, they all name, together and aloud, the objects in the pictures. Then they count to 7. For some of them, 7 is not enough and, with laughter, they continue to 10. On the shelf in the corner are colored dice and kits. The mother who was reading before takes a tower made of colored plastic chips. She takes it apart chip by chip. The children name the color of each chip she is holding in her hand. They also name the colors violet and pink, but these are not basic colors, and a preschool child does not have to know them yet.

Outdoors the snow is white. With their job well done, the children joyfully run to a small patch of open land, where they pelt each other and their mothers with snowballs. Just a moment ago they were learning with their mothers, grandmothers, and other family members. They are cheerful and happy.

In the poorest homes, there were no pictures, handicrafts, or books, and no place to write. Yet a flat space was found for a group to write and draw. In the relatively affluent homes in the settlement, there was more comfort and accommodation for home teaching (see Photo 4) and the space used for the preschool program at the Community Center was also more spacious (see Photo 5).

5. THE STEP BY STEP PROGRAM IN SLOVAKIA

As indicated throughout this report, the education system sponsored by Step by Step is based on respecting and exercising children's rights to an education. In the Slovak Republic as elsewhere, these are rights of national minorities and ethnic groups, as well as of the majority culture. The Constitution of the Slovak Republic codifies the right of minorities and ethnic groups to be educated in their own language.

According to the 2001 census, 89,920 citizens of the Slovak Republic described themselves as Roma. However, this statistic does not indicate the actual number of people belonging to the Roma national minority, for various reasons. Many Roma declare themselves to be another nationality, such as Slovak or Hungarian. According to authorities at the Demographic Research Center, the estimated number of Roma in the Slovak Republic in 2000 was 379,200. The estimate of Roma children under 14 years of age was 139,833.

The social conditions of the Roma population, particularly regarding education, were alarming. According to the statistics of the Institute of Information and Prognoses of Education, in the school year 2002–2003, the total number of pupils in Slovakia's primary schools reached 600,888. Of those, 15,597 were failing in school. Almost 60% of those failing were pupils from socially disadvantaged environments, and most of these were of Roma origin. The low educational level of the Roma minority had a direct impact on the entire society, because it resulted to some extent in unemployment, overdependence on social benefits, increased criminality, drug addiction, low levels of hygiene, and poor health conditions and housing.

In general, the Slovak educational system was not (and still is not) adjusted to the specific needs and conditions of the Roma minority. Most Roma children attended schools with Slovak (the majority language) or Hungarian as the language of instruction. They were regularly confronted with linguistic barriers. Moreover, in a distressing number of cases, children were denied access to the regular schools.

The number of Roma children enrolling in preschool education was decreasing year by year. Much of a child's personality and creativity is formed within preschool education at the sensitive ages of 3–6 years. Preschool unpreparedness of a child from a socially disadvantaged home environment results in his or her immaturity in the early grades of primary school. Therefore, many Roma children were sent to special schools for mentally disabled children. According to the statistics of the Institute of Information and Prognoses of Education, in the school year 1998–1999, only 8% of the children from disadvantaged home environments[2] were progressing successfully at the regular primary schools. In 2000, this estimate was only 6%.

In order to avoid a high rate of school failure at the standard primary schools, experimental preparatory classes were established in 1992 by the Slovak Ministry of Education. According to an evaluation of these preparatory classes in the school year 1998–1999, two-thirds of the pupils from disadvantaged environments attending the preparatory classes were successfully continuing their education at regular schools.

Only a very low percentage of Roma youth were continuing their studies in secondary schools. The overall educational level of those children completing compulsory school attendance did not reflect their time spent in school. That is, these children satisfied school attendance requirements but did not attain minimum academic preparedness, partly because they were held back for at least 1 year in primary school. Approximately 50% of 15-year-old Roma students had repeated at least a year of primary school or had finished their formal schooling in special schools for mentally disabled children.[3]

In the school year 2002–2003, the total number of students attending secondary vocational schools was 215,856, including only 190 known Roma students. According to local sources, the proportion of Roma who went beyond basic education was only 6%. In other words, even most of those who obtained basic education did not continue their studies— either at secondary grammar schools, at another type of secondary vocational school, or at apprentice schools. Instead, most of them completed the compulsory 10 years of schooling and then registered at the Labor Office.

Substandard education was therefore one of the first obstacles the Roma faced in approaching their full potential in Slovakia. Without equal opportunity to attend schools of high quality, the Roma were condemned to living their lives undereducated and unemployed.

Many Roma children were tracked into the special schools for mentally disabled children on the basis of apparent unreadiness, but with little consideration of their capacity for benefiting from these schools. This

---

[2]"Disadvantage" included low standards of living, inadequate education, unemployment, dependence on social benefits, criminality, drug abuse, lack of cultural activities, health problems, unsuitable housing, and poor hygiene.

[3]This estimate was based on local information sources.

tracking perpetuated a discriminatory link between race and disability. At the Roma settlement of Jarovnice, the biggest opportunity to help Roma children and their families begin reaching their potential appeared to be through implementing the Step by Step program. Such a program might create culturally appropriate conditions for children's self-realization in the education system.

Under the guise of aptitude or readiness testing, a pervasive, institutionalized racism existed at all levels of the school system. It resulted in a segregated education system that was inherently discriminatory. This segregated system poorly addressed the needs of Roma youth for skills and credentials. A more appropriate solution was offered for Roma children by the Step by Step program. Its initiative contained the following ideas:

- Educational goals to be reached in ways sensitive and respectful of the Roma culture and language and the aspirations of the Roma community, with decision-making power in the hands of Roma leaders.
- Equal opportunity in the operations of the education system, following legislation eliminating all segregation and discrimination.
- Free, high-quality preschool education for economically disadvantaged children, and curriculum reform connected with the professional development of teachers.
- A comprehensive approach for children ages 0–18 and their families, including prevention of school failure; intervention to decrease the dropout rates; and development of rehabilitation (mentoring and tutoring) for dropouts.

The Step by Step plan was designed for all levels of the school system and all levels of government policy. The strategy called for supporting action in other sectors, such as health, employment, economic development, social protection, and civic participation.

5.1. Nadácia Skola dokorán—the Wide Open School Foundation

Slovakia's Wide Open School Foundation started its work in 1994. According to its director, Eva Koncoková,

"Our beginnings were modest, without great ambition. I was an early childhood professional, Eva Duríková was a psychologist, and

Jozefka Schmidtová was an administrator. The three of us teamed up to cooperate with Slovakia's Head Start program.[4]

"Our goal was to support preschools having a high proportion of children from less supportive family environments and, following the example of Head Start, to give them comprehensive care. The Open Society Institute gave us strong support. This was the beginning of our journey to help Roma children and their families. It was the beginning of Step by Step in Slovakia, in a period of deep social change.

"The beginning was full of excitement. It brought teaching methods from the United States. We got excellent training on teaching methods, provided by great trainers. They brought new perspectives, helping us in implementation and development. We got funds for furnishing kindergarten spaces and later the primary schools.

"Our master teacher trainers soon gained prestige. Today they are university teachers, supervisors, and experts in other NGOs. They bring the teachings of the Open Society Institute to other programs. Among our partners are Eva Duríková, Stefan Porubský, and Eva Wagnerová. Some, such as Peter Repinský, have become international master teacher trainers. Each of them contributed to the education of children, youth, teachers, and parents in Jarovnice.

"A foundation staff member belongs to an exciting and hazardous profession. Ours is not a routine job. As executive director, I head the staff. Jozefka Schmidtová is responsible for administration and financial matters. Other members of the team are young women who manage the day-to-day agenda, correspondence, and administrative details. Recently, Bohuslav Ilavský and Vincent Cerven joined us as project managers, methodologists, and master teacher trainers. A few university colleagues help us draw up contracts. Across the country, we have an extended team of professionals. They are staff members of the 15 regional centers at kindergartens, primary and secondary schools, and universities. Our teacher trainers are on staff at these centers. They interact with research centers, local authorities, and professional institutions.

---

[4]Step by Step was called the Head Start Program from 1994 to 1996. In 1996 the OSI changed the name of the program to Step by Step to avoid confusion with the U.S. Head Start Program. The new name was proposed and selected by Step by Step country teams at an international meeting in Prague.

"One of our strategic partners, the Plenipotentiary of the Slovak Government for Roma Communities, headed by Klára Orgovánová, supported the establishment of our foundation, helping us define our mission in Roma communities, including the project in Jarovnice.

"In all, it is a colossus, yet managed by a small, highly interactive team. Together we work to keep the lights set aglow by OSI Bratislava diretor Alena Pániková, and with education experts and researchers Ludmila Simcáková and Zita Badúriková. Together, in professional partnership, we support the mission of the Soros Foundation in Slovakia and other countries. The benefits to Slovakia of that mission include the following:

- Acceleration of school success for Roma students.
- Experimental verification of Step by Step methodology for preschools and primary schools.
- Reintegration of Roma students from the socially and educationally less supportive environments of special schools into participation in the life of the majority population.

These accomplishments have brought the foundation the acknowledgment and respect of the Ministry of Education.

"Despite its small size, our staff has a far-reaching professional network—a wide base of devoted teachers, parents, and master teacher trainers. With each passing month, the Foundation is more firmly sustained in its implementation of the local processes of Slovak education. The schools supported and furnished by us increasingly function as resource centers and become independently able to seek support from the European Union [EU] and other funding bodies.

"The Jacobs Foundation and other donors have provided us with long-term grants focused on development of computer skills for young Roma people. Our goal is to help coordinate assistance from all sources to develop the hidden potential of Roma communities such as Jarovnice. We seek to find still other donors to mitigate the discrimination within segregated communities. For both children and parents, we hope to develop key competencies necessary for the labor market.

"Without the resources of EU programs—for example, Phare, Socrates, and Gruntvig—a comprehensive approach cannot be achieved. Of course we continue to apply for these resources. It is a never-ending challenge for the communities. None of them can do it alone.

"Our goal is not to provide 'fish' for the impoverished and held-back Roma children, but to teach them and their segregated communities 'how to fish.' "

Since 1994, Eva Koncoková and the Wide Open School Foundation have implemented a variety of educational initiatives in the area of Roma and general education. These include:

- Roma minority education support.
- Institutional change.
- Inclusion of children with special needs.

Through the Institutional Change programs, WOSF offers the Step by Step systemic early childhood education reform program introducing child-centered methods and parent engagement into the general education system serving children from birth through age 10. Inclusion of children with special needs aims to move children with disabilities from segregated to integrated child-centered settings with appropriate support.

But the core of their work is in Roma minority education. Through a series of interconnected programs, WOSF works to ensure school success for Roma children to promote their integration into schools with non-Roma children and to prevent their misplacement in special education. For example, initiatives focus on improving second-language teaching in early education settings and on preparing Roma teacher assistants to work in classrooms. Community-based initiatives for older children support youth clubs, computer courses, and counseling centers.

In 1996, the foundation established 15 regional centers in Slovakia, each a model of child-centered education based on the Step by Step program. The staffs of the regional centers now include 96 teacher trainers, all qualified teachers and professors of education. Through coordination of the Wide Open School Foundation, the staffs have fulfilled the requirements of the Slovak Ministry of Education for accrediting programs for professional development in the schools. The accreditation was partly based on longitudinal studies and research.

The Wide Open School Foundation was the first foundation to take the risk of coming into Jarovnice. This was a place where for a long time the ethnic minority had been a numerical majority. And life there was especially risky for the Roma. In 1998, the small stream running through the settlement, the Malá Svinka, flooded its banks and inundated Karice. It swept away not only the property of these poor people, but also their most precious possession, their children. Forty-four of them died. After the flood, the Roma built their new church (described earlier) with charity gifts from the neighboring villages. It was not clear that they could rebuild their lives, however.

In the same year as the flood, the Wide Open School Foundation started its cooperation with the settlement. It offered the Roma help in improving the educational level of their children. In a short time, two simple buildings—the Community Center and a Roma church—were built. In the newly built Roma church, director Eva Koncoková helped establish the Pastoral Center. She remembered:

> "I met the people from the settlement after the flood in 1998. I was strongly affected by the misery of a mother holding a dead child in her arms. They were scared, panicked people with devastated dwellings.
>
> "Many charity organizations visited Jarovnice to bring humanitarian help, but the people needed new hope—not compassion so much as the impulse to start the hard work. I felt they needed to acquire abilities that would help them overcome their adversity. I knew we could help them find a lost sense of life.
>
> "We addressed their spirits with the help of the priest and the philosophy of Step by Step. We started to build a community center. Later I found an institutional partner, the Special Primary School. Together we looked for allies. We were stimulated to build the Pastoral Center, which soon became the place for meetings and planning for the future.
>
> "At first the Roma were distrustful. They did not believe in strange organizations, people who are different.
>
> "We taught a few people to be trainers. We got the Roma involved in leisure, taking the edge off their work, and later into educational training. The people found a space for self-realization. In small but important ways, they found hidden potential, felt joy, experienced success, and acquired skills to prove their human worth.
>
> "People from the community—believers and nonbelievers, educated and illiterate—were involved in the first social training. All had the same conditions, the same chances.
>
> "The content of community programs fulfilled the philosophy of Step by Step in the real and practical life of the Roma. The Step by Step standards acquired a new dimension, 'a dimension of mutual enrichment.' "

Eva Koncoková knew that Roma family environments did not (and often still do not) provide the preschool experiences required by the formal education system. Young mothers in Karice gave birth to their first children very early, often at the age of 12 or 13. And soon more were on the way. It was not unusual for a 29-year-old father with seven children to leave his wife for another woman expecting his baby. The care of his first seven would be taken up partly by the grandmother or even the great-grandmother, who no longer had children of her own to care for.

6. SPECIAL PRIMARY SCHOOLS

In one form or another, the Special Primary School had long existed in Jarovnice for children found to be unready for admission to the village regular primary school. It was intended to provide special education for children with disabilities, using specialized instructional methods, tools, and forms. The pedagogy and materials were developed nationally for students with mental, sensory, or physical handicaps; students with behavior problems; and ill or weakened students placed in medical facilities. With its lowered standards, it was meant to prepare them for accommodation to the workplace and social life.

Education at special primary and secondary schools in Slovakia was linked to the educational plans and curricula of regular schools, supposedly with only minor modifications in offerings, but with lower expectations of performance. Officially, an education attained at these schools was equivalent to that attained at regular schools. The actual training of the students in the special school, however, did not meet the regular schools' practices. The quality of these students' education and of their preparation for future careers was below standard. At best, these students continued their education in vocational schools. Some received apprenticeships in selected study courses. Students with more serious mental disabilities or multiple disabilities went to schools of practical training. The objective there was to prepare young people for independent living, family life, basic assistance at homes, or auxiliary work under supervision. The special schools usually accepted students on the recommendation of pedagogical, psychological, or specialized advisory centers. Teachers working at the special schools had been trained at a university and had received pedagogical instruction in one of the specializations.

Most Roma children in special schools were classified as having language delays and related disabilities, such as dyslexia or dysgraphia. Placement in special schools was determined by tests administered by psychologists and special committees. The tests were given in Slovak, a language that many Roma children did not understand well. The tests also often included references to objects outside the children's experience, thus making them culturally as well as linguistically discriminatory. For both these reasons, the tests were seen by reform groups as unfair.

For financial and other reasons, most Roma children did not have access to preschools where experience with the Slovak language could be obtained. Their lack of fluency and their cultural and behavioral disadvantage, combined with a lack of other school readiness skills, resulted in their being labeled "handicapped." Many Roma parents agreed to place their children in special schools without understanding the long-term consequences. However, most of those parents who did realize the constraints these schools placed on their children's future thought they had no alternative.

6.1. The Special Primary School in Jarovnice

The Special Primary School in Jarovnice was located in a building on church property. Sixty-four pupils not admitted to the regular primary school attended it; 59 of these students were Roma. Instruction was organized in two shifts. The school was an active place, with places for parents and grandparents to be together. The rooms were crowded with visual stimulation, including paper constructions made by the children. In good weather, mothers and grandmothers continued some of the instruction in an ample playground (see Photos 6 and 7).

One classroom was affiliated with the international project *School Success for Roma Children*, a Step by Step special school initiative. The initiative was created to promote equal education for Roma children, giving them appropriate conditions for learning, pedagogy, and personal support. The goals for this classroom were as follows:

- To identify Roma children who were misplaced in special schools.
- To improve their academic skills and integrate them into the mainstream.
- To develop a viable model of school success for Roma children.
- To support implementation of such a model.
- To propose changes in national education policies.

The long-term strategies of this project were combined in a comprehensive approach to increase school success for Roma children through prevention, intervention, and rehabilitation. The project model had five key components:

PHOTO 6. After-school activity at the Community Center focuses on the second-language approach and expanding vocabulary through rhymes and rhythmic games. Photo copyright Nadácia Skola dokorán. Reproduced by permission.

PHOTO 7. A child is assisted in a hands-on math activity by a mother who volunteers at the Pastoral Center. Photo copyright Nadácia Skola dokorán. Reproduced by permission.

- The mainstream primary school curriculum to replace the special school curriculum.
- Step by Step early childhood methodology as the vehicle for delivering the curriculum.
- Anti-bias education for all teachers and administrators in the project.
- Appropriate methods to support second-language learners.
- A Roma teacher assistant at each project site.

The international project included an experiment. The hypothesis studied was that Roma children were being misplaced in the special schools; that some of them had average or above-average mental ability, however obscured it might be by social disadvantage; and that even a majority of Roma children, when given appropriate conditions for learning, would be capable of meeting the regular schools' academic achievement standards. The Step by Step classroom in the Special Primary School at Jarovnice was one of five classrooms participating actively in this experiment; five other classrooms served as controls.[5]

Teachers of the treatment participated in selected professional and personal development. Step by Step pedagogical methods were introduced to teachers of the treatment classes. They took part in the following training seminars: *Step by Step Methodology*; *Education for Social Justice*; *School Improvement*; *Tutoring and Mentoring of Roma Students, Especially Dropouts*; and *Critical Thinking*. All teachers at the special treatment group schools, including some of their administrators, parents, and community members, participated in these training sessions. They adopted an anti-bias stance and worked at developing intercultural understanding of Roma communities. They examined their own biases and explored how these biases were manifested. They developed a protocol to reach out to Roma communities and make the people feel welcome in the school.

The teachers of the treatment group taught according to the state curriculum, the same used by mainstream primary schools. Use of the mainstream school curriculum was the central component of the model and was the most difficult challenge of this project. The students in both the treatment and control classes were tested on Slovak language and mathematics according to the expectations of the mainstream primary schools.

---

[5]The Special Schools Project was an initiative of the Open Society Institute and Step by Step organizations in Bulgaria, Hungary, Slovakia, and the Czech Republic. From 1999–2003 the project tested the hypothesis that many Roma children are misplaced in special educational settings. By providing appropriate support, the program was able to demonstrate that 64% of these children across the four countries could reach the regular curriculum standards by grade 3.

Roma teacher assistants placed in each of the five treatment classes assisted the teachers, integrating Roma language, culture, and history into the curriculum. They also served as liaisons between the families and the school. In contrast, the control classes did not have Roma teacher assistants participating in the process of instruction.

The teachers and Roma teacher assistants paid special attention to the unique needs of each student, with recognition of the child's abilities and disabilities. Each student learned according to an individual educational plan, in keeping with Step by Step methodology. The Wide Open School Foundation provided furnishings for the treatment classrooms.

Based on the results of achievement testing, the goals for the Step by Step classrooms set at the beginning of the project were seen as met. Almost all test results were higher in the treatment classrooms, whether these were measurements of intellectual abilities, communication skills, social and emotional skills, or speech and language development. This initiative was seen as demonstrating that Roma children were capable of academic success when provided with appropriate conditions for learning.

The process of changing the attitudes and practices of school staff members was seen as holding major implication for the design, delivery, and funding of professional development at both the preservice and in-service levels. The staffs at the pilot sites identified aspects of the Step by Step methodology and anti-bias education as some of the most important things they did to try to meet the needs of students in their classes. They also indicated that more information on Roma culture, strategies for involving parents, and training sessions would help them be even more effective in the future. Almost all staff members in the pilot classes said that participating in this project would have long-term benefits for them. These benefits were most often identified as relating to improved teaching methods.

Eighty percent of the students in the five treatment classrooms passed the tests with a score of 75% or higher. The five components of the program mentioned above were seen to contribute to the success rate of these students. Although all elements of the project were interrelated and mutually supportive, the single component that the research identified as most highly correlated with academic achievement was good early childhood practice.

6.2. The Headmistress

Eva Lukácová, headmistress of the Special Primary School, was a woman who had worked professionally in Jarovnice for 20 years. She was considered an excellent manager and a highly competent teacher. Her expressed dream was to expand the capacity of the school and, with Step by Step, to create an integrated system of education emphasizing individualized learning. She knew well that not all her enrolled children belonged in special education, notwithstanding the fact that each had a special education certificate from a psychologist.

Eva Lukácová was friendly and open, yet had a strong and demanding personality. She had special abilities to bring people together and encourage them to develop their skills, knowledge, and inner power. She created for her colleagues a school environment supporting their personal development and professional career.

Lukácová had had many opportunities for career "advancement" elsewhere, but had always refused. For her, this work gave her contentment and enriched her personal as well as professional life. She said:

> "Despite many financial problems, problems with school attendance, and difficulties in involving parents, this work makes sense. It gives me energy when I see changes in student and parent attitudes toward school.
>
> "Step by Step is a methodology seen by a wide audience of school staff members and parents as effective for Roma children in preschool and mainstream primary schools. With its philosophical commitment to students from diverse cultural backgrounds, and an established infrastructure providing ongoing training and support for teachers, this methodology became the platform for all the foundation initiatives in Jarovnice.
>
> "We utilize the following Step by Step principles in our classrooms:
>
> • Developmentally appropriate educational practices.
> • Child-centered teaching based on individualization.
> • Learning as an active process.
> • Parents as partners in their children's education."

Lukácová went on to say:

> "Visible, positive changes in teaching process occur when we apply the Step by Step methodology. Our classrooms have more motivating environments.
>
> "This is an alternative model for teaching and learning. Step by Step teachers use interactive teaching strategies to develop cooperative, critical, problem-solving thinking in their students. It influences student thinking. It develops their personal and social abili-

ties, including their self-esteem. It accepts cultural differences and the social context of Roma children. The cognitive and speech development of Roma children is better stimulated when this methodology is used to augment the national curriculum.

"This pedagogy has brought about positive relationships between teachers and students, emphasizing partnering and mutual trust, help and cooperation. There is reason to believe that the learning style of the classroom is reflected in school–family cooperation. It increases parents' interest in the education of their children.

"Children from Step by Step classrooms appear to show more empathy toward their peers. I think that the Step by Step methodology, with its forms and techniques, leads to better school readiness of Roma children. It increases their independence and ability to solve problems. This methodology becomes a kind of guarantee of further cognitive, emotional, and social growth."

Speaking of parents, Headmistress Lukácová continued:

"Step by Step methodology helped us build trust and rebuild connections between the school and the community. We had to change our definitions of parent involvement. Parent–teacher conferences, open-house days, report cards, and notes sent home were merely invitations to start a conversation, not real opportunities for conversation.

"Activities such as parents' helping children with homework and parents' helping teachers in the classroom do not accomplish much if the parents themselves have low levels of literacy and if they feel that they have nothing to offer. None of these are likely to work if the parents themselves have had negative experiences in schools. If they were unsuccessful in school as children, in returning they feel that the schools, where once they were criticized as students, are now criticizing them as parents.

"We did not train them to be parents. We should not judge the quality of their parenting. We should help empower parents to engage in equal-standing conversations in the school and in the community. In order to avoid 'power-trip' conversations, we need to acknowledge that parents and community members have expertise that can help us do our job better.

"We sought ways to get the home culture incorporated into the school culture. Through home visits, we learned more about their children. We asked questions such as 'What do you enjoy about your children?', 'What things have you taught your children to do at home?', 'About what do you talk to your children?', 'What do you do together as a family?', and 'What are your dreams for your children?'

"Some parent stories emerge in the process of instruction, such as the story of Marika and the *marikle* bread [presented earlier in this chapter]. From such stories, teachers learn about the knowledge, skills, and values that exist in the community.

"Another way we initiated dialogue with parents was by having them listen to a story that their child heard in class—for example, the story of 'House, house, does anyone live here?'

"We teachers have been involved in training where we learned how to acknowledge and defer to the home and family. At the same time, the parents worked at identifying learning goals for their children."

6.3. Parent Participation

Karol Conka, a parent from the Roma settlement participating in the *Education for Social Justice* program, said:

"This training was completely different. I had to share a story from my life. It was not easy to speak for 5 minutes. Later, I felt more relaxed and I became more open, and a period of 5 minutes was not enough to express my feelings.

"It surprised me to find that I am full of mistrust, withdrawal, isolation. I blame non-Roma people for unemployment and for lack of concern about our social conditions. I have felt that all non-Roma people are racists. They have power. The law is on their side. They are unable to appreciate us. They just judge us.

"Once my children were attacked by skinheads. Twice, actually. I was hurt. If I went to the police station, they would not help my children. I knew that this majority society was unjust and discriminating. I felt powerless. I felt despair. I reacted in a typical way: I went to the pub and stole a bike.

"During this training, I learned how to cooperate better with others, express feelings, communicate, strengthen my self-esteem and self-confidence, and how to get rid of stereotypes. (First I had to learn the meaning of the word.)

"In discussions with non-Roma participants, I figured out that they struggle with similar problems. They have stereotypes too. And they had to learn to speak out more. They discussed it with me, but I still felt a barrier between us.

"This training helped me to identify my strengths. I remember one activity called 'I am an expert on . . . ' Each of us had to demonstrate a skill. I demonstrated wood carving. I'm good at it.

"But in normal, everyday life, I do not have opportunities to express my strengths. I am disappointed. People still label me as someone who steals and refuses to work and obey the law. The non-Roma people I meet are different from those I met during our training.

"I expect to change. For this reason, I have started to work as a volunteer at the Community Center. I made a book for children. It is about carving things such as animals, birds, and handles for kitchen utensils. Iveta helped me put Slovak and Roma names on them. I am proud of it. This book is used for teaching at the Community Center."

Other Karice parents in the *Education for Social Justice* program also wrote books for their children's classrooms. It was one of the activities that opened new connections to the school, helping parents feel appreciated for their words, experiences, and life stories. Most of the books were collections of pictures of the community and books of proverbs, folk tales, and legends. The parents participated in dialogues about the stories and pictures. They had opportunities to discuss important issues in their lives and to learn ways of maintaining traditions; in particular, they came to recognize the power of oral history.

All the activities included acknowledgment of and dialogue about the parents' role as teachers in their children's lives. The parents increasingly realized that they had teaching skills. Even illiterate and semiliterate parents were seen to be modeling literacy skills for their children. They perceived the "hidden literacies" in such routine behaviors as shopping, paying bills, cooking, gathering wood, and caring for sick people. The parents and all members of the extended family practiced various forms of oral literature, such as telling legends, folk tales, and family history, in addition to singing songs and playing games.

6.4. Whole-Language Strategies

Some workshops for community volunteers, teachers, and parents were entitled *Literacy Development with Second-Language Learners: Whole-Language Strategies*. For professionals and laypeople alike, they provided a theoretical and practical base for the whole-language approach to the development of literacy in children. This methodology was considered especially important for working with children with a weak language background and for children whose home language was not the one used in the schools. The objectives of the workshops were as follows:

- Understanding the processes of language acquisition.
- Identifying conditions in the environment that promote second-language development, and devising strategies for their use in classrooms.
- Developing strategies to promote reading and writing.

Through discussions and activities, the participants practiced ways to promote language development in Step by Step classrooms. These ways included thematic teaching, cooperative learning, peer tutoring, interactive journals, use of alternative forms of assessment, use of manipulatives in math, use of concrete objects, large- and small-group discussions, and use of home language.

Following a language experience approach, some participants wrote "I can" books, modeling how to develop interest in the story and going over new vocabulary. They practiced other examples of using language experience, including writing about events such as field trips and holidays, writing stories from pictures, and scribing retold stories. As part of their morning message, teachers learned more about how to teach phonics, semantics, and syntax in context.

The participants were involved in discussions about ways of helping pupils become better readers and writers. They created murals and illustrations for stories. For composing new stories, they developed such mechanisms as timelines, rebus books, board games, songs, and dioramas. They created journals for story writers. Even the least pedagogically oriented parents became acquainted with rudimentary forms of these literary devices.

6.5. Differentiated Instruction

A workshop for teachers of the Special Primary School in Jarovnice on *Differentiated Instruction* offered ideas for developing plans to accommodate differences in student readiness and learning styles. It facilitated recognition of the uniqueness of the individual child and fostered the philosophy of child-centered education. The principal said, "The more we differentiate, the more our students are all able to succeed in gaining new skills and knowledge."

During this workshop, the teachers came to better understand how students can become more involved in their learning. The participants developed strategies to promote learning and learned a new format for lesson plans that would help them provide differentiated instruction in their classrooms.

The teachers practiced the three main roles they play in the classroom: as learners, observers, and facilitators of learning. After reviewing strategies, they practiced development of active thinking and listening. They considered techniques such as webbing new information, story maps, Venn diagrams, writing process notes, varied texts, literature circles, independent studies, and group investigation. The teachers wrote examples of lesson plans for various levels of expectation of student performance, including activities to acknowledge "multiple intelligences" and potential grouping arrangements. The principal was supportive of this kind of teacher training, saying:

> "Our teachers believe that all students can learn. Lowering expectations for students who come from at-risk environments does not encourage development of traits and attitudes that will help them cope with difficult situations to be faced in their lives."

6.6. The Teacher Assistants

Placing teacher assistants from the local community in classrooms was a strategy used by Step by Step schools to bridge cultural and linguistic gaps between school and community. The premise behind this practice was that the inclusion of teaching assistants from marginalized groups enabled children from those groups to be more successful academically. In particular, the assistants helped children with little facility in the Slovak language. They served as a link between the home culture and the culture of the educational system. They cultivated parent support for their children's schooling.

The concept of having Roma teacher assistants as equal partners was consistent with the Step by Step philosophy. The Roma teacher assistants too were specialists—specialists in bringing a disrespected culture into respect. Technically, they were employed in classrooms to raise Roma students' academic performance toward mainstream levels.

In the national experiment described earlier, one important condition of the experimental treatment was the use of Roma teacher assistants. It was one of the components seen to contribute to the subsequent success of these students. According to Eva Koncoková,

> "The placement of Roma teacher assistants in the Slovak educational system and institutional recognition of their role has been a goal of the Wide Open School Foundation since 1994. The first step was to define what Roma teacher assistants needed to do. The following specifications were developed for the position:

- Comes from the same community as his or her pupils.
- Knows the parents and other community members.
- Demonstrates enthusiasm for working with them.
- Speaks the local Romani language.
- Has respect and appreciation for Roma customs and traditions.
- Has some experience in working with children.
- Participates in training on Step by Step methods and anti-bias education.
- Is actively involved in the education of the students, both during the official school day and after school."

At the initiative of the foundation, the Labor Office authorized a training course both for prospective Roma teacher assistants and for teachers who welcomed them into their classrooms. This course ran for 150 hours of theory and practice. It was accredited in September 2001 and was authorized as part of the educational system of Slovakia.

The content of the course included not only Step by Step methodology, but also the history, ethnography, and sociology of the Roma people. In addition, the course included the following topics:

- Basics of student-centered instruction.
- Development of an inclusive classroom environment, with emphasis on Roma sociocultural features.
- Development of a multicultural and anti-bias classroom climate.
- Identification of individual and cultural characteristics of Roma students.
- Methods and forms for creating a classroom community.
- Individualized instruction and intervention techniques.
- Control and organization of instruction.
- Personal and social development of the Roma teacher assistant.
- Development of communication skills.
- Partnership and cooperation between family and school.
- Community education, both organizational and cultural.
- History, ethnography, and sociology of Roma ethnicity.
- Writing projects.

Four Roma teacher assistants in the Community Center and Special Primary School in Jarovnice were graduates of the special course. They provided tutoring and carried out after-school activities. They exhibited the theoretical knowledge and practical skills necessary for working with Roma pupils in school and outside it, contributing to communication, organizational efforts, and cultural work within the Roma community.

Martin Kaleja, one of the Roma teacher assistants working at the Community Center, said:

"The teacher I work with is Iveta. She treats me as an equal partner. I really like the atmosphere that we create in the Community Center. The children feel good about being here, because their culture and traditions are not just understood but valued. When I started, I was surprised how much my presence helped the children. Because I speak Romani, I am able to explain Slovak words that they do not understand. I found that the students began to express themselves more freely. Another thing I do is bring Roma culture into the classroom by telling the children stories in Roma. Some of the stories come from the community, and others I make up myself.

"We invite parents to the classroom to assist and to create new stories with their children. They are included in the classroom and are involved in the teaching process. They express their views on what and how the children are learning. I think that the parents feel more comfortable because I am there. They see me as an ally and have become our partners. Even if they do not have much formal education, they contribute in their own ways. They come to the classroom to speak about customs of their own families or to prepare the children's favorite Roma meals. I think they feel welcome here and at school, and they have something to contribute."

Iveta added:

"The Roma teacher assistants are not seen as persons telling the community what to do, but as people who listen, share, and help the community search for possible ways to solve problems. They establish confidential and safe opportunities for the parents to express their feelings. They talk about the future of the children and the role of the school in improving opportunities for the children."

A body of educational research[6] has found that educators who feel empowered themselves have higher aspirations for their students, and their students develop a greater ability, confidence, and motivation to

---

[6]Cummins, J. (1989). *Empowering minority students.* Sacramento, CA: Association for Bilingual Education.

Fine, M. (1991). *Framing dropouts: Notes on the politics of an urban high school.* Albany: State University of New York Press.

Lee, V. E., Bryk, A., & Smith, J. (1993). The organization of effective secondary schools. In L. Darling-Hammond (Ed.), *Review of Research in Education* (Vol. 19, pp. 171–267). Washington, DC: American Education Research Association.

succeed academically. With Step by Step, the Slovak schools and communities are expanding teacher roles to empower the Roma teacher assistants. These new roles include the following:

- As coteachers who take charge of small-group cooperative learning activities.
- As teachers who devise activities to maintain and strengthen Roma culture.
- As family advocates who bring elements of the home culture into the school, and who help resolve issues between home and school when they arise.

The role of Roma teacher assistants at school was appreciated by the Special Primary School's principal, Eva Lukácová:

"Having assistants working as coinstructors helps teachers individualize instruction for their students. The academic success of our students was raised by the amount of classroom instruction and practice done in small groups working cooperatively. Another factor allowing Roma teacher assistants to support student success was the input of Roma culture into the classrooms. Into the process of instruction, our teachers incorporated Roma stories, songs, and art. Many of the activities were led solely by the assistants. They helped us improve communication between school and homes. Our students and their families see Roma teacher assistants as valued members of the teaching team."

One study[7] found that when schools had a strong commitment to reducing the gap between home and school cultures by building on the values, languages, and culture of the students' homes, even the most reluctant parents became involved. Eva Koncoková pointed out:

" . . . this idea was replicated in Slovakia by the Roma teacher assistants, inviting parents and community members to school to tell stories, to talk about the history of the community, and to engage in other home activities done at school, such as cooking and making things. Our focus on family involvement went well beyond such traditional practices as parent–teacher conferences, parent meetings, and helping children with homework.

---

[7]Fruchter, N., Galleta, A., & White, J. L. (1993). New directions in parent involvement. *Equity and Choice, 9*(3), 33–43.

"The advent of the Roma teacher assistants has had a positive effect not only on the academic performance of students, but on the entire school and community. The professional development of the teacher assistants and teachers motivates the rest of the school to become more professional. I feel it is important to expand the definition of learning environment from just the school to the entire community. This way the Roma teacher assistants can have positive influence on all of the children's environment, not just on their school environment. By empowering the teacher assistants, who are members of the local community, the program empowers its other members.

"Recalling John Dewey's words on educating 'some into masters and others into slaves,' we know that a dominant group can make a nondominant group into slaves, dependent on their masters. Then many fewer have power to solve a problem.

"In our country, the goal has been to make the teacher assistants familiar with resources that are available to community members. They helped as well to develop new programs and resources for the community. The Roma teacher assistants, not a person from the dominant group, became agents of change in their communities."

6.7. Community Resource Mobilization

Miroslav Sklenka was coordinator of the project *Improved Conditions for Mutual Tolerance between Roma and Non-Roma Inhabitants*. Speaking of the Wide Open School Foundation, he said:

"The foundation has had strong professional and methodical management. Its communication and cooperation with other beneficiary institutions—mainly the Ministry of Education of the Slovak Republic, and the Plenipotentiary of the Slovak Government for Roma Communities—has been distinctive. It has reinforced and enhanced the services provided to the Roma community and secured their long-lasting sustainability."

Mobilization of the potential of the Roma settlement Karice continues. The settlement has been involved in many programs and projects aimed at enabling the Roma to gain structural and practical skills that will foster their inclusion in society, and to overcome social exclusion by mobilizing and renewing their learning capacities. Through training and other activities tailored to their needs, the people have gained greater self-awareness, knowledge, and skill.

The Wide Open School Foundation's partnered program of multicultural activities has stimulated Roma families' interest in the formal education of their children. It has strengthened relations between the Roma and non-Roma communities, especially between representatives of the municipality and the Roma parents and community leaders.

Now we encapsulate the positive results of the Roma community's involvement in the foundation's educational activities. The Roma people have become committed to facilitating the learning processes of their children. They have gained a better understanding of the policy issues involved, as well as of the role of social environment. Recognizing their own knowledge, they have started to become involved in decision-making processes. At all levels they have demonstrated a capacity for problem solving, management, and self-evaluation. Thanks to lessons learned through the formal educational activities, they have improved their skills not only in intercultural communication, but in communication among families, children, and volunteers. The Roma themselves have upgraded the organizational and cultural work in their community.

Knowledge of Roma culture—particularly of the Romani language and of Roma history, ethnography, and sociology—has improved the self-identity and self-awareness of Roma youth and has enriched their ability to face oppression and conflict. In the words of Eva Koncoková,

"The non-Roma community has moved toward respecting the cultural differences, newly acknowledging the potential of the Roma community and their intercultural competencies, leading to a greater mutual tolerance and opposition to prejudice.

"The newly gained skills, knowledge, and competencies of the local Roma people have been demonstrated. There is also greater acceptance of the cultural and ethnic values of the Roma community by the non-Roma community. We are moving ahead with the project *Improved Conditions for Mutual Tolerance between Roma and Non-Roma Inhabitants*.

"Community targeting has been the most effective way of responding to the needs of the new generation. The government and various agencies and organizations have adopted an enormous number of supportive policies and programs. Evaluation data to assess the merits of change are still to come. We are at a critical juncture. We cannot afford to continue to waste human potential—a unique social resource. We need to extend mutual understanding of what is happening, the inertia of the sources flowing, in order to enact and refine effective educational agendas. Education remains the key."

CHAPTER 8

The Romania Case Study

Teacher professional development was the most common topic of the case studies in the 28 countries participating in the multicase study. In some countries, such as Romania, the Step by Step programs had been accredited by the countries' ministries of education to offer courses satisfying the professional requirement for in-service teacher education. Sometimes this helped establish good relations with the traditional teacher colleges; sometimes it did not.

The Romania case study team chose to study teacher training at Kindergarten 3 in Tulcea, a small city close to the Danube Delta. Because we circled wide to avoid Bucharest rush-hour traffic, the first drive to Tulcea turned from a 4-hour into a 7-hour drive for team members Ioana Herseni, Luciana Terente, and Catalina Ulrich, along with myself. Once we were there, we observed 2 days of a 3-day teacher-led training model. Principal Ana Pantea was the lead trainer.

On the first day, at a tablecloth lunch in the principal's office, the team members made a propitious discovery: They found an "informant." Case study fieldwork is greatly facilitated by locating a person who thoroughly knows the history, the people, and the territory, and who is inclined to talk about them and to steer the researchers to good data sources. The informant in Tulcea was Mihai Albota, former general inspector for the Tulcea County School Inspectorate (nicknamed "the General" because of his former job title). The General joined them for lunch and for much of the 2 days. (His stature and wisdom did not, of course, excuse him from triangulation.)

Case study researchers need also to be blessed by people to read draft copies of observations, interviews, and sections of reports. In this matter, Romania found little blessing: Most of the possible readers were too busy.

Often Catalina (writing) and I (editing) were the only ones reading the drafts. But she met the deadlines. The design for data gathering in Romania is shown in Figure 8.1.

Romania is a country preparing to join the European Union in 2007. With a population of 21,733,556 (in July 2003), GDP of 2,596 per capita, and recorded unemployment levels of 6.2% in 2004, it will be among the poorer of the EU members after it joins, though it is wealthier than many countries in southern and eastern Europe. As a precondition to joining the Step by Step program, preschools in Romania were challenged by CEDP Step by Step to provide appropriate child-centered furniture and

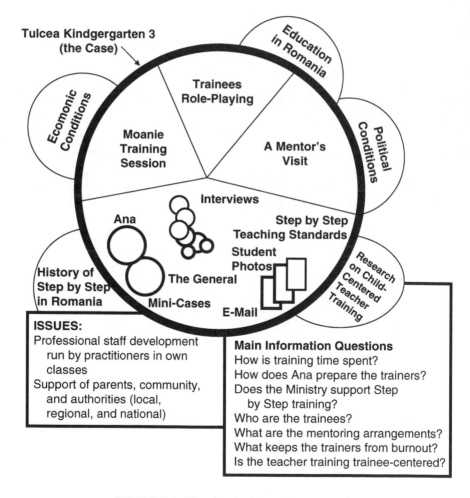

FIGURE 8.1. Plan for the Romania case study.

learning materials. By scrimping and saving, by wheeling and dealing, by creating their own materials, Kindergarten 3 had risen from the rubble, more or less. But the visitors found classrooms with luxurious napping space, high-quality activity materials, and teachers (and also teacher trainers) with high qualifications. So what were the researchers to make of the economic picture? Here, as much as in any of the other case studies, the research team was pressed to come to an understanding of the case as influenced by the situation. How can the international Step by Step program be understood unless the conditions of Tulcea, the Danube Delta, Bucharest, Romania as a whole, and all of Eastern Europe are understood—not only as regions, but as separate aggregates of classrooms and particular aggregates of people?—R. E. S.

The Romanian Case Study: Center for Educational and Professional Development, Step by Step Romania—Teacher Staff Development at the Tulcea Model Training Site[1]

CATALINA ULRICH

"Alternatives give oxygen to the system," commented a Ministry of Education and Research (MER) official, referring to alternative teaching methods. The fact that Step by Step methodology was accepted as invigorating did not make it easy to train teachers and administrators to use it. By observing complex training and teaching activities, we of the Romania Step by Step research team explored challenging central questions such as the following:

- What kinds of support and difficulties are influencing individual and institutional change in implementing Step by Step child-centered practices?
- How is teacher professional development being improved?

We also explored such additional questions as these:

- What are teachers' urgent needs for professional development?
- How can Step by Step training be improved?
- What are the methods of communication and networking between the teacher trainees and their mentors?
- How is a balance between heeding standards and valuing spontaneity achieved?

SUMMARY

Based on legislation adapted to European Union (EU) integration, the Romanian educational system promoted pluralism as a key value in a democratic society. Despite good educational policies, reform of the system moved slowly. The teachers were not sufficiently trained to transfer the policies into daily school life. Here we describe the ways Step by Step Romania was promoting child-centered practices through teacher training. The implementation of Step by Step alternatives required changes at both institutional and individual-teacher levels.

We studied the Center for Education and Professional Development (CEPD) of Step by Step Romania as a teacher-training provider, within a "market" traditionally composed of universities, teacher-training centers, pedagogical high schools, and (recently) a few accredited nongovernmental organizations (NGOs). Preschool education had been neglected within plans for educational reform. Training is one of the means for development. Model Training Site (MTS) Kindergarten 3, Tulcea, was the case we studied, noting several contexts and the internally contradictory heritage of a former Communist country. Our issues gave attention to the tensions between planning and spontaneity, alternative and traditional pedagogy, support and challenge within the context of teacher-training activities, and Step by Step methodology implementation at school and classroom levels. Our structure reflects the chronological phases of Step by Step training: attending the two required training modules (which embedded theoretical and practical activities undertaken by both trainers and trainees) and participating in monitoring activities. We also explored important issues of educational pluralism, drawing from a national symposium that was something of a retrospective on 15 years of educational alternatives in Romania.

Our methods were primarily qualitative data collection, including *observations* (of training sessions, conferences and workshops, and classroom activities), semistructured interviews (with the CEPD staff, Ministry and school inspectorate representatives, trainers, and trainee teachers), a focus group interview (with the CEPD staff), document review, and a survey questionnaire (for trainee teachers who attended the training at Kindergarten 3, Tulcea).

LIST OF CHARACTERS

- Ana Pantea—principal of MTS Kindergarten 3, Tulcea
- Mihai Albota (the General)—former general inspector for Tulcea County School Inspectorate
- Carmen Lica—executive director of CEPD, Step by Step Romania
- Jeni Batiste—trainer and teacher in MTS Kindergarten 3, Tulcea
- Marinela Peiciu—trainer and teacher, MTS Kindergarten 3, Tulcea
- Professor Ioan Neacsu—general director, Direction Evaluation, Prognosis, Strategies, and Programs for Preuniversity Education, Ministry of Education and Research
- Agafia Ghenciu (Galea)—trainer and teacher, MTS Kindergarten 3, Tulcea
- Daniela Mocanu (Dana)—trainer and teacher, MTS Kindergarten 3, Tulcea
- Maria Cîrstoiu—trainer and teacher, MTS Kindergarten 3, Tulcea
- Eliza Caramilea—trainer and teacher, MTS Kindergarten 3, Tulcea
- Silvia Craciun—inspector for preschool education, Tulcea County
- Gabriela Nichifor—teacher, School 5, Tulcea
- Ionica Mogos (Nela)—trainee and teacher, Kindergarten 41, Galati
- Elena Stratila—trainee and principal, Kindergarten 41, Galati
- Rodica Tircavu—trainee and teacher, Kindergarten 41, Galati
- Florica Paula Nistor—trainee and teacher, Kindergarten 41, Galati
- Maria Rauta—inspector for preschool education, Galati County
- Professor Viorel Nicolescu—president, National Commission for Educational Alternatives in Romania
- Dr. Gheorghe Felea—executive secretary, National Commission for Educational Alternatives in Romania
- Dr. Carmen Anghelescu—program coordinator, CEPD
- Elena Mihai—director of programs, CEPD

- Mariana Bandea—president, Romanian Association for a Modern School; representative of the Freinet educational alternative
- Liliana Dumitriu—executive director, Waldorf Federation
- Monica Cuciureanu—researcher (III), Institute of Sciences of Education; representative of the Jena Plan educational alternative
- Dr. Elisabeta Negreanu—head of department, Institute of Sciences of Education; representative of the Montessori educational alternative
- Laura Belibov—Step by Step teacher and trainer; primary school inspector, Constanta County
- Viorica Vladila—trainer and teacher, MTS Kindergarten 13, Târgoviște
- Carmen Eftimie—former site manager, MTS Kindergarten 3, Tulcea

GLOSSARY

- CCDs—Casa Corpului Didactic training centers
- CEPD—Center for Educational and Professional Development
- MER—Ministry of Education and Research
- MTS—Model Training Site

1. INTRODUCTION AND HISTORICAL/POLITICAL BACKGROUND

1.1. Staff Development at the Tulcea MTS

March 18, 2004, 9:00. Twenty-one teachers have gathered in Tulcea in Kindergarten 3 for Module Two, a 3-day Step by Step professional development activity. The lead teacher, Ana Pantea, is the principal of the kindergarten and coordinator of the training. Wearing a modish, two-piece, professional black suit, Ana welcomes the teachers to what the children call the "Smart Bunnies" room.

To help the 21 visitors and 7 staff members reacquaint themselves with each other, Jeni Batiste, a trainer, asks them to stand facing each other, give their names, and describe themselves in a word starting with the initial letter of their name. Maria Cîrstoiu, another trainer, says "moderate"; Ana says "agitated"; others say "interested," "curious," "vivacious," "fearful," "voluble," "calm," "caregiving," "thoughtful," "generous," "malleable," "timid," and "dynamic." Of course, each person is some of all of those.

It is a quiet, attentive group that sits again at the tables, opening folders and listening to Ana. She goes through the Step by Step standards, one by one. She also shows the teachers how to make classroom observations, noting on a flip chart four frequencies at which each standard may be present: "always," "often," "seldom," or "never." The room is comfortable, with lots of kids' artwork and lace curtains at the high windows. Well-worked wood framing supports a deck above almost half the room—a place for children's naps, sleeping 16. Ana's presentation of Step by Step standards during the first hour is a rerun of Module One, held 6 months ago. No direct explanation is given today as to why Step by Step was needed in the first place. No questions are posed; no questions are asked.

For the remainder of the morning, the trainees divide and go to three classrooms. Soon the children emerge from breakfast. In Classroom Three, there are three trainers, seven trainees, 10 kids, and three observers. (Seventeen other children are missing; they have the mumps.) Eliza Caramilea, a trainer and the regular teacher in this room, gathers the children about her on the floor for talk about their town and themselves. "Who is here? One person has a red sweater and blonde hair. Who is that?" "Eloise!" Eliza animates their talking, especially Ghulghi's. Maria keeps a loose hand on Marius. The trainees watch quietly.

The children are invited to choose an activity center: Blocks, Manipulatives, Arts, Sand and Water, Literacy, or Library. Each center displays a message for parents about what can be done there, with encouragement for them to be involved too. Two to four kids quickly move to each center, with or without a teacher. Soon they are drawing, slicing bread, and so forth. At the photo board, the teacher is pretending to go with three kids on a tour of Tulcea, passing the monument and the harbor. One child wears the driver's cap. The photos are ones the class took on a recent field trip. One exercise is to match 8″ × 12″ photographs with much smaller photos of the same scenes.

Some trainees are taking notes in their logs, but most are just watching. They saw similar activity last October. One comments to another on the material, "These large blocks give a child a quick sense of accomplishment," and "Feel the texture of these soft blocks." It looks as if, within their own minds, the trainees are laying out a space and scope for activity.

A boy is drawing a bus. "Do you have any children in the bus?" "I'm going to draw the driver." Later he struggles to write a sign on the bus. Eliza writes the name he tells her, "DELTA CONS," on a scrap of paper, so he can draw it on the bus. The Step by Step idea is not to do it for him. The trainees do not interact yet with the children. Mostly they watch. They notice how hard the trainers are working. They check standards. For them, it is a morning of passivity. A final session for the morning has trainees listening to a succession of their peers' commenting on how the standards had been pursued.

1.2. The Growth of Step by Step Teacher Training in Romania

In Romania, Step by Step was linked to the twin ideas of "educational alternatives" and "teacher training." Begun in 1994 under the name of Head Start, the program was recognized as an alternative to the public educational system by the Ministry of Education, in May 1995. Carmen Lica, the executive director of CEPD, remembered:

> "We started in January 1994, with training. We had few expectations at that time. We hardly knew what Step by Step was. After 10 years, it has become more than any of us imagined. We hardly had a plan; it was an adventure. Gradually, the plan became more comprehensive. We grew together with the people who were involved—the teachers, the parents."

The start of this adventure in 1994 was made easier by people wanting a change. Carmen Lica added, "People were thinking of trying new things, drawing from parts of their lives. . . . Still, the long years of the Communists left some people being resistant." She described the Step by Step program as

> " . . . one of the most generous opportunities for people at the school level. Within a centralized educational system, Step by Step in some ways operated differently: It was [a child-centered approach] appearing directly in schools, not going through many levels of decision. It was something designed for teachers, for children, and for parents. I think one of the most important characteristics was that Step by Step teachers were supposed to contribute their own experience in adapting Step by Step to the national requirements."

Remembering the beginning of the Step by Step "adventure," the former general inspector for the Tulcea County School Inspectorate, Mihai Albota, said that he first accepted the idea of alternative education because, as a math teacher, he knew "that a problem can be solved in various ways. There is the direct way, and then there are the indirect ways." As a teacher, he said he never claimed that a certain method was the only right one. He supported the idea of educational pluralism from kindergarten to high school. "Any alternative form brings something new." As a general inspector, he was a pragmatist, saying:

"If George Soros offers to help us, to give us furniture and other facilities, say one hundred dollars to buy school materials, why refuse? Why refuse help that creates better conditions for children in need? That's my initial idea. Why refuse someone's help?"

Later on, by paying attention to the matter of human resources and by anticipating opposition, he encouraged practitioners to identify the best methods of implementing alternative teaching. He described what he said to teachers proposing an alternative:

"I said, 'Launch the program. If you're not able to get used to it, then go back to our old curriculum. In time we'll see whether the program is working, whether the method is right.' I said, 'Accept it for starters, and if you don't like it, we'll give it up.' Little by little, the teachers got used to the new system. But sometimes they also taught in the traditional manner."

Referring to his arguments supporting the Step by Step alternative, "the General" (as Mr. Albota was generally called) said that he had noticed that each child's personality was respected and that the children became more sociable:

"Step by Step kids are allowed to think by themselves, to work with the team, in order to discover their skills and whether they are responsible for their own actions. They are not afraid of inspection. Before, they were shaking, with their hands behind their backs. You should not raise children like that. You should give them some space."

He saw Step by Step as bringing a special professional orientation to each child. The personality of the child becomes better understood by the teachers. They observe the skills of the child and know some of the directions in which the child should be educated. They encourage a different type of motivation for learning. The General continued:

"The children learn not because they fear the teachers, but because the teachers are well trained. Teachers who know how to stimulate children are better than those who know how to give bad marks.

The teachers trained by Step by Step will know better how to work with children. We have a great deal to win."

Moving now from the local perspective to the national, we recognized a gradual increase in support for Step by Step across Romania. Professor Ioan Neacsu, general director of Direction Evaluation, Prognosis, Strategies, and Programs for Preuniversity Education in the MER, drew attention to the government effort to increase the number of alternative education approaches:[2]

"A positive attitude toward Step by Step has been created in the public consciousness. This can be seen in the demand for Step by Step expansion. The Ministry is open to such activities. The balance between human and financial resources is important. There is good cooperation between CEPD, the inspectorates, and the Ministry."

The demand for extension grew each year. In the school year 2003–2004, there were 26,000 children in the Step by Step program, divided into the following groupings:

- 27 day nursery groups (ages 0–3), in 20 day nursery centers in 14 towns in 13 counties.
- 655 kindergarten groups (age 3–7), in 290 kindergartens in 38 counties.
- 404 primary classrooms (120 first-grade, 117 second-grade, 92 third-grade, and 75 fourth-grade), in 140 schools in 35 counties.
- 36 lower secondary classrooms (17 fifth-grade, 11 sixth-grade, 6 seventh-grade, and 2 eighth-grade), in 10 schools in 8 counties.

1.3. Teacher Training: The Engine of Educational Reform

An Organisation for Economic Co-operation and Development (OECD) report in 2001[3] included the "alternatives as the engine of reform" metaphor. An articulation of this new philosophy of teaching and learning had appeared in major educational policy documents in Romania several

---

[2]The discussion with Professor Neacsu was held March 22, 2004, at MER. Neacsu acknowledged that there were views different from his within MER.

[3]OECD, Centre for Co-operation with Non-Members (CCNM), Directorate for Education, Employment, Labor and Social Affairs, Education Committee, *Thematic Review of National Policies for Education—Romania*, Stability Pact for South Eastern Europe, Table 1, Task Force on Education, November 2001.

years earlier. These include the *Education Law* of 1995, and the new *National Curriculum Framework* of 1998. It appeared as well as in the rhetoric of many Romanian educators. A challenge for the coming years was to increase understanding of this new approach to education and its implications for classroom practice and teaching/learning methodology. Pedagogy and supervision would continue to change for monitoring classroom practice. Preservice and in-service training programs would continue to change, partly to model the new approaches and to identify ways to reward teachers who exemplified the new values.

Contemporary Ministry and other government reports emphasized that there should be concerted efforts among national and local institutions to debate articulations of the new alternatives to teaching and learning. The implications needed study, including assessment of their impact on learning. Monitoring was needed to assure that the new approaches were modeled and rewarded in policies, programs, and even the out-of-school activities of teachers and pupils.

As described above, there appeared to be widespread agreement in Romania that teacher training was one of the weakest links in the system. Much reform-related training had been delayed, due to the lack of clarity about the roles and responsibilities of such key players such as universities, the regional training centers (called Casa Corpului Didactic training centers, or CCDs), and the inspectorates.

Preschool education had been excluded from contemporary emphases within education reform. Speaking about Internet access and networking among trainers and trainees, the executive director of CEPD, Carmen Lica, drew attention to the issue of Step by Step sustainability:

> "Fund raising is needed for two-thirds of our budget. The real problem is that preschool education is not a high priority for any of the big funders. We are continually trying to identify funders. There is no sign that the Ministry of Education recognizes the need for bringing computers into preschool education. We hear of no such strategy. Officials are focusing on elementary and secondary schooling."

A timely report[4] included these words:

> This oversight may induce high long-term costs in the education system. In a country with a rate of poverty of more than 22%, there is significant prob-

---

[4]See OECD, CCNM, *Romania: Education Goals and the Transition, Education and Skills*, Paris, 2000, p. 148.

ability of large gaps developing between the preparedness for primary school of children coming from different social strata.

Ignoring this risk was seen as likely to be detrimental for students and wasteful of systemic resources. Director Neacsu, trying to make an estimate, said:

"The most profitable investment should be in preschool education. We have the experience of other countries investing in children under school age and reaching high levels: Europe, Japan, the United States."

International integration represented an immediate political challenge for Romania. Within the present context, the educational system was seen as both a tool and a target for European Union integration.

1.4. The European Union and Romania

Although Romania was the first country in Central or Eastern Europe to have official relations with the European Community (now called the European Union), there was little reason to believe that Romania would be able to join the EU before 2007. In 1974, an agreement included Romania in the European Community's *Generalized System of Preferences*. An *Agreement on Industrial Products* was signed in 1980. Over the 1990s and into the new century, Romania moved increasingly from the margins of the European integration process toward full inclusion in the EU. But it was not certain that full inclusion would result. The envisaged date of accession—2007—was fast approaching. Although the country had applied for membership in June 1995, economic reform had proceeded at glacial pace, and expressions of dissatisfaction with government inefficiencies and economic policies led to a wave of protests.

Romania has a surface area of 238,391 square kilometers. Agriculture represented 15%, industry 35%, and services 50% of the economic activity in 2002. According to preliminary data for 2002, the total population was 22,698,000, of which approximately 53% were urban. Some 89% of the population was ethnic Romanian, while the most important minorities were Hungarian (7%), Roma (2%), and less than 1% each of Ukrainian, German, Turkish, Tatar, Serb, Russian, and Jewish.

From 1948 until 1989, Romania had a Soviet-style economy in which nearly all agricultural and industrial work was state-controlled. Running a neo-Stalinist police state from 1967 to 1989, Nicolae Ceausescu wound the Iron Curtain tightly around Romania, turning a moderately prosperous country into one at the edge of starvation. During those years, its economy was based largely on heavy industry. Now Romania remains one of the poorest European countries.

Enormous economic and social changes took place in Romania after 1989, resulting in upheaval for the population. With official statistics (2003) for unemployment at 9%, Romania remained in poor economic condition. The private sector also lagged behind that in the more advanced Central European countries, but nevertheless accounted for more than 50% of the GNP and foreign trade. Further economic reform measures, delayed by successive governments, threatened a substantial rise in unemployment and an additional short- to medium-term decline in living standards for the majority of the people.

Social conditions remained poor. Life expectancy (71 years in 2001) was considerably lower than in Western European countries. Infant mortality has dropped to 18 per 1,000 live births (in 2001), but remains high by European standards. Rapidly falling birth rates since 1989, together with increased general mortality, mean that Romania has had negative population growth since 1992. The decline of the human development index (0.733 in 2001) reflects the hardship of a painful transition.

The year 2004 seemed to be decisive for Romania. "The process of the European Union's enlargement is irreversible, and it will inevitably also include Romania," President Ion Iliescue said on his return from Dublin, where ceremonies were held on the occasion of EU's enlargement by 10 new members (May 3, 2004). Some people were wondering whether the rhetorical commitment to a "continuous, inclusive, and irreversible" enlargement process would survive the 2004 enlargement. Would the EU be freed from a rhetorical entrapment and feel at liberty to revise its commitment to enlargement?

The timetable for EU accession in 2007 necessitated Romania's reaching agreements on all membership chapters (*acquis communautaire*), as well as gaining the status of a "functioning market economy." The government reasserted its resolve to implement reforms that would allow Romania to close the accession talks in 2004, sign an accession treaty in 2005 and actually join in 2007, as targeted in the accession calendar.

The World Bank classified Romania as a lower-middle-income country (according to its *A Country Risk Research Report*, published in 2004). With a gross domestic product of only $7,500 (U.S. dollars) per capita in purchasing power parity, the country remained the poorest of the 12 in line for future EU membership. Some saw this poor country as another burden for EU members.

For Romania, therefore, completing the journey from marginality to inclusion would depend very much on the extent to which the country successfully grappled with education and the other issues mentioned above.

1.5. Traditional and Alternative Teacher Education

In general, educators and teachers employed in preschool education in Romania are graduates of the pedagogical high schools, colleges, or other higher education institutions, with a training course in psychopedagogy. For some activities (foreign languages, drawing, music, and dance), teachers holding higher education qualifications are employed.

At this writing, almost all preservice teacher training (including that for preschool) is the domain of university faculties. Many observers find these faculties unconcerned with the actual needs and conditions of teachers, however. Bolstered by university autonomy, the pedagogical departments on campus have evidenced little motivation to adapt their curricula to changes required by the new national curriculum for schools and the evolving social environment.

The Department of Teacher Training of MER recently published the *Development Strategy for Preservice and In-Service Teacher Training for Preuniversity Education (2001–2004).*[5] According to this policy paper, soon there would be development of an educational market in the field of in-service teacher training, based on a competitive system, and teachers would have richer offerings from teacher-training providers.

Also pertinent was an OECD report, *Thematic Review of National Policies for Education—Romania.*[6] It commented on changes in the "educational market" as follows:

> Traditionally seen as a public service, the education system has become more and more open to private initiatives and educational alternatives. After 1990, the private education sector developed mainly at the tertiary and secondary level, but also at [the] primary level in the alternative education domain (i.e., Freinet, Petersen, Waldorf, Montessori). This trend is seen by educationalists as a way to facilitate access to higher levels of education, and increase equity, especially for higher education. Public confidence in state education is high, however, and the emergence and development of private systems do not affect the equity in access to education.

---

[5]This document is available on the MER's website (www.edu.ro).
[6]Stability Pact for South Eastern Europe, Table 1, Task Force on Education, November 2001, p. 17.

A teaching staff trained in the traditional system would have difficulty fitting its teaching repertory within the Step by Step principles of education. The traditional educational repertory induces—often without apparent intention—an authoritative teacher; generalization and standardization of the process of education; ranking the children; and attention to uniform outcomes instead of attention to discovery. All these things run counter to Step by Step principles. Moreover, a majority of teachers still applaud compliance with traditional practice.

The principles and theory of child development require techniques and a specific mentality to stimulate individualized development and to evaluate the development of every child. The Step by Step alternative offers repeated training and improvement sessions for teachers, program managers, and parents. It extends sustained technical assistance.

The Step by Step educational alternative works within the national curriculum set by the Ministry. In April 1998, through Minister's Order No. 3618, two teachers were approved as the staff for a Step by Step classroom. In February 1999, the CEPD of Step by Step Romania was authorized by the Ministry of Education and Research (by Partnership Convention No. 9693) to provide training courses for teachers. At this writing, the CEPD of Step by Step Romania, in partnership with the Ministry of Education and Research, is developing a program of training and education for preschool, primary, and lower secondary education.

Speaking about the training provided in 2003 by the CCDs and CEPD, Carmen Lica commented:

> "Last year we started designing training modules for teachers interested in Step by Step, but not necessarily willing to implement Step by Step methodology. The legislation requires that each institution have accreditation. We . . . consider CCDs our competitors. They are already . . . doing that. We tried to do training at Model Training Sites for monitoring the sites who join the program every year, and we are trying to design training modules."

Besides training modules aimed at preschool and primary school teachers who join the Step by Step educational alternative, CEPD has organized training courses on the following topics:

- Introduction to alternative pedagogies.
- Child-centered school curriculum and educational practices.
- Learning through play.
- Philosophy for children.
- Methods and techniques for better knowing each child.

- Democratic educational practices in school.
- Alternative evaluation methods.
- The significance of the attachment relationship.
- Creating educational materials for small children.
- Adult learning.
- School–family–community partnership.

With such offerings included in the CEPD business plan, teacher training was expected to become financially self-sustaining.

1.6. Professional Development from the Bottom Up: The General

Tulcea was one of the first counties in Romania where Step by Step was introduced. Mihai Albota, the former general school inspector mentioned earlier, told us about the Romanian educational system in general and about Step by Step history in Tulcea.[7] With no more than 2 years of teaching practice—he was just 24 years old—Mr. Albota became the leader of the Tulcea County School Inspectorate in 1959 and remained until 1992. He recalled:

> "Those were hard times. They summoned me to a meeting. By Decision No. 125, I was assigned this position without being asked if I wanted it or not. It was an order from the Party."

Albota did his homework. He studied the necessary laws and regulations. He organized briefing meetings with other inspectors. He had to manage 2,700 people. Eventually he learned everybody's names.

> "I knew their names, their problems, their sorrows. By the time we had our conferences in September 1959, I could talk to them as if we had known each other forever."

Little by little, people began to like him. He said that he never wronged or insulted anyone who was "hierarchically inferior." His reputation, built long ago, proved to be of great significance later on. Because he was a general inspector, people addressed him and referred to him by the nickname of "the General" in later years.

---

[7]We had two meetings in Tulcea with Mr. Albota (in March and May 2004). During the second meeting, we had a semistructured interview on May 13, 2004, in Tulcea.

His first task, assigned by the Communist Party in 1959, was (based on political criteria) to fire 60 teachers, all duly qualified. He said he gave the Party a blunt refusal. At the county level at the time, only half of the teaching staff was made up of qualified teachers. The rest lacked the proper pedagogical high school or university degrees. Those targeted by the Party's decision were the *most* competent. So the General threatened to remove himself from the education system.

> "My attitude made people trust me. They said, 'This kid saved us all. Let's help him out.' I acquired a fabulous capital of human trust."

To be a "school person" became his leading professional principle. "I am not ashamed of what I leave behind," Albota proudly stated. His heritage was impressive. During 38 years of uninterrupted leadership (28 years as a general inspector, another 10 in higher positions), he was responsible for building 132 schools, including most of the existing high schools. His highest priority was to train unqualified personnel. He commented that helping other people solve their problems was part of his nature.

> "I have probably helped over 2,000 young teachers get proper qualifications. I got them to complete their studies. I offered jobs as substitute teachers. I made sure they were able to get study holidays. Although they came from different places, many never returned."

By 1974, Tulcea County had 99.5% of its teaching positions occupied by qualified staff members. Only qualified primary and secondary school teachers were working in the Danube Delta. Professional qualification was his most important accomplishment both before and after the 1989 Romanian revolution.

> "They could ask me to fire qualified teachers 100 times. I never did. I do not believe a school's principal should be replaced only because another party wins the elections. In Tulcea today, we have two principals who are members of the opposition party. I am not interested in their political allegiance. I got central heating, a sports hall, or paving for the schoolyard, regardless of the principal's political views."

Speaking historically about the education system, the General mentioned the fact that from 1948 to 1966, all school books were translations of Russian manuals. In the 11th grade, one had to teach Marxist theory during Romanian class, and some leading Romanian writers were completely left out. In 1964, political prisoners were granted amnesty, and the school curriculum (gradually) recovered a certain grip on reality; the schoolbooks changed too. The obligatory 10 grades were introduced in 1976. The quality of education and the social system were such that "when you graduated from school, you were competent. When you graduated from university, you were assigned a job. This made good motivation for studying." The meritocracy principle functioned at the societal level, and the children of all social classes had opportunities for achievement through education: "If I graduate from school, I can really achieve something." The General averred that planning was essential. But then it all changed: "But then we found that the young graduates did not want officially assigned jobs any more."

The General said that he appreciated the high quality of the Romanian education system, but also that he was aware of its weak points. After examining the school system in other European countries, and after having access to curricula and school books in several Western countries, he became certain that "a Romanian high school graduate could teach mathematics at any college in France." Nevertheless, upgrading the Romanian system to European standards was a major issue: "We do not yet have the technical facilities, the modern methods, or the modern concepts." He saw those difficulties as solvable. A more serious shortcoming was "the motivation for a student to find what is worth studying." He saw the Internet as a superficial, work-free, undemanding source of information, more accessible to students than to teachers.

> "And kids have lost the habit of reading books. But also the level of instruction is poorer than it used to be. Anybody can enter university and eventually graduate, more or less, by continuing to pay the tuition."

But his words of pessimism gave way to hope: "We still have very many good teachers who do their job very well. The good relations among these people are very important."

Then there was the matter of administrator training. The General said, "Perhaps the greatest problem for education is the educators." He ventured the opinion that it is much more difficult to educate an adult person than a child, especially an administrator. At first there were "no trained [officials], so the training was very difficult." The mere fact that a teaching method was good did not alone make it easy to train administrators to use it.

> "Also bad was the training strategy. We proceeded from the lower levels to the highest level. We were not vigorously training the hier-

archically superior level within the organizational structure. We did not seriously train top people. These people needed to come and observe at length. We do not have knowledgeable people at the level of the school inspectorates, or at the school management level— people who comprehend communities and policy. To be honest, we still do not have such people."

With such a low level of official involvement, the support for Step by Step in Romania has been unsteady. "I do not want to speak ill of my successors, but they have not shown great interest in alternative [teaching methods]." In some isolated situations, the lack of understanding became opposition to creating new classes. But the reaction of the "beneficiaries" soon came forth.

"When [the inspectors] saw that the teachers and even the local government agreed to create such classes, the prefect went to visit. He liked it. He said, 'These children are smart. They are daring. They know things about the society, about the prefecture, that others do not.' The inspectors changed their opinion."

1.7. Trainees' Expectations of Training

Training for implementation of Step by Step evolved over the years. At the beginning, the themes of the course were approached in the same order in all the training centers. Little by little, some changes occurred from one center to another. An expressed need for ensuring the conceptual and methodological unity of training, regardless of the place and time that it was held, led to a certain uniformity. The two training modules (see below) were to cover the same material. The themes and methods were analyzed regularly and were discussed at each annual meeting. The aim was to bring the themes up to date and to improve the methods, competency, and repertoire of the trainers. The team "at headquarters" analyzed it and tried to make all needed changes, with input from the trainers. During the training, the trainers were to be totally free for planning and organizing. Within each team, they were to choose the examples, the materials, or the methods and techniques to be used. Certain changes occurred in the enactment of training, partly because the interests and needs of the trainees differed from one group to another.

A preschool teacher who wanted officially to implement the Step by Step approach was obligated to attend two 2½-day training modules. A moderate training fee and a boarding fee were charged. The county school inspectorates covered the expenses of travel, and sometimes those of training and boarding as well. The MTS worked to keep these expenses low. In Tulcea, the trainees might eat and sleep in the kindergarten. On completion of each module, they got a certificate.

For this research, we intended to identify certain aspects of the training and implementation of the program, so we invited trainees to fill in a questionnaire. At the end of the third day of the Tulcea training we observed, the 23 trainees answered questions about the following:

- Motivation for implementing the Step by Step program.
- First reactions to a Step by Step activity (what surprised trainees, what they liked).
- Reactions to first implementation of Step by Step methods in the classroom (what was easy or difficult).
- The contribution of the training in Tulcea.
- Reflection on some main aspects of the Step by Step program during the course.
- Importance of the abundance of activity materials at Tulcea.
- The difficulties met.
- Other comments.

The reasons given for participating in the program were many:

- The existence of other Step by Step groups in the same kindergarten (4).
- Children's outcomes in Step by Step (4).
- Children's level of knowledge (4).
- Information obtained from different sources (colleagues, magazines) (4).
- Parents' demand for Step by Step (3).
- The wish for a change (2).
- The democratic character of Step by Step and the child-centered activity (4).
- The opportunities for teacher flexibility and knowledge of each child (2).
- "It is something new" (2).
- "It gives the child the possibility of having a choice, of being responsible" (1).
- "It fits me" (1).

As for the expectations of the trainees regarding the training, the most common was "planning," mentioned by 8 trainees—or, more specifically, "planning, taking into account the needs of the children at centers." The second most common expectation was solving the problems of application of the program. Other trainees mentioned specific aspects of Step by Step, such as "individualization," "the arrangement of the activity centers," "the parents' greater involvement," "getting familiar with a new perspective, totally opposed to the traditional one," "a better knowledge of the children through observation," and "a democratic education." The other answers ranged from "achievement of a pleasant environment," "the making of materials," and "the knowledge of other ways of work," to the satisfaction of the need for achievement: "to practice my own creativity," "to achieve myself what they have already achieved here," "to specialize myself," and "to trust myself."

When the "forceful ideas" of Step by Step were ranked, the one ranked most meritorious was "child-centered activity." "Respect for the child" was second, followed by "parent involvement" and "teacher dialogue."

1.8. The Romanian Teacher-Training Network

In Romania, there were five preschool Model Training Sites located in Botosani, Constanta, Satu Mare, Târgovişte, and Tulcea, collectively having 30 trainers. For the primary schools there were seven Zonal Core Training Teams at Botosani, Buzau, Cluj, Satu Mare, Sfintu Gheorghe, Târgovişte, and Tulcea, with 23 trainers (each mainly covering a single geographical area). At CEPD, there were six master teacher trainers. Among the partners collaborating with CEPD were the following:

- The National Ministry of Education and Research.
- The National Ministry of Family and Health.
- The National Authority for Child Protection and Adoption.
- The county school inspectorates.
- The county child protection departments.
- The county public health departments.
- The city halls.

Support was also provided by many international entities, including the U.S. Agency for International Development (USAID), the United Nations Children's Fund (UNICEF), the International Labour Organization (ILO), and the Open Society Institute (OSI).

Among the services provided by CEPD, teacher training was the most important. It was delivered at all levels (day nursery, preschool, primary, and lower secondary) and to a wide range of target groups (preschool teachers, primary school teachers, principals, school inspectors, day nursery nurses, babysitters, and parents).

1.9. Pluralism and Democracy

"Without educational pluralism, no democracy can exist." This was the conclusion of CEPD, Step by Step Romania's president, Professor Viorel Nicolescu, in the anniversary newsletter (No. 1, 2004). In his article, "Pleading for a Way to Be," Professor Nicolescu quoted an American, Ralph Tyler, who had spoken on the correlation between the number of options that a society supports and the value of democracy in that society. The higher the number of options, the more advanced the democracy. Freedom in a human collectivity is impossible if each individual does not enjoy freedom. At a national symposium on educational alternatives held April 1–2, 2004 (and described in more detail later in this report), the rally cry was "I choose, therefore I exist." The MER's director of Direction Evaluation, Prognosis, Strategies, and Programs for Preuniversity Education, Professor Ioan Neacsu, endorsed the idea that educational alternatives contribute to the understanding of differences in a society, and help us accept interhuman differences, to the benefit of each individual child. He added:

> "Alternative education gives us life and introduces 'best practices' into education. Other institutions can draw inspiration from Step by Step, Waldorf, and the Jena Plan, as well as from the traditional ones."

As mentioned at the opening of this report, Professor Neacsu spoke of oxygenating the education system through alternatives. Referring particularly to Step by Step, he identified six characteristics:[8]

> "1. High-quality professional expertise, achieved on the one hand by the CEPD staff and on the other hand through collaborators brought in by CEPD (universities and practitioners). Thus there is a good school for spreading out ideas. It is oxygenating!
>
> "2. A good vision of what the Step by Step movement can represent, as an innovating center for 'the management of lasting development' in education. In keeping with the data, in Step by Step reports one finds a good design, with all components growing. Now we feel [that] Step by Step [is] heading toward quality, overtaking the early tendencies that focused on quantity.
>
> "3. A good balance between the theoretical, methodological part and the practical. I think that there has been good training at the

---

[8]During the discussion held on March 22, 2004, at MER.

centers I could introduce into legislation a notification of those teachers who join the Step by Step institutions through the national contests.[9]

"4. The orientation to rural regions too, as areas of vulnerable population and education, where people are poor and need assistance. Introduction of a second teacher there would help them a lot.

"5. The concern for spreading experience and information in interested circles.

"6. A positive attitude toward Step by Step has been created in the public consciousness. This can be seen in the demand for Step by Step expansion. The Ministry is open to such activities. The balance between human and financial resources is important. There is good cooperation between CEPD, the school inspectorates, and the ministry."

2. TEACHER TRAINING IN MTS KINDERGARTEN 3, TULCEA

2.1. Day One: Presenting the Step by Step Standards

Day One—March 18, 2004

08:30–09:15 Opening session; Step by Step standards
09:15–09:30 Grouping the trainees to attend the activities carried on by the trainers
09:30–11:00 Attendance of trainers' teaching activities
11:00–11:30 Coffee break
11:30–13:00 Discussions on standards, based on classroom observations
13:00–14:30 Lunch break
14:30–16:00 Weekly planning: concept (theoretical presentation and practical preparation for the next day); trainees' grouping for practical activities to be carried on next day; role distribution
16:00–16:30 Coffee break
16:30–17:30 Materials preparation for Day Two; discussions
17:30–18:00 Evaluation of the training; open session

---

[9]Seeking a teaching job happens through national contests.

March 18, 2004, 9:05. The first session of the second training module is underway. As described in Section 1.1, Ana is responsible for making the Step by Step standards clear. She asks, "How can standards be used?", and hears "Guide," "Evaluation instruments and other responses." After Ana makes a few comments about the standards, she presents each standard separately with its indicators, the evaluation criteria (when they are used), and the observation column. Some trainees write down what is presented; others just browse through the handouts; still others just listen. Ana reads the standards, which are written carefully and tidily on the flip chart in block letters. Even the placement on the page and the indented lines of the original material received from CEPD have been retained. The text is written in small and crowded characters. As indicated earlier, no explanations or details are asked for or given. Sometimes, within the presentation, the indicators for the standards can be interchanged. The teaching team members sit behind a blackboard that faces the trainees. Marinela Peiciu, one of the trainers, helps Ana change sheets on the flip chart. The participants watch the presentation. They are often reminded that they will find examples in the practical activity to be observed soon, and that they will get material for consolidation.

The trainees are then divided into three classrooms, again as noted earlier. There they get 18 pages about the Step by Step standards. Each trainee is given some indicators to follow more attentively. Some are already studying the material while waiting for the children to arrive.This training is for consolidating the knowledge given in the first module. The theoretical sessions referring to Step by Step philosophy and methodology are followed by demonstration activities, led by either a preschool teacher trainer or a trainee.

2.1.a. A Model Training Site Principal

Ana Pantea was the principal of this Model Training Site. At the opening of the training, she said that she was "agitated." She meant that she was excited. Thinking again, she said that she was ambitious: "I am quite ambitious. This characterizes me most of the time." Her ambition was seen throughout the building. She said:[10]

> "There is ambition in this kindergarten too. And good and a fair
> competition among my colleagues. All these things point to the

---

[10]During a semistructured interview held on March 19, 2004, in Tulcea. We had other discussions during the meetings in Târgovişte (April) and Tulcea (May).

individuality of the classrooms, of the team and groups. All the teachers have ambition."

Ana placed professionalism first. Perhaps this made a difference between Kindergarten 3 and others. When she became the principal, she set forth a strategy for recruiting the personnel, having in mind clear standards and different stages in the process of selection. On the one hand, she "imposed her point of view clearly," and on the other hand, she was backed by the General. She stated:

"I wanted very much to have professionals in this kindergarten. Maybe I was a bit lucky. I told everybody what I wanted. People knew me, and so they could help me. I could also do this as I had some vacancies. One more thing that helped me in setting a higher standard for the kindergarten is the fact that I tested extremely well the people I wanted to be permanent preschool teachers here. Each preschool teacher spent at least 1 or 2 years in the kindergarten, so I could tell if they could cope with all the requirements. If I was satisfied, I let them decide, and say quite sincerely whether they wanted to stay."

Since her studies in pedagogical high school, Ana had felt that education in the "free countries" was different, and in particular that democratic education as espoused by her pedagogy teacher (who had access to foreign professional publications) was different. The Step by Step program seemed perfect to her, because it launched ideas that she had cherished since high school.

Going back 10 years to the beginning of Step by Step, Ana remembered that the eligibility criteria for the program included an appropriate physical environment. She got a shock when she was assigned her building by the authorities.

"In my heart, I had an image of the program and of what we should do. All the things I had imagined were completely different from what I found I could do here. Here there was nothing, not even a coin, not even running water or a toilet. The money I received was meant for only two classrooms."

She thought it unfair to have two classrooms all furbished, while the others had neither finished floors nor functional windows. Ana remembered it as a "horror movie," and she kept photos to remind her of this time. She felt fortunate because she and the site manager collaborated very well. "She gave me advice, but I did everything at my own risk. I had good support, particularly in Bucharest." Given the situation, Ana was afraid that her kindergarten would be rejected.

> "I told myself I would crawl to Bucharest if I needed to. I wanted that program that badly. How could they possibly reject us? It was my dream."

From dream to reality, the path was laid on Ana's persistence and ability to find resources. Speaking about sponsorship, she remembered that

> " . . . everybody thought we were asking for money. But that wasn't all. Anything could help, anything was useful: roof, wall and floor tiles, anything, 15 meters of cable. . . . Within 3 days, everything was done."

2.1.A.1. ANA'S PRIDE

Ana took pride in her accomplishments. With a determined attitude, she continued to march ahead with marketing and management based as much on trust as on daring:

> "This year we will celebrate our 10th anniversary. What I would like to do is gather all my sponsors in one place—and then get the court-yard finished too."

Ever practical, Ana mentioned that a major accomplishment was buying a car for the kindergarten. Paying attention both to costs and to parent priorities, Ana remembered the time she told the parents her intention to buy a car. She said:

> "I had carefully calculated food prices, and I told myself we needed the car to improve food quality for the kids. One of the parents gave me one of those 'You must be crazy' looks. I asked if he considered my plan foolish. He admitted he did, but later he was the first to congratulate me. We were able to improve the quality of meals, because wholesale food store prices are very different from those you find in normal stores. The parents always ask, 'What did you have for lunch today?' "

With 32 years of experience as a teacher and 14 years as the principal of Kindergarten 3, Ana admitted that part of the reason for her success was that she assumed some important responsibilities. First of all, she respected the Step by Step methodology. "The parents readily admit that this methodology is different and this program is something else, too. And I am very, very keen on it." By implementing these methods "correctly and completely, you guarantee your kindergarten prestige and image." All the problems could be settled "within the family."

> "If things aren't going well even in one classroom, I am losing a bit of the value and quality of the kindergarten. The standards won't let me rest. I always keep an eye on the methodology. No mistake is accepted, not in the least. If I notice that something is wrong, I find a way to talk about it."

2.1.A.2. ANA AS MANAGER

As a manager, Ana had to ensure all the conditions for carrying on the activities. She wanted to get the courtyard improved: "There are so many children and they need it." The courtyard was not laid out as she would have liked, but she was optimistic. Besides the material conditions, team spirit was a preoccupation:

> "I've tried to build up the team. Almost all my colleagues can take over some of the work very well. From my point of view, my colleagues support me. If I have a problem, I explain it and it is solved. I know I could leave this kindergarten for a month, and the work would go on."

The General spoke of Ana as a manager: "What you see is her idea and her sweat. She is the leader." Ana mentioned the substantial contributions of the site manager. But he drew the conversation back to her management:

THE GENERAL: In the first place, she knew how to choose her people, to create the team. If you know how to choose people, you succeed. There were some who did not fit in, so they had to go.

ANA: I fired them.

THE GENERAL: Success depends on your abilities to deal with people. Ana has this ability. The people who didn't do their business were fired. Ana has always known how to win the families, the parents, the community.

2.1.A.3. ANA'S KINDERGARTEN

Kindergarten 3 operated in an antiquated building, a former school. According to archival data, the building was built between 1908 and 1912. After the 1948 reform of education, one of its 10 classrooms was used for preschool education. Starting in 1952, there were two groups (one of Romanian children, the other of Ukrainian children). Later it was extended to seven groups with an all-day program. But due to an increasing rate of unemployment and a decreasing standard of living and birth rate, in 1994 the kindergarten had only 70 children.

The Tulcea County School Inspectorate accepted the invitation of the Open Society Foundation–Romania to start a Step by Step program. They proposed Kindergarten 3, giving Step by Step the necessary site. In response to parents' demands, 50 children from disadvantaged families, joined Step by Step in 1994. In 1995 the program was extended to all three groups in the main building plus another two groups in classes in another building, which was fitted up properly with community help. The demand for enrolling in this program was constant; from 1995 until 2004, there were seven or eight groups each year. Until 2002 the program had a site manager. As of 2004, each group had two preschool teachers, a preschool teacher assistant, and a helper. The kindergarten as a whole had two medical nurses. Some 200 children attended the kindergarten. The school's history was a history of sustainability.

After an evaluation by CEPD, Kindergarten 3 became a Model Training Site. And it has functioned as a center for publicizing the Step by Step alternative. In 1996 it was the mentor for two other kindergartens, in 1997 for eight, in 1998 for three, in 2000 for two day nursery centers, and in 2003 for another day nursery. Owing to its remarkable record, Kindergarten 3 became the first "outstanding kindergarten"[11] in the country (1998–2000). This status gave it greater autonomy, especially in that the principal was entitled to select the personnel by herself.

2.1.A.4. ANA'S TEACHERS

The teachers of Kindergarten 3 were not "stuffing the children with information." Perhaps that was one of the marks of Step by Step vitality. According to the General,

---

[11]"*Gradinita representativa*," in Romanian.

"With changes in the educational system, the teacher is no longer supposed to stuff the child with information and press to have the child obey the teacher. These changes have become irreversible. We can no longer continue the old systematic way: 'Children, work on your notebooks.' 'Pay attention,' and so on. It is outdated. Now the child must be educated to search for himself, to be freer, more independent."

In the early days of Step by Step in Tulcea, parents were selected by Ana for participation. Children from disadvantaged backgrounds got priority. The General said that later, as classrooms were added,

" . . . parents volunteered to bring their children here. Now they all want to get them into Step by Step. They drive their children from all over the city. You should see the cars lined up. The parents understand Step by Step accessibility for children. It does not stuff them with tons of information. It is like the French system. We teach the children to search for themselves."

The General spoke of an academic contest for older children named *School Olympics*:

"Its winners make Romanians proud. [But] schools should not spend so much time making 'champions,' because it neglects the slower learners. The Step by Step approach is different. It is open. It has a permissive curriculum. It teaches children to follow their own initiatives. That way, the students do not destroy their neurons. We find Step by Step children more open-minded, less forced and constrained. A child is in a formative process. We should respect his or her rhythm."

Step by Step impressed the General as promoting not only cognitive skills, but emotional development and social competence:

"The children talk to the headmaster the same way they talk to their mother. The teachers act like parents. A teacher has to be a mother as well as a teacher, a science and culture person, and all that. The children trust their elders. The parents appreciate two teachers caring for their children all day long. They take walks. They go to shops or a museum. They are not kept in the classroom all day. The parents notice."

Early difficulties were used as opportunities for problem solving and cooperation. Lacking model lessons at the beginning, the preschool teachers in this kindergarten failed many times to stick to the curriculum. They tried to overcome their fear of failure. Ana suggested to her colleagues that they should talk to each other about what was going on. They were to try to solve the problems together. They took turns playing the role of preschool teacher, of a preschool teacher assistant, and of a child. They told each other where they had made a mistake, or what still remained unsolved. These exchanges became routine. When they met once a week, anyone might say, "Something is not right here; it may work with you, but it doesn't work with me." Many problems have been experienced; many solutions have been found. The teachers regularly came back to respect for the child's individuality. They saw that each group would be unique in some ways. Sharing problems and finding solutions together helped the preschool teachers of Kindergarten 3 become trainers.

2.1.b. An MTS Trainer

"Training keeps us alert," said Jeni Batiste, a pioneer teacher trainer at Kindergarten 3. After the revolution in 1989, seeking to make a change, she participated in conferences and courses on Waldorf pedagogy for 3 years. In Tulcea she could not put it into practice, however, because the inspectorate had not granted approval of Waldorf classes.

Meeting Ana, she moved to Kindergarten 3. She greatly liked the program. Currently, after an experience of 9 years as a teacher in Step by Step and 8 years as a trainer, Jeni said she had become a good trainer. She took her responsibilities seriously. As something of "a perfectionist," she regularly felt the need to change something—to do things "differently to get good results." She was interested in ways of working with adults and in the techniques for adult learners. For all the courses she took part in, she came to know their techniques so thoroughly that she could use them in her own courses. In libraries, she sought books of psychology and pedagogy. Currently she was enrolled in university courses for primary school teachers. She studied so as to meet all the requirements and "to be in touch with everything that is going on." It was tiring and demanding,

> "The training is good for us. It keeps us alert. Our training sessions are good for the teachers. They are adults who must leave with something. One way or another, you create your image before them. This matters a lot. We motivate the trainees this way."

The trainer team in Tulcea would like to do even more training:

"Unfortunately, the fact that there are very few is not to our benefit. We would like more training sessions. There are people who would like to do their training here, with us, but they were sent to other places. There is a geographical distribution. It doesn't seem fair to me. It seems fair to avoid chaos, but when somebody chooses a place . . . it seems fair for him or her to get to choose. The image of the kindergarten is linked to that of the trainer team—that is, to the quality of the training activities here."

Speaking about training, Jeni combined pride with frustration. There was never enough time either for training or for mentoring. "The standard topics have to be presented. Other topics in which the trainees are interested get short shrift." Jeni lamented that they had little opportunity to be mentors to their trainees. She said:

"With time so short, the training needs very careful planning. Around here, planning is considered the most difficult lesson. The trainees find Step by Step planning very difficult. They come with traditional methods and can't understand, can't adapt. Better said, they can't use their present methods to conceptualize the teacher's role in child-centered activity. It seems very difficult to write down what the teacher should anticipate doing there in the kindergarten classroom.

"Study of Step by Step methodology[12] facilitates good planning and preparation for the activities. Trainee interest and motivation will differ from one cohort to another."

Jeni also said she felt that the first Tulcea cohort of trainees who went into Step by Step "were opened to the new, were willing to do something else, to put their soul into it." But the more recent cohorts of trainees, she believed, had "persons who came to get a paper required by the inspectorate or to keep from losing their job due to reorganization."

[12]She referred to Hansen, K., Kaufmann, R., & Burke Walsh, K. (1999). *Crearea claselor orientate dupa necesitatile copilului* [*Creating child-centered classrooms for children ages 3–5 years*]. Bucharest: CEPD, Step by Step Romania. This is one of the core methodological texts developed for the international Step by Step program, adapted and translated into Romanian by national experts.

2.2. Planning

2.2.a. Planning and Spontaneity in Teaching

March 18, 2004, 09:30–11:00. Eliza's demonstration is at 10:20. During the trainees' observation of a trainer teaching, a child doesn't feel comfortable and Eliza brings him nearer the front of the classroom, knowing that this will make him feel better. One activity to be observed is of three boys taking an imaginary trip around Tulcea. Tudor is the driver. Radu doesn't want to leave until he gets something for a steering wheel. The rucksack of sandwiches is not forgotten. On the way, photos taken earlier by the children on the actual trip are shown by the teacher and discussed. They are reminded of seeing the stage in the Civic Square and of what they had discussed about that stage. They recall that shows are held on that stage, and different artists come and sing and dance there. And they too will go and perform on that stage. The children fancy they are now on stage in the Civic Square, dancing the "Geamparaua" and another Dobrogean dance. They make a circle for dancing the "Hora" with two teachers and the assistant. At first some boys feel embarrassed at having to dance, but not for long. In the end, all enjoy dancing.

After dancing, Karla says, "Why don't we have a puppet show?" Eliza brightly answers, "Yes," to this unplanned activity. Jeni has come into the classroom. The children are eating the sandwiches they prepared. One of the trainees asks about the meaning of the drawing made by the children on the easel. Jeni answers, "What matters is the context and the process. The children are active." While the children are eating, Eliza and Maria bring in some puppets.

Appearing angry, a trainee addresses the children: "I am sorry you haven't invited us on the trip, at least for those wonderful sandwiches." The assistant who was in the kitchen supervising those who prepared the sandwiches answers, "If you haven't worked with us . . . " The children pay no attention.

Eliza, Maria, and the children select who will be actors in the puppet show. The others are the audience. With the help of Eliza, the actors are to improvise. "Good afternoon, children," Florina says. "Good afternoon, cute little puppy," answers a child in the audience.

Eliza is trying to start a dialogue about the town tour, but the improvisation takes another path: the fairy tale *Little Red Riding Hood*. Some trainees watch the puppet show. Others stare into space, seemingly bored. Some watch the children in the audience. At the end of the puppet show, Filepe is angry. He didn't have a chance to be a puppet.

The children leave for lunch. Maria invites the trainees to the meeting hall for a few moments of trainer–trainee talk. Organizational issues are discussed. The trainees comment that the tour recollection was a very difficult activity. Maria answers, "All our daily activities are like that."

2.2.b. Planning as an Issue

Talking with the trainers, we found out that planning was the most difficult process to teach. When the two modules are completed, the preschool teachers must be able to create a lesson plan that is child-centered. Jeni explained:

> "There are many problems. For example, sometimes we bring volunteers into the classroom, as bystanders. But it was difficult to plan activities having many adults in the classroom and to work individually too. The trainers discussed it and decided not to bring parents into the classroom during modules, because the trainees misunderstand the situation. There may be a false impression that individualizing is only possible by having parents in the classroom, because everyone takes care of the children and then it is Okay."

The teachers in a "traditional school" were seen as receiving the same wrong impression. During the demonstration classes, the preschool teacher had only the teacher assistant with her, demonstrating that it is very important to have such planning: "You should not need any other adult there." At the same time, the activity in the classroom is so intense that planning is vital. Jeni said that she tells the trainees:

> "A teacher should come from home with a certain idea of what to do today and how to watch a certain child in a particular activity center. Otherwise, it is not well organized. You can't do it spontaneously. The demand on the teacher is very high and comes from many sides. The children need a preschool teacher all the time. Observation [of individual children] is possible only by having some very good observation instruments—ones requiring little effort during the activity."

Why did so many people, both trainers and trainees, find Step by Step planning difficult? Jeni commented:

"They [the trainees] come with traditional methods in mind and they can't understand, they can't adapt, on their own. Or it is better to say that they can't use their methods to do the job. It is the same activity, the same tasks, the same targets of the respective activity in other centers. It seems very difficult to them."

Jeni explained that, due to lack of time, "They always go ahead, not knowing what should be done there [in the kindergarten]." The trainers offered the trainees some examples of planning: but

" . . . there is a tendency for the preschool teachers just to copy. But it can't go on like that. We have avoided publishing examples of plans in magazines, because what we publish is copied. It is copied word for word! Our principle is individualization. We try to make the teachers understand that each set of plans is different from one preschool teacher to another, from one group to another. The solution we've found is that the trainees should do the plans by themselves. Although they give the impression of understanding, and of working together as a team, when we check [during monitoring visits] we find their big problems are with planning."

Teaching how to plan was the great challenge for the trainers. They worked hard to teach the trainees how to create a teaching plan. As part of the plan, the teachers had to follow the formal requirements of the national curriculum and to cover a certain number of activities per week, as well as the Step by Step requirements. Main objectives and strategies had to be decided for the children's activity centers. Activities specified in the curriculum had to be detailed. Trainees had the most difficulty connecting the curriculum with specific means of implementing Step by Step methods. Jeni insisted on having time "to build coherence" during the two training modules. The conceptual (theoretical) part of the training was very important, but direct experience with individual children was essential for the trainees:

"The teachers have difficulty understanding it. We have tried to explain to them that if a child has material for exploration, one can observe how he or she plays with it. But it is very difficult. They need time and more experience in Step by Step classrooms. It would be easier if you only had to take it from a book, or the like. It has to be studied [experientially]."

Jeni's conclusion was clear:

"Training activities and monitoring visits should be tailored to the trainee. They have to study, to read the materials provided during the workshops, and to reflect upon their daily teaching practice. Sharing ideas with their colleagues and mentors, asking questions, and expressing doubts—characteristics of reflective practice—are the best ways of improving personal teaching."

2.2.c. Planning in a Training Session

March 18, 2004, 14:30. In the afternoon session, Jeni speaks to the trainees about the role of planning. The trainees are encouraged to ask questions. In groups—according to the age level of children that they work with—each group presents a plan, a weekly timetable with themes for compulsory activities. Stress is laid on the continuity of activities across the week. Materials made one day in a center are to be used the next day in another center.

Jeni explains the planning of certain activities. She gives an example of scheduling art class on Monday, as a free-choice theme. Since it is the first day of the week and the first day of the theme, the children can find their own way into the theme. Again Jeni mentions the connection between the activities planned for the whole week and the goals of these activities. The main objectives of the day and the theme of the Morning Meeting are identified. The afternoon activities continue most of the morning activities. Many of them also have free-choice themes. Again Jeni stresses the flow of the planned activities, with one linked to the next. She speaks of initiation, of consolidation, and of evaluation of the children's activities.

Another trainer, Daniela Mocanu (nicknamed "Dana"), points out that these kindergarten plans are partly an outcome of discussions with the parents, with the children, and with the whole team of preschool teachers. It is creative planning. Each day plan in Dana's group has a different color: Monday, red; Tuesday, yellow; Wednesday, blue; and Thursday, green. The color for Friday is not set in advance; the choice of this color is made with the children's help. This Friday is a day for the trainees, when they are to do all the activities, so Friday is open to all possible alternatives. Dana also stresses that planning should include some activities for the whole group, for small groups, and for individuals.

Dana notes that planning is essential for Ana too, especially at the beginning of the school year. Planning is crucial for the team of trainers (preparing their training and selecting a theme of the course) and for each preschool teacher for his or her own class activities.

2.2.d. Planning and the Issue of Trainee Readiness

March 18, 2004, 16:30. During training, the trainees are to plan, prepare, and perform teaching activities for the second day. The roles of
preschool teacher, teacher assistant, observer, and parent are written
on small pieces of paper and drawn from a hat. In front of us, Diana,
a young preschool teacher, draws the role of the preschool teacher.
She doesn't like that at all. Irritated and uncertain, she asks, "But
why me? I shouldn't have taken that ticket. I don't have the experience . . . "

Early in the discussion of the next day's activities, Diana nois-
ily rejects the others' suggestions: "Well, I am the one presenting
this activity, not you. I have no experience." Her colleagues remind her that there are no marks given. Diana stays sulky; she may
be about to burst into tears. Someone in the group suggests that
she should withdraw. Two others volunteer. Diana remains undecided. Trainers Maria and Eliza let the group settle the issue. Jeni
comes by and notices the problem. At last, roles are exchanged.
The trainees have solved it by themselves. Later on, half the group
members are discussing the incident, while others are discussing
the activities to be planned for the next day. Diana says nothing
more about it.

Two weeks later at Târgoviste, I am discussing the training with
Jeni. She remembers the incident. "Maybe it would have been better
if we had assigned roles before they came. They might have been
more ready. They should have known what they were going to do. I
noticed that Diana remained undecided, a little frustrated. The
responsibility seemed too great. I interfered. I encouraged somebody
else to get involved. Jeni, as a trainer, also raises the question of the
psychological comfort of the trainees: "The training is very demanding. Diana felt upset. The emotion was unexpected. Such incidents
haven't occurred before."

2.2.e. Planning for Supervising

Ana Pantea, the principal, told how she supervises the teaching staff in
her kindergarten. She spoke first about a meeting at the beginning of
each school year. The discussions started with talk about the group of
children that each teacher would have. Once they had established the
age and the group, each team of two preschool teachers came forth with
proposals for projects. Ana brought in new initiatives or proposals if necessary. Cooperation within the teaching staff facilitated improvement.
From then on, the supervision for the year flowed smoothly:

"Every week they choose the theme and make plans for doing it. Each day it is enough for me to go just once into a classroom, even to see only one aspect, to realize what is going on in that classroom."

Telling us about one preschool teacher who failed to meet quality standards, Ana said, "I realized she was making big mistakes, because I could see them in her planning." Planning was a common responsibility shared by all the teachers. Team spirit and good fellowship were vital. "First of all, they come up with proposals; they make the plans together; they help each other with the materials."

2.3. Day Two: Step by Step Standards in Action

Day Two—March 19, 2004

09:00–09:30 Organizing the team; review of tasks and roles
09:30–11:00 Activities at centers carried on by the trainees
11:00–11:30 Coffee break
11:30–13:00 Discussion of Step by Step standards based on lived
           experience and classroom observations; questions
13:00–14:30 Lunch break
14:30–15:30 Democratic education in Step by Step classrooms;
           community building and group membership (concepts:
           group rules, negotiation, respect for individuality)
15:30–15:45 Coffee break
15:45–16:45 Observation techniques and aspects of individualization
16:45–17:00 Coffee break
17:00–18:15 Activity centers' contribution to cognitive, language,
           socioaffective, and psychomotor development
18:15–18:30 Evaluation of the training day; open session

2.3.a. Trainee Activity

March 19, 2004, 09:35. The pace is brisk as the Morning Meeting begins. The trainee acting as teacher is Ionica Mogos (nicknamed "Nela"). She engages the 19 children with a story of children from nearby Galati writing them, sending a recipe for vegetable salad, and saying they would like to visit Tulcea. Nela's children respond warmly, saying they would like to meet the Galati children. Next, Nela gives them tags, each showing a carrot, a head of cabbage, or some other vegetable. She pins one of the tags on each child. She tells them to choose an activity center: "Veggie salad"—Kitchen, "Young mathematicians"—Manipulatives, "Tools store"—Constructions, "Pots and vases for flowers"—Arts, "Spring in the garden"—Literacy Center.

Assistant teacher Ana Maria and two "mothers," Mirela and Viorica, go to the centers to help. The other trainees are observers. Mary and Maria, both trainees, are told by the teacher how to help out. The observer trainees have checklists of standards and kids' names. Mary tries to get the children to check off their own activities with chalk on a blackboard matrix, temporarily engaging their interests, but with little success in creating an accurate record.

Tuca helps Razvan and Andrei build a shed of blocks to store the garden tools. When they finish, they add paper tags showing their names. The names fall off. Andrei looks for a solution, without success. Tuca suggests Scotch tape. There is a big roll near him, but he doesn't try to use it. Tuca goes to the cabinet and cuts a piece for him to use (although the training suggests that she should let Andrei try longer to solve the problem himself).

Mirela is teaching English to Dylara and George. She has them say, "My name is . . . " in English. She shows them a poster board of a dozen vegetables with Romanian words—*morcov* on the carrot, *ridiche* on the radish. Mirela has George point to a vegetable and say its name. She says the English name, and he repeats it. After several selections by the two boys, Mirela puts six veggie cards on the table and asks them to give the English names. They do pretty well.

The room has quieted. The kids are busy, but subdued. The children in the Kitchen Center are making good progress on the salad. The trainees are subdued. Finally, Nela calls all the children to go to the lobby to make vegetable salad, with each of them playing the part of the vegetable on their tag. They sing a song as they circle about. Then Nela calls for all *morcov* to go into the "bowl" (in the center). The children bounce about with pleasure and the teachers sing lustily as new veggies are added to the bowl. Then a teacher, Maria, sprinkles them with make-believe oil and vinegar, and they mix it all up round and round until they all fall down.

11.30. After the practice teaching activities and a coffee, the trainers and trainees gather back in the training room. The trainees who performed the teacher roles look tired. They share feelings and ideas about this activity. One trainee thanks the trainer for assistance and encouragement. Nela is happy that she was a teacher. The team assisted her in planning, in preparing materials. After the activity started, she was not anxious any more. The children helped a lot: "They did the lesson almost by themselves." Another trainee says that she was not unhappy or surprised in playing her role: "That is why I am here, to become a good preschool teacher in the Step by Step alternative approach. We took the planning seriously, and we managed pretty well."

The entire group agreed that the children had no problem with the new teacher or with working in different activity centers. It became obvious that the trainees (regardless of whether they were playing the role of teacher, teacher assistant, or volunteer) had underestimated both the children's skills in developing different playthings (e.g., TV set, mobile phone) and the grownups' efforts to handle specific tasks. The trainee who played the role of teacher assistant said that she had never imagined how difficult such an assignment could be. She was nervous about being asked by children to provide materials or helping in unexpected situations. It is not easy at all to be a volunteer parent in a Step by Step classroom.

The final conclusion was that this practice teaching, so demanding and challenging, was seen by the trainees as foundational. Experiential "learning by doing" was seen as more valuable for themselves than an expository session on theoretical or even practical aspects of Step by Step. For one trainee, this session had a "Eureka" effect: She finally understood the core essence of Step by Step. For another one, this session was evidence that half of her dissertation for the professional first teaching degree had been wrong. During these discussions, Diana made no statement. She was quiet and did not look into the others' eyes when spoken to.

2.3.b. Democratic Values

Step by Step principles, including democratic orientation in the classroom, were carefully identified in the training for the preschool teachers. On the second day of the second module, after having analyzed the practical activities of the trainees, Jeni held a session on democratic education. Based on *Education and the Culture of Democracy: Early Childhood Practice*,[13] she explained the Step by Step principles of democratic education, giving these examples:

- *Freedom of thought and expression.* "(Is it important how we apply these principles in the classroom?) In the Step by Step classroom, the

---

[13]See Hansen, K., Kaufmann, R., & Saifer, S. (n.d.). *Educatia si cultivarea democratiei: metode pentru prescolari* [*Education and the culture of democracy: Early childhood practice*]. Bucharest: CEPD, Step by Step Romania.

children are free to choose much of what they do and to express their opinions. An important difference between freedom within rules and freedom without rules is recognized—between being free and libertine."

• *Authority and respect.* "Neither children nor teachers should impose themselves authoritatively. Respect is shown by addressing each other by first names."

• *Opportunity and self-initiative.* "They can choose the centers on the same panel they choose the activities for the day. Their initiative must be taken into account. During the Morning Meeting, the children can initiate activities."

• *Efficiency for oneself and consolidation of self-confidence.* "The children should have an environment where they can work together, take responsibilities and decisions, and be efficient."

• *Joint checking.* "The activities should be based on the children's needs and interests. The teacher should carry on activities that meet the children's wishes. True-to-life activities, such as the vegetable salad, are important. The children should understand that they are efficient and can really accomplish something."

• *The classroom as a "microcosm of the community."* "The children's pictures pinned up in the classroom give assurance that they are part of the group. So they feel good in the group. They take an interest in one another. It is important to post their names, photos, and products in the classroom, as well as to provide 'pockets' for their personal belongings. Everybody should feel comfortable in the classroom group."

Following the session, Jeni asked the trainees to write two things they would change in their classroom in order to facilitate democratic education. It was apparent in the clinical observations at Tulcea that these democratic values were included in the standards taught and used.

We asked the trainers whether the standards for training teachers should be as democratic as the standards for the children's class activity. Should the trainees have choices of experience, as the children do? They answered affirmatively, but deference and choice were not as apparent as they were in the children's classes. Clearly, they were not among the dominant principles for teacher training at this site. What was to be learned were standardized procedures for creating and maintaining a pre-selected learning environment. As we saw it, the Tulcea training was oriented to knowledge predetermined by leading Step by Step trainers, not left to be partially constructed or intuited by the trainees. We did not see the trainees encouraged to combine the new with the old from their past experience, but to fix upon patterns of prescribed activities.

2.3.c. Making Observations

March 19, 2004, 15:45. Maria and Eliza lead a session on observation techniques and elements of individualization. On the flip chart sheets, the trainees read that information gathered through observation can be used for encouraging children's interests, dividing the children into twos or other groups, diversifying activities, and focusing on specific activities. Maria finds examples in the trainees' observations of the previous day.

The trainees raised some questions suggesting that some of them were confused. They discussed fact-based observations and use of a portfolio. Maria gave examples of using the information for these purposes:

- Encouraging interests (e.g., a child is not happy playing with blocks, so markers and paper are placed in the activity center for writing and drawing).
- Grouping children in twos (e.g., one child, having been ill and absent, was given a mate who had attended, so both could continue the current project; a little boy who had been absent a long time was encouraged to work with a considerate girl on making a painting, which pleased him extremely, put him at ease, and made him laugh; when one child had just understood something and another one had not, they were put together so that the former should help the latter).
- Diversifying activities (e.g., a confrontation over use of materials at the Manipulatives center was diverted by distracting the attention of one child with a special photograph).
- Centering on special needs (e.g., to develop the small muscles of the hand, different activities are involved, such as using a pair of pliers).

Then Maria asked this question: "What can you observe when a child works at an easel, or with blocks, or with manipulatives, or with scissors?" Working in small groups, the trainees shared answers to the question. Their answers were summarized by group leaders orally in a plenary session.

2.3.d. Individualization

Much of the Tulcea training focused on individualization, requiring extensive knowledge of the individual child. Each boy and girl came to the kindergarten from a particular family, having a certain level of maturity, being serious or carefree, full of energy or calm, extroverted or introverted, with particular interests, and with a certain style of learning.

March 19, 2004, 16:30. It is a Friday afternoon in the class regularly taught by Agafia Ghenciu ("Galea") and Marinela. At the outset of the practical activity set forth by Nela and the other trainees, two children come to the Literacy Center. There are optional English classes at this center.

The children repeat several English words. The lesson ends, but Teo chooses not to leave. He starts telling about dinosaurs, his new hobby. Teo continues speaking about dinosaurs until Mirela, the trainee at the center, says, "Won't you go to another center too?" Mirela turns to Marinela and murmurs, "He's driving me crazy with these dinosaurs." Marinela agrees, "Yes, this is his new hobby. He had been interested in sailboats. His dream was to become a captain, although he knew nowadays there are no sailing boats. That's why I have painted a sailboat on this cloth on the wall." She points to a cloth on the wall having a plane, a train and a sailboat painted on it. "I've brought him different books about boats . . . " Marinela goes on.

On March 20, as the training closed, Ana reintroduced the idea of individualization by asking the trainees about jigsaw puzzles. She pointed out that usually a child does a puzzle more quickly than an adult. In order to construct a puzzle, it is crucial to see the entire picture. As there are no identical pieces in a puzzle, she suggested the puzzle as an analogy to the class or to the individual child. Ana explained:

"Think of the class as a puzzle. Each piece is different. Each piece is an individual child. What do you have to do in order to work with the puzzle? You have to observe, to think hard about the people in the room. Just as every piece is different, so is every child unique. The classroom needs to be observed, just as you need to observe a puzzle. For pedagogical purposes, we must not forget the standards, so as to see where we are and to what we need to move."

2.3.e. The Learning Environment

Planning the educational supplies and auxiliaries was very important. The first things that struck us when we entered a Step by Step classroom were its aesthetic aspect and the richness of materials. These things were also noted by Dr. Gheorghe Felea, executive secretary of the National

Commission for Educational Alternatives, in his *Report on Educational Alternatives in Romania.*[14]

> During the second day of training, speaking of the materials used in class, Dana says that they must be attractive, accessible, and matched to the age and level of physical development of the children (e.g., no Legos blocks for the 3-year-olds, whose little hand muscles are not yet developed). Each child should have a variety of toys, at different levels of complexity, so that the child can choose what he or she likes. One has to pay attention to the safety and cleanliness of the materials. The teachers should allow for flexibility of centers and of the materials in these centers. (Materials should be used in every center.)

General Director Neacsu expressed his appreciation for the quality of materials used by Step by Step. Much preschool education relies on enrichment of perceptual experience as a step toward conceptualization. Announcing a new initiative of the Ministry, he said:[15]

> "We wish to improve the base of auxiliary materials. I am looking forward to organizing a traveling exhibition of new things in the field. We will start in Târgoviște, where all the alternatives will come together with their experience in the field."

The materials in the classroom impressed the new teachers. Jeni, remembering their reactions, told us that at the beginning, when they saw the materials, they said they were wonderful, most useful, and good for the children, but probably too expensive. A counterargument was offered that teachers

> " . . . can make these materials themselves. I can make a puzzle. A child and I together can make a puzzle. We can enrich this center. The children appreciate their own materials more than those purchased from a store."

Jeni compared purchased materials and the handmade ones. No matter what town she visited, she found a bookshop and looked for children's games. Even secondhand things were sought. She once found a collection of carnival costumes that were great for the children's "play your character"

---

[14]See Felea, G. (Ed.). (2003). *Alternativele educationale din Romania.* Bucharest: Editura Triade Cluj-Napoca.
[15]During the discussion held on March 22, 2004, at MER.

game. Jeni commented on the fact that teachers start with the idea that they do not have any money for these materials, but they should think that these materials can also be handmade. Jeni remembered a Step by Step training session several years ago, where they developed toys from used materials.

Speaking also of materials, Ana insisted upon a balance between accessibility and quality. She recommended purchase of the best-quality, safe materials that the children could use: "That guarantees the quality of the products made by the children." Realizing that many materials are at hand everywhere, she told this story:

> "School 3 in this same neighborhood serves many Roma people. I invited the parents, the teaching staff and the principal to visit us. They were interested in joining Step by Step. Their classroom looked really bad. We probably discouraged them when they saw our kindergarten, but I told them, 'I am convinced you would make it as beautiful as ours. You have sand and water. You can buy little buckets, notebooks, and pencils.' I outlined an accessible financial evaluation. I was invited to their place, and we discussed the involvement of parents. They joined the program in the autumn. We also helped them make their blocks kit, and other things. The teacher and the parents made all kinds of toys from different materials that they would have thrown away. They have more handmade materials than purchased materials. It can be done."

Answering Question 7 on the survey questionnaire, the trainees expressed opinions as to the importance of quality in the didactic materials for Step by Step teaching. Ten of the trainees said that the richness of materials is very important; seven described it as most important; four said that it is important; and two responded that it is of little importance. No one answered that it was unimportant.

2.4. Parent Involvement

During a March 22 discussion of efforts within the Romanian system to extend school–family relations, General Director Neacsu stated:

> "At the local level, parents are being elected into the managing committee of the school. At the district level, a schools council operates within the education board (with parents involved). At the community level, the local development committee interprets educational

statistics so as to balance local labor force demands and the school's development projects. Parents participate in this local development committee. The presence of parents in action toward qualitative education is felt at the local, district, and inspectorate levels. There is good feedback, especially when schools have certain problems. Parents have a very important part in the inspection and evaluation of a school (for school criteria and standards). At meetings of parents' representatives, they discuss school services, the behavior of the teaching staff and the extent to which they can ask for special courses (as a curricular activity of the school) and can establish a curriculum for their children.

During the Step by Step training, we saw a different approach to the matter of individualization and involvement of parents. No indicators, evaluations, proceedings, or committees were mentioned, but emphasis was placed on *celebrations*. The trainees were asked to think back to their childhood memories, because the celebrations needed to be children's celebrations. They needed to suggest beautiful memories and to be recreational, not highly competitive. "We mean to prevent the 'star' phenomenon and stress elements that frequently arise in traditional celebrations." Marinela mentioned that they did not rely on text materials; rather, they constructed new scripts for each celebration, combining songs and poems learned throughout the year:

> "One year we made a big fabric Christmas tree on the carpet, and the children became the little stars on it. Another year we had a carnival with the children choosing their characters. They rehearsed their roles in class. For the kindergarten 'graduates,' we made hats and gowns. We adapted an anthem from the 'Gaudeamus' song."

Marinela sang a portion of this song for us. Others gave examples of lines composed by the teachers. Jeni showed the trainees two paper bag costumes that parents had made for the celebration. Each teacher gave examples of celebrations they remembered. Pictures from the celebrations went around the room. One person remarked, "A traditional celebration can make parents unhappy or children excessively emotional."

Dana said that last autumn she intended to evaluate children's progress partly by bringing the parents into the classroom to see what their children were doing in kindergarten. The teachers did not prepare anything in particular; they just announced that in 2 days they would have an exhibition. They made an advertisement-type announcement, invitations for the parents, and brochures telling about the program. Former students of the kindergarten were also invited. It was a turning point for parents' attitudes. They began to get more involved. One of them said, "I never imagined how many things our children can do." On another occasion, the children sold trinkets and bottles containing colored sand. With the money, they bought a little carpet and pencils. At another event, they "body-painted." That is, the children painted one another to be their favorite characters. When the parents came, the children stood with their backs turned. The show began with music, and the children suddenly turned around. The parents were greatly surprised. (The paints had been previously tested to make sure that they would not be allergic reactions.) Dana's summary: "The main idea is not to make the celebration a competition where they win or lose, but to involve children and parents in interaction using activities and games."

Day Three—March 20, 2004

08:30–10:00 Play in activity centers; learning through play in activity centers
10:00–10:30 Coffee break
10:30–11:30 Other specific elements for Step by Step: celebrations,
            classroom environment
11:30–12:30 Partnerships: kindergarten–family, kindergarten–community
12:30–12:45 Coffee break
12:45–13:30 Open session–discussion
13:30–13:45 Evaluation of training

In the final part of the training, the complex relationships among kindergarten, family, and community were graphically represented as concentric circles, shown in the graphic here. Generally, the involvement of the parents and of the community were rather different functions, but both served to benefit the schooling.

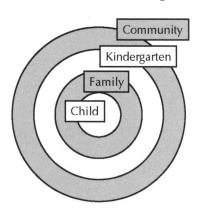

"Parents come when called by the teacher and when their opinion matters," said Silvia Craciun, inspector for preschool education for Tulcea County. She was a pedagogical high school graduate who had 29 years of classroom experience as a teacher and 1 year's experience as an inspector. She said:

> "After 1989, I never thought these parents would be so interested in what really happens in school. Teachers wish more and more that the parents would participate in the daily program of their children. This happens especially in the great traditional institutions, because it is a way to captivate the parents and stimulate competition among kindergartens. Parents are always present in the extracurricular activities, such as trips, visits to the theatre, and so on."

Ana Pantea said that within Step by Step, parents frequently participated in the classes. When they came to register their children in Kindergarten 3, they were asked why they chose Step by Step. Most answered:

- "Step by Step has didactic materials."
- "It was recommended by another parent."
- "We want something different for our children."
- "The children have important achievements."

"The parents learn about these things from other parents or from the school itself," said Pantea. Another trainer continued, " . . . because we are appreciated." Many parents did not know anything particular about the Step by Step alternative, only vague chatter heard here and there. "At first, some parents were convinced that it was good for the children; others were skeptical; and still others just wanted to take the children somewhere else." Ana took advantage of first meetings with parents interested in Step by Step to discover their purposes and to get information about the child, about the parents' jobs, about their relationships, and so forth. And appreciative parents had donated a TV set and a tape recorder and helped buy the blocks kit.

But the parents' primary contribution was not financial. Whenever necessary, they came into the classrooms and worked with the children. As the graphic above indicates, there should be a strong relationship between parents and the school. The teachers from Kindergarten 3 testified that they had regular contact with the community. Some meetings were organized so that the parents and others could give feedback to the teachers. Pantea said, "I care about relationships with persons of the community. These relationships should be maintained by inviting them into the kindergarten, by sending them a holiday postcard, or by other means."

Ana vigorously pursued her marketing strategies. Her initiative and determination made it possible for the kindergarten to obtain sponsorships. Together they renovated the building, built lavatories, had the floors parqueted, bought new furniture and educational materials, refurbished a kind of attic called "*prici*," and built handsome lofts in each classroom where the children could take naps. The kindergarten even had its own car; as noted earlier, this helped reduce the cost of supplies and making fresh food available for the children. "Without the sponsorships, we could not have transformed a building that looked like a horror movie into a large, beautiful, and welcoming kindergarten."

2.4.a. Parent Associations

In Kindergarten 3, a parents' association was created in 1998. It was called Headstart. In most schools in Tulcea, the parents expressed new ideas for classes and schools. They make decisions and sometimes constrained the teachers. The Headstart association paid for the kindergarten teacher's assistant. Some years ago, the principal of a school opposed creating a Step by Step classroom. The parents went to the Tulcea County School Inspectorate and finally to Bucharest. Their appeal reached the Minister, who supported their desire to have an alternative type of education for their children.

The Step by Step directorship in Bucharest got involved only when directly asked. Carmen Lica said:[16]

> "If we have signals from different locations in the country, from teachers or parents, that there are problems, we are willing to make an effort to solve the problem. Options like karate, music, dancing, skating—these are choices to be made at the local level. This is due to the very strong partnership created between schools and parent associations."

Parents had been involved since the beginning, explaining their feeling of ownership. Lica continued, "It is important that the parents are told what is going to happen, so they can tailor expectations accordingly."

---

[16]During a discussion on March 22, 2004, in Bucharest.

2.4.b. Diversity

We talked with Sylvia Craciun, Tulcea County's inspector for preschool education, about diversity.[17] She spoke of parents who were unhappy with the lack of opportunities for children having mild social or physical disabilities. She stated:

> "The dissatisfaction is diminishing. At the national level, some steps have been taken to integrate children with special needs into regular classrooms. But so far these have helped only isolated cases. The role of the teacher is to explain to the parents that some children need compensatory assistance through education. We should offer them what Mother Nature couldn't."

While talking to Craciun, we advanced the idea that in Step by Step they try to help children be sensitive to personal and cultural diversity. Asked whether she ever met people who did not want their children to develop wide and free thinking, Craciun answered that there had been such opinions from the parents,

> " . . . at the beginning, when the change was too sudden. After so many years, one could not expect [promoting diversity]. One had to work with the parents. It was hard to bring them into it. They would say, 'I can't/I don't have time/I learned this way . . . ' Nowadays such resistance is isolated. From what I see in the approximately 140 kindergartens I visit, the parents, regardless of their social status, want their children to be *one step ahead of where they were*."

Diversity occurs not only in children, but in parents too. Parents' expectations vary considerably. Carmen Lica spoke of two kinds:

> " 'I want my child to do top work in school.' 'I want my child to become a genius overnight.' We've met this kind of parent. And we've met the other kind of parent, saying, 'Because he's in Step by Step, my child doesn't know as many poems as my neighbor's child.' Step by Step tries to meet all the different values, principles, and attitudes."

---

[17]On March 19, 2004, at Tulcea.

3. ALTERNATIVES AND PARTNERSHIPS

3.1. The Danube Delta: A Metaphor for Alternatives

On March 20, 2004, at the end of the second module, with the General's coordination, Kindergarten 3 provided a cruise on the Danube Delta for the trainers. It was a sun-radiant Saturday afternoon. The cruise was a good opportunity for discussion and reflection. The trainers were relaxed. With the training over, they could enjoy being outdoors. The General was a member of the Local Council and of the Administrative Council of the Danube Delta Biosphere Reserve. He described the delta, Tulcea County, and the city of Tulcea.

In 2000, Tulcea had a population of 265,349. The economic activities[18] of the city of Tulcea were concentrated mainly in the metallurgical, shipbuilding, wood-processing, and food industries. Agriculture had a low standing among the area's activities, in contrast to fishing and pisciculture. The General said:

> "The Danube Delta is the mother of Europe's youngest land. It leads to the sea; [it is] predictable and unpredictable at the same time. It gives you countless options: channels and meanders, spontaneity and control. All these make up the delta we are sailing on."

From Tulcea, the Danube flows 80 kilometers before reaching the Black Sea. The river splits in two, and then into three branches—the Chilia, the Sulina, and the Sfântu Gheorghe—to create a unique and somehow exotic landscape. The water spreads into some 120 tributaries and meanders through a widening riverbed. The Black Sea waves repel the sediments of old "Danubius" brought from far away, depositing this rich earth at the mouth of the river. And this is how, in time, the youngest land of Europe came into being—a realm of reeds providing refuge for many rare species of birds, fish, and other animals.

With the passing of time, the Danube Delta ecosystem became seriously affected by careless and destructive human intervention. It suffered from cutting new water channels for shipping; from pollution of the river with sewage, industrial waste, pesticides, and nutrients; from the reduction of flooding zones as natural fish nurseries; from the construction of dams; and from ruthless exploitation of the natural resources. It was victimized by agriculture, fishing, hunting, tourism, reed cutting, and sand extraction. Much of this took place during Communist rule, especially the period 1960–1980.

---

[18]For such information, see the Danube Delta website (www.danubedelta.ro).

The Danube Delta has a particular rural acculturation of Romanians, Bulgarians, and Ukrainians. With the variety of its natural wealth and its geographically strategic position, the Danube is a bridge between lands and a gate to the whole world. The delta and the surrounding territories have a dynamism all their own.

3.2. The National Symposium in Târgovişte

April 1, 2004, 09:15. After 15 years' effort, the National Commission for Educational Alternatives is holding a national conference—an important event, the first in Romania to be dedicated exclusively to educational pluralism.[19] The 290 participants included Ministry staff members and vice-general inspectors from all around the country, as well as persons responsible for education at the local level. Conference officials refer to alternatives by a generic term: "the subsystem." The meeting is attended by representatives of five alternative schooling movements: Waldorf, Montessori, the Jena Plan, Freinet, and Step by Step. Their national leaders have a special place at the symposium—as advocates, illustrators, and honorees.

State Secretary for Preuniversity Education Irinel Chiran comments on the evolution of educational alternatives during the last decade. She recalls their hesitations at the beginning, greatly differing from the "maturity" of current alternatives. "A river delta communicates with the sea, and so do alternatives. Alternatives are loyal competitors to traditional education. They all go towards the same destination: a high-quality education, to the children's benefit and that of the whole system."

Secretary Chiran identifies three stages of educational pluralism. The first was the initial "anomalous" stage, implementation of the alternatives (1990–1995), characterized by confusion, inconsistencies, and absence of legislative recognition. The second was the provisional operation stage (1995–2000), with alternatives gaining legal status and operating licenses. And the third is a mature stage (since the year 2000), with consolidation of establishments to implement their programs. The first institutional evaluation of the system occurred during this third stage, using national parameters and standards, and producing very good results.

Leaders of the five alternatives have some reservations about the way the stages have been identified. During the following discussions, some point out that some of the alternatives have been able to operate using a clearly defined and coherent legal background from

---

[19]In 1996, the Institute for Educational Sciences organized a broader symposium.

the very beginning. A Step by Step spokesperson refers to how the initial agreements between Step by Step and the MER reflected a functional partnership between these two.[20] It is noted that Step by Step is the only alternative for which the MER pays the wages of two teachers per primary classroom.

Secretary Chiran acknowledges that the alternatives have positively influenced traditional teaching in Romania. They have had a particular influence on the attitudes of teachers, especially attitudes toward using interactive methods and certain didactic materials (tool kits). And, through the involvement of families in school life, local communities have become interested in the implementation of alternatives. Another keynote speaker, General Director Ioan Neacsu, concludes the morning plenary session by saying:

> Ministry activity should focus on the integration of alternative education into the national system of education. . . . These alternatives are credible and efficient for use in traditional education—implementing order into the system, establishing coherent policies, identifying partnership points for the transfer of good practices, creating printed materials, and advertising in national specialized magazines (*Tribuna Învăţământului*). High-quality education focuses on children and their needs.

The workshops of the afternoon[21] illustrate the approach of each alternative, but also the common aim of reducing the "magistro-centrism" (i.e., the "teacher-centered" nature) of the Romanian schools. These sessions are attended by the inspectors, but not by the Ministry people.

3.2.a. Common Goals, Different Approaches

April 2, 2004, 12:30. The participants are gathered for the afternoon plenary session. The hall is extremely crowded. The workshop rapporteurs (i.e., discussants) are called to report on the responses to the alternatives. The Waldorf representative states: "We had four workshops with 5, 10, 9, and 10 participants. These small numbers do not

---

[20]These agreements between the MER and CEPD, Step by Step Romania (dated April 27, 1998, and September 24, 2001) are included in the volume by Felea, G. (Ed.). (2003). *Alternativele education ale din Romania.* Bucharest: Editura Triade Cluj-Napoca.

[21]Our research team attended the four workshops conducted by Step by Step trainers. Jeni, Dana, and Ana organized two workshops for the preschool level on Step by Step activity centers and parents' involvement. Next day, their colleagues from the primary level conducted two workshops on the Morning Meeting and alternative student assessment instruments.

say much about the quality of the workshops. But the fact that the same persons came three times says a lot."

The atmosphere comes to life as the workshops are being evaluated. There is a mood of competition among the alternatives. "We did not want to encourage anyone to vote for us," says a rapporteur with a small number of participants. "I did not come to you because I did not know you," comments someone. Opinions are changed. The Montessori representative expresses her appreciation to the organizers. The Waldorf and Freinet representatives take a stand for cooperation among colleagues. Someone from Waldorf says, "We are all in the same boat. We need different methods as we are all different."

Gheorghe Felea, secretary of the National Commission for Educational Alternatives, calls attention to the fact that, in the minds of many, the idea of "alternatives" is not yet clearly defined and perhaps never will be, but the legitimacy of alternatives has already been established. "From them, partnership, missionary work, negotiation, and open debate can contribute to the consolidation of pluralism in Romanian education."

"The alternatives have *oxygenated* traditional education," General Director Neacsu concludes optimistically, but he also draws attention to the fact that the alternatives now benefit from a positive form of discrimination: "The financier is the one that decides," partly because of the job cuts as a result of the school population decrease. In the final discussion, he mentions again that two teachers' wages are being paid in each Step by Step primary classroom.

3.2.b. Perceptions of Step by Step

Although our research did not specifically target the ways Step by Step was perceived as an educational alternative, this topic came up (both directly and implicitly) in our interviews and discussions with people (Step by Step trainees, trainers, teachers, and other staff, as well as inspectors and MER representatives). During our study, people both inside and outside this educational alternative expressed a variety of opinions about Step by Step. Kindergarten 3 teachers expressed their pride and sense of ownership of their achievements. Some non-Step by Step teachers seemed to feel envy, and possibly a sense that Step by Step was in an unfair competition with traditional education. Most of the inspectors and MER staff members expressed a balanced valuing of the contributions of traditional education and the educational alternative movement.

Labeled both an "alternative" and part of a "subsystem," Step by Step sometimes became the target for uncomplimentary comments. It has been said to be the "monolithic otherness" of the educational system. But more often it was seen as a fair and inspired competitor. Step by Step became a "brand," desirable at both institutional and individual levels. However, the demanding activities required by the Step by Step methodology had certain side effects. Some Step by Step teachers gained a higher professional status because they became better trained; this training improved their teaching skills, as well as their knowledge of how to organize the learning environment and how to involve parents. Some colleagues in traditional classrooms were inspired by Step by Step ideas, but some perceived Step by Step to be the "spoiled child" of the educational system.[22]

The perceptions of teachers in traditional education and teachers in Step by Step were influenced by the communication between them. Still, we did not see clear efforts to improve that communication. Ana Pantea told us that the strong support from parents and the children's performance outcomes at times brought out "the envy of our colleagues" in other schools. More specifically, she commented:

> "Other kindergarten teachers say that all of our children are from wealthy homes, but it is not true. Our children come from all social classes. This is indeed something different. It is the fruit of our work. . . . Some people say that we have it easy, but they do not know how hard we work. And they wrongly believe we are paid more."

Marinela Peiciu, a Tulcea trainer, reinforced the idea that "there has been competition between Step by Step and traditional teachers." She underlined the lack of communication among teachers and the poor understanding of Step by Step philosophy. Thus the would-be complementary educational approaches were sometimes not only at odds, but contradictory:

> "There have been malicious comments that Step by Step children are left too much on their own. There was a feeling that Step by Step needs to monitor each child moving around the classroom, that one needs more adult persons in the classroom. Also that so many materials spoil the atmosphere."

More and more confident in their achievements, the Kindergarten 3 Step by Step teachers gradually gave up the idea of assisting their col-

---

[22]These comments were heard mainly from traditional teachers during the workshops of the National Symposium in Târgoviște and at Kindergarten 41, Galati.

leagues in traditional education. An increased number of "Step by Step-affiliated" teachers in Tulcea County, a sense of ownership, and the vision of child-centeredness all made it possible for the methodological study circles[23] of Step by Step teachers to operate separately from those of traditional teachers. A similar situation was reported in other counties.

Elena Mihai and Carmen Anghelescu, CEPD staff members, commented[24] on possible side effects of this tendency toward "isolation":

> "It was comfortable for Step by Step teachers to share compatible and similar professional experiences. The gap between 'traditional' and 'alternative' could deepen—which would be detrimental to education at large."

Another issue was noticed by these CEPD staffers: The cooperation between preschool and primary teachers needed strengthening. There were many examples of good communication between the two levels, especially when children who graduated from a Step by Step kindergarten continued in the program (i.e., they moved into a Step by Step primary classroom). However, in some cases, the communication was negligible.

4. MENTORING

4.1. The Mentoring Experience

May 14, 2004, 06:20. Early in the morning, we head from Tulcea to Galati. I am accompanying Marinela Peiciu to pay a monitoring visit to Kindergarten 41 in Galati. Nela Mogos and Rodica Tireavu, two of the school's teachers, started Step by Step training at Tulcea in October 2003 and completed it in March 2004. Nela did her practical training in Marinela's Step by Step class.

On the way, we discuss the monitoring. As described earlier, Marinela is a trainer in Kindergarten 3. She has worked there since she graduated from high school 8 years ago. She greatly enjoys her job, but finds the salary discouraging. She is enrolled in the manage-

---

[23]Teacher staff development in Romania, called "methodological study circles" ("cercuri metodice" in Romanian), required regular monthly activities, compulsory for all the teachers within the system. They were intended to be opportunities for sharing experience, new theoretical or practical didactic approaches, spreading results of new projects, and so on. A number of teachers gathered together in a school unit (according to class level, curriculum area, and geographical region), observed teaching lessons and other activities, and discussed issues with their colleagues.

[24]Discussion held in Bucharest at the CEPD office on June 7, 2004.

ment course of the Faculty of Economic Sciences in Dunarea de Jos University in Galati.

Among the difficulties Marinela encountered as a kindergarten mentor was inaccessible items of furniture (e.g., work spaces that are too high and cabinets that have doors). The Galati kindergartens were not able to buy the standard furniture, so they adapted the old. It was not good enough, but changes were not allowed. (Furniture parts were registered in the inventory of the institution.) "We found clever solutions. In one classroom, a teacher's desk was transformed into a dollhouse." Sometimes the classrooms were not large enough to be places where children could eat, learn, and nap together. Some classrooms were difficult to furbish. Standardized worksheets were used excessively, even when overcrowded with graphics, with no free space left.

Planning had also been a problem. Marinela said, "Some teachers do not understand that a mathematical activity can vary from center to center. Planning models have been ignored. It has been a year since the introduction of 'child-initiated activities.' Some teachers and kindergartens have given up because the activity was too demanding. They chose to go back to traditional teaching."

Marinela and I talked also about the parents' association and paying the teacher's assistant. In Kindergarten 3 in Tulcea, the association provided the pay for this assistant, as noted earlier. The parents pay the national minimum wage, using an employment contract.

We arrive at Kindergarten 41 in Galati. This kindergarten joined Step by Step in the autumn of 2003 with two groups. Its staff wishes to extend Step by Step in the kindergarten, seeing it as essential to face competition from nearby kindergartens. It has a large courtyard, a playground, a well-kept building, and good facilities. Optional classes for English, computers, sports, and dance are available. Principal Elana Stratila tells us that parents have found out about Step by Step and ask, when coming to register their child, "Do you have Step by Step?" The parents see the furnishings of other kindergartens and say, "I want Step by Step." Maria Rauta, inspector for preschool education in Galati County, says, "Step by Step is a 'brand' that increases the level of the kindergarten."

Until the previous autumn, the answer was " No, we do not have Step by Step," which caused "the best children to leave. We lost many children, actually the best." Principal Stratila is rather unhappy with the fact that the Step by Step website has not yet been updated. She says, "We now live in a different world. Parents access the Internet. They search and they don't find us. And so they believe that Kindergarten 41 does not have Step by Step. For us, it's a disadvantage."

4.2. A Trainee in Galati

At 11:35, Nela Mogos finished her morning session in Kindergarten 41 Galati. She was tired and relieved. She had completed the topic of the week, "Means of Transportation." The 16 children of the preparatory group, all dressed up for a special occasion, had worked at four activity centers: Literacy, Manipulatives, Role Play, and Arts. The Role Play Center had been crowded, with many temptations. At the back of the classroom, the children had had a fancy car with batteries, horn, music, and other accessories, and also a bike that two at a time could ride. The classroom too was crowded. In addition to the nine boys and seven girls were: Nela's colleague from an afternoon traditional class, a teacher assistant, a teacher wanting to enter Step by Step, a volunteer parent, the county inspector responsible for preschool education, Marinela, and two observers. Following the standards, Marinela wrote in the monitoring report:

> When the children are sent to the centers, a little conflict arises because all the children want to play with the new car that Luiza brought. The teacher solves the problem by letting Florin, a child from the Placement Center [a nearby residential facility], play first. Helped by a volunteer parent, the teacher manages to settle the children down.
> The educator knows and implements the Step by Step methodology by interacting with each child individually—acting like a good mediator does—in the small conflicts generated by the surprise toys that some kids bring to the kindergarten. She provides various materials, giving every child the opportunity to play and learn for a specific purpose, in accordance with every child's age and personality.

Under the "Recommendations" heading, Marinela writes:

- Make efficient use of classroom walls, with children's works exhibited.
- Children's works should be dated and signed by them.
- Buy the blocks kit for the Blocks Center.
- Place horizontal labels for the centers at child height.
- Develop the instrument through which children choose their activity center.
- Give up the special writing notebook (Type 1).
- Gather collective works for assessing certain subjects.
- Enrich the Science Center with natural elements and material.
- Draft the Nature Calendar.
- Post movable letters, figures, and words in the Literacy Center.
- Furbish the parents' room.

Marinela and Nela now speak face to face, in friendly tones, especially about Marinela's recommendations. Since Nela and a traditional education group do their teaching in the same room, some "traditional aspects" are found in Nela's teaching: She uses the same red color on children's notebooks both to mark mistakes and to draw a model letter or number. Also, the blocks kit is missing. And the children's choices are limited, because the teaching material supply is not very rich and some material is inaccessible to children, packed on high lockers. Finally, the sand and the water bowl are placed a bit too high.

The conversation becomes more animated when they talk about planning. "Planning is a problem," says Nela. Marinela asks why she planned 4 weeks ahead, and Nela answers, "This is how I've always done it." Marinela says, "You can make a weekly plan. You are working with older children who can negotiate what they want for the next week. Working with them should be so flexible that you can hardly keep to your plan. You may want to draft your plan the weekend ahead."

They talk about sections of the teaching plan, and about where to include the compulsory activities. Nela asks about changes in the plan. Marinela answers, "The changes appear after class observation. The games and activities initiated by the children are spontaneous. You can include them in the plan at the end of the week. Did you notice any activity initiated by the children today?" "Yes, they wanted to play with sand and water," Nela replies.

The dialogue continues:

NELA: The music. Where do I include music in the plan?

MARINELA: In the art section.

NELA: And the education for society? In which section do I include it?

MARINELA: In whichever section you consider appropriate. For example, environmental education can be included in the science section, in the sand and water activity, or wherever the topic seems appropriate.

NELA: Oh, I see! (*with relief*) I did not understand the connection between the two.

MARINELA: How is it going? What other difficulties did you encounter?

NELA: My difficulties are with planning. I was not quite aware of some things.

PRINCIPAL STRATILA: We do not get any help down here. I think we will take a trip to Tulcea to watch you work in the kindergarten.

Marinela gives them examples from her own teaching practice. She says that music activities can be carried out in the Blocks Center as well as in the Role Play Center, if the music deals with housewives, vegetables, or the like. Marinela's advice is "to be flexible, to see where the activity is going." Her conclusion comes right away: "We have a plan to follow, and our role is to think through the activity ahead."

The conversation then turns to balancing planning and spontaneity. Nela mentions "another problem": "During the Morning Meeting, when I announce a topic, and the children have other ideas, what do I do?"

Marinela answers: "If you plan to speak about a topic, but something interesting happens in everyday life, or if the kids have seen something on TV and want to talk about it, if you see that they are interested in something else, you should discuss it with them. Your topics are well formulated. If they had not been so, I would have told you. If something changes, go to the observation stage. What can we do for the Morning Meeting? You may have a morning when you do not plan anything special; you just tell the kids you have some thread, a pair of scissors and some other stuff, and you ask them what you can do with that. It might happen that they do not come up with any ideas, but you should not do this every day. Basically, we have to follow the plan."

Afterward, they discussed the benefit of the standards presented in Tulcea. Nela spoke of plans to communicate more with the children in class, to offer them more opportunities to express themselves. Regarding her attitude toward the kids, she planned to get closer to them. She spoke of dealing with real class situations: For instance, if there are centers that children do not like, Nela wanted to communicate with them; she might play as if one of them. As for children who required special attention, like Florin, the boy from the Placement Center, Nela tried to speak more to him, to be near him as much as possible.

There was also the "parents" issue. Nela said she had a good relationship with them: "They are good parents. They have little money. After they assisted with some classes, I asked the mothers their opinion. They went, 'Oh, we had no idea of what you were doing here. We thought our children did nothing but play. We could not believe how many poems they know already.'" Marinela suggested that, despite their modest financial means, parents can be asked to bring "old shoes, beads, and clothes, anything they can."

Marinela and Nela extended the discussion to include the kindergarten principal and the county inspector, noting problems faced generally by teachers in preschool and primary school units. The principal said that there is a vacancy for the teaching assistant job, but the standards for the applicants are high: a baccalaureate degree, computer skills, English-language abilities, and music and dance skills. Speaking about expanding the Step by Step alternative and the preschool "Eco program" in Galati County, Inspector Rauta labeled herself a strong advocate of "everything new." She invited us to visit the other two kindergartens in Galati and asked for a copy of Marinela's monitoring report, to have "proof of what's going on."

5. REFLECTION/DISCUSSION

"To do a puzzle, one has to see the entire picture . . . " So declares Ana at the end of the second training module on March 20 in Tulcea. Ana concludes by naming the trainers as permanent support for the trainees. After the second module, the trainers and the teachers continue their journey together into the philosophy and practice of child-focused education. "The difficult part is just beginning. The umbilical cord between the trainees and the mentors has not yet been cut." They still have months of monitoring. Taking into account the standards, the mentors are supposed to stay close to the trainees as they teach, among the children and together with the parents and their colleagues, in order to see *where they are and where they might go.*

This report completes the research study conducted between March 18 and July 15, 2004. The writer, Catalina Ulrich, was substantially helped by Ioana Herseni (head of the preschool department of CEPD, Step by Step Romania) and Luciana Terente (program assistant in the same department). The research team was also composed of other members of CEPD, who gave feedback during the writing process.

The research team primarily looked at the ways CEPD, Step by Step Romania provided training for preschool teachers aiming at implementing Step by Step methods at the classroom level. The training took place in Model Training Sites at kindergartens that had successfully passed an evaluation by the CEPD staff for delivering high-quality training based on Step by Step methodology.

Within the Romanian educational context in general, teacher staff development was an important issue. In 1991, education officially became a national priority. After that, education reform itself became a priority. Aiming to reform the educational system, strong and comprehensive educational policies were developed. Not unexpectedly, the practical implementation of those policies remained difficult. NGOs helped the reform efforts. The NGOs tried to address needs that seemed most difficult for the system—particularly equal opportunities for Roma children and children with special needs, education in underprivileged areas, education for democracy and human rights, and gender issues in education.

Since 1994, the contributions of CEPD, Step by Step Romania to the educational sector have transformed it into one of the most important NGOs in Romania. Both within the civil society arena and on the educational stage, CEPD was recognized for its efforts and results in promoting open-society values. These values were manifested in child-centeredness, resources for appropriate learning environments, parent participation and community involvement, interactive teaching approaches, and innovative assessment methods.

We researchers targeted MTS Kindergarten 3 in Tulcea as a Step by Step methodology training provider. We joined several main characters on their Step by Step journey—teachers and a training team led by the principal, Ana Pantea. We joined them during the second module of the training held in Tulcea, March 18–20, and then at a national symposium on teaching alternatives held in Târgovişte, April 1–2. There the trainers of Kindergarten 3 in Tulcea conducted workshops on Step by Step for preschool classrooms. And on May 14–15, we went along for a monitoring visit to a trainee teacher at Kindergarten 41 in Galati.

During this journey, we interviewed people; observed training sessions, classroom activities, and workshops; and attended conferences or mentoring meetings. In our case study, Kindergarten 3 operated like a prism. The question "How is Step by Step child-centered methodology implemented through teacher training?" was like a beam of white light entering a prism. The answers came out in a rainbow of colors at the other end.[25] The spectrum revealed the perspectives of MER and school inspectorate officials, experienced and inexperienced Step by Step teachers, Step by Step trainers and trainees, "traditional education" teachers, representatives of other teaching alternatives, and the CEPD staff.

The perspectives disclosed by the field research were not nearly as predictable as the color spectrum, however. First, Step by Step was compared (and frequently was seen as opposed) to "traditional education." In Romania at least, an educational alternative was perceived by teachers, parents, and students as "something at odds" with the educational field.

---

[25] Analogy suggested in the *Introductory Course for Step by Step Country Teams on Case Study Development*, Part 3, Module 2, 2004 (www.osi.hu/esp/resource).

The results were increasing parent demand to have more Step by Step classrooms; increasing inspectorate support for child-based teacher training; an increasing number of teachers saying it is no longer possible to teach other than "Step by Step style"; and increasing the visibility of child-centered teaching in the mass media. Step by Step was one of the alternatives seen as "different."

Deep within the national educational system at the Ministry and the school inspectorates, Step by Step has become part of an educational "subsystem." Without real endorsement of the alternatives' mission, we found that some within MER felt that Step by Step should focus on the integration of alternative education into the national system of education. "Integration" could be subject to a range of interpretations.

Many people (from teachers to officials) saw a sharp distinction between the "system" (meaning traditional education) and Step by Step (an educational alternative). More of a dichotomy than an integration was to be found both in official documents (the 2003 *Report on Educational Alternatives in Romania*, based on a national evaluation) and in the comments of the Step by Step trainers (during the training held in Tulcea).

The educational alternative subsystem approved by MER included Step by Step, Montessori, Freinet, the Jena Plan, and Waldorf. As such, they were expected to offer something different, but at the same time to respect mainstream system requirements. The five educational alternatives were, in fact, perceived as more or less homogeneous. The differences were obvious in the cases of Step by Step (the most familiar) and Waldorf (the most deviant), but all went beyond the national curriculum.

As part of the subsystem, Step by Step was seen by some as an "innovation laboratory" for the wider national educational system. At this writing, there appeared to be a robust partnership between the Ministry of Education and Research. There were official agreements accrediting the teacher training. Step by Step also benefited from "positive discrimination" measures (e.g., wages for two teachers per primary classroom).

In a newspaper article, Open Society Foundation–Romania President Renate Weber[26] stated that most of the Step by Step educational principles were being taken over in the traditional educational system. Step by Step instructional approaches were being found in the Romanian preschool and primary school curriculum, as well as specific teaching

---

[26]See "Step by Step helps children in developing their personalities," May 28, 2004, *Romania Libera*, p. 11.

methods (e.g., learning in activity centers, thematic study, replacement of marks with qualitative assessment of student performance).

Coming back to the main focus of the research, we found Kindergarten 3, Tulcea to be a regular preschool unit with an earned reputation for achievement. We learned that it had matured together with its "mentor," CEPD, Step by Step Romania. As a part of the public educational system, Kindergarten 3 was much like other Romanian kindergartens. Its Step by Step training center was also typical, having met the evaluation standards. However, Kindergarten 3 could be considered atypical in its human resources. The professional staff members were highly motivated and highly qualified; they either had university degrees or were working for them. They worked together in a climate of positive competitiveness. Its managers promoted high-quality standards both for individuals and for the staff as a team.

During our study, we perceived that the success of Kindergarten 3 was largely due to inspired leadership and strong support from the county inspectorate. The management team, represented mainly by the principal, focused on creating across the school an appropriate learning environment. Very special attention was paid to recruiting personnel. The principal had the autonomy to select the teachers herself. Ana Pantea was a proud woman—proud of her achievements, of her kindergarten and staff, and of the kindergarten's influence within the Step by Step network. Ownership and ambition made it possible for Kindergarten 3 to become a Model Training Site.

But it was not exemplary in all respects. The formal training was divided into well-conceptualized didactic presentation of the methodology, personally appealing practical observations, and role playing. The presentation sessions had limited interaction opportunities and relied little on visual and problem-based illustration. Given the child-centered philosophy, there was surprisingly little encouragement for the teachers to be coauthors of Step by Step, drawing upon their aspiration and experience. However impressive, some role-playing sessions were time-consuming and allowed only a few trainees to get a much greater understanding from the differentiated roles. The informal training, through mentoring and group work, appeared greatly underbudgeted, countering the expectation that Step by Step has a full-blown mentoring arrangement.

The staff of Kindergarten 3 stressed task specification and planning: "Planning is everything!" Planning is a heritage of the former Socialist system, as well as an aspect of the new global system. It was seen as crucial for management, for teacher training, for teaching and for supervising teaching. Planning by teachers was a key ingredient in implementing

Step by Step child-centered methods. The idea was that somebody can "afford" to be spontaneous only after careful planning in advance. It was a difficult standard for some trainees. Experience and flexibility were seen as necessary to balance planning and spontaneity.

The planning process was challenging for most of the teachers. The child-centered approach, with its attention to children's uniqueness and spontaneity, was sometimes seen as opposed to the requirements of the compulsory national curriculum, opposed to the quantitative indicators for calculating teaching loads, and opposed to the evaluation criteria used by school inspectors. The same difficulty was found, for some teachers, in the trainers' eagerness to teach about themes and topics instead of developing skills and competencies.

Becoming a Step by Step teacher required not only completion of the two modules and a monitoring visit, but a lot of time for individual study and reflective practice. The Step by Step preschool teachers were seen to be committed to working together with other Step by Step preschool colleagues, but Step by Step primary teachers were seldom available for collaboration. Because all this professional self-improvement was stressful, teachers sometimes felt vulnerable. Some new trainee teachers expressed the need for more methodological assistance through regular visits to each trainee's classroom by either trainers or CEPD staff members. Budget restraints and limited human resources at the CEPD office made the process of mentoring new teachers and sites difficult. Mentoring appeared to be a topic for future CEPD development.

A Step by Step "professional culture" was visible. It was grounded in both the child-centered approach as described throughout the Step by Step educational principles and the sense of a practice being cultivated among the Step by Step teachers. Based on this, the dialogue between traditional and Step by Step teachers covered different issues—ranging from "best-practices transfer" to frustration, from fair competition to prestige, from personal commitment to financial resources.

Step by Step was perceived as the most popular educational alternative across Romania. A greater future for Step by Step, however, requires both expansion and quality assurance mechanisms. The training sessions and monitoring discussions we observed emphasized core ideas specific to Step by Step philosophy and a "culture of standards" within Step by Step classroom practices. We expect Step by Step to become different in a few years, dealing with individual teachers meeting the educational needs of individual children coming from different backgrounds. Step by Step appears to be an educational alternative tailoring itself to the dynamics of a changing Romania.

CHAPTER 9

Step by Step
Cross-Case Analysis

First Steps

The purpose of this short final chapter is to illustrate the Track I cross-case procedure, using the three Step by Step case reports presented in Chapters 6–8. This is not the actual cross-case analysis, because that is still underway. That analysis awaits the completion of case reports from several other countries. As noted in Chapter 5, 28 studies were commissioned for the project. As of 2005, the compilation of the reports is in the hands of the project managers, Sarah Klaus and Hugh McLean, at the Open Society Institute office in Budapest.

The analysis in this chapter is based on the reports in Chapters 6–8 from Ukraine, Slovakia, and Romania, as well as on those (still in process) from three other countries: Bosnia and Herzegovina, Kyrgyzstan, and Lithuania.

After discussing the project with the team and reading the case reports, this analyst (myself) began the cross-case procedure with the preparation of a copy of Worksheet 3 (Analyst's Notes While Reading a Case Report) for each of the six reports. These filled-in versions of Worksheet 3 are included at the end of this chapter as Figures 9.1–9.6. (Note that these figures omit a few of Worksheet 3's details that are unnecessary for the present illustrations—the clarifications in parentheses of a few items, and some of the "Prominence . . . " and "Expected Utility . . . " items.)

These worksheets depend on input from the report authors, but they need to be prepared by one person, the cross-case analyst. Even one person alone has difficulty keeping the topics and ratings of the worksheets uniformly defined, conceptualized, and scaled. Each case's research will have its individuality, as will its report, and some of that individuality needs to be preserved, but the analysis itself depends on considerable standardization. The procedures described in Chapters 3 and 4 have been designed to provide that standardization.

From Worksheet 2 and the six versions of Worksheet 3 came the input for Worksheet 4 (Ratings of Expected Utility of Each Case for Each Theme). The project's themes were identified earlier on Worksheet 2. As indicated in Chapter 5, the six themes were these:

- Children's outcomes.
- Family and community engagement.
- Equal opportunities for each child to develop his or her potential.
- Teacher professional development.
- Enabling networks and partnerships.
- Program sustainability.

(These themes took the form of topics more than of research questions. From one study to the next, researchers will vary in preferences for how to express the themes.) Other important cross-cutting topics came up among the researchers during the months of data gathering and write-up, such as program development, funding, program and teacher standards, administrator staff development, trainee mentoring, and expanding the program into the upper primary grades. But such topics were subsumed under the six themes or held outside the case study project.

By the time of the ISSA's 10th anniversary celebration in 2004, it was better to express these themes more precisely, as follows:

- Promoting high-quality child-centered teaching, ISSA standards and certification.
- Family and community engagement.
- Creating child-centered environments and learning opportunities.
- Reforming and decentralizing teacher professional development.
- Reaching children outside preschools.
- Social inclusion and access to high-quality education for Roma children.
- Inclusion of children with disabilities.
- Building a network of networks, particularly Step by Step non-governmental organizations (NGOs) and the ISSA network.

The actual Step by Step Project cross-case analysis probably will be carried out using these themes or a further revision of them.

On the following pages, the illustration of cross-case analysis for this book develops just two of the original themes: "Equal opportunity" and "Teacher professional development." Equal opportunity was seen as embracing the overlapping concerns of social inclusion (particularly with Roma children); inclusion of children with disabilities; fair treatment for all children regardless of ethnicity, gender, religion, or socioeconomic status; reduction of stereotyping of people and cultures; and advancement of an open society. Teacher professional development was seen as embracing the overlapping concerns of pedagogy; classroom methods; lifelong learning and professional literature; curricula and standards of teacher training; daily planning; activity resources; classroom management; teacher mentoring; and certification. However these concerns are discussed, not every important subdivision will get attention in the final report.

Figure 9.7 is a presentation of Worksheet 4 (Ratings of Expected Utility of each Case to Enhance Themes) to illustrate some of the first steps in a Step by Step cross-case analysis. The original themes are listed, but ratings are provided for only two. Director Klaus recommended "Equal opportunity" and "Teacher professional development" as the two. The procedure calls for ratings of utility for development of the themes from the six cases as represented in the six filled-in copies of Worksheet 3 (Figures 9.1–9.6).

This analyst found high utility in two of the six case reports for Theme 3 and four for Theme 4. An analyst might discuss these estimates of utility with team members and others, expecting that different expectations would become apparent, but the final choice of data to rely on for assertions or conclusions probably needs to reside with the analyst. The estimates of utility show up in Worksheet 5A as parentheses and double parentheses—indications of the cases that seem most likely to help develop the themes "Equal opportunity" and "Teacher professional development."

Figure 9.8 is a presentation of Worksheet 5A (A Matrix for Generating Theme-Based Assertions from Case Findings Rated Important), with a few alterations. The ratings are judgments by the analyst as to the importance of each of the findings from the case reports. The analyst has kept in mind that the purpose of the study is to gain a better understanding of the Step by Step program as a whole. The cases are studied, not because this is the only way or the best way to understand the program, but because in the activities and the individual contexts at sites within these countries, the nature of the whole program can be seen in experiential and situational ways.

Twenty-two findings from the six countries are listed in Figure 9.8. These are the findings that came to the attention of the analyst as he read the case reports. Naturally he noted the findings as each country's team presented them, but he also put down what he saw as special insights and troubling concerns in each report. How well his mind captured the case while retaining the perspective of the project as a whole is critical to the cross-case analysis.

These competing foci have been referred to in earlier chapters as the "case–quintain dilemma." Each case report has a story to tell about its case. The case is an offspring of the international program, but it has other forebears, its own cast of characters, and its own life. If the case researchers or analyst pay too much attention to the themes, they fail to see the complexity and contextuality of the case. The parts are more than pieces of the whole. But if the researchers concentrate on the uniqueness of the case, they find too little for understanding the Step by Step program as a whole. The analyst, step by step, is performing ballet.

The 22 statements of findings in Figure 9.8 have been abbreviated so as to squeeze them all into fairly limited space. Most analysts do some tasks better if they can see all the ideas together in full view. But the abbreviations fail to catch the complexity of the statements of findings as given in the filled-in versions of Worksheet 3. And the statements of findings in the versions of Worksheet 3 are simplifications—often oversimplifications—of what has been said in the case reports. The analyst has to keep returning to the case reports, but really cannot. He or she can only keep some of the complexity of the findings in mind.

Different analysts will have different ways of carrying out the "case–quintain dialectic." One approach is to deal more or less equally with all the findings from all the cases. This is partly what Tracks II and III (see Chapter 3) are intended to do: to deal with the larger thrusts or clearer composites of findings. There the analyst sacrifices depth in order to be more complete in coverage. The alternative approach is to select a few findings or merged findings or factors and deal as much as one can with their complexity. There the analyst expects more or less to ignore some important findings so as to present others in depth. Whether or not the analyst makes a choice, the analyst is making a choice.

The purpose of Worksheet 5A (as shown in Figure 9.8) is to help the analyst make choices. The following findings (slightly amplified) have been rated as the most promising for Theme 3, "Equal opportunity" (i.e., they are rated high in both utility and prominence for this theme):

- The training of teachers is done by teachers with their children in their classrooms."
- "Because Liubchyk is present, the students in his classroom are learning important social skills."

- "Liubchyk is growing intellectually and academically, partly because he attends a regular classroom."
- "Step by Step in Slovakia and its partners are doing exemplary educational work with the Roma."
- "Some people of the village, including the assistant to the mayor and the priest, question the Roma's interest in integration."

Each of these five case findings is important enough to get space in the final report. But as they are, they are case findings and cannot be generalized to Step by Step as a program. Step by Step in Haiti and Mongolia does not work with Liubchyk or Roma. Nor can success in one country be presumed to be success elsewhere. The analyst looks for related findings—from unpromising cases as well as from auspicious ones; not just in Worksheet 5A, but in Worksheet 3; and even by e-mailing country team members. The analyst looks for commonality in findings across cases, but also for counterevidence anywhere. The procedure calls for interpretation. It is not an assertion-generating machine.

Continuing with Theme 3, the equal opportunity theme, moving beyond the H ratings for Ukraine and Slovakia, the analyst notes (in Figure 9.8) possible help from Ukraine Findings V and VI, and Bosnia and Herzegovina Findings I, II, and IV. He or she reads the five finding statements on Worksheet 3 for these cases, and probably returns for some scanning of the case reports. And before he is through, he probably has checked out Romania Finding II, Bosnia and Herzegovina Finding III, Kyrgyzstan Finding I, and Lithuania Finding II.

These efforts should be keeping alive the idea of the case activity and circumstance. But the multicase project has its overarching research questions. Those themes, or themes revised and augmented, will probably determine the conceptual structure of the final report. Simultaneously or dialectically, the author (who may or may not be the analyst) needs to be thinking about cases and the quintain—writing a lot about the theme, writing some about each individual case as illustration.

I won't attempt it here, not even merely to round out the example. One reason is that I do not want what I might write to be seen by anyone as an actual Step by Step cross-site analysis, for which all the data do not yet exist. For now, we cannot go further.

WORKSHEET 3. Analyst's Notes While Reading a Case Report

Code Letters for This Case: UKR

Case Study Report Title: Inclusive Education: The Step by Step Program Influencing Children, Teachers, Parents, and State Policies in Ukraine

Author(s): Natalia Sofiy and Svitlana Efimova

Analyst's Synopsis: This is a case study of Liubchyk, a first-grade boy diagnosed with autism, who was enrolled in a regular classroom largely through the advocacy of his mother, Step by Step, and the principal of the school. Common practice was formerly to send children like Liubchyk to a special boarding school. Aspirations for membership in the European Union have made it easier for economic and political leaders to welcome the Step by Step program, with its ethics of inclusion and social justice. Parents have taken a strong role, not only as supporters but as demanders. The board meeting of the health improvement center Shans is a story of parliamentary futility, but also of parental dedication to the care and education of the children with special needs in Kyiv Oblast. The research team members have a sensitivity to experiential knowing, and have told their story in a way that all readers get a vicarious experience of Step by Step in Ukraine.

Situational Constraints:

Uniqueness among Other Cases: The Ukraine program is one of the better country programs, and this school is one of the most advanced. Otherwise, the school is ordinary for a middle-class community.

Prominence of Theme 3 in This Case: (Equal opportunity) Very high

Prominence of Theme 4 in This Case: (Teacher professional development) Middling

Expected Utility of This Case for Developing Theme 3: Very high

Expected Utility of This Case for Developing Theme 4: Low to middling

Conceptual Factors (for Track III): Disability; seclusion of children with disability; demand on teacher time; parents as advocates; partnering; resources for staff development

Findings:

    I. Social learning for all children was extra high when Liubchyk was there.

    II. Parents provided not only assistance but agitation for going further.

(continued)

FIGURE 9.1. Worksheet 3 as completed for the Ukraine case study.

III. For many children with disabilities who were previously assigned to special schools, inclusion provided greater intellectual and social benefit, not distracting from the instruction of others.

IV. In Ukraine, the Step by Step teacher training was done by teachers in their classrooms who recognized trainees as individuals, with their own experiences, needs, and expectations. They appealed to the emotions, yet stayed within a strong framework of early childhood education standards.

V. The Ministry of Education and the Academy of Pedagogical Sciences, expressed support of SbS teacher training for inclusion, child-centered kindergartens, and additional teachers and parent volunteers in the classroom.

VI. Ukrainian SbS mothers participated in professional development and program planning alongside teachers, were sometimes among those speaking fervently for SbS standards.

VII. Parents obtained support from the central government more readily by forming an NGO than by appealing as citizens directly to legislators and executive branch officials.

Possible Excerpts for the Multicase Report:

Oksana (Liubchyk's teacher) said that his parents had expressed much gratitude to the teachers: "During these 6 months, Liubchyk has made significant steps in his development. Unlike at the beginning of the academic year, when he experienced a certain discomfort, now he goes off to school in high spirits." Liubchyk's grandmother, also involved in his upbringing, put it this way: "We can thank the atmosphere of this place."

Oksana worked to assure that all the children treated Liubchyk right. She said that by observing how adults treat Liubchyk, the children had the opportunity to learn how to interact with him, to rejoice in his successes, and to acquire the experience of communicating and caring for people with special needs.

Oksana attributed much of Liubchyk's academic understanding to regular communication between his parents and his teachers. Almost daily they analyzed his difficulties and successes. And there were longer meetings. Once a quarter, one of the parents (usually his mother), Oksana, Halyna, and Marianna met to reflect and plan their assistance to Liubchyk. (p. 128)

[Victor Ogneviuk, Ukraine vice-Minister of Education and Science:] "Today, the most important issue [in attaining equal opportunity for all children] is preparation of a new generation of teachers capable of helping children with special needs. Without well-prepared teachers and mentors, our talk is in vain." (p. 171)

The next assignment for each child is to color a scene from the fairy tale and place them in the order the scenes appear in the story. The children work in groups. Liubchyk chooses a picture among those offered by Halyna, the assistant teacher, but he refuses to join a group. He is not pressed to do so. "What is this bird?" she asks. Liubchyk spreads his arms and says, "A swallow." "Very good," says Halyna, and pats him on the shoulder. The children work on their scenes. When the coloring is completed, the children gather, and the scenes are laid out in order. "Liubchyk, come here, we are missing your picture," says his friend Anychka. Liubchyk gives her his neatly colored swallow, but continues to stay close to Halyna. (p. 192)

(continued)

FIGURE 9.1. *(continued)*

Commentary:

When Step by Step began its work in Ukraine and in many other former Soviet bloc countries, there was a political commitment to fully supporting care for all children. It was believed that certain children, particularly orphans, displaced children, and those with disabilities, would be able to receive appropriate services only if they were enrolled in special schools, not in the regular schools. Separate institutions were developed for different categories of children. No formal system of foster care existed, so children whose parents were not deemed fit (for example, parents who were accused of abusing their children, were alcoholics, or who lived in extreme poverty) were institutionalized. Likewise, parents of children with special needs were encouraged to enroll their children in special schools, many of which were internats, or boarding facilities. As a result, they lived in isolation from more typical children and from society at large. Even children with only physical disabilities were provided with the special education curriculum and a lower-prestige diploma.

With special attention to Liubchyk's first-grade classroom in Maliuk School, the report described his socialization, sense of membership, pride in his work, and low distraction from class instruction, as well as his reading and arithmetic. The embedded cases of his mother and his teacher were important components. And the use of role playing as a key experiential part of teacher training was nicely illustrated. The contexts of Ukraine as related to the Soviet educational system and the EU were part of the original plan.

There was a noticeable lack of expectation that it is futile to work for change.

Professionals were moving away from treating the diagnosis toward treating the child.

Trainers drew on teachers' compassion in professional development.

The national organization staff was active in training and mentoring.

FIGURE 9.1. *(continued)*

WORKSHEET 3. Analyst's Notes While Reading a Case Report

Code Letters for This Case: SLO

Case Study Report Title: Impact Step by Step at the Roma Settlement
Jarovnice-Karice: Community Resource Mobilization

Author(s): Eva Koncoková and Jana Handzelová

Analyst's Synopsis: This is a study of several Step by Step early education efforts (including home schooling and community center programs) for Roma children ages 0–6 in a Slovak village. With an impoverished, non-majority-language home environment, many Roma children were not admitted to regular schools. Once-a-week classes were organized here for preschool children and their mothers to guide home schooling the rest of the week—schooling that would accelerate development of conceptualization, communication, and socialization. Thus might the children pass tests necessary for admission to regular school and be kept out of long-standing special schools for Roma students only and/or children with disabilities.

Situational Constraints:

Uniqueness among Other Cases: Although Step by Step programs in other countries deal with educational opportunities for the Roma, this was not seen as an ordinary Step by Step initiative. The organization of the home schooling was extraordinary.

Prominence of Theme 3 in This Case: (Equal opportunity) Highly prominent

Prominence of Theme 4 in This Case: (Teacher professional development) Low

Expected Utility of This Case for Developing Theme 3: Very high

Expected Utility of This Case for Developing Theme 4: Average

Conceptual Factors (for Track III): Durability of Roma parents in home schooling; attitudes of fathers; support by social worker; attitudes of villagers; interest in integration; tolerance of Special Primary School staff; EU support for Roma

Findings:

    I. Mothers had continued the home schooling.

    II. The teaching of mothers and children emphasized preparation for primary school, but gave some attention to interpersonal respect, children's interests, and choice.

    III. Some villagers continued to think that the Roma did not seek integrated education.

    IV. Educational and institutional contributions of Step by Step and its partners were exemplary.

    V. Though doing little for Roma living conditions themselves, state and local authorities applauded Step by Step efforts.

(continued)

FIGURE 9.2. Worksheet 3 as completed for the Slovakia case study.

Possible Excerpts for the Multicase Report:

The registry of dwellings in the settlement showed 115 houses, 230 shanties or shacks, and 30 barracks. Many were in the worst possible condition. Many had poor sanitary facilities, lacked toilets, and were too small for the number of people living there. Most settlement dwellings were made of wood, sheet metal, and cardboard, minimally furbished. It was even worse in the shanties than in the regular houses, because the windows in winter had to be stuffed with cloth, plastics, and cardboard. Many of the shanties were not approved dwellings and did not have a registry number. (p. 205)

As in nearly all the larger houses here, the center of activity is a room in the middle. In it stands a big table.... Some nine children are sitting at the table. Their mothers are crowded closely behind the.... One of the mothers is holding a big, colored picture book. She reads loudly and clearly a Slovak version of the fairy tale *Cinderella*. She reads one sentence, and immediately another woman says it in the Romani language. The children are listening carefully.... The mother then asks the children about the content of the fairy tale. She checks to see that they understand all the words. (p. 217)

[One of the most devoted advocates for the Roma children, and for ultimate integration, was Mária Lichvárová, the settlement's social worker.] In 2000, Mária became involved in Step by Step training focused on philosophy and methodology; multicultural and anti-bias education; and partnership and cooperation among school, families, and the Roma community. ... With a Roma teacher assistant helping, she developed tools to reach out to the Roma community and make people feel welcome in the school.... [She said,] "It brought a new sense to my teaching." (p. 211)

Mobilization of the potential of the Roma settlement Karice continues. The settlement has been involved in many programs and projects aimed at enabling the Roma to gain structural and practical skills that will foster their inclusion in society, and to overcome social exclusion by mobilizing and renewing their learning capacities. Through training and other activities tailored to their needs, the people have obtained self-awareness, knowledge, and skill.

The Wide Open School Foundation's program of multicultural activities has stimulated Roma families' interest in the formal education of their children. It has strengthened relations between the Roma and non-Roma communities, especially between representatives of the municipality and the Roma parents and community leaders.... The Roma themselves have upgraded the organizational and cultural work in their community. (p. 240)

Commentary:

The research team concentrated on the Wide Open School Foundation's strategic plan. Cooperation of state and local authorities was substantial.

Interpersonal relationships continued to suffer from stereotypical views.

Unemployment was almost total.

Efforts were made at the primary school for Roma students only to keep up with the national school curriculum. Its principal and many around him expressed a preference for "separate but equal" schools.*

*Here, with or without justification, the Analyst recognized that the assistant to the mayor was not quoted in the report. The Analyst spoke with the authors about several matters and included this commentary.

FIGURE 9.2. *(continued)*

WORKSHEET 3. Analyst's Notes While Reading a Case Report

Code Letters for This Case: ROM

Case Study Report Title: Center for Educational Development, Step by Step Romania: Teacher Staff Development at the Tulcea Model Training Site

Author(s): Catalina Ulrich

Analyst's Synopsis: The research team studied the Center for Educational and Professional Development (CEPD), Step by Step Romania as a teacher-training provider within a "market" traditionally composed of universities, teacher-training centers, pedagogical high schools, and (recently) a few accredited NGOs. Preschool education had been overlooked during national planning for educational reform. Training was one of the means for development. Model Training Site (MTS) Kindergarten 3, Tulcea, was the case studied, in its several contexts and the internally contradictory heritage of a former Communist country. The researchers gave attention to tensions between planning and spontaneity, alternative and traditional pedagogy, support and challenge within the context of teacher-training activities, and Step by Step methodology implementation at school and classroom levels. The structure of the study reflects the chronological phases of Step by Step training: attending the two required training modules (which embedded theoretical and practical activities undertaken by both trainers and trainees) and participating in monitoring activities. The researchers also explored important issues of educational pluralism, drawing from a specially called national symposium that was something of a retrospective on 15 years of educational alternatives in Romania.

Situational Constraints:

Uniqueness among Other Cases: Although all countries are different, this appeared to be a pretty typical teacher-training venue for the SBS program.

Prominence of Theme 3 in This Case: (Equal opportunity) Apparent as an issue only regarding student differences in a regular classroom

Prominence of Theme 4 in This Case: (Teacher professional development) High

Expected Utility of This Case for Developing Theme 3: Some high, some low

Expected Utility of This Case for Developing Theme 4: High

Conceptual Factors (for Track III): Experience of trainers; close hewing to Step by Step standards; direct experience with children in their own classrooms; partnering; resources

Findings:

I. Experienced teachers found the pedagogy appealing and challenging.

II. There was diligent pursuit of equal opportunity for children enrolled here.

(continued)

FIGURE 9.3. Worksheet 3 as completed for the Romania case study.

III. Trainees generally raised technical questions; few asked about culture or open-society issues.

IV. Institutional partnering required maintenance.

V. The driving force for staff development was teacher initiative rather than institutional leadership.

Possible Excerpts for the Multicase Report:

[Mihai Albota, former general inspector for the Tulcea County School Inspectorate, nicknamed "the General":] "Step by Step kids are allowed to think by themselves, to work with the team, in order to discover their skills and whether they are responsible for their own actions. They are not afraid of inspection. Before, they were shaking, with their hands behind their backs. You should not raise children like that. You should give them some space." (p. 249)

[The General]: "Also bad was the training strategy. We proceeded from the lower levels to the highest level. We were not vigorously training the hierarchically superior people within the organizational structure. We did not seriously train top people. These people needed to come and observe at length. We do not have knowledgeable people at the level of the school inspectorates, or at the school management level—people who comprehend communities and policy. To be honest, we still do not have such people." (p. 259)

Observed: Maria and Eliza lead a [teacher-training] session on observation techniques and elements of individualization. On the flip chart sheets, the trainees read that information gathered through observation can be used for encouraging children's interests, dividing the children into twos or other groups, diversifying activities, and focusing on special activities. Maria identifies examples in the trainees' observations of the previous day. (p. 281)

Commentary:

The trainees were experienced and enthusiastic, but not all trainees were ready to allow children to make their own activity decisions. The trainers were highly competent and happy with their work, but were not obviously on a remunerative career ladder.

Heeding standards and valuing spontaneity did not automatically fit together.

Having a patron in the local educational authority was of great help to the principal. But at this time, her kindergarten catered less to underprivileged children than it did before—perhaps because many of the more privileged people were now going out of the way to get their children enrolled.

There was strong camaraderie among trainers and trainees.

FIGURE 9.3. *(continued)*

WORKSHEET 3. Analyst's Notes While Reading a Case Report

Code Letters for This Case: B&H

Case Study Report Title: Professional Development of Teachers through Networking and Partnering in Bosnia and Herzegovina

Author(s): Radmila Rangelov-Jusovic and Elvira Ramcilovic

Analyst's Synopsis: The researchers visited Training Center Jablanica to observe the training of teachers and to learn the perceptions of the staff and others about Step by Step training. Much attention was given to partnering, but an experiential account of partnering had not yet been included in this unfinished report.

Situational Constraints:

Uniqueness among Other Cases: The recent civil war made the site unique; the travel of teachers was still limited. However, the training activities seemed routine for Step by Step.

Prominence of Theme 3 in This Case: (Equal opportunity) Low

Prominence of Theme 4 in This Case: (Teacher professional development) High

Expected Utility of This Case for Developing Theme 3: Low

Expected Utility of This Case for Developing Theme 4: High

Conceptual Factors (for Track III): Supply of teachers; cultural tolerance; cultural aims of education; affiliation of organizations; participation in teacher networks; operational distance between local and state education offices; social activism

Findings:

I. In B&H there was a great need for personnel for child-centered education—not only for teachers, but for principals, mentors, and regional officials. The SbS Foundation was strongly committed to that need.

II. The public need for reconciliation, for cultural tolerance and respect, and for rebuilding of social institutions was recognized, but the need for taking responsibility at the national level for some of the teacher training was, so far, barely mentioned.

III. There was a strong recognition that educational improvement needed vigorous partnering and networking. This situation was unusual, in that the Ministries of Education were not physically remote. Independent ministries were located in each of the country's many cantons.

IV. There was little mention, so far, of equal opportunity, inclusion, or special support for Roma children in the report.

Possible Excerpts for the Multicase Report:

Although in ways an ordinary day for professional development in Bosnia and Herzegovina, it was unusual for several reasons. First of all, it was training for teachers by teachers. Based on their practical experience, this training was aimed to provide answers on how to apply new teaching methods and to help the practitioners understand better the reform requirements. Organized for the first time at the local level, this training should

(continued)

FIGURE 9.4. Worksheet 3 as completed for the Bosnia and Herzegovina case study.

establish conditions for ongoing professional development and strengthening local capacities as well as rebuilding the professional climate. It was training based on teacher needs, with full, active involvement of the participants. (p. 4)

A common weakness was the shortage of personnel and structural capacity. A total of 13 Ministries of Education have been established, but many experienced professionals had left the country, leaving few available for administering the schools. (p. 8)

... the Jablanica training team [with six full-time schoolteachers] was working intensively almost every second weekend up until the 2004 summer break. (p. 18)

[Teacher Zvonko Dzidic:] " ... in three workshops at Training Center Jablanica ... we got answers to many questions. They showed us what a working day looked like in practice, beginning with the Morning Meeting. I visited classes held by my mentor three times, and she came to my classroom twice, watching my work and providing very valuable feedback." (p. 19)

[Marko Nedic, a deputy minister of education:] "Partnerships and networking are important because they bring self-reflection and the exchange of experience. The Ministry of Education can help organize a network of all schools, institutions and persons interested in teacher professional development." (p. 20)

Commentary:

" ... all 14 primary school training centers in Bosnia and Herzegovina promoted professional development through networking and partnerships." (p. 2)

Aspirations were expressed in B&H to build schools modeled on those in developed countries, but the problems of those schools were not sufficiently acknowledged. Certainly, the aims of equal opportunity and cultural tolerance are not well modeled in many Western countries. Is it that funding agencies are more impressed with mimicking the West than with pursuing the highest ideals of B&H's own people?

[Sabaha Bijedic, director of the Pedagogical Institute:] "It is my opinion that a state body responsible for professional development, accreditation of training programs, and selection of mandatory and additional training needs to be established. This body could publish a catalogue of accredited training programs for professional development, from which every teacher would have to pass a certain number, according to their own needs and interests. Of course, this is where the problem of finances comes up." (p. 11)

The training centers do a job that, in most social perspectives, should be funded by state revenues. It often appears that they do it better than the state would. But an ethic among foundations is to support new initiatives rather than continuing operations. So the staffs of training centers, in addition to lobbying for operational funding, spend a portion of their time creating new initiatives—time that is not then available for basic training operations.

Much of the B&H case study is devoted to testimonials from SbS supported people and from others; too little of it actually tells what they do.

"Formal partnering of schools was usually limited to relations with the Ministry of Education and the Pedagogical Institute." (p. 24) Many of the activities of partnerships seemed devoted to professional development, but some were directed at a variety of other ventures. Certainly all seemed needed. Little was reported about banding together particularly for lobbying and evaluation purposes.

"The financial resources of schools and teachers were extremely low, [obligating] most teachers [to cover the] costs of professional development."

FIGURE 9.4. (continued)

WORKSHEET 3. Analyst's Notes While Reading a Case Report

Code Letters for This Case: KGZ

Case Study Report Title: Step by Step Training Centers on the Way to a Quality Education

Author(s): Anara Tentimisheva, Alima Abdyvasieva, and Nurbek Teleshaliyev

Analyst's Synopsis: This is a collection of impressions held by teachers and others of Step by Step teaching and teacher retraining. The case teacher taught in a primary school in Osh, the southern capital; her training center was at School 16. Educational conditions in the country were difficult, and the difficulties extended to teacher professional development. There were 11 Step by Step training centers in the country; this one offered 9-day units in 3-day sessions. With an emphasis on teacher creativity and lifelong learning, the training was adapted to the places where the teachers were initially trained. Democratic principles included child-oriented environment, students' right to choose, parents' participation, and placing teacher and child on an equal footing.

Situational Constraints:

Uniqueness among Other Cases: This report indicated changes in teachers' attitudes to children.

Prominence of Theme 3 in This Case: (Equal opportunity) Low

Prominence of Theme 4: (Teacher professional development) Middling

Expected Utility of This Case for Developing Theme 3: Low

Expected Utility of This Case for Developing Theme 4: High

Conceptual Factors (for Track III): Sites of previous training; differences between traditional teaching and Step by Step teaching

Findings:

    I. In the past, classes were taught via child-passive, direct instruction of a standardized curriculum. Now teachers were getting each individual child active in learning.

    II. Eleven teacher training centers were established within schools, requiring family participation, individualized teaching, and learning resources.

    III. It should not be expected that teacher training can be adequately funded through fee payment in such a poor country with a relatively tiny market demand.

(continued)

FIGURE 9.5. Worksheet 3 as completed for the Kyrgyzstan case study.

Possible Excerpts for the Multicase Report:

[A teacher's first impression of Step by Step:] "Checkup of home assignment, dictation, constant calligraphy, explanation of new material, consolidation of explained material, home assignment—the lesson was broken into pieces that were called activity centers." (p. 1)

[Deputy director:] " ... I realize that the personnel of the Osh Institute of Advanced Teacher Training need advanced training themselves." (p. 4)

[Teacher:] "This program brought me closer to children and their parents. My students became more open. Now they express their opinion freely." (p. 8)

[Teacher:] "Changes that happened to me have changed parents as well. When they saw how I tried to do my best, they offered me their help; they assisted me in making plans, organizing out-of-class activities, making visual aids, etc. They helped me to create a comfortable environment for the children." (p. 9)

[Parent:] "This strategy puts a child, with his or her abilities, wishes, needs, and motives, into first place. Communication is built upon mutual respect. Every child is helped to develop, regardless of abilities. It is good when a child actively participates in the learning process." (p. 9)

[Principal:] "One of our teachers was in a contest for Teacher of the Year. She had to conduct a lesson. The jury left before the lesson was over. The children begged to finish the lesson." (p. 13)

Commentary:

Teachers could not afford to pay for staff development, but neither could the government. Unless teachers did pay, they could not choose their training site. Director: "I don't know how long these free seminars will last." (p. 14)

SbS staff at the training center believed that lesson planning should not be done far in advance from the actual activity. It should be done by the teacher no more than a few days ahead, and should remain open to suggestions by the children and opportunities that arise. (p. 5)

There was a debate as to whether the training centers should be licensed.

Elaborate criteria for selecting training centers were given.

The camaraderie was great, but it sounded a bit cultish, not open to other ideas.

Unlike in Romania and Ukraine, the SbS trainers were pressed to protect their own family lives and limited themselves to three training programs each summer. (p. 7)

Training took place in three languages: Russian, Kyrgyz, and Uzbek.

About bureaucracy: "We have issued a teacher-training license only to the main [Step by Step] foundation. . . . Neither schools nor kindergartens can get a license. International donors caused that change. Public schools and universities are not issued a license to teach teachers. It would be possible to register a private organization and to then get a license. However, in this case they should either rent or buy an office or building. We can issue a license for the organization of courses and seminars, but they have to sign a rent contract." (p. 15)

FIGURE 9.5. (continued)

WORKSHEET 3. Analyst's Notes While Reading a Case Report

Code Letters for This Case: LTH

Case Study Report Title: Network of Step by Step Training Centers: Ongoing Professional Development—Impact after Training

Author(s): Antanas Valantinas, Regina Sabaliauskiene, Regina Rimkiene

Analyst's Synopsis: The training center at Vilnius B. Basanavicious Secondary School was selected as Lithuania's case to illustrate the best Step by Step training in the region and to identify its impact on the professional development of teachers. The researchers chose to interview various stakeholders on broad questions more than to observe training activities. Much attention was given to school choice. By "network," the researchers meant a cohort of trainees. By "impact," they meant the trainees' judgment of the quality of the workshops. The researchers did not examine SbS pedagogy in greater depth than its general prescriptions. The report is informal in tone, almost conversational.

Situational Constraints:

Uniqueness among Other Cases: The report leaves the reader thinking that SbS activity in Lithuania was no different from that in other countries. Country specifics were few.

Prominence of Theme 3 in This Case: (Equal opportunity) Low

Prominence of Theme 4 in This Case: (Teacher professional development) High

Expected Utility of This Case for Developing Theme 3: Low

Expected Utility of This Case for Developing Theme 4: Middling to high

Conceptual Factors (for Track III): Teacher creativity; parental preference for schools

Findings:

    I. In 10 years the number of Lithuanian classrooms using the SbS approach reached 1,000. Some 78 SbS staff development courses were officially recognized by the Ministry. Over 2,000 teachers were attending SbS seminars each year.

    II. College courses were introduced or changed to acknowledge the teaching methods of Step by Step.

    III. The trainees were supportive of Step by Step teaching and teacher training, and indicated readiness to help it expand in the schools.

(continued)

FIGURE 9.6. Worksheet 3 as completed for the Lithuania case study.

Possible Excerpts for the Multicase Report:

[Trainer:] "If a teacher is innovative, if he or she is creative, school children will appreciate his or her appeal. . . . Thus the success of the teaching method is determined by the personality of the teacher, exclusively. Even in the most successful cases, teachers adopt some elements of the technique, yet not the system itself." (pp. 17–18)

[Researcher:] "The training center is shaping the image of the school." (p. 18)

[Researcher:] "This made me reflect on the difference between the school principal that attracts the money into his school by the quality of teaching process and the one who brings the money into his school by administrative measures only." (p. 18)

[According to one principal,] The main obstacle for subject matter teachers to adjust to Step by Step methods is the movement of students from class to class. The factor of [Step by Step topical] integration is almost impossible for them. Current staff development does not encourage teachers cooperating with students.

[Parent, commenting on a child's transition to a traditional classroom:] "Parent: The child needs an adjustment period, and teachers and parents should cooperate on it. Subject teachers should listen to the children's opinions, yet require them to perform their responsibilities. And generate more creative tasks and encourage creativity. And show more respect for their pupils and treat them as personalities. . . . But the SbS teachers [preparing them] should spend less time in Morning Circle, but instead teach them more serious things." (p. 27)

Commentary:

The researchers said that a trainee returning to a school that was not aware of this pedagogical approach could expect to find more opposition than support.

Educational priority statements coming from the Ministry are increasingly parallel to the SbS standards.

The claim was made that one of the reasons for the case study was to find out whether there are problems to solve.

It was not revealed whether or not the trainers at the Lithuanian training centers were teachers with their own classrooms. They were paid from workshop fees.

The formal evaluation of workshops (primarily feedback from participants at the end) is not credible, because it was based largely on the social bonding that has occurred or not occurred. Bonding is good, but quality of bonding is generally a poor indicator of quality of training.

At one point, the main researcher said, "I had no time to properly inspect the environment of the classroom."

FIGURE 9.6. *(continued)*

WORKSHEET 4. Ratings of Expected Utility of Each Case for Each Theme

Utility of Cases	Case A	Case B	Case C	Case D	Case E	Case F
Original Multicase Themes	UKR	SLO	ROM	B&H	KRG	LTH
Theme 1 Children's outcomes						
Theme 2 Family and community engagement						
Theme 3 Equal opportunity for each child	H	H	M	L	L	L
Theme 4 Teacher professional development	M	M	H	H	H	H
Theme 5 Enabling networks and partnerships						
Theme 6 Program sustainability						
Added Multicase Themes						
Theme 7						
Theme 8						

H = high utility; M = middling utility; L = low utility. High utility means that the Case appears to be one of the most useful for developing this Theme. As indicated, the original Themes can be augmented by additional Themes even as late as the beginning of the cross-case analysis. Descriptions of each Theme can be attached to this worksheet, so that the basis for estimates can be readily examined.

FIGURE 9.7. Worksheet 4 as completed for Themes 3 and 4 in the six Step by Step cases.

WORKSHEET 5A. A Matrix for Generating Theme-Based Assertions from Case Findings Rated Important

	Themes					
Case A: Ukraine	1	2	((3))	4	5	6
Finding IV: Training by teachers in classroom			H	H		
Finding I: High social learning in class			H	M		
Finding V: Ministry supportive			M	H		
Finding III: Liubchyk's intellectual growth			H	M		
Finding VI: Parents in prof. development			M	M		
Case B: Slovakia … (atypical)	1	2	((3))	4	5	6
Finding IV: SbS, partners: exemplary work			H	H		
Finding III: Villager view Roma integration			H	L		
Finding I: Parents continue home schooling			L	H		
Finding V: Authorities applaud SbS effort			L	M		
Case C: Romania	1	2	3	((4))	5	6
Finding III: Trainees technical, not societal			L	H		
Finding V: Teacher initiative, not institutnl.			L	H		
Finding II: Equal opportunity within classrm.			M	M		
Finding I: Pedagogy appealing, challenging			L	M		

(continued)

FIGURE 9.8. Worksheet 5A as completed for Themes 3 and 4 in the six Step by Step cases.

Case D: Bosnia & Herzegovina	1	2	3	(4)	5	6
Finding I: Need child-centered educators			H	H		
Finding II: Reconciliation not in tchr. trng.			H	H		
Finding IV: Little report on equal opportnty.			H	M		
Finding III: Need for partnering, networking			M	M		
Case E: Kyrgyzstan	1	2	3	(4)	5	6
Finding I: Individualized student learning			M	M		
Finding II: Growth of teacher-tng centers			L	L		
Case F: Lithuania	1	2	3	(4)	5	6
Finding II: College teacher tng. aware of SbS			M	L		
Finding III: Trainees supportive of SbS meth.			L	M		
Finding I: Growth of SbS teacher tng.			L	L		

H = high importance; M = middling importance; L = low importance. A high mark means that for this Theme, the Case Finding is of high importance. Parentheses around a Theme number means that it should carry extra weight in drafting an Assertion. The notation " . . . (atypical)" after a case means that its situation might warrant extra caution in drafting an Assertion.

FIGURE 9.8. (continued)

References

Abercrombie, N., Hill, S., & Turner, B. S. (1984). *Dictionary of sociology*. London: Penguin.

Becker, H. S. (1992). Cases, causes, conjunctures, stories, and imagery. In C. C. Ragin & H. S. Becker (Eds.), *What is a case?: Exploring the foundations of social inquiry* (pp. 205–216). Cambridge, UK: Cambridge University Press.

Bickman, L., & Rog, D. J. (Eds.). (1998). *Handbook of applied social research methods*. Thousand Oaks, CA: Sage.

Blumer, H. (1969). *Symbolic interactionism: Perspective and method*. Chicago: University of Chicago Press.

Bolman, L. G., & Deal, T. E. (2003). *Reframing organizations: Artistry, choice, and leadership* (3rd ed.). San Francisco: Jossey-Bass.

Carr, W. L., & Kemmis, S. (1986). *Becoming critical: Education, knowledge and action research*. London: Falmer.

Clandenin, J., & Connelly, M. (1999). *Narrative inquiry*. San Francisco: Jossey-Bass.

Crabtree, B. F., & Miller, W. L. (1999). Researching practice settings: A case study approach. In B. F. Crabtree & W. L. Miller (Eds.), *Doing qualitative research* (2nd ed., Vol. 2, pp. 293–312). Thousand Oaks, CA: Sage.

Creswell, J. W. (1998). *Qualitative inquiry and research design: Choosing among five traditions*. Thousand Oaks, CA: Sage.

Cronbach, L. J. (1977, April). Remarks to the new society. *Evaluation Research Society Newsletter, 1*, 1.

Cronbach, L. J., & Snow, R. E. (1977). *Aptitudes and instructional methods: A handbook for research on interactions*. New York: Irvington.

Delamont, S. (1992). *Fieldwork in educational settings: Methods, pitfalls and perspectives*. London: Falmer.

Denzin, N. K. (1989). *The research act* (3rd ed.). Englewood Cliffs, NJ: Prentice-Hall.

Denzin, N. K. (2000). The practices and politics of interpretation. In N. K.

Denzin & Y. S. Lincoln (Eds.), *Handbook of qualitative research* (2nd ed., pp. 897–922). Thousand Oaks, CA: Sage.

Denzin, N. K., & Lincoln, Y. S. (Eds.). (2005). *Handbook of qualitative research* (2nd ed.). Thousand Oaks, CA: Sage.

Dreyfus, H. L., & Dreyfus, S. E. (1986). *Mind over machine: The power of human intuition and expertise in the era of the computer.* New York: Free Press.

Eckstein, H. (1975). Case study and theory in political science. In F. I. Greenstein & N. W. Polsby (Eds.), *Handbook of political science* (Vol. 7, pp. 72–138). Reading, MA: Addison-Wesley.

Elliott, J. (1991). *Action research for educational change.* Milton Keynes, UK: Open University Press.

Erickson, F. (1986). Qualitative methods in research on teaching. In M. C. Wittrock (Ed.), *Handbook of research on teaching* (3rd ed., pp. 119–161). New York: Macmillan.

Firestone, W. A. (1993). Alternative arguments for generalizing from data as applied to qualitative research. *Educational Researcher, 22*(4), 16–23.

Firestone, W. A., & Herriott, R. (1984). Multisite qualitative policy research: Some design and implementation issues. In D. M. Fetterman (Ed.), *Ethnography in educational evaluation* (pp. 63–88). Beverly Hills, CA: Sage.

Flick, U. (1998). *An introduction to qualitative research: Theory, method and applications.* London: Sage.

Flyvbjerg, B. (2001). *Making social science matter* (S. Sampson, Trans.). Cambridge, UK: Cambridge University Press.

Flyvbjerg, B. (2004). Five misunderstandings about case-study research. In C. Seale, G. Gobo, J. Gubrium, & D. Silverman (Eds.), *Qualitative research practice* (pp. 420–434). London: Sage.

Foucault, M. (1980). *Power/knowledge: Selected interviews and other writings, 1972–1977.* New York: Pantheon.

Gall, M. D., Gall, J. P., & Borg, W. R. (2003). *Educational research: An introduction* (7th ed.). Boston: Allyn & Bacon.

Geertz, C. (1973). Thick description: Toward an interpretive theory of culture. In C. Geertz, *The interpretation of cultures* (pp. 3–30). New York: Basic Books.

Glaser, B. G., & Strauss, A. L. (1967). *The discovery of grounded theory: Strategies for qualitative research.* Chicago: Aldine.

Gobo, G. (2004). Sampling, representativeness and generalizability. In C. Seale, G. Gobo, J. Gubrium, & D. Silverman (Eds.), *Qualitative research practice* (pp. 435–456). London: Sage.

Goetz, J. P., & LeCompte, M. D. (1984). *Ethnography and qualitative design in educational research.* New York: Academic Press.

Gomm, R. (2004). *Social research methodology.* London: Palgrave Macmillan.

Graue, M. E., & Walsh, D. J. (1998). *Studying children in context: Theories, methods, and ethics.* Thousand Oaks, CA: Sage.

Greene, J. (1995). *Evaluators as advocates.* Paper presented at the annual meeting of the American Evaluation Association, Vancouver, British Columbia, Canada.

Greene, J. (2000). Understanding social programs through evaluation. In N. K. Denzin & Y. S. Lincoln (Eds.), *Handbook of qualitative research* (2nd ed., pp. 981–1000). Thousand Oaks, CA: Sage.

Guba, E. G., & Lincoln, Y. S. (1981). *Effective evaluation*. San Francisco: Jossey-Bass.

Hansen, K. A., Kaufmann, R. K., & Saifer, S. (n.d.). *Education and the culture of democracy: Early childhood practice*. New York: Open Society Institute.

Herriott, R. E., & Firestone, W. A. (1983). Multisite qualitative policy research: Optimizing description and generalizability. *Educational Researcher, 12*(2), 14–19.

Holly, M. L., Arhar, J., & Kasten, W. (2005). *Action research for teachers* (2nd ed.). Upper Saddle River, NJ: Pearson-Merrill.

House, E. R., & Howe, K. R. (1999). *Values in evaluation and social research.* Thousand Oaks, CA: Sage.

Huberman, A. M., & Miles, M. B. (1994). Data management and analysis methods. In N. K. Denzin & Y. S. Lincoln (Eds.), *Handbook of qualitative research* (pp. 428–444). Thousand Oaks, CA: Sage.

Jegatheesan, B. (2005). *Ways of being at home and community: Language and socialization of children with autism in multilingual South Asian immigrant families.* Unpublished doctoral dissertation, University of Illinois, Urbana.

Kemmis, S. (1980). The imagination of the case and the invention of the study. In H. Simons (Ed.), *Towards a science of the singular* (pp. 93–142). Norwich, UK: University of East Anglia, Centre for Applied Research in Education.

Kennedy, M. M. (1979). Generalizing from single case studies. *Evaluation Quarterly, 3,* 661–678.

Lewontin, R. C. (1995, April 20). Sex, lies, and social science. *New York Review of Books,* p. 28.

Lincoln, Y. S., & Guba, E. G. (1985). *Naturalistic inquiry.* Beverly Hills, CA: Sage.

MacDonald, B., Adelman, C., Kushner, S., & Walker, R. (1982). *Bread and dreams: A case study in bilingual schooling in the U.S.A.* Norwich, UK: University of East Anglia, Centre for Applied Research in Education.

Malinowski, B. (1984). *Argonauts of the western Pacific.* Prospect Heights, IL: Waveland. (Original work published 1922, 1961)

Maxwell, J. A. (1992). Understanding and validity in qualitative research. *Harvard Educational Review, 63,* 279–300.

McCormick, S. (1994). A nonreader becomes a reader: A case study of literacy acquisition by a severely disabled reader. *Reading Research Quarterly, 29*(2), 157–176.

Merriam, S. B. (1998). *Qualitative research and case study applications in education* (2nd ed.). San Francisco: Jossey-Bass.

Messick, S. (1989). Validity. In R. L. Linn (Ed.), *Educational measurement* (pp. 13–103). New York: Macmillan.

Miles, M. B., & Huberman, A. M. (1994). *Qualitative data analysis* (2nd ed.). Thousand Oaks, CA: Sage.

Noffke, S. E. (1997). Professional, personal, and poliical dimensions of action research. *Review of Research in Education, 22*, 305–343.

Parlett, M., & Hamilton, D. (1976). Evaluation as illumination: A new approach to the study of innovative programmes. In G. V. Glass (Ed.), *Evaluation studies review annual* (Vol. 1, pp. 141–157). Beverly Hills, CA: Sage.

Patton, M. Q. (1990). *Qualitative evaluation and research methods* (2nd ed.). Newbury Park, CA: Sage.

Peshkin, A. (1986). *God's choice.* Chicago: University of Chicago Press.

Polanyi, M. (1962). *Personal knowledge: Towards a post-critical philosophy.* Chicago: University of Chicago Press.

Quinn, W., & Quinn, N. (1992). *Buddy evaluation.* Oakbrook, IL: North Central Regional Educational Laboratory.

Ragin, C. C. (1987). *The comparative method.* Berkeley: University of California Press.

Ragin, C. C., & Becker, H. S. (Eds.). (1992). *What is a case?: Exploring the foundations of social inquiry.* Cambridge, UK: Cambridge University Press.

Raisin, S., & Britton, E. D. (1997). *Bold ventures: Patterns among U.S. innovations in science and mathematics education.* Dordrecht, The Netherlands: Kluwer Academic.

Richardson, L., & St. Pierre, E. A. (2005). Writing: A method of inquiry. In N. K. Denzin & Y. S. Lincoln (Eds.), *Sage handbook of qualitative research* (3rd ed., pp. 959–978). Thousand Oaks, CA: Sage.

Ruddin, L. P. (2005). *How much can political scientists generalize from single cases?* Unpublished master's thesis, University of London, Birkbeck College.

Schön, D. (1983). *The reflective practitioner: How professionals think in action.* New York: Basic Books.

Schwandt, T. A. (2000). Three epistemological stances for qualitative inquiry: Interpretivism, hermeneutics, and social constructionism. In N. K. Denzin & Y. S. Lincoln (Eds.), *Handbook of qualitative research* (2nd ed., pp. 189–214). Thousand Oaks, CA: Sage.

Scriven, M. (1998). Bias. In R. M. Davis (Ed.), *Proceedings of the Stake Symposium on Educational Evaluation* (pp. 13–24). Urbana: University of Illinois.

Seals, T. A. (1985). *A theoretical construction of gender issues in marital therapy.* Unpublished doctoral dissertation, University of Illinois, Urbana.

Seefeldt, C., & Barbour, N. (1994). *Early childhood education: An introduction* (3rd ed.). New York: Macmillan.

Silverman, D. (1993). *Interpreting qualitative data.* London: Sage.

Silverman, D. (2000). Analyzing talk and text. In N. K. Denzin & Y. S. Lincoln (Eds.), *Handbook of qualitative research* (2nd ed., pp. 821–834). Thousand Oaks, CA: Sage.

Simons, H. (Ed.). (1980). *Towards a science of the singular.* Norwich, UK: University of East Anglia, Centre for Applied Research in Education.

Sjoberg, G., Williams, N., Vaughan, T. R., & Sjoberg, A. (1991). The case approach in social research: Basic methodological issues. In J. R. Feagin, A. M. Orum, & G. Sjoberg (Eds.), *A case for the case study* (pp. 27–79). Chapel Hill: University of North Carolina Press.

Smith, L. M. (1994). Biographical method. In N. K. Denzin & Y. S. Lincoln (Eds.), *Handbook of qualitative research* (pp. 286–305). Thousand Oaks, CA: Sage.

Smith, L. M., & Dwyer, D. (1979). *Federal policy in action: A case study of an urban education project.* Washington, DC: National Institute of Education.

Souchet, T., Stake, R., Chandler, M., Snow, D., & Burke, M. (1999). *The Teachers Academy principals study.* Urbana: Center for Instructional Research and Curriculum Evaluation, University of Illinois.

Spiro, R. J., Vispoel, W. P., Schmitz, J. G., Samarapungavan, A., & Boerger, A. E. (1987). Knowledge acquisition for application: Cognitive flexibility and transfer in complex content domains. In B. C. Britton (Ed.), *Executive control processes* (pp. 177–199). Hillsdale, NJ: Erlbaum.

Stake, R. E. (1984). An Illinois pair: A case study of school art in Champaign and Decatur. In M. Day, E. Eisner, R. E. Stake, B. Wilson, & M. Wilson (Eds.), *Art history, art criticism, and art production* (pp. 4.1–4.58). Santa Monica, CA: Rand Corporation.

Stake, R. E. (1988). Case study methods in educational research: Seeking sweet water. In R. M. Jaeger (Ed.), *Complementary methods for research in education* (pp. 253–278). Washington, DC: American Educational Research Association.

Stake, R. E. (1995). *The art of case study research.* Thousand Oaks, CA: Sage.

Stake, R. E. (2005). Qualitative case studies. In N. K. Denzin & Y. S. Lincoln (Eds.), *Sage handbook of qualitative research* (3rd ed., pp. 443–466). Thousand Oaks, CA: Sage.

Stake, R. E., & Davis, R. M. (1997). Summary of evaluation of Reader Focused Writing for the Veterans Benefits Administration. *American Journal of Evaluation, 20*(2), 323–343.

Stake, R. E., DeStefano, L., Harnisch, D., Sloane, K., & Davis, R. (1997). *Evaluation of the National Youth Sports Program.* Retrieved from www.ed.uiuc.edu/circe/nysp

Stake, R. E., & Easley, J. A. (1979). *Case studies in science education.* Urbana: Center for Instructional Research and Curriculum Evaluation, University of Illinois.

Stake, R. E., Platt, W., Davis, R., Vanderveen, N., & Dirani, K. (2003). *Integrating VBA training and evaluation.* Urbana: Center for Instructional Research and Curriculum Evaluation, University of Illinois.

Stanhope, G. R. (2005). *Illinois Learning Standards implementation and a systems perspective in four elementary schools: A multiple case study.* Unpublished doctoral dissertation, University of Illinois, Urbana.

Stenhouse, L. (1978). Case study and case records. Toward a contemporary history of education. *British Educational Research Journal, 4*(2), 21–39.

Stouffer, S. A. (1941). Notes on the case-study and the unique case. *Sociometry, 4*, 349–357.

Strauss, A. L., & Corbin, J. (1990). *Basics of qualitative research: Grounded theory procedures and techniques.* Newbury Park, CA: Sage.

Tierney, W. (2000). The observation of participation and the emergence of public ethnography. In N. K. Denzin & Y. S. Lincoln (Eds.), *Handbook of qualitative research* (2nd ed., pp. 537–554). Thousand Oaks, CA: Sage.

Tobin, J. (1989). *Preschool in three cultures*. New Haven, CT: Yale University Press.

Vaughan, D. (1992). Theory elaboration: The heuristics of case analysis. In C. C. Ragin & H. S. Becker (Eds.), *What is a case?: Exploring the foundations of social inquiry* (pp. 173–292). Cambridge, UK: Cambridge University Press.

Yin, R. K. (1992). *Evaluation: A singular craft*. Paper presented at the annual meeting of the American Evaluation Association, Seattle, WA.

Yin, R. K. (1994). *Case study research: Design and methods* (2nd ed.). Thousand Oaks, CA: Sage.

Index

About the Author

Robert E. Stake, PhD, is a specialist in the evaluation of educational programs and case study methods. He is director of the Center for Instructional Research and Curriculum Evaluation at the University of Illinois. Dr. Stake is the author of *Quieting Reform: Social Science and Social Action in an Urban Youth Program* (1986), about Charles Murray's evaluation of Cities-in-Schools, and three other books on research methods: *Evaluating the Arts in Education: A Responsive Approach* (1975), *The Art of Case Study Research* (1995), and *Standards-Based and Responsive Evaluation* (2003). With his wife, Bernadine, Dr. Stake has four children, nine grandchildren, and four great-grandchildren.

Contributors

Svitlana Efimova, Senior Teacher, Department of Pedagogy and Psychology, Lviv Oblast Institute of Postgraduate Pedagogical Education, Lviv, Ukraine

Jana Handzelová, Staff, Nadácia Skola dokorán (Wide Open School Foundation), Bratislava, Slovakia

Sarah Klaus, Executive Director, International Step by Step Association and Open Society Institute, Budapest, Hungary

Eva Koncoková, Director, Nadácia Skola dokorán (Wide Open School Foundation), Bratislava, Slovakia

Cassie Landers, Consultant to International Step by Step Foundation, New York, New York

Natalia Sofiy, Director, Ukrainian Step by Step Foundation, Kyiv, Ukraine

Catalina Ulrich, Lecturer, Faculty of Educational Sciences, University of Bucharest, Romania